Tales from
the Jungle

Tales from the Jungle

A Rainforest Reader

EDITED BY DANIEL R. KATZ
AND MILES CHAPIN
FOREWORD BY GEORGE PLIMPTON

Crown Trade Paperbacks
New York

We dedicate this book to our fathers,
who allowed us to pursue our own visions,
and explore our own jungles

Published by Crown Trade Paperbacks, 201 East 50th Street, New York, New York 10022. Member of the Crown Publishing Group.

Random House, Inc. New York, Toronto, London, Sydney, Auckland

CROWN TRADE PAPERBACKS and colophon are trademarks of Crown Publishers, Inc.

Manufactured in the United States of America

Text printed on recycled paper

Design by Renato Stanisic
Cover illustration, "Secrets of the Rainforest," copyright © 1991 by Charles Lynn Bragg. Licensed by Seiffer and Assoc., Bethel, CT 06801.

Library of Congress Cataloging-in-Publication Data
Tales from the jungle : a rainforest reader / [compiled] by Daniel
   R. Katz and Miles Chapin : foreword by George Plimpton.
     1. Rainforests—Literary collections. 2. Jungles—Literary
collections. I. Katz, Daniel R. II. Chapin, Miles.
   PN6071.R35T35   1995
   810.8'036—dc20
                                                                94-13056
                                                                CIP

ISBN 0-517-88160-8

10   9   8   7   6   5   4   3   2   1

First Edition

Contents

ADVENTURE GONE BAD:
THINGS THAT GO BUMP IN THE NIGHT

THE JUNGLE IN THE MIND: THE FORESTS IN FICTION

The Fate of the Forests: The Future

Acknowledgments

Thanks are due to a special group of people who made this book possible. They include: Anna Basoli, Barbara Bristol, Kris Dahl, Patty Eddy, Jake Ehlers, Florence Eichan, Paul Ewing, Michael Goulding, Dorothea Herrey, Julian Hope, Diane Jukofsky, the W. K. Kellogg Foundation, Maya Kennedy, Jessica Murrow, Roger Pasquier, Andy Revkin, Paula Russo, Lauren Shakely, Helene Weitzner, Diana Widener, Chris Wille, Richard Zacks, Jenny Chapin, Jessica Robinson, and the board and staff of the Rainforest Alliance.

Special thanks to Tom Lovejoy for letting us raid his library.

Finally, the editors wish to thank all the authors who gave their material for this book.

Foreword

As you'll read in this volume's introduction, many have felt that the rainforests were burdensome parts of the world, especially for those who were visitors in such places for an extended period of time. Indeed, before taking a trip myself into the rainforests in the eastern part of Zaire, formerly the Congo, I read up on the area, and began wondering what I was getting into. The German explorer Adolphus Frederick, Duke of Mecklenburg, wrote of where I was going: "I believe a long stay in this forest would lead to heavy mental depression in sensitive men. The unutterable feeling of oppression which makes itself felt in the course of time lies in the absence of any free view, the impossibility of permitting the eye to roam freely across a wide space, or of once catching a glimpse of sky and earth merging in the far horizon. You are hemmed in by thickets which prevent you from penetrating the green depths on either side, and, on gazing upward, the dense canopy of foliage overhead forbids an untrammeled view of the heavens to eyes so wearied with eternal green. On coming to a glade, the green walls rise implacably up to a height of forty metres, and the traveller can only be compared to a prisoner who has exchanged the narrow confines of his cell for the prison courtyard. The forest is oppressive in its monstrous hugeness and density, filling up all the space from the ground to the highest treetops. Thus we could understand how the Belgian officials found their *forêt vierge* deadening and soul-killing, and often spoke with mild horror of the march through the forest from Stanleyville to their stations on the eastern boundary."

Who was I to disagree with a German duke! But when I found myself in the rainforest he describes, I immediately felt quite differently about it—that comparing the green foliage flanking a rainforest game trail to the bleak wall of a prison compound was ill chosen. First of all, to my eyes at least, the smallest patch of jungle turned out to be a splendid tangle of botanical variety . . . a hodgepodge of insect life. I made notes of huge spiderwebs high above. The shades of light on the forest floor changed dramatically when the sun, unseen above the forest canopy, ducked behind a cloud. What I particularly remember were the occasional thunderstorms that passed through. They thrashed the treetops, darkening the forest floor in deep shadows, which were lit occasionally by the fitful flickering of lightning, and then they moved on, muttering into the distance. It was there, as the forest floor once again brightened up, that a slender beam or two of sunlight dappling the leaves, a sudden deluge of raindrops showered down. It took that long for the storm, now long gone, to percolate through the canopy, the lianas, the creepers, the outsized leaves and vines, past those spiderwebs to reach us on the forest floor. The hum of insects rose in the thick, humid air.

I was in the Congo looking for the Congo peacock—one of the four species of bird that ornithologists rank as the most exciting to find on the African continent. The others are the lyre-tailed honey guide, the bald crow, and the whale-headed stork. The criteria was that each bird had to be rare, unique, and difficult to track down. To my knowledge, no ornithologist has ever seen all four. The first two—the honey guide and the crow—live in eastern Nigeria, and the stork (the easiest of the four to find), in the papyrus swamps of Lake Victoria and marsh areas in the Sudan and Zambia. Of the four, the peacock is the most difficult. Indeed, the bird, which looks somewhat like a hen pheasant with a small white crown on its head, was only discovered in 1924.

When I arrived in the Congo, the other three birds were already on my list. We trekked into the jungle after the peacock. Late one afternoon, one of those thunderstorms came through. We were wearing our safari hats because we knew the raindrops would soon reach us. After the storm had gone by, our little group moved across the sun-dappled forest—Alec Forbes-Watson, the ornithologist, leader of the expedition; my sister, Sarah, who is an avid bird-watcher, much more skilled than I am; and I. Two trackers were ahead of us. I was last in line, my sister just in front of me. Suddenly, to one side and slightly behind me, I heard a rush of movement, a beat of wings, and saw just a glimpse of a dark shape moving quickly up through the thick undergrowth before it disappeared. I have always insisted that it was the Congo peacock. My sister disagrees. She says I was "seeing things." She is very competitive. Forbes-Watson doesn't take sides.

I like to think that my bird list is complete, and that I am the only living soul to have on his list those four prized African birds. Such a thought does a lot to lift the "heavy mental depression" that the German duke feels affects "sensitive men" in the rainforest.

It is, of course, a somewhat limited reason to hold the rainforests in such high esteem—that one of them in the eastern fastnesses of Zaire contains this unique bird. A far more obliging and sensible view is that I was privileged to spend some time in one of the most remarkable areas of the world—rainforest county, or "jungle" in Rudyard Kipling terminology. Indeed, it occurs to me that my favorite books during childhood were the Kipling "jungle books." I envied Mowgli not only his glamorous friends of the Indian rainforests—the python Kaa, the panther Bagheera, Ikki the porcupine, Akela, the great grey wolf, and the rest of them—but also the country over which these animals roamed. I envied Mowgli when the Monkey People picked him up by the arms and swung him through the treetops a hundred feet above the ground, twenty feet at a bound.

Last year, I spent some time in Kiplingesque country—at Ranthambhore, once the private hunting preserve of the Maharajah of Jaipur, where tens of thousands of tigers were killed by the maharajahs and the English sahibs who fired from hunting towers and the safety of elephants' backs—in an area more recently decimated by poachers. There is a vast room in the Pink Palace at Jaipur that is covered entirely with tiger skins, so that one can walk a hundred yards or so across the backs of tigers. Now, in the thousands of acres of Ranthambhore, there are perhaps twenty tigers left, maybe fewer. We spent five days looking for them, and saw none.

Our guide shook his head in disbelief. He said, mournfully, "The tiger is the king of the jungle, and once he is gone, the jungle will go with him. And then we will have nothing." He looked at us. "Is it not the same everywhere?" We nodded our heads in agreement.

Afterward I remembered Mowgli's "Song Against the People" in which he urges the forests themselves to take action: "I have untied against you the club-footed vines/I have sent in the Jungle to swamp out your lines/The trees—the trees are on you!/the house-beams shall fall. . . ."

—GEORGE PLIMPTON
New York City

Introduction

"The horror! The horror!"

It is with these dying words that one of the best-known characters in all of jungle literature, Joseph Conrad's creation Mr. Kurtz, sums up life in the torrid zone. Kurtz's encounter with the jungle was by no means typical, but his words perfectly express the attitude held by most other Westerners for centuries. For them, the jungle was a dreadful and darkly mysterious place full of horrifying beasts, strange and incurable diseases, and unspeakable dangers.

It is only in the last few decades that this general perception of jungles has been supplanted by a more benign view. The grandchildren of readers who cringed in fear while reading chilling jungle tales now learn of the many ways these places contribute to their lives; and these children learn a new word, *rainforests,* for these once-forbidding realms. Governments, businesses, and conservation groups around the globe desperately work to keep forests standing as biologists gradually discover what makes these unique environments tick. Jungles themselves, or at least those parts of jungles still untouched by human hands, have changed less than nearly anywhere else on Earth in the past few centuries, but our attitudes about them could hardly have changed more.

When did this shift occur? How can we track the *idea* of jungles in literature as well as their images? What about biological reality? And, we must ask, is there still hope for their future survival? These are a few of the questions this volume seeks to explore.

Growing up as two white males from the urban jungles of the United States, we shared the common consciousness of jungles. Anyone who has spent a lazy afternoon watching a Tarzan movie or a Saturday morning laughing as "George of the Jungle" slammed into a tree while swinging from a vine will know what we're talking about. For earlier generations the adventure stories of H. Rider Haggard, or the regular dispatches of ace newspaperman Henry Morton Stanley, served the same purpose.

Jungles are a part of our collective fantasies, our folklore, and our very fiber. Even today, when jungles are represented by far more wholesome images than before, the fascination remains. The nightmarish visions of shrunken heads and quicksand pits presented by the media, such as in Ripley's "Believe It Or Not!" series, may persist to a certain degree, but today families pay dearly to visit "jungle" theme parks. And still we are entranced by the images coming out of the real thing: researchers scouring the forests to find miracle cures for life-threatening diseases, indigenous peoples fighting bravely to protect their homelands, and biologists discovering new species, proving that nature still holds many surprises.

This volume celebrates a range of writers' responses to the jungles, but it is also an effort to bring their current state into sharper focus. Reports from the forest can be confusing, though, alternately uplifting and depressing. The irrefutably rich biology of these regions is providing a wealth of useful species at the same time as their very survival is threatened. The struggle for control of the forests has created martyrs such as Chico Mendes and, possibly, some heroes for the future. But the destruction continues.

The stories in this collection are mostly the work of explorers, naturalists, journalists, scientists, and, of course, great authors. We offer them to you in the hope that you can see the source of our perceptions of jungles, and see where our attitudes might lead. Wherever colonialism and the expropriation of foreign territory took place along the equator, tales from the jungle were soon to follow. In this book, they date back as far as the 1500s and take a cautious look at the future. They are a mixed bag, a smorgasbord, provided for your enjoyment, entertainment, and elucidation.

Most of these stories provide perceptions of the forest from the outside looking in. That is, their viewpoints have little to do with the needs, desires, or realities of the forest and its inhabitants. Indeed, over the course of history our opinions were shaped much less by local voices than by the imaginations of those who may never have walked down a jungle trail. There has always been a market for sensationalistic books, written to be enjoyed by an audience at a safe remove—often by lamplight in a comfortable armchair, far from the equator. Of course, there were other types of jungle sojourns, and other kinds of jungle tales. Naturalists ventured into tropical areas to collect species or to better their understanding of how nature works. Much of our knowledge of natural history is based on their findings. Others searched for lost cities, or tracked the source of unimaginable riches. Some went into the jungle simply to be the first of their society to do so, and then to claim it as their own "discovery."

We have, however, noted some striking similarities in jungle stories, whether fact or fiction. First, most of them are by European males. Second, most of the pieces reflect the cultural biases of their day, which sometimes astonish the reader, although the degree of prejudice varies from author to author and from era to era. These pieces often reveal more about the author than about the forest itself. Third, the writings generally exhibit a disdain for native peoples and lack of respect for their wisdom, culture, and rights. Thankfully, as time has passed, sensitivity and concern for indigenous peoples has increased dramatically, at least among Western authors. To be sure, cultural biases still exist, but they have certainly evolved in a more benign direction. Who can say for sure how our current attitudes will be perceived by the generations that follow?

The tragedy in the tropical forests today encompasses more than racism, more than simple misunderstanding, and more than a lack of tolerance for other ways of living. We now know much more than those early explorers did about what is lost when the forests disappear and what the greater implications of that loss are. We have learned to chuckle at the exaggerations of most big-as-your-thigh snake stories, but there is no exaggeration in stating that tropical rainforests are in serious danger. It is with a different sort of horror that we discover the alarming rate at which these areas are disappearing from our globe. Indeed, in the almost 150 years that have passed since Alfred Russel Wallace totaled up his remarkable list of 125,660 different species collected in the tropics, these areas have been whittled to half their original size—from four billion acres to under two and a half billion in less than a flash of geological time. And the rate of destruction has increased: Even the most conservative scientist would probably agree that today about eighty acres of tropical forest are being converted to some other type of landform *every single minute.*

What do we lose when these lush, vigorous, and seemingly impenetrable walls of green are leveled for roads, cattle ranches, logging operations, and agriculture? These surprisingly fragile ecosystems, which cover only seven percent of the planet's surface, actually contain more than half of the planet's biodiversity—the different species that currently exist in our world. Many of these species are still not known to science and could be of tremendous benefit. According to Dr. E. O. Wilson of Harvard University, whose writing appears in this collection, three species an hour are lost to extinction, and most of these are not even named by scientists. When we lose the species that have been part of a larger whole for several millennia or more, the results can be catastrophic, both locally and globally. The first rule of intelligent tinkering, said Aldo Leopold, is to save all the parts. Moreover, aside from all of the economic reasons for conserving rainforests, we strongly believe the forests have a right to exist for their own sake, and for the sake of the life within them.

There are ways both to conserve rainforests for future generations and to provide for people today. They revolve around two central ideas: common sense and alternatives. Common sense is needed in order to prove that if the forest is used more sparingly and thoughtfully now, humankind will reap benefits for a longer period of time. Alternatives to deforestation are necessary to provide different—less damaging—ways to use the forests. This is the mission of the Rainforest Alliance. Since 1987 we have been working with a broad range of constituencies, from the smallest local community to the largest multinational corporation, to find common ground and practical solutions to deforestation. And we have been successful. For example, the staff of our Smart Wood Certification Program works with logging operations to prove that "good logging" is not an oxymoron. The Smart Wood program awards a seal to operations and companies following guidelines that result in less damage to the forest. In a similar fashion, our ECO-OK Certification Program awards a seal to companies that grow their tropical agricultural products in an environmentally friendly manner. It is hoped that one day all bananas, vanilla, coffee, chocolate, and other tropical products will come from environmentally friendly sources.

The Rainforest Alliance has many other programs as well, and we encourage you to find out more (see the Afterword for our address). Please write or call us for more information. In fact, if you make your way through the maze of pieces included in this book, each a glimpse of a part of the whole of the amazing variety of nature (human and otherwise) that can be found in tropical forests, we feel confident that you will have a greater understanding and appreciation for them. If you are then moved to do something about their plight, you will be glad to hear that you already have: the profits of this volume are supporting the work of the Rainforest Alliance. If you want to reach out further, then get involved! Read more, think more, and act with great responsibility—for this is the world we have inherited from our forebears, and the only world we can pass along to future generations. They might like to visit a rainforest someday, too, and not just within the pages of a book.

Our collection starts with "The Explorers," including some of the early ones and a few of more recent vintage, then moves on to a section we have titled "Observations." Here, you will find attempts to understand, describe, enjoy, and in some cases simply survive the rigors of travel in tropical forests. We have included a section on "Things That Go Bump in the Night," to borrow a phrase from James Thurber, that contains some of the gory business one expects to find in any volume with the word *jungle* in the title. We then move on to take a look at jungles in fiction, where the evolution of the West's image of jungles is readily apparent. Finally, we end with a section that takes a cautious look at the future.

So grab an armchair and your pith helmet, and prepare yourself to venture into the unknown jungle darkness! But please, watch where you step.

—The Editors

Beyond Here
Be Dragons:
The Explorers

*I can understand the mad passion for travel books and their
deceptiveness. They create the illusion of something that
no longer exists but still should exist, if we are to have any
hope of avoiding the overwhelming conclusion that the
history of the last twenty thousand years is irrevocable.*

—Claude Lévi-Strauss

*Up there, in the dark places of the Amazon, Nature is cruel,
a monster which guards its secrets well and gives no quarter
to intruders.*

—F. W. UpdeGraff

The Finding of Livingstone

From The Autobiography of Sir Henry Morton Stanley *(1909)*
By Henry Morton Stanley

"Find Livingstone." That was the assignment James Gordon Bennett of the New York Herald *gave Henry Morton Stanley, an ace journalist who had been covering an insurrection in Spain. Bennett had heard that David Livingstone, the most famous explorer of the day, might be returning from Africa. Bennett wanted a jump on the story, certain that it would sell newspapers. So, from late in 1869 until Friday, November 10, 1871, Stanley dedicated himself entirely to finding the elusive Dr. Livingstone.*

Eventually, of course, Stanley succeeded, but only to discover that Livingstone had no longing to return home immediately and that he craved not rescue but supplies. And although Stanley later went on to make some real advances in exploration, the main prize he received for his search for Livingstone was a reputation as an arrogant seeker of fame and fortune.

Nevertheless, the meeting of Stanley and Livingstone remains one of history's most famous encounters, in or out of the jungle. Aside from questions of truth, honor, ethics, or morality, this meeting near Lake Tanganyika made for a fascinating story. The following is Stanley's version. (DRK)

Though fifteen months had elapsed since I had received my commission, no news of Livingstone had been heard by any mortal at Zanzibar. According to one, he was dead; and, according to another, he was lost; while still another hazarded the conviction that he had attached himself to an African princess, and had, in fact, settled down. There was no letter for me from Mr. Bennett, confirming his verbal order to go and search for the traveller; and no one at Zanzibar was prepared to advance thousands of dollars to one whom nobody knew; in my pocket I had about eighty dollars in gold left, after my fifteen months' journey!

Many people since have professed to disbelieve that I discovered the lost traveller in Africa! Had they known the circumstances of my arrival at Zanzibar, they would have had greater reason for their unbelief than they had. To me it looked for a time as though it would be an impossibility for me even to put foot on the mainland, though it was only twenty-five miles off. But, thanks to Captain Webb, the American consul, I succeeded in raising a sum of money amply sufficient, for the time being, for my purpose.

The "sinews of war" having been obtained, the formation of the expedition was proceeded with. On the 21st of March, 1871, it stood a compact little force of three whites, thirty-one armed freemen of Zanzibar, as escort, one hundred and fifty-three porters, and twenty-seven pack-animals, for a transport corps, besides two riding-horses, on the outskirts of the coast-town of Bagamoyo; equipped with every needful article for a long journey that the experience of many Arabs had suggested, and my own ideas of necessaries for comfort or convenience, in illness or health, had provided. Its very composition betrayed its character. There was nothing aggressive in it. Its many bales of cloth, and loads of beads and wire, with its assorted packages of provisions and medicine, indicated a peaceful caravan about to penetrate among African tribes accustomed to barter and chaffer; while its few guns showed a sufficient defensive power against bands of native banditti, though offensive measures were utterly out of the question.

I passed my apprenticeship in African travel while traversing the maritime region—a bitter school—amid rank jungles, fetid swamps, and fly-infested grass-lands, during which I encountered nothing that appeared to favour my journey. My pack and riding-animals died, my porters deserted, sickness of a very grievous nature thinned my numbers; but, despite the severe loss I sustained, I struggled through my troubles.

My mission to find Livingstone was very simple, and was a clear and definite aim. All I had to do was to free my mind from all else, and relieve it of every earthly desire but the finding of the man whom I was sent to seek. To think of self, friends, banking-account, life insurance, or any worldly interest but the one sole purpose of reaching the spot where Livingstone might happen to rest, could only tend to weaken resolution. Intense application to my task assisted me to forget all I had left behind, and all that might lie ahead in the future.

In some ways, it produced a delightful tranquility which was foreign to me while in Europe. To be indifferent to the obituaries the papers may publish to-morrow, that never even a thought should glance across the mind of law-courts, jails, tombstones; not to care what may disturb a Parliament, or a Congress, or the state of the Funds, or the nerves excited about earthquakes, floods, wars, and other national evils, is a felicity few educated men in Britain know; and it compensated me in a great measure for the distress from heat, meagreness of diet, malaria, and other ills, to which I became subject soon after entering Africa.

Agreeably to this determination, for twenty-two days we travelled in a south-westerly direction, during which I estimated we had performed a journey of two hundred and forty miles. At a place called Mpokwa, Mirambo's capital lying due north ten days distant, I turned westward, and after thirty-five miles, gradually turned a little to the westward of north. At the 105th mile of this northerly journey we came to the ferry of the Malagarazi River, Mirambo [a warring chief] being, at that point, eight days' march direct east of us, from whence I took a north-westerly course, straight for the port of the Arab colony on the great Lake. With the exception of a mutiny among my own people, which was soon forcibly crushed, and considerable suffering from famine, I had met with no adventures which detained me, or interrupted my rapid advance on the Lake. At the river just mentioned, however, a rumour reached me, by a native caravan, of a white man having reached Ujiji from Manyuema, a country situated a few hundred miles west of the lake, which startled us all greatly. The caravan did not stay long. The ferriage of the river is always exciting. The people were natives of West Tanganyika. The evidence, such as it was—brief, and given in a language few of my people could understand—was conclusive that the stranger was elderly, grey-bearded, white, and that he was a man wearing clothes somewhat of the pattern of those I wore; that he had been at Ujiji before, but had been years absent in the western country; and that he had only arrived either the same day they had left Ujiji with their caravan, or the day before. To my mind, startling as it was to me, it appeared that he could be no other than Livingstone. True, Sir Samuel Baker was known to be in Central Africa in the neighbourhood of the Nile lakes but he was not grey-bearded; a traveller might have arrived from the West Coast, he might be a Portuguese, a German, or a Frenchman, but then none of these had ever been heard of in the neighbourhood of Ujiji. Therefore, as fast as doubts arose as to his personality, arguments were as quickly found to dissipate them. Quickened by the hope that was inspired in my mind by this vague rumour, I crossed the Malagarazi River, and soon after entered the country of the factious and warlike Wahha.

A series of misfortunes commenced at the first village we came to in Uhha. I was summoned to halt, and to pay such a tribute as would have beggared me had I yielded. To reduce it, however, was a severe task and strain on my patience. I had received no previous warning that I should be subjected to such extortionate demands, which made the matter worse. The inevitable can always be endured, if due notice is given; but the suddenness of a mishap or an evil rouses the combative instincts in man. Before paying, or even submitting to the thought of payment, my power of resistance was carefully weighed, but I became inclined to moderation upon being assured by all concerned that this would be the only instance of what must be endured unless we chose to fight. After long hours of haggling over the amount, I paid my forfeit, and was permitted to proceed.

The next day I was again halted, and summoned to pay it again. The present demand was for a bolt of cloth. This led to half-formed resolutions to resist to the death, then anxious conjectures as to what would be the end of this rapacity. The manner of the Wahha was confident and supercilious. This could only arise from the knowledge that, whether their demands were agreeable or not to the white man, the refusal to pay could but result in gain to them. After hours of attempts to reduce the sum total, I submitted to pay one bale and a quarter. Again I was assured this would be the last.

The next day I rose at dawn to resume the march; but, four hours later, we were halted again, and forfeited another half bale, notwithstanding the most protracted and patient haggling on my part. And for the third time I was assured we were safe from further demands. The natives and my own people combined to comfort me with this assurance. I heard, however, shortly after, that Uhha extended for two long marches yet, further west. Knowing this, I declined to believe them, and began to form plans to escape from Uhha.

I purchased four days' rations as a provision for the wilderness, and at midnight I roused the caravan. Having noiselessly packed the goods, the people silently stole away from the sleeping village in small groups, and the guides were directed, as soon as we should be a little distance off, to abandon the road and march to the southward over the grassy plain. After eighteen hours' marching through an unpeopled wilderness, we were safe beyond Uhha and the power of any chief to exact tribute, or to lay down the arbitrary law, "Fight, or pay." A small stream now crossed was the boundary line between hateful Uhha and peaceful Ukaranga.

That evening we slept at a chief's village in Ukaranga, with only one more march of six hours, it was said, intervening between us and the Arab settlement of Ujiji, in which native rumour located an old, grey-bearded, white man, who had but newly arrived from a distant western country. It was now two hundred and thirty-five days since I had left the Indian Ocean, and fifty days since I had departed from Unyanyembe.

At cock-crow of the eventful day, the day that was to end all doubt, we strengthened ourselves with a substantial meal, and, as the sun rose in the east, we turned our backs to it, and the caravan was soon on full swing on the march. We were in hilly country, thickly wooded, towering trees nodding their heads far above, tall bush filling darkly the shade, the road winding like a serpent, narrow and sinuous, the hollows all musical with the murmur of living waters and their sibilant echoes, the air cool and fragrant with the smell of strange flowers and sweet gums. Then, my mind lightened with pleasant presentiments, and conscience complaisantly approving what I had done hitherto, you can imagine the vigour of our pace in that cool and charming twilight of the forest shades!

About eight o'clock we were climbing the side of a steep and wooded hill, and we presently stood on the very crest of it, and on the furthest edge looked out into a realm of light—wherein I saw, as in a painted picture, a vast lake in the distance below, with its face luminous as a mirror, set in a frame of dimly blue mountains. On the further side they seemed to be of appalling height. On the hither side they rose from low hills lining the shore, in advancing lines, separated by valleys, until they terminated at the base of that tall mountain-brow whereon I stood, looking down from my proud height, with glad eyes and exultant feelings, upon the whole prospect.

On our admiring people, who pressed eagerly forward to gaze upon the scene, contentment diffused itself immediately, inspiring a boisterous good-humour; for it meant a crowning rest from their daily round of miles, and a holiday from the bearing of burdens, certainly an agreeable change from the early reveillé, and hard fare of the road.

With thoughts still gladder, if possible, than ever, the caravan was urged down the descent. The lake grew larger into view, and smiled a broad welcome to us, until we lost sight of it in the valley below. For hours I strode nervously on, tearing through the cane-brakes of the valleys, brushing past the bush on the hill-slopes and crests, flinging gay remarks to the wondering villagers, who looked on the almost flying column in mute surprise, until near noon, when, having crossed the last valley and climbed up to the summit of the last hill, lo! Lake Tanganyika was distant from us but half a mile!

Before such a scene I must halt once more. To me, a lover of the sea, its rolling waves, its surge and its moan, the grand lake recalls my long-forgotten love! I look enraptured upon the magnificent expanse of fresh water; and the white-tipped billows of the inland sea. I see the sun and the clear white sky reflected a million times upon the dancing waves. I hear the sounding surge on the pebbled shore, I see its crispy edge curling over, and creeping up the land, to return again to the watery hollows below. I see canoes, far away from the shore, lazily rocking on the undulating face of the lake, and at once the sight appeals to the memories of my men who had long ago handled the net and the paddle. Hard by the lake shore, embowered in palms, on this hot noon, the village of Ujiji broods drowsily. No living thing can be seen moving to break the stilly aspect of the outer lines of the town and its deep shades. The green-swarded hill on which I stood descended in a gentle slope to the town. The path was seen, of an ochreous-brown, curving down the face of the hill until it entered under the trees into the town.

I rested awhile, breathless from my exertions; and, as the stragglers were many, I halted to re-unite and re-form for an imposing entry. Meantime, my people improved their personal appearance; they clothed themselves in clean dresses, and snowy cloths were folded round their heads. When the laggards had all been gathered, the guns were loaded to rouse up the sleeping town. It is an immemorial custom, for a caravan creeps not up into a friendly town like a thief. Our braves knew the custom well; they therefore volleyed and thundered their salutes as they went marching down the hill slowly, and with much self-contained dignity.

Presently, there is a tumultuous stir visible on the outer edge of the town. Groups of men in white dresses, with arms in their hands, burst from the shades, and seem to hesitate a moment, as if in doubt; they then come rushing up to meet us, pursued by hundreds of people, who shout joyfully, while yet afar, their noisy welcomes.

The foremost, who come on bounding up, cry out: "Why, we took you for Mirambo and his bandits, when we heard the booming of the guns. It is an age since a caravan has come to Ujiji. Which way did you come? Ah! you have got a white man with you! Is this his caravan?"

Being told it was a white man's caravan by the guides in front, the boisterous multitude pressed up to me, greeted me with salaams, and bowed their salutes. Hundreds of them jostled and trod upon one another's heels as they each strove to catch a look at the master of the caravan; and I was about asking one of the nearest to me whether it was true that there was a white man in Ujiji, who was just come from the countries west of the Lake, when a tall black man, in long white shirt, burst impulsively through the crowd on my right, and bending low, said,—

"Good-morning, sir," in clear, intelligent English.

"Hello!" I said, "who in the mischief are you?"

"I am Susi, sir, the servant of Dr. Livingstone."

"What! is Dr. Livingstone here in this town?"

"Yes, sir."

"But, are you sure; sure that it is Dr. Livingstone?"

"Why, I leave him just now, sir."

Before I could express my wonder, a similarly-dressed man elbowed his way briskly to me, and said,—

"Good-morning, sir."

"Are you also a servant of Dr. Livingstone?" I asked.

"Yes, sir."

"And what is your name?"

"It is Chuma."

"Oh! the friend of Wekotani, from the Nassick School?"

"Yes, sir."

"Well, now that we have met, one of you had better run ahead, and tell the Doctor of my coming."

The same idea striking Susi's mind, he undertook in his impulsive manner to inform the Doctor, and I saw him racing headlong, with his white dress streaming behind him like a wind-whipped pennant.

The column continued on its way, beset on either flank by a vehemently-enthusiastic and noisily-rejoicing mob, which bawled a jangling chorus of "Yambos" to every mother's son of us, and maintained an inharmonious orchestral music of drums and horns. I was indebted for this loud ovation to the cheerful relief the people felt that we were not Mirambo's bandits, and to their joy at the happy rupture of the long silence that had perforce existed between the two trading colonies of Unyanyembe and Ujiji, and because we brought news which concerned every householder and freeman of this lake port.

After a few minutes we came to a halt. The guides in the van had reached the market-place, which was the central point of interest. For there the great Arabs, chiefs, and respectabilities of Ujiji, had gathered in a group to await events; thither also they had brought with them the venerable European traveller who was at that time resting among them. The caravan pressed up to them, divided itself into two lines on either side of the road, and, as it did so, disclosed to me the prominent figure of an elderly white man clad in a red flannel blouse, grey trousers, and a blue cloth, gold-banded cap.

Up to this moment my mind had verged upon non-belief in his existence, and now a nagging doubt intruded itself into my mind that this white man could not be the object of my quest, or if he were, he would somehow contrive to disappear before my eyes would be satisfied with a view of him.

Consequently, though the expedition was organized for this supreme moment, and every movement of it had been confidently ordered with the view of discovering him, yet when the moment of discovery came, and the man himself stood revealed before me, this constantly recurring doubt contributed not a little to make me unprepared for it. "It may not be Livingstone after all," doubt suggested. If this is he, what shall I say to him? My imagination had not taken this question into consideration before. All around me was the immense crowd, hushed and expectant, and wondering how the scene would develop itself.

Under all these circumstances I could do no more than exercise some restraint and reserve, so I walked up to him, and, doffing my helmet, bowed and said in an inquiring tone,—

"Dr. Livingstone, I presume?"

Smiling cordially, he lifted his cap, and answered briefly, "Yes."

This ending all skepticism on my part, my face betrayed the earnestness of my satisfaction as I extended my hand and added,—

"I thank God, Doctor, that I have been permitted to see you."

In the warm grasp he gave my hand, and the heartiness of his voice, I felt that he also was sincere and earnest as he replied,—

"I feel most thankful that I am here to welcome you."

The principal Arabs now advanced, and I was presented by the Doctor to Sayed bin Majid, a relative of the Prince of Zanzibar; to Mohammed bin Sali, the Governor of Ujiji; to Abed bin Suliman, a rich merchant; to Mohammed bin Gharib, a constant good friend; and to many other notable friends and neighbours.

Then, remarking that the sun was very hot, the Doctor led the way to the verandah of his house, which was close by and fronted the market-place. The vast crowd moved with us.

After the Arab chiefs had been told the latest news of the war of their friends with Mirambo, with salaams, greetings, and warm handshakings, and comforting words to their old friend David (Livingstone), they retired from the verandah, and a large portion of the crowd followed them.

Then Livingstone caught sight of my people still standing in the hot sunshine by their packs, and extending his hand, said to me,—

"I am afraid I have been very remiss, too. Let me ask you now to share my house with me. It is not a very fine house, but it is rainproof and cool, and there are enough spare rooms to lodge you and your goods. Indeed, one room is far too large for my use."

I expressed my gratification at his kind offer in suitable terms, and accordingly gave directions to the chiefs of the caravan about the storing of the goods and the purchase of rations; and Livingstone charged his three servants, Susi, Chuma, and Hamoyda, to assist them. Relieved thus happily and comfortably from all further trouble about my men, I introduced the subject of breakfast, and asked permission of the Doctor to give a few directions to my cook.

The Doctor became all at once anxious on that score. Was my cook a good one? Could he prepare a really satisfactory breakfast? If not, he had a gem of a female cook—and here he laughed, and continued, "She is the oddest, most eccentric woman I have ever seen. She is quite a character, but I must give her due credit for her skill in cooking. She is exceedingly faithful, clean, and deft at all sorts of cooking fit for a toothless old man like myself. But, perhaps, the two combined would be still better able to satisfy you?"

Halima, a stout, buxom woman of thirty, was brought at once to our presence, grinning, but evidently nervous and shy. She was not uninteresting by any means, and as she opened her capacious mouth, two complete and perfect rows of teeth were revealed.

"Halima," began Livingstone, in kind, grave tones, "my young brother has travelled far, and is hungry. Do you think you and Ferajji, his cook, can manage to give us something nice to eat? What have you?"

"I can have some dampers, and kid kabobs, and tea or coffee ready immediately, master, if you like; and by sending to the market for something, we can do better."

"Well, Halima, we will leave it to you and Ferajji; only do your best, for this is a great day for us all in Ujiji."

"Yes, master. Sure to do that."

I now thought of Livingstone's letters, and calling Kaif-Halek, the bearer of them, I delivered into the Doctor's hands a long-delayed letter-bag that I had discovered at Unyanyembe, the cover of which was dated November 1st, 1870.

A gleam of joy lighted up his face, but he made no remark, as he stepped on to the verandah and resumed his seat. Resting the letter-bag on his knees, he presently, after a minute's abstraction in thought, lifted his face to me and said, "Now sit down by my side, and tell me the news."

"But what about your letters, Doctor? You will find the news, I dare say, in them. I am sure you must be impatient to read your letters after such a long silence."

"Ah!" he replied, with a sigh, "I have waited years for letters; and the lesson of patience I have well learned!—I can surely wait a few hours longer! I would rather hear the general news, so pray tell me how the old world outside of Africa is getting along."

Consenting, I sat down, and began to give a résumé of the exciting events that had transpired since he had disappeared in Africa, in March, 1866.

When I had ended the story of triumphs and reverses which had taken place between 1866 and 1871, my tent-boys advanced to spread a crimson table-cloth, and arrange the dishes and smoking platters heaped up profusely with hot dampers, white rice, maize porridge, kid kabobs, fricasseed chicken, and stewed goat-meat. There were also a number of things giving variety to the meal, such as honey from Ukawendi, forest plums, and wild-fruit jam, besides sweet milk and clabber, and then a silver tea-pot full of "best tea," and beautiful china cups and saucers to drink it from. Before we could commence this already magnificent breakfast, the servants of Sayed bin Majid, Mohammed bin Sali, and Muini Kheri brought three great trays loaded with cakes, curries, hashes, and stews, and three separate hillocks of white rice, and we looked at one another with a smile of wonder at this Ujiji banquet.

We drew near to it, and the Doctor uttered the grace: "For what we are going to receive, make us, O Lord, sincerely thankful."

From M'Fetta to Egaja

From Travels in West Africa *(1897)*
By Mary Kingsley

Think of it: In 1893 Mary Kingsley, a proper Englishwoman, daughter of the popular novelist Henry Kingsley, decides to visit the Dark Continent. She travels solo, except for native Fan and Ajumba guides, and visits only briefly at colonial settlements. Her ostensible aim is to collect specimens of fishes and insects, and so she journeys along the southern coast of West Africa and penetrates the interior several times, into Sierra Leone, the Cameroons, and the Congo. She greets native African and colonial European as equals, she travels much of the way as a native African would, and she does all this simply because she wants to.

Would that all of us who wish to travel and experience nature could do so with such grace and produce a report that ages as well as Travels in West Africa. *Mary Kingsley wrote two other books in her lifetime,* West African Studies *(1899) and* The Story of West Africa *(1899). Kingsley died of typhoid fever in South Africa in 1900, while working as a nurse during the Boer War.* (MWC)

On one occasion, between [the villages of] Egaja and Esoon, Wiki [the great elephant hunter] came back from [a] quest [for bush-ropes] and wanted me to come and see something, very quietly; I went, and we crept down into a rocky ravine, on the other side of which lay one of the outermost Egaja plantations. When we got to the edge of the cleared ground, we lay down, and wormed our way, with elaborate caution, among a patch of Koko; Wiki first, I following his trail.

After about fifty yards of this, Wiki sank flat, and I saw before me some thirty yards off, busily employed in pulling down plantains, and other depredations, five gorillas; one old male, one young male, and three females. One of these had clinging to her a young fellow, with beautiful wavy black hair with just a kink in it. The big male was crouching on his haunches, with his long arms hanging down on either side, with the backs of his hands on the ground, the palms upwards. The elder lady was tearing to pieces and eating a pine-apple, while the others were at the plantains destroying more than they ate.

They kept up a sort of whinnying, chattering noise, quite different from the sound I have heard gorillas give when enraged, or from the one you can hear them giving when they are what the natives call "dancing" at night. I noticed that their reach of arm was immense, and that when they went from one tree to another, they squatted across the open ground in a most inelegant style, dragging their long arms with the knuckles downwards. I should think the big male and female were over six feet each. The other would be from four to five. I put out my hand and laid it on Wiki's gun to prevent him from firing, and he, thinking I was going to fire, gripped my wrist.

I watched the gorillas with great interest for a few seconds, until I heard Wiki make a peculiar small sound, and looking at him saw his face was working in an awful way as he clutched his throat with his hand violently.

Heavens! think I, this gentleman's going to have a fit; it's lost we are entirely this time. He rolled his head to and fro, and then buried his face into the heap of dried rubbish at the foot of a plantain stem, clasped his hands over it, and gave an explosive sneeze. The gorillas let go all, raised themselves up for a second, gave a quaint sound between a bark and a howl, and then the ladies and the young gentleman started home. The old male rose to his full height (it struck me at the time this was a matter of ten feet at least, but for scientific purposes allowance must be made for a lady's emotions) and looked straight towards us, or rather towards where that sound came from. Wiki went off into a paroxysm of falsetto sneezes the likes of which I have never heard; nor evidently had the gorilla, who went off after his family the moment he touched the forest, and disappeared as they had, swinging himself through it from bough to bough, in a way that convinced me that, given the necessity of getting about in tropical forests, man has made a mistake in getting his arms shortened. I have seen many wild animals in their native wilds, but never have I seen anything to equal gorillas going through bush; it is a graceful, powerful, superbly perfect hand-trapeze performance.

I have no hesitation in saying that the gorilla is the most horrible wild animal I have seen. I have seen at close quarters specimens of the most important big game of Central Africa, and, with the exception of snakes, I have run away from all of them; but although elephants, leopards, and pythons give you a feeling of alarm, they do not give that feeling of horrible disgust that an old gorilla gives on account of his hideous appearance.

After this sporting adventure, we returned, as I usually return from a sporting adventure, without measurements or the body.

About five o'clock I was off ahead and noticed a path which I had been told I should meet with, and, when met with, I must follow. The path was slightly indistinct, but by keeping my eye on it I could see it. Presently I came to a place where it went out, but it appeared again on the other side of a clump of underbush fairly distinctly. I made a short cut for it and the next news was I was in a heap, on a lot of spikes, some fifteen feet or so below the ground level, at the bottom of a bag-shaped game pit.

It is at these times you realise the blessing of a good thick skirt. Had I paid heed to the advice of many people in England, who ought to have known better, and did not do it themselves, and adopted masculine garments, I should have been spiked to the bone and done for. Whereas, save for a good many bruises, here I was with the fullness of my skirt tucked under me, sitting on nine ebony spikes some twelve inches long, in comparative comfort, howling lustily to be hauled out. The Duke came along first, and looked down at me. I said, "Get a bush-rope, and haul me out." He grunted and sat down on a log. The Passenger came next, and he looked down. "You kill?" says he. "Not much," say I; "get a bush-rope and haul me out." "No fit," says he, and sat down on the log. Presently, however, Kiva and Wiki came up, and Wiki went and selected the one and only bush-rope suitable to haul an English lady, of my exact complexion, age, and size, out of that one particular pit. They seemed rare round there from the time he took; and I was just casting about in my mind as to what method would be best to employ in getting up the smooth yellow, sandy-clay, incurved walls, when he arrived with it, and I was out in a twinkling, and very much ashamed of myself. Then we closed up, for the Fans said these pits were symptomatic of the immediate neighbourhood of [the village of] Efoua. We sounded our ground, as we went into the thick plantain patch, through which we could see a great clearing in the forest, and the low huts of a big town. We charged into it, going right through the guard-house gateway, at one end, in single file, as its narrowness obliged us, and into the street-shaped town, and formed ourselves into as imposing a looking party as possible in the centre of the street. The Efouerians regarded us with much amazement, and the women and children cleared off into the huts, and took stock of us through the door-holes. There were but a few men in the town, the majority, we subsequently learnt, being away after elephants. But there were quite sufficient left to make a crowd in a ring round us.

As a result of the confabulation, one of the chiefs had his house cleared out for me. It consisted of two apartments almost bare of everything save a pile of boxes, and a small fire on the floor, some little bags hanging from the roof poles, and a general supply of insects. The inner room contained nothing save a hard plank, raised on four short pegs from the earth floor.

I shook hands with and thanked the chief, and directed that all the loads should be placed inside the huts. I must admit my good friend was a villainous-looking savage, but he behaved most hospitably and kindly. From what I had heard of the Fan, I deemed it advisable not to make any present to him at once, but to base my claim on him on the right of an amicable stranger to hospitality. When I had seen all the baggage stowed I went outside and sat at the doorway on a rather rickety mushroom-shaped stool in the cool evening air, waiting for my tea, which I wanted bitterly. Pagan came up as usual for tobacco to buy chop with; and after giving it to him, I and the two chiefs, with Gray Shirt acting as interpreter, had a long chat.

One old chief was exceedingly keen to do business, and I bought a meat spoon, a plantain spoon, and a gravy spoon off him; and then he brought me a lot of rubbish I did not want, and I said so, and announced I had finished trade for that night. However the old gentleman was not to be put off, and after an unsuccessful attempt to sell me his cooking-pots, which were roughly made out of clay, he made energetic signs to me that if I would wait he had got something that he would dispose of which Gray Shirt said was "good too much." Off he went across the street, and disappeared into his hut, where he evidently had a thorough hunt for the precious article. One box after another was brought out to the light of a bush torch held by one of his wives, and there was a great confabulation between him and his family of the "I'm sure you had it last," "You must have moved it," "Never touched the thing," sort. At last it was found, and he brought it across the street to me most carefully. It was a bundle of bark cloth tied round something most carefully with tie-tie. This being removed, disclosed a layer of rag, which was unwound from round a central article. Whatever can this be? thinks I: some rare and valuable object doubtless, let's hope connected with fetish worship, and I anxiously watched its unpacking; in the end, however, it disclosed to my disgust and rage, an old shilling razor. The way the old chief held it out, and the amount of dollars he asked for it, was enough to make any one believe that I was in such urgent need of the thing, that I was at his mercy regarding the price. I waved it off with a haughty scorn, and then feeling smitten by the expression of agonised bewilderment on his face, I dashed him a belt that delighted him, and went inside and had tea to soothe my outraged feelings.

As soon as all my men had come in, and established themselves in the inner room for the night, I curled up among the boxes, with my head on the tobacco sack, and dozed.

After about half an hour I noticed that the smell in the hut was violent, from being shut up I suppose, and it had an unmistakably organic origin. Knocking the ash end off the smouldering bush-light that lay burning on the floor, I investigated, and tracked it to those bags, so I took down the biggest one, and carefully noted exactly how the tie-tie had been put round its mouth; for these things are important and often mean a lot. I then took its contents out in my hat, for fear of losing anything of value. They were a human hand, three big toes, four eyes, two ears, and other portions of the human frame. The hand was fresh, the others only so, and shrivelled.

Replacing them I tied the bag up, and hung it up again, I subsequently learnt that although the Fans will eat their fellow friendly tribesfolk, yet they like to keep a little something belonging to them as a memento. This touching trait in their character I learnt from Wiki; and though it's to their credit, under the circumstances, still it's an unpleasant practice when they hang the remains in the bedroom you occupy, particularly if the bereavement in your host's family has been recent. I did not venture to prowl round Efoua; but slid the bark door aside and looked out to get a breath of fresh air.

It was a perfect night, and so no mosquitoes. The town, walled in on every side by the great cliff of high black forest, looked very wild as it showed in the starlight, its low, savage-built bark huts, in two hard rows, closed at either end by a guard-house. In both guard-houses there was a fire burning, and in their flickering glow showed the forms of sleeping men. Nothing was moving save the goats, which are always brought into the special house for them in the middle of the town, to keep them from the leopards, which roam from dusk to dawn.

Our second day's march was infinitely worse than the first, for it lay along a series of abruptly shaped hills with deep ravines between them;

each ravine had its swamp and each swamp its river. This bit of country must be absolutely impassable for any human being, black or white, except during the dry season. There were representatives of the three chief forms of the West African bog. The large deep swamps were best to deal with, because they make a break in the forest, and the sun can come down on their surface and bake a crust, over which you can go, if you go quickly.

The worst sort of swamp, and the most frequent hereabouts, is the deep narrow one that has no crust on, because it is too much shaded by the forest. The slopes of the ravines too are usually covered with an undergrowth of shenja, beautiful beyond description, but right bad to go through. I soon learnt to dread seeing the man in front going down hill, or to find myself doing so, for it meant that within the next half hour we should be battling through a patch of shenja. I believe there are few effects that can compare with the beauty of them, with the golden sunlight coming down through the upper forest's branches on to their exquisitely shaped, hard, dark green leaves, making them look as if they were sprinkled with golden sequins. Their long green stalks, which support the leaves and bear little bunches of crimson berries, take every graceful curve imaginable, and the whole affair is free from insects; and when you have said this, you have said all there is to say in favour of shenja, for those long green stalks of theirs are as tough as twisted wire, and the graceful curves go to the making of a net, which rises round you shoulder high, and the hard green leaves when lying on the ground are fearfully slippery. It is not nice going down through them, particularly when nature is so arranged that the edge of the bank you are descending is a rock-wall ten or twelve feet high with a swamp of unknown depth at its foot. It is still less pleasant, however, going up the other side of the ravine when you have got through your swamp. You have to fight your way upwards among rough rocks, through this hard tough network of stems; and it took it out of all of us except the Fans.

These narrow shaded swamps gave us a world of trouble and took up a good deal of time. Sometimes the leader of the party would make three or four attempts before he found a ford, going on until the black, batter-like ooze came up round his neck, and then turning back and trying another place; while the rest of the party sat upon the bank until the ford was found, feeling it was unnecessary to throw away human life, and that the more men there were paddling about in that swamp, the more chance there was that a hole in the bottom of it would be found; and when a hole was found, the discoverer is liable to leave his bones in it. If I happened to be in front, the duty of finding a ford fell on me; for none of us after leaving Efoua knew the swamps personally. I was too frightened of the Fan, and too nervous and uncertain of the stuff my other men were made of, to dare show the white feather at anything that turned up. The Fan took my conduct as a matter of course, never having travelled with white men before, or learnt the way some of them require carrying over swamps and rivers and so on. I dare say I might have taken things easier, but I was afraid to be afraid. I am very certain I should have fared very differently had I entered a region occupied by a powerful and ferocious tribe like the Fan from some districts on the West Coast, where the inhabitants are used to find the white man incapable of personal exertion, requiring to be carried in a hammock, or wheeled in a go-cart or a Bath-chair about the streets of their coast towns, depending for the defence of their settlement on a body of black soldiers.

All the rivers we crossed on the first, second, and third day I was told went into one or other of the branches of the Ogowé, showing that the long slope of land between the Ogowé and the Rembwé is towards the Ogowé. The stone of which the mountains were composed was that same hard black rock that I found on the Sierra del Cristal. They look like very old parts of the same range worn down to stumps by the disintegrating forces of the torrential rain and sun, and the dense forest growing on them. Frost of course they had not been subject to, but rocks, I noticed, were often being somewhat similarly split by root-lets having got into some tiny crevice and by gradual growth enlarged it to a crack.

I had suffered a good deal from thirst that day and we were all very nearly tired out with the athletic sports since leaving Efoua. One thing only we knew about [the next village] Egaja was that not one of us had a friend there, and that it was a town of extra evil repute, so we were not feeling very cheerful when towards evening time we struck its outermost plantations. Fortunately, after we passed the first plantation, we came upon a camp of rubber collectors—four young men; I got one of them to show us the way into the town.

At last we came to a sandy bank, and on that bank stood Egaja, the town with the evil name among the Fan, but where we had got to stay, fair or foul. We went into it through its palaver house, and soon had the usual row.

I had detected signs of trouble among my men during the whole day; the Ajumba were tired, and dissatisfied with the Fans; the Fans were in high feather, openly insolent to Ngouta, and anxious for me to stay in this delightful locality. I kept peace as well as I could, explaining to the Fans I had not enough money with me now, because I had not, when starting, expected such magnificent opportunities to be placed at my disposal; and promising to come back next year—a promise I hope to keep—and then we could go and have a grand time of it. This state of a party was a dangerous one in which to enter a strange Fan town, where our security lay in our being united. When the first burst of Egaja conversation began to boil down into something reasonable, I found that a villainous-looking scoundrel, smeared with soot and draped in a fragment of genuine antique cloth, was a head chief in mourning. He placed a house at my disposal, quite a mansion, for it had no less than four apartments. The first one was almost entirely occupied by a bedstead frame that was being made up inside on account of the small size of the door.

This had to be removed before we could get in with the baggage at all. While this removal was being effected with as much damage to the house and the article as if it were a quarter-day affair in England, the other chief arrived. He had been sent for, being away down the river fishing when we arrived. I saw at once he was a very superior man to any of the chiefs I had yet met with. It was not his attire, remarkable though that was for the district, for it consisted of a gentleman's black frock-coat such as is given in the ivory bundle, a bright blue felt sombrero hat, an ample cloth of Boma check; but his face and general bearing was distinctive, and very powerful and intelligent; and I knew that Egaja, for good or bad, owed its name to this man, and not to the mere sensual, brutal-looking one. He was exceedingly courteous, ordering his people to bring me a stool and one for himself, and then a fly-whisk to battle with the evening cloud of sand-flies. I got Pagan to come and act as interpreter while the rest were stowing the baggage. After compliments, "Tell the chief," I said, "that I hear this town of his is thief town."

"Better not, sir," says Pagan.

"Go on," said I, "or I'll tell him myself."

So Pagan did. It was a sad blow to the chief.

"Thief town, this highly respectable town of Egaja! a town whose moral conduct in all matters was an example to all towns, called a thief town! Oh, what a wicked world!"

I said it was, but I would reserve my opinion as to whether Egaja was a part of the wicked world or a star-like exception, until I had experienced it myself. We then discoursed on many matters, and I got a great deal of interesting fetish information out of the chief, which was valuable to me, because the whole of this district had not been in contact with white culture; and altogether I and the chief became great friends.

In Captivity

From Hans Staden: The True History of His Captivity *(1557)*
By Hans Staden, translated and edited by Malcolm Letts

What follows is an excerpt from the amazing—but entirely true—story of Hans Staden, a hapless German worker caught in the wrong place at the wrong time.

Drawn by the "New World" like a moth to the flame, Staden left his home in Holland for Lisbon, a perfect point from which to embark—the Portuguese were at that time making their mark all over the Americas. In 1547, he found his boat: a ship carrying convicts to Brazil, which Portugal had claimed as a colony in 1500.

Staden arrived in Brazil to find that conflict between indigenous Indians and their would-be rulers had intensified to the point of all-out war. Stranded in San Vincente, Portugal's first Brazilian colony, Staden was put to work manning a Portuguese cannon. His weapon was of little use against the Tupi Indians, however, who captured him during a raid.

This is by far the oldest piece in this collection, and the language takes some getting used to. Staden's original narrative was written in German more than four hundred years ago. Even in translation, it is clearly a language with a vocabulary a wee bit different from our own. (DRK)

I had a savage man for a slave of the tribe called Carios who caught game for me, and it was my custom to make expeditions with him into the forest.

As I was going through the forest I heard loud yells on either side of me, such as savages are accustomed to utter, and immediately a company of savages came running towards me, surrounding me on every side and shooting at me with their bows and arrows. Then I cried out: "Now may God preserve my soul." Scarcely had I uttered the words when they threw me to the ground and shot and stabbed at me. God be praised they only wounded me in the leg, but they tore my clothes from my body, one the jerkin, another the hat, a third the shirt, and so forth. Then they commenced to quarrel over me. One said he was the first to overtake me, another protested that it was he that caught me, while the rest smote me with their bows. At last two of them seized me and lifted me up, naked as I was, and taking me by the arms, some running in front and some behind, they carried me along with them through the forest at a great pace towards the sea where they had their canoes. As we approached the sea I saw the canoes about a stone's throw away, which they had dragged out of the water and hidden behind the shrubs, and with the canoes were great multitudes of savages, all decked out with feathers according to their custom. When they saw me they rushed towards me, biting their arms and threatening me, and making gestures as if they would eat me. Then a king approached me carrying the club with which they kill their captives, who spoke saying that having captured me, they would now take vengeance on me for the death of their friends, and so carrying me to the canoes they beat me with their fists. Then they made haste to launch their canoes, for they feared that an alarm might be raised at Brikioka, as indeed was the case.

Before launching the canoes they bound my hands together, but since they were not all from the same place and no one wanted to go home empty-handed, they began to dispute with my two captors, saying that they had all been just as near to me when I was taken, and each one demanding a piece of me and clamouring to have me killed on the spot.

Then I stood and prayed, expecting every moment to be struck down. But at last the king, who desired to keep me, gave orders to carry me back alive so that their women might see me and make merry with me. For they intended to kill me "Kawewi Pepicke": that is, to prepare a drink and gather together for a feast at which they would eat me. At these words they desisted, but they bound four ropes around my neck, and I was forced to climb into a canoe, while they made fast the ends of the ropes to the boats and then pushed off and commenced the homeward journey.

My captors passed by an island and ran the canoes ashore, intending to spend the night there, and they carried me from the canoe to the land. I could scarcely see, for I had been wounded in the face, nor could I walk on account of wounds in my leg, but could only lie down on the sand. Then they stood round me and boasted that they would eat me.

So in mighty fear and terror I bethought me of matters which I had never dwelt upon before, and considered with myself how dark is the vale of sorrows in which we have our being. Then, weeping, I began in the bitterness of my heart to sing the Psalm: "Out of the depths have I cried unto thee." Whereupon the savages rejoiced and said: "See how he cries: now is he sorrowful indeed."

Then they considered and decided that the island was not a suitable place in which to spend the night, and they returned to the mainland where there were huts which they had erected previously, and it was night when we came there. The savages beached the canoes and lit a fire and afterwards took me to it. There I had to sleep—in a net which they called in their tongue Inni. These nets are their beds and they make fast to two posts above the ground, or if they are in the forest they tie them to two trees. So I lay there with the cord which I had about my neck tied high up in a tree, and they lay round about me all night and mocked me saying in their speech: *Schere inbau ende*, which is to say: "You are my bound beast."

Before daybreak we were once more on our way and rowed all day, so that by Vespers we were some two miles from the place where they intended to spend the night. Then great black clouds arose behind me which were terrible to see, and the savages laboured at the oars, striving to reach land and to escape the wind and darkness. But when they saw that their efforts were in vain they said to me: *Ne mungitta dee Tuppan do Quabe, amanasu y an dee Imme Ranni me sisse,* which is to say: "Speak with your God that we may escape the wind and rain." I kept silent, but prayed in my heart as the savages required of me: "O almighty God, Lord of heaven and earth, who from the beginning hast succoured those that call upon thee, now among the heathen show thy mercy to me that I may know that thou art with me, and establish thee among these savages who know thee not, that they may see that thou hast heard my prayer."

I lay bound in the canoe and could not turn myself to regard the sky, but the savages looked steadfastly behind them and commenced to say: *Oqua moa amansu,* which means: "The great storm is departing." Then I raised myself as best I could and looked back and saw that the clouds were passing, and I praised God.

When we came to land they did with me as before and bound me to a tree, and lay about me all night telling me that we were approaching their country where we should arrive on the morrow about evening, at which I rejoiced not at all.

On that same day about vesper time (reckoning by the sun) we came in sight of their dwelling. The place to which I had come was thirty miles distant from Brikioka where I had been captured.

When we were near the dwellings I saw that the place was a small village with seven huts, and it was called Uwattibi (Ubatúba). We landed on the beach close by the sea, and there were the women folk in a plantation of mandioca roots. They were going up and down gathering roots, and I was forced to call out to them and say: *A junesche been ertmi vramme,* which means: "I your food have come."

As we landed, all the women, young and old, came running out of the huts which were built on a hill, to stare at me. The men went into their huts with their bows and arrows, leaving me to the pleasure of the women who gathered round and went along with me, some in front and some behind, dancing and singing the songs they are wont to sing to their own people when they are about to eat them.

They then carried me to a kind of fort outside the huts called Ywara, which they defend against their enemies by means of great rails made like a garden fence. When I entered this enclosure the women fell upon me and beat me with their fists, plucking at my beard and crying out in their speech: *Sehe Innamme pepikeae*, which is to say: "With this blow I avenge me of my friend, that one who was slain by your people."

At this time I knew less of their customs than I knew later, and I thought to myself: now they are preparing to kill me. In a little time the two men who had captured me, namely Jeppipo Wasu and his brother, Alkindar Miri, came near and told me that they had presented me in friendship to their father's brother, Ipperu Wasu, who would keep me until I was ready to be eaten, when he would kill me and thus acquire a new name.

This Ipperu Wasu had captured a slave a year before, and had presented him in friendship to Alkindar Miri, who had slain him and gained a new name. This Alkindar Miri had then promised to present Ipperu Wasu with the first prisoner he caught. And I was the prisoner.

My two captors told me further that the women would lead me out Aprasse. This word I did not then understand, but it signifies a dance. Thus was I dragged from the huts by the rope which was still about my neck to the dancing place. All the women came running from the seven huts, and seized me while the men withdrew, some by the arms, some by the rope about my throat, which they pulled so tight that I could hardly breathe. So they carried me with them, for what purpose I knew not, and I could think only of our Saviour Jesus Christ, whereat I was comforted and grew more patient. They brought me to the hut of their king, who was called Vratinge Wasu, which means the great white bird. In front of this was a heap of fresh earth, and they brought me to it and sat me there holding me fast. I could not but think that they would slay me forthwith and began to look about me for the club which they use to kill their prisoners, and I asked whether I was now to die, but they told me "not yet." Upon this a woman approached carrying a piece of crystal fastened to a kind of ring and with it she scraped off my eyebrows and tried to scrape off my beard also, but I resisted, saying that I would die with my beard. Then they answered that they were not ready to kill me yet and left me my beard. But a few days later they cut it off with some scissors which the Frenchmen had given them.

After this they carried me from the place where they had cut off my eyebrows to the huts where they kept their idols. Here they made a ring round me, I being tied with two women in the centre, and tied my legs with strings of objects which rattled. They bound me also with sheaves of feather arranged in a square, which they fastened behind at my neck so that they stood up above my head. This ornament is called in their language Arasoya. Then the women commenced to sing all together, and I had to keep time with the rattles on my legs by stamping as they sang. But my wounded leg was so painful that I could hardly stand upright, for the wound had not been dressed.

When the dance was ended I was handed over to Ipperu Wasu who guarded me closely. He told me that I had some time to live. And the people brought the idols from the huts and set them up around me, saying that these had prophesied that they would capture a Portuguese. Then I replied that the idols were powerless and could not speak, and that even so they lied, since I was no Portuguese, but a kinsman and friend of the French, and that my native land was called Allemania. They made answer that it was I who lied, for if I was truly the Frenchmen's friend, how came it that I was among the Portuguese? For they knew well that the French were as much the enemies of the Portuguese as they were, and that they came every year in their boats, bringing knives, axes, mirrors, combs and scissors, and taking in exchange Brazilian wood, cotton, and other goods, such as feathers and pepper. These men were their good friends which the Portuguese were not. For the Portuguese, when they came to the country and settled there, had made friends with their enemies. Moreover, the Portuguese had come to their country, desiring to trade with them, and when they had gone down in all friendship and entered the ships, as they are to this day accustomed to do with the Frenchmen, the Portuguese had waited until sufficient numbers were on board, and had then seized and bound them, carrying them away to their enemies who had killed and eaten them. Others the Portuguese had slain with their guns, committing also many further acts of aggression, and even joining with their enemies and waging frequent war, with intent to capture them.

The savages said moreover, that the Portuguese had wounded the father of the two brothers, my captors, and had shot off one of his arms so that he died of his wounds, and that they intended to take vengeance on me for their father's death. To which I made answer that they should not visit this upon me, since I was no Portuguese, but had arrived some time since with the Castilians, and had been shipwrecked among the Portuguese, for which reason I had remained with them.

There was a Frenchman four miles distant from the village in which I was, and when he heard news of me he came and entered one of the huts opposite to the one in which I was kept. Then the savages came running to me and said: "Here is a Frenchman. Now we shall see whether you are in truth a Frenchman or not." At this I rejoiced greatly, for I told myself that he was at least a Christian and would do his best for me.

Then they took me to him, naked as I was, and I found him to be a youth known to the savages by the name Karwattuware. He commenced to speak to me in French, which I could not well understand, and the savages stood round about and listened. Then, when I was unable to reply to him, he spoke to the savages in their own tongue and said: "Kill him and eat him, the good-for-nothing, for he is indeed a Portuguese, your enemy and mine." This I understood, and I begged him for the love of God to tell them not to eat me, but he replied only: "They will certainly eat you." Whereupon I bethought me of the words of the Prophet Jeremy when he said: "Cursed be the man that trusteth in man," and I departed with a heavy heart. I had on my shoulders a linen cloth which the savages had given me, although I know not where they can have obtained it. This I tore off and flung it at the Frenchman's feet, saying to myself (for the sun had burnt me severely) that it was useless to preserve my flesh for others if I was to die. And they carried me back to the hut which was my prison where I stretched myself in my hammock. God alone knows the misery that I endured, and weeping I commenced to sing the verse: "Let us now beseech the Holy Ghost to save and guard us when death approaches and we pass from sorrows into peace." But the savages said only: "He is indeed a true Portuguese. Now he cries. Truth indeed he is afraid to die."

The Frenchman remained for two days in the huts, and on the third day he departed. The savages had resolved to make their preparations and to kill me on the day when everything should be ready. In the meantime they kept me very closely and mocked me continuously, both young and old.

It fell out during my misery, just as men say, that troubles never come singly, for one of my teeth commenced to ache so violently that by reason of the pain I could not eat and lost flesh. Whereat my master enquired of me why I ate so little, and I replied that I had a toothache. Then he came with an instrument made of wood, and wanted to pull out the tooth. I told him that it had ceased to trouble me, but nevertheless he tried to pull it out with force, and I resisted so vigorously that he gave up the attempt. Then he threatened that if I did not eat and grow fat again they would kill me before the appointed day. God knows how earnestly, from my heart, I desired, if it was his will, to die in peace without the savages perceiving it and before they could work their will on me.

In the meantime the twenty-five canoes of the savages who were friendly with the Portuguese came out in warlike array, and one morning they attacked the village.

Now when these Tuppin Ikins commenced to attack and were shooting at us, there was consternation in the huts and the women prepared to flee. But I said: "You take me for a Portuguese, your enemy, now give me a bow and arrows and free me, and I will help you to defend the huts." This they did, and I called out and shot my arrows, doing as they did, and encouraging them to be of good heart and no evil would befall them. My intention was to break through the stockade surrounding the huts and run towards the attackers, for they knew me well and were apprised that I was in the village, but my captors guarded me too well. And when the Tuppin Ikins saw that they could do nothing they returned to their canoes and departed, and as for me I was watched all the more closely.

News came the next day from a village called Mambukabe that the Tuppin Ikins, after they had departed leaving me a captive, had descended upon the village and burnt it, but the inhabitants had escaped except a small boy who had been captured. Upon this Jeppipo Wasu, who had charge of me and who did me many injuries, hurried off, since the people of the village were his friends, to help them to rebuild their huts. And with him went all his companions from the huts. His intention was to bring back clay and root metal in order to prepare the feast at which I was to be eaten, and as he departed he gave orders to Ipperu Wasu, to whom he had presented me, that I was to be closely guarded. They were absent for more than a fortnight making their preparations.

When I was daily expecting the return of the others who, as I have reported, were preparing for my death, I heard one day the sound of howling in the huts of the king, who was absent. I was much afraid, for I thought that they had now returned, since it is the custom of the savages, when one of them has been absent not longer than four days, to cry over him with joy when he returns. Presently one of the savages came to me and reported that the brother of him who owned a share in me had returned with the news that the others were all sick, whereat I greatly rejoiced, for I told myself that now God would show his might. Not long afterwards this brother himself came to the hut where I was, and sitting down by me he commenced to cry out aloud, saying that his own brother, his mother, and his brother's children had all fallen sick, and that his brother had sent him to me with the message that I was to make my God restore them to health; and he added that his brother was persuaded that my God was wrath with them. To which I replied: "My God is indeed angry with you for threatening to eat me, and for going to Mambukabe to prepare the feast, and for falsely accusing me of being a Portuguese." I told him, further, to return to his brother and bid him come back to the huts, and I would intercede with my God to make him well again. He replied that his brother was too ill to come, but that he knew and had observed that if I desired he would recover. Whereupon I made answer that he must wait until he was strong enough to come home to these huts, and that then he would be restored to health. With this answer he returned to Mambukabe, which is situated four miles from Uwattibei, where I was.

After some days the sick persons all came back. Then I was taken to the king's huts, and he told me how the sickness had come upon them, and that I must have known it, for he well remembered my saying that the moon was wrath with them. When I heard this I told myself that it was indeed God's doing that I had spoken on that evening, and I rejoiced greatly and said: "This day is God with me."

I told the king that this misfortune had befallen him because he had threatened to eat me, although I was no enemy of his, and he promised that if he recovered his health no evil should happen to me. But I was at a loss to ask of God, for it seemed to me that if the savages recovered they would kill me at once, and if they died the others would say: "Let us kill him lest greater misfortunes befall us" as indeed they had already begun to say, and I could only submit the whole matter to God, the king beseeching me anew to make them well again. I went to and fro laying my hands on their heads as they desired me to do, but God did not suffer it and they began to die. A child died first, and then the king's mother, an old woman whose business it was to prepare the pots for the drink with which I was to be eaten. Some days later a brother died, and then again a child, and then another brother, that one who had first brought me news of their illness.

When the king saw that his children and his mother and brother were dead he began to fear that he and his wives would die also, and he begged me to tell my God to make an end of his wrath so that he might live. I comforted him mightily, telling him not to despair, and that when he recovered his health he must give up all thought of killing me, which he promised, giving orders to those in his huts to cease from mocking me and threatening to eat me. He remained sick for a time, but finally he recovered, as did one of his wives who had been stricken, but there died of his family some eight persons, besides others, all of whom had treated me with great cruelty.

The old women about the huts who had done me much injury, beating me and threatening to eat me, now called me *Scheraeire*, which signifies: "Son, do not let me die," saying that when they ill-treated me they thought I was one of the Portuguese whom they had hated. Further that they had eaten many Portuguese whose God had never been as angry as mine, and that it was clear that I was not a Portuguese at all.

After this they left me alone for a time, for they did not know what to do with me, nor whether I was in truth a Portuguese or a Frenchman. They remarked that I had a red beard like the Frenchmen, whereas the Portuguese, although they had seen some with red beards, had in general black beards.

Some days later the savages made preparations to eat one of their captives. These preparations took place in a village called Teckquarippe, about six miles away, and a company of people set out for the village, taking me with them. The slave who was to be eaten belonged to a nation called Marcaya, and he travelled thither in a canoe.

Now it is their custom when they are about to kill a man for the people to brew a drink from roots called Kawi, and after they have drunk this they kill their victim. I went to the prisoner on the eve of the day on which they were to drink in preparation for his death and said: "All is ready for your death," and he laughed and said: "Yes." Now the rope with which they bind their victims is called Mussurana, and it is made of cotton, being thicker than a man's finger, and the man agreed that all was in order, only the rope was too short, for it wanted some six fathoms in length, and he added that with his people the matter would have been better arranged. And he spoke and acted as if he were going to a merrymaking.

I had with me a book in the Portuguese tongue, which the savages had taken from a ship they had captured with the help of the French, and they had given it to me. I departed from the prisoner and read in the book, and was consumed with pity for him. I therefore returned to him, for the Portuguese are friendly with the Marcaya tribe, and told him that I also was a prisoner as he was, and had not come to eat him, but had been brought there by my masters. He replied that he knew well that we did not eat human flesh. I then told him to be comforted for they would eat his body only, but his soul would be gathered to another place with the people of our nation where all was happiness and joy, but he doubted whether this was true, for he said he had never seen God. I told him that he would see him in another life, and so left him.

That night a great storm of wind arose and blew so furiously that pieces of the roofs of the huts were carried away. Then the savages began to murmur against me, saying in their speech: *Apo Meiren geup-pawy wittu wasu Immou:* "This evil fellow, the magician, has brought this wind upon us, for he looked by day into his book of thunder," meaning the book which I had, and they insisted that I had done this because the prisoner was a friend of the Portuguese, saying that I intended, perchance, to hinder the feast with bad weather. Then I prayed to God and said: "Lord, thou hast protected me until now, protect me still further," for they murmured much against me.

When the day broke it was fine weather and the savages drank and were merry, but I went to the victim and told him that the great wind was my God, and that he had come to claim him. At dawn the following day he was eaten.

There was a king over certain huts which were close to my hut, named Tatamiri, and he had charge of the roasted flesh. He caused drink to be prepared, according to their custom, and all the savages gathered together, drinking, singing, and making very merry. The day following they cooked the flesh again and ate it. But the flesh of Hieronymus remained in the hut where I was, hanging in the smoke, in a pot over the fire for three weeks, until it was as dry as wood. This was due to the fact that one of the savages named Parwaa had gone to collect roots with which to prepare drink to be served when Hieronymus was eaten, and so the time passed. The savages would not take me to the ship until they had celebrated their feast and eaten the remains of Hieronymus, and in the meantime the ship had departed, for it lay about eight miles from the place where I was.

When I heard the news of this I was much cast down, but the savages assured me that the ship came every year, and with this I had to be content.

I had made a cross of reeds and set it up in front of my hut, and it was my custom to say my prayers there. I had told the savages not to remove it, lest some misfortune should befall them. But they gave no heed to my words, and once I was away fishing, a woman tore up the cross and gave it to her husband to use for rubbing down the charms which they make from the shell of sea-snails, since it was round. At this I was very sad, and some days later it began to rain heavily. The rain endured for several days, and the savages came to my hut and asked me to tell my God to stop the rain, for if it continued it would spoil their planting, the time for which then arrived. I replied that it was their own fault for they had angered my God by pulling up the wooden stick in front of which I used to speak with him. When they heard that this was the cause of the rain, my master's son helped me to set up another cross, and it was then about an hour after midday, reckoning by the sun. As soon as the cross was set up the weather, which before noon had been very stormy, began at once to improve. And they all marvelled, saying that my God, in truth, did as I told him.

One day I went fishing with the chief named Parwaa, the man who had roasted Hieronymus, and as I stood fishing with him and another at the close of day, there arose a great storm of rain and thunder not far from where we stood, and the wind blew the rain in our direction. Then the two men begged me to ask my God to see to it that the rain did not hinder us, so that we might catch more fish since, as I knew, there was nothing to eat in the hut. Thus moved, I prayed to God from the depths of my heart, that he might show his power in me and make plain to the heathen that he was with me at all times. As I finished my supplication the wind, blowing mightily, carried the rain towards us, so that it was raining heavily some six feet away from us, but on the place where we stood we felt nothing. Then the savage Parwaa spoke again: "Now I see that you have indeed prayed to your God," and we caught a number of fish.

When we returned to the huts the two men told the others what had happened when I spoke to my God, and they were all amazed.

When all was made ready, as I have already related, the savage Parwaa caused drink to be prepared which was to be served when Hieronymus was eaten. When they had finished drinking they brought out the two brothers and another named Anthonius who had been captured by my master's son, and we four Christians were there together. We were forced to drink with the savages, but before doing so we prayed to God to have mercy on the dead man's soul, and to us also when our time came. And then the savages spoke with us and were merry, but we were full of sorrow. The next day, early in the morning, they cooked the flesh again and ate it very quickly.

They now took me to be given away, and as I parted from the two brothers they begged me to pray to God for them, and I advised them, in case they should escape, what direction they should take in the mountains, and how to cover their tracks, for I knew the mountains well. They were able to take advantage of my counsel, for I heard later that they had escaped, but whether they were recaptured I know not.

The savages now carried me to a place called Tackwara Sutibi, where they intended to give me away. When we were a short distance from the shore I looked behind me towards the huts and saw a black cloud hovering over them. I pointed this out to my companions, and told them that my God was wrath with the whole village for having eaten Christian flesh. When we arrived at the end of our journey I was presented to a king called Abbati Bossange, and the savages warned him that he was not to injure me or suffer me to be injured, since my God was very mighty against those that did me evil, which thing they had seen while I was with them. And I added my own warning, saying that my brother and friends would shortly arrive with a ship full of goods, and if they took care of me I would make them large gifts; for I knew full well that my God would send my brother with the ship right speedily. This pleased the savages greatly, and the king called me his son and I went with his sons hunting.

I remained some fourteen days in the place Tackwara Sutibi with king Abbati Bossange, and one day it happened that certain of the savages came to me and reported that they had heard the sound of shooting, which must have come from the harbour of Iteronne, or Rio de Jenero. As I was sure that a ship must have arrived there, I told them to carry me to it, for this was doubtless my brother's ship. They agreed to do this, but detained me for a few days more.

In the meantime it happened that the Frenchmen who had arrived there heard that I was a prisoner among the savages, and the captain sent two of his men, together with certain native kings, their friends, to the place where I was, and they came to a hut, the chief king of which was called Sowarasu. My hut was close at hand, and the news was brought to me that the two men had arrived from the ship. At this I rejoiced greatly, and went to them and bade them welcome in the native tongue, and when they saw my misery and nakedness they were full of pity and shared their clothes with me. I asked them why they had come and they said that it was on my account, and that their orders were to take me to the ship and to use force if necessary. Then my heart overflowed with gratitude to God and I told one of the men, who was called Perot and knew the savage tongue, that he must make believe he was my brother, and that he was to say that he had brought me certain chests full of merchandise and must take me with him to the ship to fetch them. He was to tell the savages also that I would then return to collect pepper and other things and wait until the ship came again the next year. Then they took me to the ship, my master going with us, where they received me in all pity and showed me great kindness. After we had been some five days in the ship, the king Abbati Bossange, to whom I had been given, asked me for the chests which they had brought me, so that we might now return home. I reported this to the ship's captain who told me to put him off until the ship had taken in the full cargo, in case the savages should become angry and work some mischief, since they were a people in whom no trust could be placed. My master still thought that he would take me back with him, but I held him with empty words, telling him not to hurry, for he knew that when good friends came together they could not part at once, and that when the ship left we would return to the huts. And so I satisfied him.

At last the ship was ready and the Frenchmen were all mustered together and I with them, the king, my master, with his people, being also there. Then the ship's captain spoke to the savages through his interpreter, and said that he was well pleased that they had not killed me when they captured me from among their enemies. He said also, in order to make it easier for him to take me away, that he had ordered me to be brought to the ship so that he might reward them for their care of me. Further, that it was his intention to give me goods and wares, and as I was known to them, to leave me there to collect pepper and other useful commodities until he came again. Meanwhile we had arranged between us that some ten of the crew, who were not unlike me, should gather round and say that they were my brothers and wanted to take me home. And so it fell out. My brothers would not suffer me to land, saying that I must return with them, as my father longed to see me once more before he died. Upon this the captain told the savages that he was captain of the ship and would have preferred that I should return with them, but that he was only one against many and could do nothing. All this was ordained so that we might part from the savages on friendly terms. I told the king, my master, that I should greatly like to return with him, but that, as he could see, my brothers would not allow me to do so. Thereupon he began to howl and cry in the ship, saying that if they took me away I must return with the first boat, for he looked upon me as his son, and was wrath with those of Uwattibi for threatening to eat me. And one of his wives who was in the ship began to cry over me, according to their custom, and I cried also. Then the captain gave them goods, some five ducats' worth of knives, axes, looking-glasses, and combs, and the savages returned with them to their dwellings.

On the last day of October 1554 we sailed from the harbour at Rio de Jenero, and made for France. We had favouring winds, so that the crew marvelled saying that such weather must have been sent specially as a gift from God (as indeed it was), for the hand of God was upon the waters. Amen.

The River of Doubt

From Through the Brazilian Wilderness *(1914)*
By Theodore Roosevelt

Here's an interesting piece from our own Bull Moose president himself. Teddy Roosevelt was our twenty-sixth president and is generally credited as our most environmentally conscious one. A great outdoorsman his entire life, after his time in the White House (1901–1909) he took to a life of travel and manly sport, mostly under the aegis of "collecting specimens" for the American Museum of Natural History in New York. His famous African safari was immortalized in his book African Game Trails, *and the book from which this excerpt is taken did the same for his Brazilian sojourn.*

This is not low-impact camping here. The phrase "take nothing but photos, leave nothing but footprints" comes to mind, but with T.R., his son Kermit, and their cronies at large in the wilds of Brazil, such moderation is definitely not on the program. (MWC)

On February 27, 1914, shortly after midday, we started down the River of Doubt into the unknown. We were quite uncertain whether after a week we should find ourselves in the Gy-Paranà, or after six weeks in the Madeira, or after three months we knew not where. That was why the river was rightly christened the Dúvida.

We had been camped close to the river, where the trail that follows the telegraph-line crosses it by a rough bridge. As our leaden dugouts swung into the stream, Amilcar and Miller and all the others of the Gy-Paranà party were on the banks and the bridge to wave farewell and wish us good-by and good luck. It was the height of the rainy season, and the swollen torrent was swift and brown. Our general course was to be northward toward the equator, by waterway through the vast forest.

We had seven canoes, all of them dugouts. One was small, one was cranky, and two were old, waterlogged, and leaky. The other three were good. The two old canoes were lashed together, and the cranky one was lashed to one of the others. Kermit with two paddlers went in the smallest of the good canoes; Colonel Rondon and Lyra with three other paddlers in the next largest; and the doctor, Cherrie, and I in the largest with three paddlers. The remaining eight camaradas—there were sixteen in all—were equally divided between our two pairs of lashed canoes. Although our personal baggage was cut down to the limit necessary for health and efficiency, yet on such a trip as ours, where scientific work has to be done and where food for twenty-two men for an unknown period of time has to be carried, it is impossible not to take a good deal of stuff; and the seven dugouts were too heavily laden.

The paddlers were a strapping set. They were expert river-men and men of the forest, skilled veterans in wilderness work. They were lithe as panthers and brawny as bears. They swam like water-dogs. They were equally at home with pole and paddle, with axe and machete; and one was a good cook and others good men around camp. They looked like pirates in the pictures of Howard Pyle or Maxfield Parrish; one or two of them were pirates, and one worse than a pirate; but most of them were hard-working, willing, and cheerful. They were white—or, rather, the olive of southern Europe—black, copper colored, and of all intermediate shades. In my canoe Luis the steersman, the headman, was a Matto Grosso negro; Julio the bowsman was from Bahia and of pure Portuguese blood; and the third man, Antonio, was a Parecís Indian.

My canoe ran ahead of the surveying canoes. The height of the water made the going easy, for most of the snags and fallen trees were well beneath the surface. Now and then, however, the swift water hurried us toward ripples that marked ugly spikes of sunken timber, or toward uprooted trees that stretched almost across the stream. Then the muscles stood out on the backs and arms of the paddlers as stroke on stroke they urged us away from and past the obstacle. If the leaning or fallen trees were the thorny, slender-stemmed boritana palms, which love wet, they were often, although plunged beneath the river, in full and vigorous growth, their stems curving upwards, and their frond-crowned tops shaken by rushing water. It was interesting work, for no civilized man, no white man, had ever gone down or up this river or seen the country through which we were passing. The lofty and matted forest rose like a green wall on either hand. The trees were stately and beautiful. The looped and twisted vines hung from them like great ropes. Masses of epiphytes grew both on the dead trees and the living; some had huge leaves like elephants' ears. Now and then fragrant scents were blown to us from flowers on the banks. There were not many birds, for the most part the forest was silent; rarely we heard strange calls from the depths of the woods, or saw a cormorant or ibis.

My canoe ran only a couple of hours. Then we halted to wait for the others. After a couple of hours more, as the surveyors had not turned up, we landed and made camp at a spot where the bank rose sharply for a hundred yards to a level stretch of ground. Our canoes were moored to trees. The axemen cleared a space for the tents; they were pitched, the baggage was brought up, and fires were kindled. The woods were almost soundless. Through them ran old tapir trails, but there was no fresh sign. Before nightfall the surveyors arrived. There were a few piums [a kind of sand fly] and gnats, and a few mosquitos after dark, but not enough to make us uncomfortable. The small stingless bees, of slightly aromatic odor, swarmed while daylight lasted and crawled over our face and hands; they were such tame, harmless things that when they tickled too much I always tried to brush them away without hurting them. But they became a great nuisance after a while. It had been raining at intervals, and the weather was overcast; but after the sun went down the sky cleared. The stars were brilliant overhead, and the new moon hung almost cool, and we slept soundly.

Next morning the two surveying canoes left immediately after breakfast. An hour later the two pairs of lashed canoes pushed off. I kept our canoe to let Cherrie collect, for in the early hours we could hear a number of birds in the woods near by. The most interesting birds he shot were a cotinga, brilliant turquoise-blue with a magenta-purple throat, and a big woodpecker, black above and cinnamon below with an entirely red head and neck. It was almost noon before we started. We saw a few more birds; there were fresh tapir and paca tracks at one point where we landed; once we heard howler monkeys from the depth of the forest, and once we saw a big otter in mid-stream. As we drifted and paddled down the swirling brown current, through the vivid rain-drenched green of the tropic forest, the trees leaned over the river from both banks. When those that had fallen in the river at some narrow point were very tall, or where it happened that two fell opposite each other, they formed barriers which the men in the leading canoes cleared with their axes. There were many palms, both the burity with its stiff fronds like enormous fans, and a handsome species of bacaba, with very long, gracefully curving fronds. In places the palms stood close together, towering and slender, their stems a stately colonnade, their fronds an arched fretwork against the sky. Butterflies of many hues fluttered over the river. The day was overcast, with showers of rain. When the sun broke through rifts in the clouds, his shafts turned the forest to gold.

This evening we made camp on a flat of dry ground, densely wooded, of course, directly on the edge of the river and five feet above it. It was fine to see the speed and sinewy ease with which the choppers cleared an open space for the tents. Next morning, when we bathed before sunrise, we dived into deep water right from the shore, and from the moored canoes. This second day we made sixteen and a half kilometres along the course of the river, and nine kilometres in a straight line almost due north.

The following day, March 1, there was much rain—sometimes showers, sometimes vertical sheets of water. Our course was somewhat west of north and we made twenty and a half kilometres. We passed signs of Indian habitation. There were abandoned palm-leaf shelters on both banks. On the left bank we came to two or three old Indian fields, grown up with coarse fern and studded with the burned skeletons of trees. At the mouth of a brook which entered from the right some sticks stood in the water, marking the site of an old fish-trap. At one point we found the tough vine hand-rail of an Indian bridge running right across the river, a couple of feet above it. Evidently the bridge had been built at low water. Three stout poles had been driven into the stream-bed in a line at right angles to the current. The bridge had consisted of poles fastened to these supports, leading between them and from the support at each end to the banks. The rope of tough vines had been stretched as a hand-rail, necessary with such precarious footing. The rise of the river had swept away the bridge, but the props and the rope hand-rail remained. In the afternoon, from the boat, Cherrie shot a large dark-gray monkey with a prehensile tail. It was very good eating.

We camped on a dry level space, but a few feet above, and close beside, the river—so that our swimming-bath was handy. The trees were cleared and camp was made with orderly hurry. One of the men almost stepped on a poisonous coral-snake, which would have been a serious thing, as his feet were bare. But I had on stout shoes, and the fangs of these serpents—unlike those of the pit-vipers—are too short to penetrate good leather. I promptly put my foot on him, and he bit my shoe with harmless venom. It has been said that the brilliant hues of the coral-snake when in its native haunts confer on it a concealing coloration. In the dark and tangled woods, and to an only less extent in the ordinary varied landscape, anything motionless, especially if partially hidden, easily eludes the eye. But against the dark-brown mould of the forest floor on which we found this coral-snake its bright and varied coloration was distinctly revealing; infinitely more so than the duller mottling of the jararaca and other dangerous snakes of the genus lachesis. In the same place, however, we found a striking example of genuine protective or mimetic coloration and shape. A rather large insect larva—at least we judged it to be a larval form, but we were none of us entomologists—bore a resemblance to a partially curled dry leaf which was fairly startling. The tail exactly resembled the stem or continuation of the midrib of the dried leaf. The flattened body was curled up at the sides, and veined and colored precisely like the leaf. The head, colored like the leaf, projected in front.

We were still in the Brazilian highlands. The forest did not teem with life. It was generally rather silent; we did not hear a chorus of birds and mammals as we had occasionally heard even on our overland journey, when more than once we had been awakened at dawn by the howling, screaming, yelping, and chattering of monkeys, toucans, macaws, parrots, and parakeets. There were, however, from time to time, queer sounds from the forest and after nightfall different kinds of frogs and insects uttered strange cries and calls. In volume and frequency these seemed to increase until midnight. Then they died away and before dawn everything was silent.

At this camp the carregadores ants completely devoured the doctor's undershirt, and ate holes in his mosquito-net; and they also ate the strap of Lyra's gun-case. The little stingless bees, of many kinds, swarmed in such multitudes, and were so persevering, that we had to wear our head-nets when we wrote or skinned specimens.

The following day was almost without rain. It was delightful to drift and paddle slowly down the beautiful tropical river. Until mid-afternoon the current was not very fast, and the broad, deep, placid stream bent and curved in every direction, although the general course was northwest. The country was flat, and more of the land was under than above water. Continually we found ourselves travelling between stretches of marshy forest where for miles the water stood or ran among the trees. Once we passed a hillock. We saw brilliantly colored parakeets and trogons. At last the slow current quickened. Faster it went, and faster, until it began to run like a mill-race, and we heard the roar of rapids ahead. We pulled to the right bank, moored the canoes, and while most of the men pitched camp two or three of them accompanied us to examine the rapids. We had made twenty kilometres.

We soon found that the rapids were a serious obstacle. There were many curls, and one or two regular falls, perhaps six feet high. It would have been impossible to run them, and they stretched for nearly a mile. The carry, however, which led through woods and over rocks in a nearly straight line, was somewhat shorter. It was not an easy portage over which to carry heavy loads and drag heavy dugout canoes. At the point where the descent was steepest there were great naked flats of friable sandstone and conglomerate. Over parts of these, where there was a surface of fine sand, there was a growth of coarse grass. Other parts were bare and had been worn by the weather into fantastic shapes—one projection looked like an old-fashioned beaver hat upside down. In this place, where the naked flats of rock showed the projection of the ledge through which the river had cut its course, the torrent rushed down a deep, sheer-sided, and extremely narrow channel. At one point it was less than two yards across, and for quite a distance not more than five or six yards. Yet only a mile or two above the rapids the deep, placid river was at least a hundred yards wide. It seemed extraordinary, almost impossible, that so broad a river could in so short a space of time contract its dimensions to the width of a strangled channel through which it poured its entire volume.

This had for long been a station where the Nhambiquaras at intervals built their ephemeral villages and tilled the soil with the rude and destructive cultivation of savages. There were several abandoned old fields, where the dense growth of rank fern hid the tangle of burnt and fallen logs. Nor had the Nhambiquaras been long absent. In one trail we found what gypsies would have called a "pateran," a couple of branches arranged crosswise, eight leaves to a branch; it had some special significance, belonging to that class of signals, each with some peculiar and often complicated meaning, which are commonly used by many wild peoples. The Indians had thrown a simple bridge, consisting of four long poles, without a hand-rail across one of the narrowest parts of the rock gorge through which the river foamed in its rapid descent. This sub-tribe of Indians was called the Navaïté; we named the rapids after them, Navaïté Rapids.

We spent March 3 and 4 and the morning of the 5th in portaging around the rapids. The first night we camped in the forest beside the spot where we had halted. Next morning we moved the baggage to the foot of the rapids where we intended to launch the canoes, and pitched our tents on the open sandstone flat. It rained heavily. The little bees were in such swarms as to be a nuisance. Many small stinging bees were with them, which stung badly. We were bitten by huge horse-flies, the size of bumblebees. More serious annoyance was caused by the piums and boroshuda flies during the hours of daylight, and by the polvora, the sand-flies, after dark. There were a few mosquitos. The boroshudas were the worse pests; they brought the blood at once, and left marks that lasted for weeks. I did my writing in head-net and gauntlets. Fortunately we had with us several bottles of "fly dope"— so named on the label—put up, with the rest of our medicine, by Doctor Alexander Lambert; he had tested it in the north woods and found it excellent. I had never before been forced to use such an ointment, and had been reluctant to take it with me; but now I was glad enough to have it, and we all of us found it exceedingly useful. I would never again go into mosquito or sand-fly country without it. The effect of an application wears off after half an hour or so, and under many conditions, as when one is perspiring freely, it is of no use; but there are times when minute mosquitos and gnats get through head-nets and under mosquito-bars, and when the ointment occasionally renewed may permit one to get sleep or rest which would otherwise be impossible of attainment. The termites got into our tent on the sand-flat, ate holes in Cherrie's mosquito-net and poncho, and were starting to work on our duffle-bags, when we discovered them.

Packing the loads across was simple. Dragging the heavy dugouts was labor. The biggest of the two water-logged ones was the heaviest. Lyra and Kermit did the job. All the men were employed at it except the cook, and one man was down with fever. A road was chopped through the forest and a couple of hundred stout six-foot poles, or small logs, were cut as rollers and placed about two yards apart. With block and tackle the seven dugouts were hoisted out of the river up the steep banks and up the rise of ground until the level was reached. Then the men harnessed themselves two by two on the drag-rope, while one of their number pried behind with a lever, and the canoe, bumping and sliding, was twitched through the woods. Over the sandstone flats there were some ugly ledges, but on the whole the course was downhill and relatively easy. Looking at the way the work was done, at the good-will, the endurance, and the strength of the camaradas, and at the intelligence and unwearied efforts of their commanders, one could but wonder at the ignorance of those who do not realize the energy and power that are so often possessed by, and may be so readily developed in, the men of the tropics. Another subject of perpetual wonder is the attitude of certain men who stay home, and still more the attitude of certain men who travel under easy conditions, and who belittle the achievements of the real explorers of, the real adventurers in, the great wilderness. The imposters and romancers among explorers and would-be explorers and wilderness wanderers have been unusually prominent in connection with South America (although the conspicuous ones are not South Americans, by the way); and these are not subjects for con-demnation and derision. But the work of the genuine explorer and wilderness wanderer is fraught with fatigue, hardship, and danger. Many of the men of little knowledge talk glibly of portaging as if it were simple and easy. A portage over rough and unknown ground is always the work of difficulty and of some risk to the canoe, and in the untrod-den, or even the unfrequented, wilderness risk to the canoe is a serious matter. This particular portage at Navaïté Rapids was far from being unusually difficult; yet it not only cost two and a half days of severe and incessant labor, but it cost something in damage to the canoes. One in particular, the one in which I had been journeying, was split in a manner which caused us serious uneasiness as to how long, even after being patched, it would last. Where the canoes were launched, the bank was sheer, and one of the water-logged canoes filled and went to the bottom; there was more work in raising it.

We were still wholly unable to tell where we were going and what lay ahead of us. Round the camp-fire, after supper, we held endless discussions and hazarded all kinds of guesses on both subjects. The river might bend sharply to the west and enter the Gy-Paraná high up or low down, or go north to the Madeira, or bend eastward and enter the Tapajos, or fall into the Canumà and finally through one of its mouths to enter the Amazon direct. Lyra inclined to the first, and Colonel Rondon to the second, of these propositions. We did not know whether we had one hundred or eight hundred kilometres to go, whether the stream would be fairly smooth or whether we would encounter waterfalls, or rapids, or even some big marsh or lake. We could not tell whether we would meet hostile Indians, although no one of us ever went ten yards from the camp without his rifle. We had no idea how much time the trip would take. We had entered a land of unknown possibilities.

We started down-stream again early in the afternoon of March 5. Our hands and faces were swollen from the bites and stings of the insect pests at the sand-flat camp and it was a pleasure once more to be in the middle of the river, where they did not come in any numbers, while we were in motion. The current was swift, but the river was so deep that there were no serious obstructions. Twice we went down over slight riffles, which in the dry season were doubtless rapids; and once we struck a spot where many whirlpools marked the presence underneath of bowlders which would have been above water had not the river been so swollen by the rains. The distance we covered in a day going down-stream would have taken us a week if we had been going up. The course wound hither and thither in sometimes sigmoid curves; but the general direction was east of north. As usual, it was very beautiful; and we could never tell what might appear around any curve. In the forest that rose on either hand were tall rubber-trees. The surveying canoes, as usual, went first, while I shepherded the two pairs of lashed cargo canoes. I kept them always between me and the surveying canoes—ahead of me until I passed the surveying canoes, and then behind me until, after an hour or so, I had chosen a place to camp. There was so much overflowed ground that it took us some little time this afternoon before we found a flat place high enough to be dry. Just before reaching camp Cherrie shot a jacu, a handsome bird somewhat akin to, but much smaller than, a turkey; after Cherrie had taken its skin its body made an excellent canja. We saw parties of monkeys; and the false bell-birds uttered their ringing whistles in the dense timber around our tents. The giant ants, an inch and a quarter long, were rather too plentiful around this camp; one stung Kermit; it was almost like the sting of a small scorpion, and pained severely for a couple of hours. This half-day we made twelve kilometres.

The 7th, 8th, and 9th we spent in carrying the loads and dragging and floating the dugouts past the series of rapids at whose head we had stopped.

The first day we shifted camp a kilometre and a half to the foot of this series of rapids. This was a charming and picturesque camp. It was at the edge of the river, where there was a little, shallow bay with a beach of firm sand. In the water, at the middle point of the beach, stood a group of three burity palms, their great trunks rising like columns. Round the clearing in which our tents stood were several very big trees; two of them were rubber-trees. Kermit went down-stream five or six kilometres, and returned, having shot a jacu and found that at the point which he had reached there was another rapids, almost a fall, which would necessitate again our dragging the canoes over a portage. Antonio, the Parecís, shot a big monkey; of this I was glad because portaging is hard work, and the men appreciated the meat. So far Cherrie had collected sixty birds on the Dúvida, all of them new to the collection, and some probably new to science. We saw the fresh sign of paca, agouti, and the small peccary, and Kermit with the dogs roused a tapir, which crossed the river right through the rapids; but no one got a shot at it.

Except at one or perhaps two points a very big dugout, lightly loaded, could probably run all these rapids. But even in such a canoe it would be silly to make the attempt on an exploring expedition, where the loss of a canoe or of its contents means disaster; and moreover such a canoe could not be taken, for it would be impossible to drag it over the portages on the occasions when the portages became inevitable. Our canoes would not have lived half a minute on the wild water.

On the second day the canoes and loads were brought down to the foot of the first rapids. Lyra cleared the path and laid the logs for the rollers, while Kermit dragged the dugouts up the bank from the water with block and tackle, with strain of rope and muscle. Then they joined forces, as over uneven ground it needed the united strength of all their men to get the heavy dugouts along. Meanwhile the colonel with one attendant measured the distance, and then went on a long hunt, but saw no game. I strolled down beside the river a couple of miles, but also saw nothing. In the dense tropical forest of the Amazonian basin hunting is very difficult, especially for men who are trying to pass through the country as rapidly as possible. On a trip such as ours getting game is largely a matter of chance.

On the following day Lyra and Kermit brought down the canoes and loads, with hard labor, to the little beach by the three palms where our tents were pitched. Many pacovas grew round about. The men used their immense leaves, some of which were over twelve feet long and two and a half feet broad, to roof the flimsy shelters under which they hung their hammocks. I went into the woods, but in the tangle of vegetation it would have been a mere hazard had I seen any big animal. Generally the woods were silent and empty. Now and then little troops of birds of many kinds passed—wood-hewers, ant-thrushes, tanagers, flycatchers; as in the spring and fall similar troops of warblers, chickadees, and nuthatches pass through our northern woods. On the rocks and on the great trees by the river grew beautiful white and lilac orchids—the sobralia, of sweet and delicate fragrance. For the moment my own books seemed a trifle heavy, and perhaps I would have found the day tedious if Kermit had not lent me the Oxford Book of French Verse. Eustache Deschamp, Joachim du Bellay, Ronsard, the delightful La Fontaine, the delightful but appalling Villon, Victor Hugo's "Guitare," Madame Desbordes-Valmores's lines on the little girl and her pillow, as dear little verses about a child as ever were written—these and many others comforted me much, as I read them in head-net and gauntlets, sitting on a log by an unknown river in the Amazonian forest.

The 15th of March, we started in good season. For six kilometres we drifted and paddled down the swift river without incident. At times we saw lofty Brazil-nut trees rising above the rest of the forest on the banks; and back from the river these trees grew to enormous proportions, towering like giants. There were great rubber-trees also, their leaves always in sets of threes. Then the ground on either hand rose into bowlder-strewn, forest-clad hills and the roar of broken water announced that once more our course was checked by dangerous rapids. Round a bend we came on them; a wide descent of white water, with an island in the middle, at the upper edge. Here grave misfortune was narrowly escaped.

Kermit, as usual, was leading in his canoe. It was the smallest and least seaworthy of all. He had in it little except a week's supply of our boxed provisions and a few tools; fortunately none of our food for the camaradas. His dog Trigueiro was with him. Besides himself, the crew consisted of two men: João, the helmsman, or pilot, as he is called in Brazil, and Simplicio, the bowsman. Both were negroes and exception-ally good men in every way. Kermit halted his canoe on the left bank, above the rapids, and waited for the colonel's canoe. Then the colonel and Lyra walked down the bank to see what was ahead. Kermit took his canoe across to the island to see whether the descent could be better accomplished on the other side. Having made his investigation, he ordered the men to return to the bank he had left, and the dugout was headed up-stream accordingly. Before they had gone a dozen yards, the paddlers digging their paddles with all their strength into the swift current, one of the shifting whirlpools of which I have spoken came down-stream, whirled them around, and swept them so close to the rapids that no human power could avoid going over them. As they were drifting into them broadside on, Kermit yelled to the steersman to turn her head, so as to take them in the only way that offered any chance whatever of safety. The water came aboard, wave after wave, as they raced down. They reached the bottom with the canoe upright, but so full as barely to float, and the paddlers urged her toward the shore. They had nearly reached the bank when another whirlpool or whirling eddy tore them away and hurried them back to midstream, where the dugout filled and turned over. João, seizing the rope, started to swim ashore; the rope was pulled from his hand, but he reached the bank. Poor Simplicio must have been pulled under at once, and his life beaten out on the bowlders beneath the racing torrent. He never rose again, nor did we ever recover his body. Kermit clutched his rifle, his favorite 405 Winchester with which he had done most of his hunting both in Africa and America, and climbed on the bottom of the upset boat. In a minute he was swept into the second series of rapids, and whirled away from the rolling boat, losing his rifle. The water beat his helmet down over his head and face and drove him beneath the surface; and when he rose at last he was almost drowned, his breath and strength almost spent. He was in swift but quiet water, and swam toward an overhanging branch. His jacket hindered him, but he knew he was too nearly gone to be able to get it off, and, thinking with the curious calm one feels when death is but a moment away, he realized that the utmost his failing strength could do was to reach the branch. He reached, and clutched it, and then almost lacked the strength to haul himself out on the land. Good Trigueiro had faithfully swum alongside him through the rapids, and now himself scrambled ashore. It was a very narrow escape. Kermit was a great comfort and help to me on the trip; but the fear of some fatal accident befalling him was always a nightmare to me. He was to be married as soon as the trip was over; and it did not seem to me that I could bear to bring bad tidings to his betrothed and to his mother.

Simplicio was unmarried. Later we sent to his mother all the money that would have been his had he lived. The following morning we put on one side of the post erected to mark our camping-spot the following inscription, in Portuguese:

In These Rapids Died Poor Simplicio

On an expedition such as ours death is one of the accidents that may at any time occur, and narrow escapes from death are too common to be felt as they would be felt elsewhere. One mourns sincerely, but mourning cannot interfere with labor. We immediately proceeded with the work of the portage.

The Black Beach

From The Windward Road *(1956)*
By Archie Carr

Almost everything you have ever heard, read, or even thought about sea turtle conservation can be traced back to Archie Carr, the man who put sea turtles on the map and created the first major programs to promote their long-term survival.

With endless fascination, Carr studied the behavior and biology of myriad turtle species around the world and particularly in the Caribbean. On sandy islands and coasts throughout this region, he spent countless days checking out turtle eggs of all varieties: green, loggerhead, ridley, hawksbill, trunkback, and others.

When he wasn't in the field, Carr devoted much of his time to writing, a pursuit in which he clearly felt as much at home as he did on a deserted stretch of tropical sand. Among the jewels his pen produced is "The Black Beach," a piece that first appeared in Mademoiselle *magazine and was selected for the O. Henry Award as one of the best short stories of 1956. Ironically, the O. Henry Award is given for fiction, yet "The Black Beach" is a nonfiction essay; an expertly described day in the life of a turtle conservationist was clearly as enter-taining as any of that year's flights of fancy. This anecdote is just one of ten lively essays found in* The Windward Road, *a collection of Carr pieces that received the John Burroughs Medal from the American Museum of Natural History.* (DRK)

It was on the black beach that I met Mrs. Ybarra. It was the long, lonesome, log-strewn stretch from Tortuguero to Parismina. You don't see many people on that beach. Perhaps the chances against our meeting reinforced the impression Mrs. Ybarra made on me and caused her to seem more noteworthy than she really was. That you must judge when you have learned the circumstances.

I was looking for nests of trunkback turtles. I had walked five miles and had found no sign—no fresh trail that was not clearly that of hawksbill or green turtle. Even the greens were scarce. There was just a sprinkling of early layers in the van of the big nesting migration—the "fleet," as the people on the beach call it—which was already long overdue. It was nearing noon of a flaming cloudless day and the land breeze had killed the trade wind.

Two miles back I had met the Siquirres dogs—the seasonally feral packs of curs that Paco had pointed out from the plane two days before. Each May or June the dogs gather on the beach from Siquirres and the other towns along the railroad far inland, called by some unknown cue to cross as much as thirty miles of jungle, marsh, and mangrove swamp and meet the fleet, and batten on turtle eggs for the season. There were eight dogs in the pack I met, and they were hungry and irritable. They ran yapping before me for a while, as if they thought I was somehow to blame for the lateness of the fleet, and then they dashed off over the low dunes and disappeared among the coco plums. Besides the dogs and a scurrying sand crab now and then, I had seen no living thing on land.

Seaward there was little more—no boat to watch, no cruising fin; no whitecaps, even, nor any bar or promontory to break the sweeping surf line. Once in a thousand steps there came the thin, lost cry of a tern, hidden out among the heat waves.

Once, for a little while, a black patch showed on the burnished, blue-white swells just beyond the breakers where a shoal of anchovies had come up from wherever they had been to flip and play and circle at the surface. I stopped to see what hungry things would gather from the sea and the air, as they always gather about such schools. Almost at once the jacks came—big, flat, gleaming five-pounders that slashed and ripped at the edges of the anchovy cloud, knocking chunks of it into the air in showers of chrome splinters; and sometimes throwing themselves out, too, in short parabolas, head-over-tail, stiff and sheepish-looking. I thought what I could do among the jacks with a bass rod and a Johnson spoon.

The crying tern saw the shoal and came in to circle and wail above it, never changing the sad key of its song. A gray pelican sailed up silently from behind me, rose and dropped head-first into the fish cloud and then emerged to float with the scattering school and solemnly appraise the catch in his sack, while the longshore drift carried him and the anchovies slowly southward. Suddenly, in one split second, the million fish sounded in mindless unison. At once the tern caught a ballooning thermal with one thin wing and soared off into the glare; and the pelican was left floating alone.

I shuffled on through the fine hot sand. It was light, powdery dust of pumice and black glass that let you sink ankle-deep. It was so hot it burned my shanks above my shoe tops. The beach was piled with stranded timber—immense, silver trunks of cedar and *laurel* and *cedro macho* from the Costa Rican rivers and mahogany from Panama or Nicaragua, stolen from the loggers by decades of June floods and then thrown back again onto the black beach by the wild seas that batter this open coast. No tropical beach is fun to walk on at cloudless, windless midday. This one, with its endless monstrous jetsam to send you weaving from the deep, hot dunes down into the brawling surf and back again, made following the narrow strip above high-water mark, where turtle trails are laid, a trying job. My ardor for trunkback nests was failing under the sun and I was on the point of crawling beneath a propped log to sleep out the midday calm when I saw what I had come after.

It was a short, broad-limbed V, deeply engraved in the beach above the tide zone. The open end of the wedge had been truncated by the lap of the last, highest wave, and the apex merged with a broad plowed and scuffed patch in the soft blown sand just seaward of the dune front. The limbs of the V—the trails to and from the disturbed patch—were nearly as wide as the wheel trail of a tractor, and indeed the whole system of marks seemed to show that a heavy, wheeled vehicle had come up from the sea, had sunk deep in the sand drift, and after a great deal of backing and filling and churning had returned to the water.

It was the nest of a trunkback. It was the first I had ever seen but there was no mistaking it. It was the first ever recorded for Central America, but its significance to me far transcended that statistic. To me it was the long-sought land-sign of a sea creature I had looked for since childhood—a monster of the deep ocean guided ashore one time in each year by the primal reptile drive to dig a hole in earth and drop in it the seeds of trunkbacks for tomorrow, and cover the hole with toeless flat feet, and pound back down to the sea never looking behind. It was the work of a water reptile pelagic as a whale or a plesiosaur and at home in the oceans of the world—the last vestige of landcraft left to a bloodline seabound for a hundred million years, and left then but to one sex for one hour on one night in the year.

You will gather that I am curiously, perhaps almost psychotically, susceptible to the color of the trunkback. For a while, then, what with my thoughts and the sun and the quaking air, I just stood and looked at the nest.

After a while the trance of lightheaded exultation ran out and I put down my camera bag and canteen and set about appraising the site where the turtle had worked. There was a great deal of it. A female trunkback often weighs a thousand pounds or more and is full of a fantastical kind of gland-given zeal that would almost pass for ingenuity. Everything she does is calculated, in a purely mechanistic sense of course, to keep her eggs from being dug up again, by either herpetologist or coatimundi. She can't hide the fact that she was out on the beach, so she confounds the egg-hunter with a plethora of clues. In this case the area of flung sand in which I had to prospect for the egg chamber was at least fifteen feet in diameter and roughly circular in outline. Since it offered no evidence, at least to my eye, by which the field for search might be narrowed down, I had to cover every square foot of it; and since the clutch of eggs might lie waist-deep beneath the sand, the job ahead was imposing.

I took up my egg stick. After making a few random test holes here and there, I began moving systematically back and forth across the site, punching as deeply as I could drive the stick. When I had completed a regular and closely spaced gridwork of holes and had found nothing, I began to realize that the slim section of cane that I had found effective enough in prospecting for the nests of hawksbills and green turtles was too feeble for the work at hand. To get down through the hard sand that lay below the surface drift I needed a pole with backbone—something I could plant and swing my weight on.

I began looking about the beach for something suitable. This was an open shore and a heavy sea washed it, and there was no dearth of driftwood, as I have said. I tested one silvery stick after another, but all were either crooked as a snake or punky and spineless from salt water and sun. I found a section of timber bamboo that was sound, but you don't split stuff like that with a pocketknife, which was the only tool I carried. Halfheartedly I trimmed and sharpened a leaf stem of coco palm, and this collapsed at the first thrust.

I wanted the nest badly, and with the mounting realization that I probably would not get it my frustration grew apace. I cursed my lack of foresight in not bringing a machete. I grabbed up a sphere of drifted pumice stone and tried to put an edge on my knife blade with it, but the rounded face of the stone collapsed like sugar candy and only polished the metal. In a peevish fit I threw the stone at the face of a *laurel* log and it went to pieces there.

Suddenly, a slight, blue feist dog burst from behind the log and started shrieking at me, lifting its feet in indignation and looking backwards at intervals as if for support from a source hidden from me by the rise of the log.

Then, for an instant, I saw a face above the six-foot loom of the trunk, and then the face was gone. I ran around the end of the log and saw a woman on horseback retreating at a dead run in the direction from which she had come. I could hear the splatting of the horse's feet in the wave wash and I could see in the slant of the rider's back that she was not party to the flight but was trying to stop and turn the horse. It was the horse who was alarmed at the sudden, unprecedented sight and stink of gringo behind a log on the black beach—not Mrs. Ybarra.

Mrs. Ybarra no doubt took an unenthusiastic view of me too. But she was a woman inured to the shocks of life on this beach. She was not the sort to turn back because of a stranger there, no matter how unaccounted for. She gradually dominated the horse and brought it to a grudging halt a hundred yards down the beach and turned it. I could see that it was an ash-colored *criollo* stallion—one of the tough, runty, and cruelly selected remnant of the old Spanish horse that somehow survived the odds against horseflesh on this tropical shore and that now, salt-cured, parasite-proof, and vampire-tolerant, and economical with its tissue-water as a camel, will single-foot all night in sand fetlock deep. The horse of the Mosquitia is almost a breed apart. Æsthetically it compares unfavorably with a true horse, but it is right for its milieu.

The example under Mrs. Ybarra had the odd, ratlike face and ewe-necked silhouette they all have. He came back toward me under pressure, against his judgment, his eyes rolling. He came because the will of his rider was stronger than his will.

As she approached, Mrs. Ybarra steered her mount down beach to pass well seaward of me, gripping the reins firmly and drumming at the horse's tight belly with her heels. She gave me a quick look.

"*Adios,*" she said.

Adios said that way means you are going on by. In a matrix of circumstances such as this it becomes a bivalent greeting, a salutation with connotation that a parting will follow immediately. It is a hello-goodby, and a word that, as far as I know, has no counterpart in English or North American. Spanish can be shaded delicately. It is nowhere near so simple as my textbooks and teachers made out.

There was of course no reason at all why Mrs. Ybarra should not go on by. But at the moment she spoke I saw the pearly gleam of new turtle eggs in two arroba baskets swinging from her saddle; and this made it unthinkable that she should ride on and leave me with my dilemma.

So I said: *"Buenas tardes,"* and the shift in salutation changed our relationship at once and made it a point of courtesy for her to rein up, a bit warily, and see what my intentions were.

She was not the sort of woman you would expect to see on this beach, even supposing you were expecting women of any sort. She was a short, turnip-shaped woman with a thin-lipped Madonna's face and a mass of snuff-colored hair piled under a man's old felt hat tied on with a scarf. She had spindly Spanish legs and a big bosom bound in by a bodice of muslin. She wore a brown cotton smock, and a skirt of the same stuff was cleverly tucked under and around her legs, because she rode astride and not sidesaddle like the women in Honduras. Her racial origin and place in life were not evident from her appearance. Her skin was very dark, but she had nothing to do with the dark people of Tortuguero, who run mostly to Mosquito and Black Carib interbreeds with a sprinkling of black creoles from Bluefields and San Andrés. She looked like no Costa Rican I ever saw. Except for her almost black skin and reddish hair, and for the shameless way she strad-dled the high wooden packsaddle, she more closely approached the kind of women you see in the mountains of Matagalpa or of southern Honduras, where the century of hardship the old revolutions brought bred thin-faced women with more than their share of character. She had much in common with them and much in common with her horse. She was weatherbeaten, but she had the quiet confidence that goes with a full stomach.

"Buenas tardes," she said, stopping her horse. "The widow of Ybarra from Panal, this side of Parismina."

I told her my name. I said I was studying the ways of turtles. I motioned toward the trunkback nest.

"Do you know what kind of turtle did that?" I said.

"Why not? *Es de canal*—a trunkback."

"That's what I thought," I said. "How do you know?"

"Only a trunkback tears up the beach like that. All this beach is torn up by trunkbacks. It's hard to ride except near the water."

I looked up and down the beach and for the first time noticed that the sand in front of the dunes had an oddly uneven topography that was not part of the wind-piled dune system, and not like any beach I had ever seen before.

"Some of that is where animals dig for eggs when the fleet of green turtles comes, but mostly it's trunkbacks that pile the sand like that. Like this nest here . . . But why don't you go on a way? I saw several carey nests in the light sand yonder, and some of green turtles—various. I dug two." She patted the side of one of the egg baskets.

"I don't want hawksbill eggs," I said, "or green turtle either. I'm looking for trunkback eggs."

"They're not as good as carey eggs. They have a little taste."

"I don't want to eat them," I said. "I want to measure them."

She looked at me deprecatingly. "They're this big. *Asi de grande.*" She cupped her hand to show me how big.

"I mean exactly. And I want to take pictures of them."

"They are very deep. A yard—yard and a half. The animals can't find them. Even the tigers. Even the Siquirres dogs that dig out all the rest don't try to dig trunkback eggs."

"I don't care how long it takes," I said. "I would dig all afternoon if I knew there was a nest there. Maybe this one scratched and went back. Loggerheads do that."

She studied the tumbled sand for a moment. Then she wagged her finger from side to side in front of her face in the gesture of negation that all Latins use.

"Puso—" she said. *"Ahí puso."*

"But how do you find the nest?" I asked. "I've punched all around here and couldn't find a soft place anywhere."

Again she wagged her finger at me. "You didn't punch deep enough. There is no soft place in a *canal* nest. You just have to find it. Please, what time is it? Midday?"

I brushed the sweat-soaked sand from the face of my watch.

"A quarter after. Are you in a hurry?"

"Today the Spaniard pays the Mosquitos. I am going to collect a debt and I want to get there before they are all drunk. I saw the airplane Thursday, and they will all be drunk by dark."

I thought of the milk can of rum I had flown with and saw that she was probably right. The Spaniard she was talking about was Don Pedro, Yoyo's *mayordomo* at the Atlantic Trading Company at Tortuguero.

"How much is the debt?" I said.

"There are two of them. They add up to eight colones."

"All right, look. I'll pay you ten if you will help me find the turtle nest."

She looked at the sand in front of the horse again, and then up at the sun. She sighed and swung a leg over the tall saddle frame and stepped to the ground.

"We will try it." She said it with no great enthusiasm.

She led the horse into the sprinkled shade of a ragged old mangineel, the only real tree anywhere on the foreshore, and tied the reins to a branch.

"That is a poison tree," I said.

"It doesn't molest horses."

"But how about your hands? You have to hold the reins."

"Don't worry. It doesn't molest me either. Only the juice, or the smoke when it burns."

"I wouldn't tie a horse to that tree for anything," I said.

"It's all right. You are a stranger here and haven't found yourself."

She drew a wasted sliver of a machete from a rawhide scabbard tied to the saddle. She walked back to the turtle nest and called to the feist and it came bouncing down from the beach grass, eager to serve her with all its talents. She leaned and scratched suggestively at the sand to interest the dog in the place.

"Huevos," she said.

I winced, because this word said by itself like that usually means something quite different; but the dog understood and began to dig in a crab hole six feet from the turtle nest.

"Don't be an imbecile," Mrs. Ybarra said. "Here—dig here!"

The dog dropped his ears, hurt by the tone of the words; then he moved over and started digging in the turtle nest.

"With green turtles and *careyes* Filin never deceives himself. With trunkbacks he doesn't serve. Let him dig here awhile. I have to go back there." She waved a hand toward the low scrub a hundred yards inland.

"*Bueno.*" I thought she was excusing herself from me and prepared to stay and give what encouragement I could to the dog.

"No—I have to cut a stick. You come too. You can climb better."

We pushed through the sea grapes and sea oats and coco plums, and behind the dunes we came to a coppice of tightly spaced saplings. We stopped and Mrs. Ybarra peered about in the dense thicket until she found what she wanted.

"*Aquel.*" She pointed into the dim interior of the thicket. "If you climb that *palito* and trim it, we can get it out."

I shinnied up the slim, smooth stem and trimmed off all the branches I could reach. Then I slid down and cut the trunk through at the ground and dragged it out into the clear. Mrs. Ybarra cut a five-foot section from the stem, skinned the bark from it, and tapered one end to a point.

"*Ya.*" She said. "Maybe with this."

When we got back, the feist had lost interest in the turtle nest and was digging out another sand-crab hole.

"He doesn't serve," Mrs. Ybarra said.

She planted the tip of the stick in the center of the nest and pushed. The point grated to a stop in the dense sand two feet down. She tried again a foot away, with the same result. She punched a dozen holes and from each the stick emerged only dusted with the fine sand. She stopped and studied the site again on hands and knees, plucking at each twig or bit of debris that protruded above the plowed surface. After a while she found a newly broken end of beach morning-glory stem, and when she pulled on this a good three feet of green vine came out of the sand.

"Maybe here," she said. "The *canal* buried the vine."

She took up the stick and probed carefully all around where the vine had been. Still the rod broke through no nest roof and came out smeared with no yolk. Finally she stopped and shook her head, and sweat silently.

"It is *fregada*, this question of the *canal* nests," she said.

She wiped her eyes with the backs of her forearms. Her hair was falling out from under her hat, and the sweat-stuck sand had frosted the dark shine of her face. I thought I could see misgiving in her expression. I thought she must be leaning toward my view that this was a trial nest without eggs, such as loggerheads make.

"I don't believe there's anything here," I said.

"Don't deceive yourself. *Aquí puso*—she laid here. It is sure. Always it is like this. The *canal* is—ooo—very big. Her leg is like this—" She measured against her own thigh. "She reaches to a great depth, and she is heavy and she packs the sand back with her belly, harder than it was before. And the worst is, she plows so much ground it is hard to locate the nest. If you do find the eggs they are too big to eat with comfort. It is not worth the trouble. But maybe if we both pushed on the stick— The place should be exactly there."

I have seen a water-witch point out the spot for a well with the judicious precision with which Mrs. Ybarra aimed the tip of her stick. She sighted as if she were aiming a rifle at the head of a snake.

"Exactly there," she repeated.

She stuck the point in the sand and we both leaned on the shaft. It broke with a snap and split back to our hands.

"It broke," Mrs. Ybarra said. "The wood was tender. Look, do you want to try any more? I think it will be easier if you go out at night and find the *canal* when she is laying and before she has covered. Any time when the moon is over the sea, not over the land. In the black sand pieces they come out every night—one, two, three—to lay."

I said I thought she was right. I dug in my pocket and from under the sand there brought out some Costa Rican bills. I counted ten colones and held them out to her, saying that I was grateful for her help and was sorry she had got so hot and sandy.

"Ah, no," she said. "I can't accept that. I said I would find the eggs. You owe me nothing. I'll reach the village in plenty of time."

"No, look—I stopped you. I'm going to put the money in your saddlebag."

I turned and walked toward the mangineel tree behind the screen of tall sea oats. My first sight of Mrs. Ybarra's horse was his feet waving and kicking in the air, all four of them. I ran toward him in sudden panic, burst through the grass, and saw him on his back writhing and jerking and bending his short, stiff backbone in impossible, convulsive arcs. The limb to which he had been tied was broken and the reins had tangled about the bit shafts. His contortions had pushed the saddle around onto his belly and broken loose most of the bundles, which were scattered about in the sand. The two baskets of turtle eggs had been dumped on the ground, and the horse was rolling in them.

"Come, quick, look at your horse," I yelled. "Quick! What is the matter with him?"

She came running.

"Oh, my sainted mother, is he scratching! Yes, my God, he is scratching! He always scratches when he is hot, and I forgot to watch—and look at my *carga*! *A la*—! Get up! You! Flojo! Stand up!"

She seized a piece of driftwood and began pounding the horse on his unprotected underside. He stopped rolling and in awkward haste floundered to his feet and stood with flaring nostrils, ears back, and eyes rolling at his mistress, stung and puzzled at her attitude.

He was a frightful thing to see. The bridle was bunched at his chin. The saddle and the empty egg baskets and some bundles that had not broken their moorings hung beneath him, and a disheveled game rooster dangled from a cinch ring between his forelegs. His back and sides were heavily smeared with a thick, uneven mixture of egg yolks and whites and black sand, in which, here and there about his surface, leaves and rotting mangineel apples and empty turtle-egg shells were stuck. He looked as if a two-year-old child had made a frosting for him. He shook himself violently, but looked no better for it.

A feeling of despondency spread over me. This poor woman—what misery I had brought her! How utterly my stubbornness had wrecked her hopes and her day! I turned to her, in my shame ready to crawl, or to force on her every last colon I could claw out of my pockets.

She was laughing.

She was pointing at the horse with one hand and beating helplessly at the air with the other, and shaking with silent mirth. I looked at her narrowly, to make sure her joy was real and not a symptom of deep nervous shock. Suddenly she found her voice.

"What a barbarity!" she shrieked. "What a brutal animal! Oh, my sainted mother, what animal more brutal!"

She was so clearly delighted that I looked back at the horse with new eyes, and this time he looked funny to me too and I started to laugh. We both laughed for a long time.

After a while I said: "I am sorry. The blame is all mine. What can we do?"

"No," she said, "it doesn't matter. I only have to bathe the horse."

She began to untangle the bridle, stopping at intervals to bend over and shake and screech with laughter. I helped her unfasten the cinches and disengage the confusion of saddle and *carga*. She took the machete and cut some clumps of grass, which she doubled and bunched and bound to make a brush. She shed her shoes and smock and skirt and strode off to the surf clad only in a sacklike nether garment, leading the horse by the bridle.

I hurriedly made a crude copy of her grass brush; then I rolled up my trousers and followed her into the water.

Within fifteen minutes the little horse was clean, or nearly so. His blue barb skin showed through matted wet hair and only a few patches of coagulated yolk clung to him here and there. Mrs. Ybarra led him back to the tree and rubbed his back with handfuls of dry grass and spread on it the burlap saddle blanket. She tidied up the saddle a bit and I heaved it on the horse and fastened the cinches while she rearranged the *carga*. The gamecock was dead, but seemed remarkably intact for having been under a horse. Mrs. Ybarra chopped part way through his neck with the machete and hung the body low on the saddle to bleed on the ground. Then she slipped on her skirt and dropped her shoes in one of the baskets. She brushed at the sand on her arms and put on her smock, then swung herself into the saddle.

Once again I held out the thin sheaf of bills.

"*Vea,*" I said cajolingly. "It was my fault that you lost the eggs and the cock died."

"*¡Qué va!* The cock was to kill, and there will be eggs enough. There is no lack of carey eggs and the fleet will not be long coming. Will you be going back now?"

I told her I was going on. I must have seemed depressed at the prospect, because she said:

"All right, there's a *cocal* [a coco fringe] no more than there—just a little way. You can get a *pipa* there [a drinking coconut], and there is shade. Then if you go on six miles there is another *cocal*, and my house is there. If you go that far, it is almost certain that I can show you a *canal* tonight, laying on the high tide."

I thanked her and said I couldn't go that far. Without her noticing, I slipped the money into the basket where her shoes were.

"I'm going to dig another *canal* nest," I said. "I don't believe this one laid."

"Ay-eeee," she yelped. "You will kill yourself for nothing. She laid. This one laid. Right there. No *canal* nest will be easier to dig than this one."

"O.K.," I said. "But I'm not going to dig here any more. I'll be seeing you."

She gave me a look of what I think was pity, then set her mount in motion with her bare heels, guided him into the surf-wash, and squeezed him into the mincing single-foot he would hold all the way to Tortuguero. Then she turned and waved.

"*Adios, pues,*" she said.

The little feist saw her leaving and ran to take the lead. A first sudden breath of the afternoon breeze wiped the gleam from the water and turned it black. The hoof-splash of the horse faded in the distance, and when it was gone the only sounds were the roll of the waves and the fitful piping of the tern as it slipped and tilted on the swelling trade wind.

Cahill Among the Ruins in Peru

From Jaguars Ripped My Flesh *(1987)*
By Tim Cahill

⌒

Add a new name to the list of the world's great explorers. Columbus, Drake, Vespucci, Marco Polo, Scott, Peary, Burton, et al., make way for Tim Cahill. On assignment for Outside *magazine, where this piece originally appeared, Cahill traveled in the high mountains of Peru searching out unnamed, un-mapped, and un-"discovered" traces of a cloud forest civilization that flourished in the years before the reign of the Incas. His story is told in the humorous, unique style that readers of* Outside, *and before that* Rolling Stone *magazine, have come to expect from this adventurer-correspondent.*

There are very few places left on the planet that can be said to be unexplored; this montane region of the Peruvian Amazon is one of them. So come along with Cahill and his hearty band as they hack their way through the thickets of the Andean highlands, slip in the mud, and survive massive hangovers from the local beverages. (MWC)

In the northeastern section of Peru there is a state called Amazonas, and the capital city of six thousand is Chachapoyas. Three blocks off the Plaza de Armas, down the narrow streets between clean pastel houses, there is a high wooden door that leads into a courtyard, and just off that courtyard, under his second-story apartment, Carlos Gates, the supervisor of Archaeological Monuments for Amazonas, keeps an office. For Chachapoyas, it is a luxurious affair. The floor is poured concrete, not dirt, for one thing, and for another, there is an electric light. On the walls there are various certificates and diplomas, along with the obligatory framed painting of Christ showing the Sacred Heart glowing in His chest.

A man in his middle years, Gates, like most of the people of Chachapoyas, is short, no more than five feet two inches, and very broad in the shoulders and chest. Despite his exuberant gestures, Carlos exuded grace and dignity. He smiled often, in a kindly fashion, and gave us no help at all.

"It is very difficult for you to explore here," he said in Spanish. "You must have a permit to dig."

Laszlo Berty, who spoke the best Spanish, said, "But we do not wish to dig. Only explore." The other two members of the expedition—Tom Jackson and I—nodded our assent.

"To explore, you must have a permit. You must have a permit to go into certain areas," Gates said. He suggested we visit the known ruins: Kuélap, Congona, and others.

Laszlo explained that we would certainly want to see those ruins, for we had read of them and we understood that they were beautiful. Still, our research indicated that there were other, unexplored ruins in Amazonas, and our goal was to find some of them. Señor Gates knew more of these ruins than any man alive. Could he not give us help on our expedition?

Gates stared at his desk top in what appeared to be great sorrow. Sometimes, he said, it is not good when new ruins are discovered. Men come searching for the gold and they destroy what is left of the ruins. *Huacos*—prehistoric objects—are removed and sold to wealthy collectors, and the work of scientists is made difficult.

Laszlo explained that he intended to run commercial trips down the rivers of Amazonas and that he wanted to find ruins near the rivers where he could take his clients. Tom Jackson worked for the South American Explorers' Club and he would note our discoveries, in a scientific fashion, in that club's journal. I intended to publish the results of our expedition in an American magazine. We would not dig and we were not *huaqueros*, not grave robbers.

Gates apologized profusely. He did not mean to suggest that we were huaqueros—never. It is the men who come later, like vultures, who defile the ruins. He was referring to those men and not to us.

There was silence. We were getting nowhere. Finally Laszlo said, "It is true that we are not professors of anthropology or professors of archaeology. We are adventurers. But adventurers with an object." He fixed Gates with his most sincere stare. "In the life of a man," he said with great dignity, "it is important for adventure. What else is in life?"

I am incapable of uttering a statement like that. It would wither and die on my tongue like a snake in the sun. But it was Laszlo's genius, when dealing with Peruvians, to say the right thing at the right time. Carlos nodded sagaciously as if he agreed that, yes, it is adventure and adventure alone that is important in the life of man.

Laszlo knew enough not to push any further at this point. We would visit Kuélap, he said, and the others. When we returned to Chachapoyas, perhaps Señor Gates would be able to help us then.

Yes, Carlos said, if he could find the time, perhaps.

There is, in northern Peru, a unique area known as the *montaña* located just east of the Andes and west of the awesome forests of the Amazon basin. It is a wet, mountainous, transitional surface between the mightiest mountains of the Americas and the largest jungle in the world.

The montaña is close to the equator; and, along rivers such as the Utcubamba, people grow tropical fruits and rice and sugar cane. But the vegetation of the surrounding mountains seems strangely inverted to those familiar with ranges in the temperate region. The lower slopes are poor and sandy—a cactus and mesquite environment similar to what we call high chaparral. Above the cactus the land becomes fertile—it is much like the American Midwest—and here people raise livestock and grow corn and potatoes and melons on small terraced farms called *chacras*. Above the chacras, one comes upon the strangest inversion. The terraced fields rise into thick, choking jungles. It is as if the tropical forests of the Amazon basin had made one last effort to claim the entire continent. These mountaintop jungles of the montaña are known as the *ceja de selva*, the eyebrow of the jungle.

From the highest points on the ridgetops, it is possible to watch clouds form, wispily, in the great river basins four thousand and five thousand feet below. They rise to the ridge, thicken into great roiling banks, drop a hard cold rain, and fall again into the valleys.

The ceja, then, is a jungle formed of clouds—a cloud forest—and one thousand years ago there was an Indian people, the Chachapoyas, who lived among the clouds, in fortresses constructed high on jungle ridgetops. It is thought that they chose the cloud forests for their cities for obvious defensive purposes, and also to avoid the malaria and other tropical diseases endemic to the river valleys.

Conquered by the Incas in 1480—who were, in turn, conquered by the Spanish in the 1530s—the Chachapoyan empire fell into obscurity and ruin. The great fortresses, the graceful stone cities, the grand plazas of the Chachapoyas were abandoned, left to the jungles. Many are known to archaeologists, but they are little studied. Other cities and fortresses—dozens of them, perhaps hundreds—lie undiscovered, undisturbed in a millennium, in seldom-visited frontier country the Peruvians describe as *silvestre* and *salvaje*, wild and savage.

During the month of July, *Outside* magazine launched an expedition into the montaña of northeastern Peru. Our objective was to locate undiscovered jungle ruins of the people of the clouds.

The expedition was the brainchild of Laszlo Berty, thirty, of Erie, Pennsylvania, the owner of Amazon Expeditions, a fledgling Peruvian river-running operation. Berty had been both a computer systems analyst and a Marine, and he managed to combine the fine attributes of both these professions into one remarkable personality.

Puns and jokes were lost on Laszlo. The English language is best suited for issuing orders so that one may achieve specifically stated goals.

"Don't do that," Laszlo would say.

"What?"

"Put that cup on the filthy ground."

Laszlo had outfitted the expedition—tent, sleeping bags, stove, cooking equipment—and it was important to him that these things be kept spotless. He didn't like me putting the sleeping bag I was using—his bag—on the filthy ground. He didn't like Peruvians to drink out of his canteen because you can never tell what strange diseases they might have. Driving along the broiling river basins, we were frequently obliged to bake in the car with the windows up because Laszlo is *allergic to dust.*

In the little cafes, Laszlo ordered the waiters to stop wiping his bottle of Amazonas Kola with their towels. The towels were invariably *sucio,* filthy. My hands were usually sucio, Tom Jackson's hands were sucio, even Laszlo's hands were sucio at times, a condition which disturbed him greatly. He'd examine his fingers and utter, "Filthy, filthy."

It is fair to say there was tension between Laszlo and me. By the morning of the third day—no later—we had come to an unspoken agreement. At odd intervals I'd simply explode. Laszlo would regard me with injured dignity and apprehension—you can never tell what a crazy person will do—and I'd shout in his face for five or ten minutes at a crack, walk off stiff-legged and steaming, think of something else and charge back to stand inches from him, waving my arms and pointing. After one of these berserk tirades, Laszlo and I would be very polite to each other for, oh, two or three days. Then the cycle would start over.

Tom Jackson, twenty-five, the third member of the expedition, watched these outbreaks in noncommittal silence. He was a slight, handsome fellow, and a missing tooth in the front of his mouth gave him a boyish, Huck Finn look. Tom had accompanied Laszlo on a previous river trip, and I assumed that he had sided with Laszlo during that first high-volume confrontation. I was wrong.

"Naw," he told me privately, "I was hoping you'd punch his lights out."

Jackson swallowed what I interpreted as a lot of abuse from Laszlo: orders issued in bored disgust, as if Tom were some witless incompetent. Because *Outside* had funded the expedition and Laszlo had organized and outfitted it, Tom attempted to remain neutral regarding the basic unsettled question of who was to lead the party. It took him a week to break. When he finally did, he erupted, burning Laszlo with a number of acid and intolerable comments. After some time I was invited to arbitrate. Who would continue with me, who should return to Lima?

Wrong approach, I said. Stupid. Together we were a complete entity. Apart our chances of success were minimal. We were all pretty fair woodsmen, but Laszlo had a knack for getting information out of Peruvians. Tom was the most accomplished climber, the hardest working, the most adept at fixing mechanical things. I was the strongest swimmer—we would have to get our equipment across a number of rivers at the rapids—and I had done more reading on the area, more recently. Decisions, I suggested, should be a three-way affair.

In the end, my position prevailed. Still, we spent the next few weeks gnawing on one another's nerves like rats on a rope. Laszlo had to put up with incredible stupidity on my part, and at times Jackson was even dumber. Once we found ourselves halfway up a mountain just as the sun set. We were on a grassy flat and we could see several two-story wattle-and-daub huts: two feet of mud and clay packed onto a frame of branches and thin tree trunks. The huts were empty.

We had drunk all our water on the çlimb. We were exhausted and sweated out and my tongue was stuck to the roof of my mouth. I suggested that our first order of business should be to find water.

Laszlo could hardly believe I had said such a thing. "There's no water up here," he said. It should have been self-evident. "That's why there's no people here. They only come up in the wet season." He paused to let this sink in. "When there's water."

Still, you can't talk good sense to cretins. Tom and I decided that since there was new corn and wheat in the chacras, and since we could see horses in a pen, and since there had been a fiesta in the town below, that the people who lived in the huts were at the fiesta, that there had to be water for the crops and livestock, and that we would look for that water. Laszlo, who knew the search was fruitless, lay on his back in the grass, wisely conserving energy.

At dusk Tom found a small pool, about two feet in diameter, behind a stand of trees. Later, after dinner and over coffee, I expressed the opinion that Tom had saved our ass, finding the water.

Laszlo sighed heavily. "Of course you found water," he explained. "Water runs down the side of a hill. You guys walked across the side of the hill. *Anybody* could have found water."

This was the kind of irritating idiocy Laszlo had to put up with *every single day*.

Shortly after our second visit to Carlos Gates, we drove south from the city of Chachapoyas to Tingo, where we started the long walk to Kuélap. That fortress, discovered by Juan Crisóstomo Nieto in 1843, was the keystone of known Chachapoyan culture. It is simply massive— the largest pre-Inca construct in Peru—and the fort is set like a ship upon high, crumbly cliff walls. The battlements rise some sixty feet above the cliffs and stretch for nearly half a mile. One stands before the main gate feeling dwarfed and impotent.

Kuélap had been cleared in spots, but for the most part it belonged to the jungle. It was an easy matter to become lost *inside,* and wander about, stumbling into typical Chachapoyan circular habitations. These are round stone buildings, usually open at some point to form a door, and constructed out of what appears to be local limestone. They are five, ten, fifteen, sometimes twenty feet high. In all probability, the circular habitations (or "circle habs," as we soon began to call them) had been covered with the same kind of thatched roof we had seen on the huts below. They were now, of course, open to the sky, and countless generations of jungle plants had grown in their interiors— grown and died and provided the loam for other plants so that most of the constructs were filled with soil. Flowers and trees and thorns grew where the roofs had been.

There were more battlements, rising in concentric circles behind the main walls, and everything there built by the hand of man, even the outer walls, was curvilinear. Small trails wound among the circle habs and underground chambers and mossy walls. Off the trails, the jungle was so thick it took a good fifteen minutes of machete work to move a hundred yards.

The vegetation was thick and rank and thorny. To walk it was necessary to clear an area from head to thigh. It was impossible to see more than three feet ahead, and the odor was intense. Everywhere there was the smell of faded lilacs, a sickly sweet odor, that combined with something thick and dead and skunklike.

We camped for a night atop a tower situated at the highest point in the fort. Twenty-seven feet high with crumbling steps to the top, it had been cleared, and there was a grassy spot for our tent. We could see forever, in every direction.

As the sun set, we listened to the jungle. At twilight there was a last frantic avian burst: green parrots shrieked over the constant chatter of smaller birds and occasionally we heard a series of strange, high-pitched whoops. As darkness fell, the birds gave way to crickets and the odd frog, croaking deep and resonant, like the sound of two rocks striking together underwater. Fireflies flashed in the jungle and, this night, there was a full moon; the tops of the trees shown silver in its light. Occasionally, there was a deep-throated wail, probably a monkey, followed by about half a dozen barks or grunts.

I slept the sleep of a Chacha warrior, secure in this fort at the center of the universe.

Virtually nothing is known of the Chachapoyan people (also called Chachas) before the Incas. We have some information—about a page and a half—in a book written by Garcilaso de la Vega. Born in 1539, Garcilaso was in a unique position to record the events of the conquest of Peru by the Spanish; his mother was the granddaughter of the Inca Túpac Yupanqui, his father was a conquistador with Pizarro. Combining his own memories of the conquest and interviews with Inca court historians—the Indians had no written language, but their historians memorized a set chronology, using colored ropes in which various knots had been tied as mnemonic devices—Garcilaso wrote his massive Royal Commentaries of the Incas.

The Chacha women, he tells us, were considered especially beautiful and the men fierce fighters. They worshiped the serpent and they lived in a hard, mountainous land where travelers were routinely required to raise and lower themselves by rope. In the late 1470s, the eleventh Inca, Túpac Yupanqui, moved north from the Inca capital of Cuzco on a march of imperial conquest. In 1480, his armies conquered the Chachapoyas and subdued seven major cities. Garcilaso placed these cities in a rough geographical context: one can be found on the other side of a certain snowy pass, another located atop a sloping hill so many leagues long.

In the mid-1960s, an American explorer, Gene Savoy—inspired by the exploits of Hiram Bingham, who discovered Machu Picchu in 1911—launched a series of expeditions into the montaña in search of the cities mentioned by Garcilaso. A University of Portland dropout and former newspaperman, Savoy was not a professional scientist. "I taught myself what I know about archaeology, anthropology and history from reading, study and practical field experience," Savoy states in his book, *Antisuyo*. (The name refers to that quarter of the Inca empire east of the Andes.) In his last expedition, Savoy may have discovered as many as six of the seven cities mentioned by Garcilaso.

In his travels, Savoy hoped to examine a theory first propounded by Dr. Julio C. Tello, one of the fathers of Peruvian archaeology. Having discovered one of the first full-blown Peruvian cultures—the Chavín, dated about 900 to 400 B.C.—Tello postulated that the forerunners of the Chavín may have originated in the jungle.

More accepted theories say that culture there first evolved among less sophisticated local peoples or that it was imported by Central American or Mexican peoples who migrated to northern Peru. The idea that culture in Peru might have originated in the montaña or jungle is not taken seriously by most archaeologists. The jungles of both regions, it is thought, could not have supported a high culture.

But what if a major migration had taken place along long-forgotten jungle trails? If so, it was possible that the remains of a culture earlier than the Chavín existed, undiscovered, somewhere in the tropical rainforest.

Savoy's expeditions in Amazonas did not prove, conclusively, that ancient man in Peru rose up out of the jungle. However, the dozens of cities, the hundreds of curvilinear Chachapoyan ruins Savoy found, did prove, he wrote in *Antisuyo,* that the mountaintop jungles of the ceja de selva "could support a vigorous civilization whose monumental remains are as imposing as if not superior to anything found on the coast or sierra." Potsherds taken from Savoy's finds were carbon-dated and found to be between 800 to 1400 A.D. All were from superficial grave sites, and test pits undoubtedly would have yielded older specimens.

Throughout *Antisuyo* one senses an obsessiveness: "Where did the Chachapoyas originate and who were their forerunners . . . from an explorer's point of view, the work has only just begun—with three million square miles of tropical forest still to be archaeologically explored, one hardly knows where to begin. I believe that tropical Amazonas holds the vestige of ancient cultures of which we know nothing—perhaps a civilization of far greater magnitude than we suspect (the size of the Chachapoyan ruins, which surpass those of Cuzcoá, hint at such a possibility)." Unstated in *Antisuyo* is a glittering vision: the great mother metropolis with its massive towers and battlements and plazas, out there—somewhere—in Amazonia. The cradle of the continent's civilization. The final discovery.

When Pizarro landed in 1532, Peru was bleeding in the aftermath of a brutal civil war. Following the death of the Inca Huayna Cápac in 1525, Atahuallpa, the Inca's son by a concubine, launched a war against Huáscar, the legitimate heir. Huáscar's forces were defeated, he was imprisoned, and Atahuallpa assumed the throne.

Pizarro and less than two hundred men crossed the mountains and established themselves in the great Inca plaza at Cajamarca. Atahuallpa and an unarmed retinue of thousands entered the plaza in good faith to meet the strange white men. There, Pizarro's chaplain approached the Inca and informed him that a certain God the Father, who was actually a Trinity, had created the world and all the people in it. But, because people had sinned, God the Father had to send His Son, part of the Trinity, to earth, where He was crucified. Before that happened, the chaplain explained, the Son, whose name was Jesus Christ, had conferred His power upon an Apostle, Peter, and Peter had passed that power on, successively, to other men, called Popes, and one of these last Popes had commissioned Charles the Fifth of Spain to conquer and convert the Inca and his people. Atahuallpa's only hope of salvation, the chaplain concluded, was to swear allegiance to Jesus Christ and to acknowledge himself a tributary of Charles the Fifth.

Atahuallpa then informed the chaplain that he, the Inca, was the greatest prince on earth and that he would be the tributary of no man. This Pope, he said, must be crazy to talk of giving away countries that didn't belong to him. As for Jesus Christ who had died, the Inca was sorry, but—and here he pointed to the sun—"my God still lives in the heavens and looks down on his children."

The conquistadores lay in wait, hiding in the massive buildings that surrounded the square. When the chaplain returned with the Inca's reply, Pizarro, his foot soldiers, and cavalry erupted into the plaza. Muskets and cannons firing, they slaughtered between two thousand and ten thousand unarmed Indians that day and took the Inca prisoner.

Atahuallpa, in captivity, spoke often with the Spanish, and he understood soon enough—all talk of Popes and Trinities notwithstanding—that it was the love of gold which brought the white men to his country. He offered Pizarro enough gold to fill a room measuring seventeen by twenty-two feet to a height of nine feet.

It would be a simple matter, Atahuallpa told his captors, for the interiors of the temples at Cuzco were literally plated with gold and all ornaments and utensils used in religious ceremonies were fashioned of gold or silver. There were immense silver vases and statues, and silver reservoirs to hold water. Even the pipes which carried water into the sacred buildings were made of silver. In the temples and royal palaces there were gardens of gold and silver: sculpture representing corn, potatoes, and other crops grew from a glittering soil of gold dust.

Before the king's ransom had been completely paid, Huáscar was murdered in his prison cell. Pizarro said Atahuallpa had issued the order, and a swift trial was followed by a swifter execution. Pizarro had seen that the Inca empire was an absolute theocracy and that without the Inca—especially in the wake of a bloody civil war—the Indians would fall into disorganization and despair.

The gold and jewels that the Spaniards took out of Peru in the following years is estimated at over $11 billion. And yet, after the conquest, the Incas themselves told the Spaniards that they had seen only a small fraction of the actual wealth of the empire. During the time of the ransom, most of the gold—tears of the sun, the Incas called it—had been hidden in the jungles or thrown into the lakes. (One treasure, mentioned in some chronicles, is a massive chain of gold, *seven hundred feet long,* fashioned in celebration of Huáscar's birth.) Many historians and treasure hunters believe that the gold of the Incas was smuggled over the Andes, into the eastern land that was called Antisuyo.

The day after our night on Kuélap, we drove south along the Utcubamba River to the town of Leimebamba. This area must have been important to the cloud people, judging by the number of ruins to be found there. Leimebamba itself consists of a paved square and about half a dozen rock-strewn mean streets where black wiry-haired pigs doze in the sun and goats root among the rocks, and the old white-haired Indian women in black robes sit cross-legged in the dust, spinning wool.

We sat at a rickety table in the Bar El Caribe, a dank, dirt-floored restaurant just off the square, and studied our maps and diagrams. The owner, a sly, hatchet-faced man with a severe crewcut, lurked about— a pace or two away—staring over our shoulders.

"You have come for the gold," he informed us. "You have a metal detector."

Laszlo told him that we were only tourists, not interested in gold, and that metal detectors are too heavy to carry up mountains in a backpack.

The man would not be taken for a fool. "There are portable metal detectors," he said.

As was usual in Amazonas, where gringos are seldom seen, we were surrounded by friendly people who simply stared for minutes on end before opening up with questions.

"You search for gold?"

"No."

"You are huaqueros?"

"No."

"Why have you drawn your own maps then?"

Leimebamba was rife with rumors about Gene Savoy: he had come into the area with experts, had followed the old Inca road, and had found a body of water which he called the Lake of the Condors. There he sent a scuba diver down, and when the diver came up he and Savoy had a fight about the gold. People believe that the treasure of the Incas is buried in the ruins; that it is gleaming there, beneath the waters of the Lake of the Condors.

Savoy, so the rumor goes, returned to Leimebamba alone. Later he was seen, it is said, crossing the mountains on the trail to Balsas, which is on the Marañón River. With him were two heavily laden mules. No one who tells the story doubts that those mules carried gold. Here the details get a little fuzzy. At Balsas, Savoy was arrested, or perhaps only detained. Some say he was deported as a huaquero. Others say he escaped to Ecuador.

The owner interrupted to show us a prize possession. It was a cassette tape recorder and he stroked it as if it were a favorite pet, then slipped a tape into its mouth. It was American music, country and western, and the song we heard was about a bunch of cowboys who find a fortune in gold and end up killing each other.

There are, in Amazonas, several stories of people who have entered or violated ruins and these people invariably have sickened and died, victims, it is said, of el abuelo—the grandfather—an unpleasant transference in which all the diseases of the gathered dead enter and infest the interloper's body.

The first person we met who actually showed fear approaching the ruins was one Manuel Anunsación Hidalgo Garcia, nineteen, but he was very cagey about it. After guiding us along an easy trail from

Leimebamba to a high meadow near the mountain ruins of Congona, he simply pointed into a wall of thorny brush and left us to machete our way the remaining quarter-mile.

The odor was sharper than at Kuélap, more like licorice or anise, though still pervaded by that melancholy smell of faded lilacs. Congona was thick with a massive-trunked tree that adapts itself to the jungle canopy by sending out thick branches in grand horizontal thrusts. These branches were hung with green streamers and moss, and wherever a branch found the sun, there were large, sharp-petaled red flowers.

The first circular habitations we saw were unimpressive, but as we moved higher, they became larger and more ornate. In places, the branches of these massive trees had burst through the walls of the ruins. At the summit, we found a grassy meadow fronting a magnificent double tower with a winding stairway to the top.

Where Kuélap had been awesome, Congona was a marvel of symmetry and grace. There was an ineffable beauty to it, even in ruin. Huge yellow flowers grew around the rim of the central towers and green creepers fell along the mossy walls. There was no apparent military value in the towers and they suggested nothing so much as a place of worship, a cathedral in the jungle.

After we established camp at the top of the towers, I hacked my way, alone, through vines and creepers, the odor of licorice thick in the dying twilight. The inside of one of the less ornate circle habs I found had been cleared, and the work had been done, at a guess, two or three years previously. Moving into the ruin, I saw something wrong and bad, something that seemed palpably evil, and I felt, for a chill moment, the Thing that had caused Manuel Anunsación Hidalgo Garcia to leave us at the lip of the jungle.

There, dead center in the floor of the ruin, I saw a grave-shaped hole, five feet deep, three wide, four long. The sides of the hole were covered with thick green moss. Huaqueros—grave robbers—had been to Congona.

A few feet above the hole, four or five flat black insects, like wasps or hornets, hovered in formation. It was a simple matter, in the near darkness, to let oneself go, to feel a dread like paralysis taking hold of the arms and legs. I could imagine the golden priests atop the central towers and the people of the clouds strolling among the most graceful achievements of their culture. Momentarily, in that mood and in the presence of a defilement, I tried to believe that we were wrong to be there, that these ruins were best left to time and the jungle.

In the morning, that shivery sense of blasphemy seemed a conceit, a romance. Early that afternoon we returned to Leimebamba, walking three abreast and filling the narrow streets. There were scratches on our arms and faces and our machetes swung by our sides. We were giants, taller and heavier than the biggest men in town. The old women gathered up the children and shooed them indoors as we passed. We had come from Congona, and something in the eyes of the people begged us to swagger. We were brave men, foolish men. Soldiers of fortune. Huaqueros.

When the owner of the Bar El Caribe delivered our drinks and asked if we had found gold, we smiled and gave noncommittal answers.

There is no such thing as a good map of Amazonas, and we have Ecuador to thank for that. In July of 1941, that country, claiming the land from its border south to the Marañón River, launched an undeclared war against Peru. At the battle of Zarumilla, Peruvian forces won a stunning victory and Peru retained control of 120,000 square miles of land. There are Ecuadorians who object to this state of affairs and, in the hinterlands of Amazonas, one still hears of sporadic border clashes.

Good, detailed contour maps of the state, then, have a military significance and they are impossible to obtain. Additionally, the Guardia Civil, a national police force, maintains control points along the only road into the jungle; there foreigners must show their passports and explain what they are doing in that area of Peru.

Hotels are required to obtain the same information, as is the PIP (pronounced "peep"), the Peruvian Investigative Police, an FBI analog. Officers of the PIP—we called them pipsqueaks—wear plain clothes and strut around looking significant. My favorite was the chief—El Jefe—of the Chachapoyas division. One night at the Bar Chacha, four pipsqueaks surrounded our table and told us there was some problem with our papers and that we must go with them to headquarters. We were shown into a large room where El Jefe, a fat man of middle years, pretended not to notice us. His flowing black hair gleamed under the electric light and smelled strongly of rose water. He wore blue-tinted aviator glasses, an iridescent blue raincoat, and a blue-and-white polka-dot ascot. On one side of his desk there was a neat pile of official documents without stamps. On the other side was a smaller pile of official documents that had been stamped. In the middle of the desk, just behind the nameplate that read "Miguel Zamora," there were half a dozen different stamps. Miguel took his time with a couple of documents, looked up with an oleaginous smile, and asked, "What can I do for you gentlemen?"

"Can you walk like a duck?" is the only appropriate response to that question; but, of course, we didn't say that. There were many things we didn't say to police officers during our stay.

Carlos Gates, the supervisor of archaeological monuments, was actually beginning to like us. We were well read, well prepared, and we were persistent. Between trips to the known ruins we visited him a total of four times, and missed him on three other passes. Finally, Señor Gates stopped talking about permits and broke out the gin in the middle of one of our visits. We were getting somewhere.

Because our Spanish was not the best, Gates spoke slowly and distinctly, and tended to shout a bit, as if we were also hard of hearing. He helped us out with gestures and expressions. If something was large or interesting or beautiful, Carlos would widen his eyes as if awestruck. If something was difficult or dangerous, he would snap into a serious expression and pretend to brush lint off his shirt front with his right hand.

Yes, Gates said, he was the man mentioned in Savoy's book, and no, he didn't believe for a moment the rumors we had heard in Leimebamba. People in Amazonas, he said, are jealous of their history and they delight in its mystery. He knew Savoy wasn't a huaquero because he had worked with him, had helped the American plan his expeditions.

And now he was willing to help us. We knew, of course, that most of the known Chacha ruins were located on high forested peaks near the Utcubamba River. This was clear. Many of the ruins were fortified cities: a fortress at the highest point surrounded by circle habs. There were a dozen or more of these in the Utcubamba basin and the main doors of the forts always faced Kuélap. Gates drew a simplified sketch.

The known ruins lay in a rough semicircle, east of Kuélap. The area west of Kuélap had yet to be explored. Gates drew a second diagram.

On this diagram Gates indicated that there would be ruins in the area west of Kuélap. It was his theory that the Chachas would have had cities or fortresses there for reasons of defense and symmetry. If we were willing to share our findings with him, Carlos said, he would introduce us to Don Gregorio Tuesta, a landowner in the area, who could find us a guide who knew the trails there.

We looked at our map. There were no trails marked in the area, and only one pueblo. "What's the land like there?" Laszlo asked.

Carlos said he'd never been there, but from what he'd heard, it was (here Señor Gates popped his eyes for us), but also (he brushed lint off his shirt).

One cool, misty morning I found myself just outside of a seven-hut pueblo called Choctamal, a four-hour walk west of Kuélap. Not far away, on a heavily forested ridge, there was a fortress known as Llaucan, the last known Chacha ruin west of the Utcubamba. This day we were to push on: climb the mountains separating the Utcubamba River basin from the Marañón River basin. There would be, we fervently hoped, unknown ruins ahead. In a sense, it was the start of our expedition.

I was squatting in the bushes with the last of the confetti they call toilet paper in Peru. The local pigs had just demonstrated to me, in the most concrete manner, that they would eat *anything*. Not only that, but they seemed to prefer it directly from the horse's mouth, as it were. For this reason, I was clutching a long sturdy stick, the better to crack the porcine bastards as they made their move. So they milled about, just out of range, squealing and grunting and fixing me in their beady little hungry pink eyes. Not an auspicious start for an expedition of discovery.

Don Gregorio Tuesta, fifty-five, the man whom we had met through

Carlos Gates, was big, five feet ten inches and 175 pounds—a giant of a man for Amazonas. He had eleven children, was a rich man, and walked a lot like John Wayne, only faster. Carlos Cruz, twenty-two, a local potato farmer and hunter, tended the mule carrying our supplies. Carlos was a little over five feet tall, dark of skin, and poor. He and Tuesta chewed coca leaves together in a friendly fashion.

"You need coca to make you strong to climb to the ruins," Tuesta said. Strictly in the interests of good journalism, I chewed about a pound of primo coca. Taken along with a taste of quicklime, called *cal,* it tended to depress the appetite, deaden the tongue, and overcome fatigue. The rush was minor and somewhat disappointing: about what you'd expect from a chocolate bar eaten late in the afternoon of a particularly hectic day.

"What's the trail like ahead?" we'd ask Tuesta.

"Muy fácil," very easy, he would lie. We came to calibrate the difficulty ahead by a system I called the coefficient of coca. If Carlos and the Don plunged on with only a single mouthful, it would be a bearable climb; three or more mouthfuls meant we were in for hell on a hill.

At ten thousand feet we came on some small circle habs. There were three of them, in very poor condition. It was not an impressive set of ruins, but it was unknown to scientists and explorers.

It was there, at our first discovery, that I was treated to an example of Carlos's humor. In a steep clearing, the loose forest loam turned muddy and I slid a fast dozen yards down the slope on my back. Dirt poured into my pants, and, when I finally managed to turn over and pull myself to a halt by grabbing handfuls of ground cover, I saw Carlos laughing like a lunatic at a parade.

"Don Timoteo," he said, *"ichunga."*

Ichunga, I found to my discomfort some moments later, is a small prickery plant that imparts a painful chemical sting that lasts for half an hour. The palms of my hands were on fire and the dirt in my pants was full of ichunga. Carlos could hardly stand it. He kept muttering "Don Timoteo" and chuckling to himself for minutes at a stretch. I was convinced that he had the brain of a hamster.

An hour above the first circle habs, we explored a sparse, almost dry jungle where we came upon a series of high, natural rock walls. Where these walls met the forest floor there were a number of overhangs, some of which contained small caves. In a rock pile under one of the overhangs, Don Gregorio spotted a human jawbone. Tom crawled back into a cave and came out with three complete skulls, two of which were bleached pure white and one was a pale muddy brown.

We found nearly a dozen skulls in all. The beige pottery fragments scattered among the skulls had a red line around the inside lip, just above a contiguous series of broad red spirals. The fragments were similar in size, shape, color, and design to a bowl I had seen in Lima at the National Museum of Anthropology and Archaeology. That bowl had been taken from Kuélap and was dated at 1000 A.D.

These bones had lain in place perhaps a thousand years or more. They were not, as I had expected, brittle, but were, instead, very flexible. Perhaps it was the dampness or the acid in the soil, but you could squeeze these skulls at the temple and they would give several inches. Then, slowly, they would settle back into shape. The urge was strong to squeeze each skull.

A heavy cloud rolled up from the Rio Tingo below and cast everything in a pale, leaden light so that the dry moss on the trees hung gray and lifeless. What had earlier been a slight breeze became a chill wind and, at odd intervals, we heard the caw of an unseen bird. It was a harsh, mechanical sound and it contrasted eerily with another animal noise, a soft mournful cooing that seemed to be very near.

Don Gregorio anointed our fingers with a fragrant oil; protection, he said, against the *antimonia,* a supposed disease caused by breathing the dust of archaeological excavations. A person suffering from the antimonia, it is said, will die coughing up the entire volume of his body's blood.

The mountains that form the watershed between the Utcubamba and Marañón rivers rise to 12,000 feet and higher. Above 10,400 feet or so, the jungle gives way to *puna,* cold, wind-whipped grasslands. At night the temperature drops well below freezing and cold stars howl in the sky.

There was a pass, Abra Asomada, behind us, and we were making our way through a region of intermontane passes that seldom dropped below eleven thousand feet. (Don Gregorio had returned to Chachapoyas, and now Carlos led, forging the trail with uncanny skill.) The ground looked like easy walking, but it was treacherous. High green-brown grasses hid impassable marshes and there were sinkholes deep enough to drop a man from the face of the earth.

Coming out of the marshes, we followed a ridge toward a high stone outcropping. Nearing the outcropping, we came upon a round grassy indentation. It was, unmistakably, a circular habitation. The hill above was pockmarked with circle habs, twenty-five to thirty of them scattered like a skirt before the rock above. To the north, over a gentle ridge, there were twenty more.

And the rock outcropping itself: where there were gaps in the natural stone, we saw high limestone walls. It was a fort, and we hurried to climb our way to the top. At 11,720 feet, the highest point in the fort proper, there was a small tower, similar in shape to the one we had seen at Kuélap.

To my knowledge, this miniature Kuélap was the first Chachapoyan fort to be found *above* the cloud forests. Located as it was, on a commanding position over a natural Marañón-to-Utcubamba route, I imagined the fort was Kuélap's defense early warning point. The vision goes like this:

The tower lookout spots suspicious movement from the Marañón side. A staggered series of runners is dispatched to Kuélap. A drum sounds, and those in the circle habs, warriors all, march out to meet the invading army. Repulsed by superior numbers, they retreat to the fort, which they can hold indefinitely. The invaders, anxious to claim richer prizes below, march off toward the Utcubamba.

Where the warriors of Kuélap are lying in ambush.

I don't know why this should be, but finding a fort, a military installation, is more thrilling than coming upon the remains of an ancient but apparently peaceful community. It has an effect on the ego and, I suspect, this is especially true of rank amateurs like myself who enter into expeditions not really convinced there is anything out there to find. We become Explorers, with a capital E, and that gives us the right to call things by any name we choose.

Never mind the handful of local hunters who know of the place and call it something or other in some goddamn foreign language. Just because a sheer accident of birth and geography put them there first, just because we are talking about their country and their ancestors, these arrogant bozos think they have the right to go around slapping names on things willy-nilly. The hell with them, I say.

It's up to us Explorers to name these places. We rush into print, the better to screw our expeditionary friends. It gives us near orgasmic pleasure to consider the other fellow—Laszlo Berty, let's say—reading our report in a mounting fury. We like to think that now—at this very moment—the color is rising in his face, making it all red and mottled, like a slice of raw liver. We chuckle over our typewriters. We are Explorers. We get to name things.

Okay?

Okay.

Henceforth, let the fort above Abra Asomada be known as Fort Big Tim Cahill. This is a good name, and I think it sings.

The passes and the puna formed a natural boundary line, like a river, and I imagined that Fort Cahill would be the last Chacha construct we would find west of the Utcubamba. I was wrong. We swept down out of the cold grasslands onto a forested ridge with three prominent peaks. There were dozens of circle habs on each peak, and, inexplicably, there was not evidence of fortification. In case of attack, the people of Three Peaks must have retreated back over the puna—which seemed unlikely because of the distance and the cold—or they massed at some yet-undiscovered fort, another Kuélap perhaps, on the Marañón side.

Dropping from 10,500 feet at Three Peaks to 9,250 feet at a grassy area called Laguna Seca, we chose a steep ridge-running trail and, rising with the ridge, we found dozens more. This was one of the wetter jungles we had seen and the walls of the ruins were badly crumbled. In places we would come upon a high, unnaturally round mound of earth. A machete sank two feet into soft loam before striking solid stone. We attempted to clear one of these buried circle habs, but it was painstaking work. Wrist-thick roots had burrowed through the stone, and it was difficult to remove them without damaging the structure.

There were perhaps a hundred circle habs on the ridge, and still we found no evidence of fortification. At one point, we came upon three rectangular buildings, each thirty feet long, sixteen across, separated by alleys six feet wide. Rectangular construction was characteristic of the Incas, and a good guess would be that these had been built sometime in the 1480s, just after Túpac Yupanqui conquered the Chachas.

Following the ridge from about 9,500 feet to 8,300 feet, we found over a hundred more circle habs and about twenty-five rectangles among them.

Below the ridge, the jungle opened into bright green broadleaf plants, and the trees were hung with brilliant red and yellow and green creepers, so that it was rather like walking through a continuous bad curtain. Dozens of large black butterflies with white Rorschach patterns on their wings rested on the broadleafs and darted among the creepers.

On my map of the area, I found one pueblo, Pisuquia, and the trail brought us there early one steamy afternoon. The pueblo consisted of four or five stone and mudpack houses, a few huts, one haggard young man, a stout señora, two bony pigs, a flock of decrepit chickens, and half a dozen of the dirtiest, most sullen children in the universe. There were, the young man told us, ruins on that ridge—he pointed south—and that one—east—and that one—west. Not to mention the two hundred and some ruins we found on the ridge that brought us into Pisuquia.

The people of Pisuquia farmed with wooden plows and lived in dirt-floored huts that crumble in about twenty years. It was boggling to think that a thousand years ago there were not only *more* people living in the area, but that they were certainly more accomplished builders, and probably better potters, jewelers, and farmers than the present locals. The Chachas of prehistoric Peru were, by all objective standards, more civilized than the people of Pisuquia.

Three hours beyond Pisuquia, there is a pueblo called Tribulón, and Carlos directed us to a large house where some of his relatives lived. Half a dozen men sat on a low bench in front of the house and in front of them there was a dented metal can that might once have held kerosene. Occasionally one of the men would rise unsteadily and dip their only cup, a cracked wooden bowl, into the can. He would then shout *"jugo de caña"* and down the pale liquid in a rush that left half the contents streaming down his shirt front. The men had a glazed and sanguine look about the eyes and their lips were green from the coca they chewed.

It was the eve of the feast of the Virgin of Carmen, reason enough to drink, and the men greeted us warmly. We were offered bowls of jugo de caña, which is fermented sugar-cane juice. Tom took a few polite sips, but Laszlo and I downed several bowls. It had a thin, sugar-water taste, rather like super economy orange Kool Aid, and the alcoholic content seemed small. It tasted good after a long, hot walk and Laszlo and I drank quite a lot of it.

An hour or two after sunset, when things started getting blurry, we were ushered into a dark, smoky, dirt-floored room some eight feet wide and thirty long. We sat with the men at a low table with benches a foot or two off the ground and ate corn soup with what I took to be bits of grilled pork floating on top. There were eight or nine women who didn't eat, but who sat opposite us, on the floor, talking quietly among themselves. In the far corner, one of the women tended a small wood fire and she hurried to pour more soup when the men called for it. The only other light in the room was a small candle set high on a wooden ledge above the women. There were bits of stringy-looking meat hanging out to dry on the underside of the ledge.

Between bowls of jugo de caña and sips of soup, I watched the guinea pigs, called *cuy,* scurrying about in the corners of the room. The small ones made high keening sounds and hid under the women's skirts. Larger ones, snow white and the size of small rabbits, moved across the room in a stately waddle. Cuy have been a source of protein in Peru since prehistory. I glanced up at the meat hanging under the ledge, watched one of the big guinea pigs relieve itself near my foot, and examined the little piece of gray meat on my spoon.

"Más jugo de caña," I said. Every time I drank, I seemed to lose half the bowl down my shirt front. Laszlo was developing the same problem.

Tom noted that Carlos had turned out to be a terrific guide: he knew the jungles and trails as if by instinct. I drank to that. Then I drank a couple of bowls in celebration of Carlos's rotten sense of humor.

Laszlo said that he noticed that *"caramba"* was the strongest word Carlos ever used. *Caramba* translates to something like "Great Scott." Laszlo said he really liked Carlos and was going to teach him some great American swear words and how they could be used in potent combination. He started with the word "fuckload" to indicate a great amount. Carlos seemed acutely embarrassed by this information.

Sometime later, after more bowls of jugo de caña, I found myself in another room where Tom was playing "Oh! Susanna" on his harmonica and I was dancing with Carlos's brother-in-law, who was sweating profusely and whose lips were green. The thing to do, it seemed, was hop around on one foot or the other, machete flopping by your side, with the right hand raised in a fist high above your head and the left held steady behind the back, like a fencer. Faces swam up out of the crowd and most of them seemed to be laughing hysterically.

About midnight we were allowed to spread our bags out in a room on the second floor. Laszlo held forth for some time about all the things he had to do and about how he was going to get up at 3:00 A.M. in order to accomplish them all. There was no doubt about this. He would be up at three. Absolutely. He could do it. He didn't see how all the Peruvians could have gotten so drunk on jugo de caña since he had drunk more than anybody and didn't feel a thing. I was stricken with sudden unconsciousness just after that last statement.

About 6:30 the next morning, I woke to a very imperfect world. Laszlo was still there and I would have said he was dead except that he was snoring painfully. Though seriously ill, I made one of those superhuman efforts you read about—a young mother lifts an auto off her child, that sort of thing—and worked up a passably bright and alert tone.

"Laszlo, Laszlo," I shouted, alarmed and concerned, "it's after three. You have things to do, places to go, people to meet."

He opened one eye. The lid came up slowly, as if it were operated by several tiny men straining away at some heavy internal crank.

"Shut up," he croaked.

Laszlo lurched to his feet several hours later and, despite the fact that he hadn't been drunk, even though he drank more than anybody, his bladder had failed in the night. He had to hang his bag up to dry. It was absolutely filthy. Sucio. Laszlo would have to sleep in that stained and stale bag for the remainder of the expedition. You can imagine how I felt.

In a remote valley called Santa Rosa there is a town called Pueblo Nuevo, and just above the town there are two wattle-and-daub huts belonging to Marino Tuesta, the brother of Don Gregorio Tuesta. We had a letter of introduction.

Marino took us above his farm to a forest where most things—tree trunks, rocks, the ground itself—were covered with a soft ferny moss called *musco*. Everything felt fuzzy and gentle, even the circle habs we found there. Somewhat below the highest point, we came to a gently sloping area where the sun burst through the jungle canopy in oblique golden pillars, highlighting a high, sharp-cornered wall. Probably Inca. I cleared away the foliage while Tom paced off the wall for his map of the city. This is an inexact process because you must walk on broken ground and over fallen trees, hacking your way through where the jungle is thick.

Twenty-five minutes later I caught sight of Tom. *He was coming the other way.* It had taken him nearly half an hour to pace off the building. It was immense—150 feet by 150 feet—and I saw on Tom's face a glazed and incredulous expression. His map indicated that this, the largest single ruin we had found, was the central plaza of a symmetrical jungle city. The arrangement recalled governmental plazas seen in many modern American cities, and something about that realization set the mind diving into chilly waters. There is, in us all, an idiot pride which argues that our age alone possesses civilization. Standing in the midst of indisputable proof to the contrary can be terrifying, like a sudden premonition of death.

The city of the great plaza had been discovered by Miguel Tuesta, the father of Gregorio and Marino. He called it Pueblo Alto, the high city, and Marino said we were the only other people he knew who had ever seen it. He considered the ruins beautiful and went up there often, to think.

On another day, we walked across the Santa Rosa Valley to explore a mountain visible from Marino's front door. There, in a jungle thick with *bejuco*—moss-covered hanging vines the size of a man's wrist—we came on another city. The grand plaza here was larger than the one at Pueblo Alto—270 feet by 261 feet—and it was apparent that the two cities would be visible to each other when the jungle was cleared. We called this place Pueblo Alto South.

On a rise above the plaza we found three very large, very well-preserved circle habs. One had a bisecting wall inside as well as a number of small niches set at about chest level. In the niches we found five hibernating bats. Carlos plucked them from the niches, threw them in a heap on the ground, and, before we could stop him, stomped them all to death with a satisfied smile. They were, he said, vampire bats, and they preyed on the local livestock.

Within minutes, we were engulfed in a heavy downpour during which I reflected on the *relámpago*. This is a belief, common in Amazonas, that those who venture too close to the ruins will hear the thunder roll before they are incinerated by a bolt of lightning. As it was, we only got a little wet. None of us ever spat up any blood, so the antimonia didn't get us; and we didn't have any problems with el abuelo, unless all those dead Chachas suffered from chronic loose bowels. I like to think that our expedition succeeded and that we escaped retribution because we took nothing from the ruins, because we weren't huaqueros. I'm pretty sure it wasn't because we were pure of heart and lived in harmony with one another.

Back in Lima, we took our notebooks to Dr. Ruth Shady of the National Museum of Anthropology and Archaeology. We told her about the burial site and the fort above Abra Asomada, about the city on Three Peaks, about the hundreds of ruins on Pisuquia's ridge, about Pueblo Alto and Pueblo Alto South. Dr. Shady took a few sketchy notes and excused herself. The new American ambassador to Peru was visiting and she didn't have time to listen to a lot of excited talk and speculation about the Chachapoyans, none of whom had ever paid a cent to visit the museum.

So I am forced to draw my own conclusions. We proved that the Chacha culture existed west of Kuélap and extended, in force, into the Marañón River basin. I think there may be a Kuélap-like fort somewhere near the area we explored. We found no evidence of fortification past Fort Cahill, although the Chachas of the Marañón must have had at least one strong defensive position. I think our findings tend to support Savoy's hypothesis: the jungles of the montaña could and did support a vigorous culture. That culture was probably larger and more far-flung than most archaeologists now believe. It is, then, all the more possible that part of the great migration south from Mexico and Central America took place overland, through the jungles. The mother metropolis could be there still, somewhere in the vast rainforest of the Amazon basin.

In the end, I am pleased with the lack of response from the museum and Dr. Shady. It means that vast areas of our world are going to remain unexplored and unstudied. Mystery is a resource, like coal or gold, and its preservation is a fine thing.

There were many ruins our expedition didn't reach for simple lack of time. There are said to be circular habitations above Pisuquia, and in the mountains surrounding Pueblo Alto and Pueblo Alto South. One valley over from Santa Rosa, people talk of finding perfectly preserved mummies. On a mountain across from Fort Cahill we saw a series of ancient terraces, obviously man-made, and their size suggested impressive ruins to be found there. In a place called Chilchos there are said to be mountaintop fortresses. An ancient pre-Inca road leads out of Chilchos into the jungle. No one knows where it goes.

I keep thinking about that road. It leads out of Chilchos. Into the jungle. And no one knows where it goes.

Pa Lampung Padan's Sewing Machine

From Stranger in the Forest *(1988)*
By Eric Hansen

Who would be naive enough to attempt a 1,500-mile trek across the mammoth island of Borneo without an iota of jungle experience or the ability to speak the local language?

Eric Hansen, for one. In 1982, led by his zest for the unknown, Hansen set out to traverse Borneo's remote forests. In addition to an abundance of natural charm, Hansen was equipped with only a bedsheet, a change of clothes, and a basket filled with trinkets to barter. He returned with a wealth of anecdotes to share with the world.

In this excerpt from Stranger in the Forest, *Hansen brings us face-to-face with people who perhaps are lost in time but who quickly figure out nonetheless that time does equal money. He also makes some pertinent observations on what happens when a once well-groomed gringo spends a little too much time in the bush. (DRK)*

Three hundred miles from the east coast and two days' walk from where the longboat sank, I climbed to the top of a mountain ridge smothered in giant trees. It was the morning of my 115th day in the jungle. Like an island, the ridge sat half-submerged in a sea of blue-white valley mist. Each day before noon those cool rising mists would submerge the jungle mountains like an ocean tide.

My two guides and I slashed a small clearing in the dense undergrowth with our parangs and sat down to make tea. After collecting wood and splitting it, Bo 'Hok showed me how fire was made before the Penan discovered Bic lighters. He cut a two-foot length of green bamboo with his parang and from his tin tobacco box produced a smallish flake of flint. He called it *batu api*, the fire rock. Holding the flint and a thin mat of tinder between his thumb and first two fingertips, Bo 'Hok vigorously struck the smooth surface of the bamboo at an oblique angle. To my astonishment sparks appeared. The tinder soon glowed red in patches and was then placed into a prepared handful of dried fibrous sago bark mixed with ash from burned leaves. This mixture, he explained, was *tidak takoot angin*, not afraid of the wind. Bo 'Hok added wood shavings, blew two or three times, and within seconds we had fire. Flames danced around the base of the blackened cooking pot, and we brought out our enameled mugs and a plastic bag of Lipton tea.

As the water heated, I watched the column of smoke meandering up through the twisted network of branches. Three swallows appeared briefly against a patch of blue sky to dart across the one small opening in the jungle canopy. Far off, black cicadas intermittently droned their predictable phrases.

I tried to wash daily, but hadn't been able to the previous afternoon; the streams on the steep slopes were too small to bathe in, so by morning I smelled of stale sweat and mosquito repellent. Living in the perpetual shade was beginning to make me feel confined and irritable. The sunlight was only 150 feet above my head, but there was no way of getting to it. My inclination was to climb hand over hand up through the layers of the forest canopy to poke my head above the highest branches and feel the sun's warmth on my face and forearms. I imagined that the rolling expanse of closely clustered tree crowns would look like a densely planted garden of giant broccoli. Bo 'Hok and Weng could have managed the climb, but they didn't feel the need. For me, it was an impossible feat. I had to abandon the thought.

It was during moments of relative inactivity such as this that I would start thinking about how completely alone I felt. The sounds, the smells, and especially the terrain were still unfamiliar. I had chosen to come, wanted to come, but that did not dissipate the sense that I was isolated in a place that wasn't my own. I was completely restricted to a pace dictated by circumstances beyond my control: the weather, the moods of Bo 'Hok and Weng, and the availability of wild game. I felt I had become fluent enough in Indonesian, but the cultural gap between my Western middle-class background and that of these two nomadic hunters had come to feel like a sociological Grand Canyon. The three of us had experienced so many intimate, humorous, touching moments, but I knew I didn't really matter to them. We were physically together, but separated by our histories, thoughts, perceptions, and expectations. To them I was a slightly amusing stranger who had some shotgun shells that they needed. One day soon we would say goodby, and they would return to the forest without me. The likelihood that I would be forgotten troubled me because I knew that the memory of these months in the rain forest would stay with me forever. I needed someone to reflect the intensity of my experience in order to validate it. Bo 'Hok and Weng didn't think in such terms. They had a much more immediate sense of the world, based primarily on survival. I spent much of my time thinking; they spent theirs looking for food and a place to sleep.

Few outsiders had ventured into this part of the rain forest. None had come as alone and vulnerable as I was. Nieuwenhuis had brought 110 porters and bodyguards this way in 1898; then there was the story of poor George Muller. In 1824, as a representative of the Dutch Colonial government, he had set out to cross the island from east to west. He wanted to be the first white man to accomplish the journey. Traveling up the Mahakam River from Samarinda with twelve Javanese soldiers, he succeeded in negotiating the maze of smaller rivers that led into the rugged central mountains that now bear his name. He crossed the watershed, and with his goal seemingly possible, yet still months away, he set up his last camp on Sungai Bungan at the headwaters of the Kapuas River. The next morning the longboats were loaded, but as Muller made his final preparations to leave he and his soldiers were attacked and cut down by a band of marauding natives. One of the Javanese men managed to escape and somehow found his way through hundreds of miles of unknown rain forest to reach Pontianak with news of Muller's death.

Even with this knowledge, I felt comfortable that I would not share Muller's fate. I gradually came to realize that by traveling as a total novice—ignorant of even the basics of jungle survival—the highland people gave me special treatment. I was viewed as being either very brave or very mad, and I don't think anyone was quite sure which. I wasn't certain myself. It was clear that I was doing something they would never consider—traveling without tribal companions beyond the boundaries of their land. There was a practical reason for my traveling this way. I wanted to avoid intimidating anyone. Having white skin, long feet, and standing nearly twelve inches above most people were provocative enough. Had I traveled with a group (of Westerners), the community response would have been completely different. They would have been inhibited. On my own I was in the minority, always off balance, completely vulnerable. I was the stranger, and the people treated me exactly as they saw fit. The quickest and most accurate way of judging a community, it seems to me, is to observe how its members react to strangers. Traveling on my own was the only way to see what the people were like. I had consciously put myself in a position where I was the one who had to adapt—both to the people and to the environment. It was my ability to adapt to change in response to what was going on around me that ensured my continuing survival. By living in their leaf huts, eating their food, learning their language, joining the hunt, and dancing with them at night, I let the people know I accepted them and wished to be accepted by them in return. I felt comfortable making a fool of myself, and the people responded to my openness with hospitality and good humor. Their sympathy and friendship surrounded me with an aura of safety that no passport, weapon, map, or radio could ever have provided.

I hadn't slept well the previous night because of the damp, so I held the teacup close to my face and blew the steam into my eyes to help clear them. Over the rim of the cup I could see Bo 'Hok and Weng sitting on the other side of the fire. They were preoccupied with the task of oiling their gun barrels with stomach fat from an eight-foot snake they had hacked to pieces the day before.

A nearby rustling and crunching of twigs caught my attention. Something large was moving towards us on the trail. Bo 'Hok and Weng instinctively slipped cartridges into their shotguns, eased the breeches shut, and waited quietly. Staggering into view, a man suddenly appeared on the narrow game trail. He was bent double beneath the weight of what looked like a large hardwood box. His arrival came as a surprise because we hadn't seen any other human being in six weeks.

The man was dressed in blue satin jogging shorts, black hightop tennis shoes without socks, and a red T-shirt. It wasn't until he got closer that I recognized what he was carrying. It was an old-fashioned treadle sewing machine mounted on a cast-iron frame within a hardwood cabinet. I knew there wasn't a village for more than eighty miles in the direction from which he was walking. I stared at him in disbelief. He walked up to us and with a half-smile, raised his eyebrows slightly in greeting, then lowered himself to his haunches, gently placing the heavy machine upright on the ground. Cast into the metal base I read the word "Singer."

I had absolutely no idea what this man and his sewing machine could be doing in the jungle. It seemed unlikely that he was a mad nomadic tailor, but no other possibility presented itself. The timing of this man's arrival was perfect. For the previous few days I had been congratulating myself on my great adventure, and now I was confronted with serious competition. There is a perverse sort of one-upmanship that obliges travelers all over the world to outdo one another with stories. This man didn't have to utter a single word. One glance at his sewing machine and I felt my journey fade into insignificance.

I later learned his name was Pa Lampung Padan. I offered him *sugee*, but before our conversation began I was distracted by a metallic clanking sound. The commotion grew louder, and soon a second man appeared on the trail. His rattan pack was filled with a mass of shiny aluminum rice-cooking pots. Dozens more were attached by their handles to the sides of the pack. His footsteps were accentuated by the sound of many pots striking one another. The pot man sat down next to the sewing machine with a resounding crash of metal. Immediately another man arrived carrying a 25-horsepower Johnson outboard motor and a brace of rainbow-colored golfing umbrellas. The group continued to grow as three more men appeared. The pile of booty was impressive. There were tape recorders manufactured in Java, Stihl chain saws from Sweden, a battered World War II British Commando Special Z Unit jerry can full of gasoline, red and blue plastic buckets, and four large tins of Huntley and Palmer's Superior Reading Biscuits. I was unfamiliar with this brand name and incorrectly assumed the biscuits were to be eaten while reading. I imagined myself seated comfortably in an armchair by a fireplace—a bone china teacup and saucer on the polished mahogany side table, the fragrance of bergamot, a small dish of reading biscuits, and P. G. Wodehouse in hand.

The men sat on the jungle floor surrounded by their remarkable loads with expressions of total nonchalance. They might have been simply returning from the corner store with a bottle of milk and the newspaper. I caught sight of Bo 'Hok covetously admiring the umbrella man's right forearm. It displayed three identical stainless steel Seiko 5 wristwatches. The three of us were very impressed by this caravan of coastal goods.

Pa Lampung Padan told me that for the previous four weeks they had been shuttling this tremendous amount of newly purchased tools and gifts over the mountains from Sarawak. According to his story, there must have been two or three thousand pounds of the stuff stacked on the banks of a nearby stream. There is no air service between Sarawak and central Kalimantan, and the only way to transport these goods is by longboat and on foot.

For generations men have left the isolation of the highland communities to travel out into the world. It is considered "good" to travel far. This practice is called *peselai* (the long journey) by the Kenyah, and *bejelai* (to walk) by the Iban. This tradition goes back to headhunting days. The fact that men are now returning with sewing machines and tape recorders rather than with heads has not significantly changed the purpose of the journey or the rituals of spirit worship. Before World War II a man's wealth was calculated in terms of ceramic rice-wine jars, brass gongs, salt, and cloth. Today the items of consequence are radios, batteries, medicines, chain saws, outboard motors, and front teeth sheathed in gold by Chinese dentists on the coast.

The coastal boomtown economy—created by the timber, oil, and natural-gas industries—was evident in the selection of the goods the men had brought. These products of modern technology made me reflect upon how one culture measures what is of value in another culture. When the Kalimantan Kenyah go to the coast, they return with utilitarian objects such as tools, kerosene, and cooking pots. Other items, such as sunglasses, Milo (a health drink similar to Ovaltine or Horlicks), plastic toys, printed T-shirts, and plastic dinnerware sets, are purchased primarily for social status. Back in the upriver longhouses some of these products of Western industry become ritual power objects. During my two-month reconnaissance through Iban country in Sarawak, I once saw a lurid pink plastic suitcase used as a portable shrine. Instead of neatly folded clothes and a shaving kit, the suitcase contained steaming fresh pig livers for divining the future. In another Iban village chain saws and famous headhunting swords were lashed to the upright roof supports and draped with red hibiscus flowers. People danced around these temporary displays during *Gawai*, the June rice-harvest celebrations. We might laugh at the notion of plastic tea sets in the jungle, but it is a time-honored ritual for Western travelers to collect preindustrial artifacts to use as home decorations. A woven rattan sago mat on a living-room wall creates a lifestyle image with that ethnic touch. Possession of primitive artifacts suggests worldly knowledge, just as in highland communities of Borneo an electric wristwatch that plays "Happy Birthday" is the mark of a great traveler. Funny thing how travel can narrow the mind.

The man with the Seiko watches asked me what I was doing in the jungle. I told him I was collecting plants and trading shotgun shells and beads for stories. I'm afraid this explanation didn't make much of an impression.

"How far is your home, *Tuan?*" asked Pa Lampung Padan.

"From the coast, two hundred days by longboat with two 40-horse-power outboard engines," I answered with my standard reply.

I could see the men measuring this distance in their minds. How many tins of gasoline? How many *gantangs* of rice? Would the fishing be good? This great distance was "too far" for them to imagine. How could all the supplies for two hundred days be carried in the boat?

The men were more impressed by the Borneo rivers I had traveled and the names of the villages where I had stayed. They nodded and occasionally conferred privately as I correctly recited the succession of headmen who had passed me from one tribal area to another. The list stretched from the coast to the last village in Kalimantan Pow-O-Pan. When I finished, Pa Lampung Padan exclaimed, "*Tuan*, you are not just collecting leaves and tree bark. You have come far from your home. You, too, are on *peselai*. You are the same as us." I agreed, to help them make sense of what I was doing, but I felt that in no way did my wanderings compare with their stupendous journey.

The purpose of *peselai* is to acquire wealth and social status. In many ways these trips are also spiritual journeys and provide an opportunity for young men to establish or enhance their sense of self. It is a time for the men (and some women, too, these days) to test themselves in new places. A successful trip will add prestige to the individual and his or her community. *Peselai* serves other practical purposes as well. Young women put considerable pressure on eligible bachelors by asking them pointedly, "Have you gone on *peselai*? What is your story? What have you done?"

In a lifetime there are few opportunities that allow men the time to leave their villages and farms to go on these long journeys. It is also unusual to meet a man who has not made at least one extended trip to the coast. There is an expression in the highlands of Kalimantan: Four trips to the coast and you are an old man.

Traditionally, before leaving on *peselai*, the men must first receive proper omens from the jungle. One waits for the first call of the *isit* bird (the spider hunter, *Arachnothera chrysogenys*). Then the *elang* bird (white-headed hawk, *Haliaster intermedius*) must be seen flying from right to left. Then men also wait for the call of the crested rain bird (*Platylophus porphyromelas*) and finally for the deceptive doglike sound of the barking deer (*Cervulus muntjak*). Waiting for the omens and preparing the proper food offerings can take a minimum of two weeks, usually much longer.

"How long did it take for you to receive the omens?" I asked Pa Lampung.

"Oh, I don't consult the birds now. I am a Christian. I pray to the forest spirits with help from Jesus and God. One quick prayer is enough."

"As well it should be," I agreed.

Pa Lampung Padan had said goodby to his wife and children two years earlier. He left his village, Long Peliran, one morning with two friends. Carrying parangs and light packs, the three men wandered for weeks through the giant forest. They traversed the great dividing range to the north and eventually located a river flowing through Sarawak towards the South China Sea. They lived off the jungle and traveled downstream for another five days before arriving in the twentieth century. Their longboat was beached at the Holly Stone Quarry on the banks of the Baram River. The local people called the place Batu Gading (The Ivory Rock), named for the tremendous bread-loaf–shaped white stone monolith that rises dramatically out of the green jungle at a tight bend in the river. Pa Lampung Padan and his two friends found work at the quarry. For twenty months he drilled holes in Batu Gading, set explosive charges, and blew up the dense blue-gray rock. The stone rubble was reduced to gravel and sent downriver on barges to pave the coastal roads of Brunei and Sarawak.

As illegal workers in Sarawak, the Indonesians are taken advantage of by the Chinese camp manager. They are paid less and sleep on the floors of corrugated metal hovels, twenty men to a room. The toilet facilities are unspeakable, and most workers prefer the river. The starting wage for Indonesians was less than three U.S. dollars per day. This was two-thirds the local wage, but twice what they could earn in Indonesia. Consequently, the coastal Malays and nearby longhouse workers looked down on the Indonesians because they represented cheap imported labor that deprived them of jobs.

Pa Lampung Padan persevered and eventually became a relatively highly paid laborer. He did well for himself and never lost sight of how his efforts would benefit his family.

"In a month I could save 400 Malay dollars [175 U.S. dollars] from my 500-dollar wage," he told me. "The other 100 dollars went for rice, sugar, canned drinks, biscuits, soup, salt, and soap. We made kerosene lamps out of old soft-drink cans. The wicks were made from twisted cloth and stuck into the tops. We bought our own food, also fuel for cooking, work clothes, and made our own entertainment. There was the river for swimming and one dirt badminton court. We bought the nets, racquets, and shuttlecock. Everything we bought (at inflated prices) from the company store."

The combined pressures of hard labor, nowhere to go after work, and the loneliness of being separated from their families and land caused some men to grow despondent and to squander their meager wages on petty luxuries from the company store. They also spent their money on card games, alcohol, and the camp prostitutes. For the two hundred workers the Chinese shop owner had contracted six women from the coast. A new group of women came each month. For twenty dollars (one to two days' wages) a man could spend an hour with one of these women, as others waited their turn.

Credit was readily extended by the company store, so that some of the workers were laboring merely to service their debts and to feed themselves. I was told that one Indonesian man had been at the stone quarry for nineteen years and hadn't saved any money. He had lost contact with his family, and the shame of returning to his village empty-handed kept him at Batu Gading.

After twenty months of this life, Pa Lampung Padan had saved enough money. He left the blasting pits of Batu Gading and traveled downstream to the Marudi bazaar. There, after testing the weight of several models, he bought a sewing machine for his wife—the best one he could find. There are other sewing machines in the highlands, but such a marvelous new machine had never been seen by the people of Long Peliran.

From Marudi Pa Lampung Padan joined five other Kenyah men for the return journey to Kalimantan. They traveled upstream to the village of Long Moh near the border then hacked a longboat out of a single tree trunk with short handled axes and an adz. The longboat was loaded and poled upstream to the headwaters of Sungai Janan, the last river in Sarawak. From there Pa Lampung Padan carried the sewing machine over the precipitous mountain ridges to the first stream in Kalimantan. Another longboat was built of hand-hewn planks lashed together with rattan vines. Pa Lampung described the half-submerged bamboo raft piled high with the sewing machine and other precious cargo, slowly floating along quiet jungle waterways. Pa Lampung had traveled more than seven hundred miles roundtrip in the previous two years and was now within four days of his home village. He had risked blowing his body to pieces in a dust-filled quarry where no one cared about him and had lived among strangers in a miserable shack eating cheap tinned food for both those years. The loneliness must have been unbearable. His wife had been through her own ordeal. She had not heard from her husband since he had left and had continued to take care of the farm and the children while he was gone, with no idea that her husband would be home in a matter of days.

Pa Lampung finished the story of his journey, and I was speechless. There was something almost too touching about his efforts. What more was there to be said about "man, the loving, the thoughtful provider," or "woman, the faithful home keeper"? These values had long ago been reduced to clichés in modern culture, but listening to Pa Lampung, I was moved by his sense of devotion to his family, exemplified by his sacrifice and the incredible physical strain to return with his gifts.

The cooking pot with the tea had gone cold for the third time, and the steadily rising valley mist was now creeping through the trees. It was time to start walking again. The men began stripping the bark from freshly cut six-foot-long saplings. With steady strokes of their knife blades, they decorated the ends of the poles with long spiral ribbons of wood shavings. The six poles were placed in the ground at the edge of our clearing to thank the spirit of the omens as well as *balai utung*, the spirit of each man, for the successful journey. This was the final ritual for their *peselai*, as they were now entering their own country.

Pa Lampung Padan squatted in front of the sewing machine. He adjusted his shoulder straps and placed a pounded, bark fiber tumpline across his forehead before struggling to his feet. Bo 'Hok, Weng, and I watched them go. One by one the men lifted their packs and in single file disappeared into the jungle. The sound of clanking pots was eventually replaced by the bird and insect sounds of the forest.

The Last Eden

From Time Magazine *(1992)*
By Eugene Linden

It is 1993 in the Ndoki, a remote region in the northern West African country of Congo. Like Henry Morton Stanley, the journalist who ventured into the African jungle more than one hundred years earlier, this roving reporter, Eugene Linden, is searching for nothing less than "the last Eden."

As a senior staff writer for Time *magazine, Eugene Linden has gained a reputation not only as an excellent journalist and adventurer, but also as an outspoken, dedicated friend of the environment.*

There aren't many spots left on Earth that remain unscathed by Western development. But Eugene Linden found just such a place in the Ndoki, a world that, at the time of his visit, not only had escaped the effects of modern civilization but perhaps had eluded the touch of humankind altogether. (DRK)

Ndokanda, a BaNgombe Pygmy, hunkers down beside me. Holding the bridge of his nose, he lets out a loud bray—his dead-on imitation of the cry of small rainforest animals called duikers. These deerlike creatures make the noise in the throes of giving birth, and Pygmies imitate it because other duikers come running when they hear the call. This time, however, the braying attracts a large band of chimpanzees, drawn by the prospect of dining on vulnerable duikers. For a moment I feel the shiver of being hunted.

But when the chimps spot the Pygmy and his three white companions, the animals stop dead in their tracks. Their bloodlust gives way to astonishment, as if they are seeing something they have never seen before. They begin stamping their feet, shaking their arms, calling to one another and throwing branches at us. As many as 25 animals scream from all sides. Each time we make a move, a new round of calls erupts among the chimps, but they never show signs of fleeing.

Instead, for more than two hours, the mesmerized chimps hover around us, drawing to within a few arm lengths. I am flabbergasted. Wild chimps do not react this way to humans in any other part of the African rainforest. But this is no ordinary meeting of fellow primates. For the chimps surrounding us, seeing humans amounts to an ape version of *Close Encounters of the Third Kind*.

In this drama, we are the aliens. We have ventured into the last vast unexplored rainforest on earth—the unsullied Ndoki region of northern Congo—a place where the animals do not know what to make of us because they have never seen humans before.

The word Ndoki (pronounced en-*doe*-key) means "sorcerer" in Lingala, and this is indeed an enchanted, mysterious place. Guarded by swamps to the south and east, hills to the north and the forbidding Ndoki River to the west, the region is almost inaccessible. Pygmies have crisscrossed central Africa for thousands of years, but there is no evidence that they have entered beyond the fringes of this 3 million–hectare (7.5 million–acre) expanse of virgin forest, which is about the size of Belgium.

Our 15-day expedition, led by botanist Michael Fay of Wildlife Conservation International, has taken us to parts of the forest we believe no human has ever seen. We are catching a glimpse of the rarest treasure on this crowded planet: an ecosystem as pristine today as it was

12,000 years ago, before humans began to transform the earth. Our journey into unknown territory is a grand adventure, one that is as exciting as it is daunting. At one point, Fay must persuade apprehensive Pygmy trackers to continue through the Ndoki, for legend holds that the forest is home to Mokele Mbembe, a dinosaur-like creature that can kill elephants.

Mokele Mbembe could hardly create more of a stir than we do in this previously undisturbed land. Gorillas stare and scream at us, and sometime charge, but almost never run away. Colobus and cercopithecus monkeys crane their necks to eye us from high tree branches. Gloriously fat wild pigs, elsewhere the favorite game of hunters, look up from their rooting and peer at us calmly through the low brush for several minutes before moving off toward new forage.

But most intriguing is the curiosity shown by highly intelligent chimps. "What do they think of us?" I wonder. They must recognize our apelike features, but our clothes and equipment are novelties in this world. While our size and lack of fear make them cautious, they clearly have no awareness of how deadly our species can be. Otherwise they would flee as wild chimps do in other parts of Africa where apes are part of the human diet.

If the apes are bewildered, we are in awe of the wild innocence of their world. Was this how the wandering Asians felt more than 10,000 years ago when they crossed to Alaska and marched southward through the Americas, going where no man had ever gone? On today's fully occupied planet, there are few places left where indigenous peoples do not hunt and trap or where loggers and mining companies have not sent in teams of surveyors. The great forests east of the Ndoki River may be this earth's last Eden.

I first heard about the Ndoki three years ago, when Fay told me about this wondrous forest where gorillas, chimps and other animals do not run away at the sight of humans. At the time, I was researching an article on great apes, and I thought Fay was exaggerating. I had spent fruitless days trying to get glimpses of chimps and gorillas in forests just to the north of Ndoki, and it was hard for me to imagine that Africa might still contain forests so remote that the animals had never learned to fear mankind. Western lowland gorillas, hunted for centuries, are among the shyest, least-known animals on earth, and scientists in Gabon and the Central African Republic have invested years trying to gain trust so they could study the animals at close quarters.

Not long after my talk with Fay, I encountered Japanese primatologist Masazumi Mitani, who along with Suehisa Kuroda established the first research camps at the edge of the Ndoki region in 1987. Since then, the Japanese researchers, in cooperation with Congolese scientist Antoine Ruffin Oko, have conducted a groundbreaking survey of animal populations in the Ndoki and have closely studied the primates, including gorillas and chimps. Mitani told me the animals were indeed unafraid of humans, but warned that conditions in the region were "very, very difficult." Knowing the extreme privation Japanese primatologists regularly endure, I took these cautionary words very seriously.

Yet my desire to visit this extraordinary place was tempered not so much by the prospect of hardship as by the feeling that perhaps the Ndoki should be left alone. It has been protected for millenniums by its inaccessibility. Should there not be somewhere on earth where nature can be safe from the heavy hand of humanity? Journalists, explorers and scientists can inadvertently set in motion the destruction of the places they are trying to protect.

Later conversations with Fay and others disabused me of the notion that the Ndoki would be safe if simply left alone. Only lack of funds has stymied government plans to build a road through northern Congo that would open the region to development. And in 1990 only the arguments of Fay and Japanese researchers, backed by the U.S. government and the World Bank, persuaded Congolese authorities that there were alternatives to giving a logging concession for the Ndoki region to an Algerian-Congolese consortium.

Even now, the Ndoki is almost entirely surrounded by logging concessions. Moreover, had an international convention not banned the sale of ivory in 1989, poachers almost assuredly would have braved the swamps and rivers and invaded the region, which is among the last places in central Africa with substantial numbers of elephants. Finally, a 30-year dry spell and overgrazing to the north have pushed migrant human populations southward through the Central African Republic and into northern Congo, ever closer to the edges of the Ndoki.

In response to these pressures, Fay began working in 1989 with the World Bank, the U.S. government, the Japanese scientists and conservation organizations to encourage the Congolese government to establish a Ndoki park. The goal would be to protect the core of the region while allowing some tourism on the more accessible fringes. The involvement of the World Bank, however, aroused the ire of groups such as the Environmental Defense Fund and Greenpeace, which argued that the project might bring on the human intrusions it was designed to prevent.

So I put aside my reservation and arranged to join Fay on an expedition into Ndoki in late May. He planned to renew his search for two unnamed clearings in the interior of the forest that showed up on aerial maps but that he had failed to locate in a foray two years earlier. He also hoped to test a battery-operated geographical positioning device that he would need during a longer surveying expedition later this summer.

Our trip begins in Ouesso, a frontier town of 13,000 on the Sangha River in northern Congo. There three Americans—Fay, Karen Lotz, a photographer, and I—set off in a 14-meter (46-foot) motorized dugout canoe for the nine-hour trip up the Sangha River, past a logging camp to Bomassa, a Pygmy village adjacent to the headquarters being set up for the proposed park.

Outside interest in northern Congo forests dates to the turn of the century; colonial records include an outraged letter by an expatriate who demanded compensation from the French government for the death of his son, who was eaten by cannibals. But intensive logging began only in the mid-1980s. "If the loggers weren't here, we could leave as well," says Fay. He finds it frustrating that logging continues despite studies commissioned by the World Bank and the Congolese showing that almost all of these operations lose money and cheat the government by welshing on debts to state-owned companies. As if that were not enough, Libyan employees of Socalib, a Libyan-Congolese logging company, were implicated in the 1989 bombing of a passenger jet over Niger. Scores of Congolese people died. "Forestry's been great for this country," remarks Fay sarcastically. "They cut the forests, stiff the Congolese on taxes and debts, and then kill the citizens."

Fay is a small but durable 35-year-old New Jersey native nicknamed "Concrete" by the Pygmies for his willingness to endure the hardships of the jungle. Accustomed to spending unscheduled nights outdoors, Fay has become rather haphazard and fatalistic about planning. As a result, when darkness falls we are still several kilometers short of Bomassa. The boat runs aground time after time as we try to pick our way with a flashlight through constantly shifting sandbars. Fay is unperturbed, which is more than I can say, and he will be equally sanguine about many other mishaps in the coming days.

When we finally get to Bomassa, Fay sends word to the village that he wants to hire trackers and bearers. A ragged, somewhat inebriated group shows up the next morning. Fay chooses Ndokanda and Joachine, trackers he has worked with before, but rejects one Pygmy whose feet are swollen with elephantiasis. He fills out the team of bearers by lifting our packs and duffels and estimating how many men it will take to carry the load: "That's half a Pygmy, that's three-quarters and this one (he grunts as he hefts a 132-pound pack) a whole Pygmy." Standing nearly 5 feet, the BaNgombe and BaNbengele peoples are taller than most other Pygmies but still seem impossibly small to haul the loads they agree to carry. Seraphin, an auspiciously named employee of Fay's who has come downriver from his home in the Central African Republic, offers to come along as cook.

The 25-kilometer (15-mile) hike from Bomassa to the crossing point on the Ndoki River takes two or three days, depending on how much the bearers have had to drink. We make the mistake of traveling ahead of the Pygmies, and our hung-over crew drags its feet, forcing us to camp just before the Djeke River, 16 kilometers outside Bomassa. Fay says he cannot push the porters too hard or they will simply abandon us in the middle of the forest as they did him on a prior trip into the Ndoki.

After a meal of soup, salami and cookies, I settle into sleep, wondering whether the dire reports I had heard from the Japanese researchers had overstated the dangers of the area. A few minutes later, I awake feeling an insect on my finger. Flicking it off, I feel another take its place, and then suddenly thousands of bugs seem to bite me at once. Seconds later, I hear a strangled cry from Karen as she is attacked as well. Stumbling blindly over roots and a massive column of ants, we tear down a path and dive into the river. Crushing the ants seems to release some chemical distress signal: as we emerge from the river, the aggressive creatures drop on us from everywhere.

Stamping, slapping and at a loss, I rouse Fay, whose tent is out of the line of attack. Surveying the insects that still cover my legs, he says drowsily, "Driver ants can really be a problem; they can kill a tethered goat," and then goes back to sleep. Moving my hammock away from the column of ants, I wince with pain as I drive a spiky vine clear through my thumb and watch blood spurt out. Then it starts to rain. By 2:30 A.M. the ants have moved on, and I miserably return to my tent for what's left of the night.

The next day we hit the swamps that have long deterred those curious about the Ndoki. We pick our way through the quicksand-like muck by feeling with our toes and walking sticks for a series of thin logs Japanese researchers have previously laid down. I slip once and fall up to my chest in mud before grabbing a root. Sobered by the slip, I ask Fay how deep the mud is. "Who knows?" he says, shrugging.

The Ndoki River is the real barrier. Unnavigable and meandering, it is 3 meters (10 feet) deep in places and spreads out into swamps several kilometers wide. Even at its shallowest points, it can take eight hours to cross on foot and is impassable much of the year. We use a pirogue that Kuroda's team has built to resupply his tiny station. Parched by the precarious walk to this point, we cool ourselves with the absolutely pure waters of the Ndoki as we pole through the river grass. Fay thinks he knows why the Pygmies have historically kept to the west side of the river. With ample game in the more accessible forests, they have no need to risk a crossing. At this point, though, I am not thinking of hardship but rather of the beauty of the grassy river, the fragrant smells floating through the clean air, and the world that lies beyond the east bank of the Ndoki.

After landing, we begin our journey back in time. The forests in these wet areas are open and cool, even though the equatorial sun beats down on the upper stories of the canopy. At one point we discover leopard droppings containing black hair and some bone bits. The Pygmies claim it is gorilla hair, though only DNA analysis could tell for sure. Fay thinks it's possible, since he has documented leopard attacks on gorillas. Samory, one of the trackers, claims leopards kill the immensely strong apes with surprise attacks in which the cat quickly snaps its jaws around the gorilla's throat. The Ndoki may be innocent of humans, but it is not a peaceable kingdom.

There is, in fact, a civilization in these forests, even if it is nonhuman. The area is latticed with trails, some as wide as boulevards, that have been cut and maintained by elephants. Says Ndokanda: "This is the elephant's city, and the leopard's and other animals' too." The grid of paths leads to the elephants' favorite spots: mineral licks and clearings, where they socialize with relatives and friends; baths, where they cover themselves with mud; knobby trees, where they rub the mud off, stripping their skin of ticks in the process; and trees such as the *Balanites wilsoniana* and *Autranella congoensis,* beloved by the big animals for their fruits.

We have left behind the overhunted west bank of the Ndoki, where elephant trails are abandoned and overgrown. On the east side we see fresh signs of elephants everywhere. We do not, however, see the great beasts. Because of the vast territory they roam, and perhaps because of their ability to communicate with one another, they are the only creatures in this ecosystem that know about humans. They stay away from us.

The elephant paths and clearings open up the forest for other big animals such as buffalo, and the trails certainly make walking easy for us. As we head down one path, Joachine suddenly pauses. The brush erupts as a male gorilla charges, then abruptly stops and drops down in the vegetation to stare. Fay observes that gorillas favor the herbaceous plants growing in marshy lowlands and in places where elephants have created clearings. Farther from the water, the canopied forest suits chimpanzees. With both populations at very high levels, the Ndoki is one of the few places on earth where chimps and gorillas live close together.

Fay and the Japanese researchers have even seen gorillas and chimps feeding in the same fig tree.

Now that we are far away from the nearest village and the temptation of palm wine, the Pygmies begin to come into their own. Even with 14 years' experience, Fay can still lose a trail, but Ndokanda, a former elephant hunter, or any of the other Pygmies can read the very faintest imprint with a glance. In the forest they are utterly self-reliant, creating cord from vines, cups from leaves, and bed mats from bark. Still, they are apprehensive about this forest, and when Fay tells them where we are going, Samory says, "Mokele Mbembe lives there." Fay is convinced that the Pygmies are describing a black rhinoceros, an animal that does occasionally fight elephants.

That night the termites reduce Fay's one T-shirt to tatters. This gives him the excuse to try his "new system," which means stripping down to a bathing suit and sandals. "Come back in two years, and you will find me completely naked, living in the middle of the Ndoki with six Pygmy wives," he jokes. He thinks that the Pygmies have it right: the less you wear, the faster your skin dries after a rainfall and the less likely you are to get parasitic fungi and footworms. Fay has already accumulated four nasty footworms, which burrow under the skin until they discover that you are not a pig or elephant—their proper hosts. The worms then die, but the bacteria in the little corpses infect your feet.

The second day after crossing the Ndoki, Fay announces that we are entering the "unknown," and we set off in search of the two clearings, called *bais* by the Pygmies, that he failed to find in 1990. Fay is certain that the *bais* are elephant strongholds. According to maps drawn from aerial reconnaissance, we have to cross at least 15 kilometers of dry land before reaching the next watershed. Unless we find a stream by dusk, we face a waterless night after a full day's hike. Ndokanda sets an uncharacteristically slow pace, so Fay decides to shame him by taking the lead. As we set off ahead, he remarks, "The one thing Pygmies can't stand is for a white guy to lead in the forest."

Entering dryer land, we come across disturbing signs that humans are affecting this forest from afar. Everywhere we see fallen *Gilbertiodendron dewevrei* trees with no sign of regrowth. Fay says this tree species dominates during wet periods and may be dying out because of the long dry spell that has reduced rainfall more than 10 percent over the past 30 years. Many scientists believe the shortage of rainfall stems from the widespread deforestation by humans in other parts of Africa, which may have changed the continent's weather patterns. Already the Ndoki is one of the driest tropical rainforests on earth, and if rainfall keeps decreasing, the woodland may be doomed no matter what legal protection it receives.

By afternoon I'm all sweated out and parched, but still we see no sign of water—or of the Pygmies straggling behind us. At one point Fay sees a thick vine and says, "Aha!" He hacks off a section at just the right spot, and pure water spurts into his mouth. I grab his machete and hack away but manage to taste only a few drops.

As the sun sinks and it appears that we will spend a dry and desperate night, we finally hit sandy soil—a good sign. Soon we find elephant footprints filled with water. It looks pure, and I drink greedily. Fay's hand is so tired from hours of hacking with the machete that he cannot open the water bottle I have just filled.

As soon as we settle down to wait for the rest of the group, Ndokanda comes motoring by us. Not bothering to stop, he yells at Fay in Sango, "You fool, I know this place. Right ahead there is plenty of water." Ndokanda is right, of course, and we are left openmouthed, wondering what enabled him to recall this tiny part of a vast forest from a brief visit years earlier.

That night, with Fay interpreting, I ask the Pygmies how they would feel if a road were built through the Ndoki and led to the destruction of the forest and the animals. At first they scoff, saying there is no way anyone can kill off the forest—it is just too big. Then they get excited. "So that's what you are doing here," says Samory, "building a road. Great! Pay us well, and we'll build it for you." Joachine chimes in, "But you've got to build it in a straight line, not that zigzag path you took today." They then launch into a debate about how much they should be paid and whether they should be allowed to bring their women.

Listening, Fay shakes his head sadly. The forests have always yielded food and wood during the millenniums Pygmies have hunted in central Africa. They cannot conceive of the devastation that roads and logging have wrought upon tropical woodlands beyond their charmed world.

If we are dumbfounded by Ndokanda's photographic memory for terrain, it is soon his turn to be impressed. Using a compass and a battery-operated geopositioning system, we look for the two clearings. The system works by using signals sent from satellites and can pinpoint a position within 100 meters. By taking a reading in the middle of a swamp near the camp (trees block the satellite signals), we are able to determine the way to the clearings.

It takes us two days to find and explore them. The excitement of the discovery, however, gives way to disappointment that elephants no longer frequent these clearings. Ndokanda seizes on that fact as a face-saving way of explaining why he had not found the spots on the earlier expedition.

While we are exploring, Seraphin goes off with two Pygmies and discovers the remains of an elephant. Fay worries that this may be the work of poachers, but Seraphin points out that the elephant has its tusks. The Pygmies can find no sign that any humans have been in the area. The elephant could have died of natural causes, or it could have been wounded outside the Ndoki and then run inside for refuge.

Every foray into the forest brings us face-to-face with wildlife, most notably gorillas. In one day we tally four separate encounters, and by the end of the trip we have found 15 gorilla groups. A couple of silverbacks, or mature males, go through the motions of halfhearted charges, but most do not come forward even in response to distress calls and hand clapping by apprehensive females when we get between them and the males. We take to calling these circumspect males the "pacifist gorillas of Ndoki." The gorillas also seemed blithely unaware that they are supposed to be ungainly in trees. One giant silverback jumped between several trees and ended up 50 meters (160 feet) from the ground at the very top of the canopy.

Exploring this rich, fecund world is the high point of the expedition. In camp we eat pasta flavored with dried soups and sausages, but Fay uncovers more exotic treats on the forest floor. He likes to pick up half-eaten fruits left by the animals and to sample the untouched parts. I try the juicy kernels of a *Myrianthus arboreus* fruit and decide that gorillas know a good taste when they find one.

Fay's attitude toward the question of what foods people might take from the Ndoki has changed over the years. During his first ventures into the forest, he allowed the Pygmies to catch a duiker every two days, arguing that such brief hunts would in no way affect the forest. Since then, however, he has realized that conservationists should not introduce hunting where animals have never learned to fear humans. Moreover, only if there is a total ban on hunting will the Pygmies resist the temptation to exploit this immensely productive ecosystem.

It is during our hike back toward the Ndoki River that we come upon the band of chimps—an encounter Fay calls "the signal wildlife experience" of his 14 years in Africa. The ruckus the apes raise begins with threats and distress calls, but some of them seem to let out hoots that chimps use to greet one another. I would like to think those chimps have the capacity to welcome the apelike aliens into their forest.

We hike out of the Ndoki in two days, covering more than 30 kilometers in the last 24 hours. It would be rough going for a distance runner, but I am in no shape for the trip at all. An insect has apparently injected me with one of the countless toxins found in the jungle, and I come down with pleurisy-like symptoms that make every breath painful. It is probably dengue fever, also called breakbone fever. Whatever it is, the final day's march is sheer hell. As at the beginning of the trip, darkness falls when we are still several kilometers from Bomassa, and we walk the last stretch by failing flashlights. At 9 P.M. I stumble, exhausted, aching and 14 pounds lighter, into the base camp.

The ardors of the trip remind me of why this area has remained unchanged since the last Ice Age. Amid our planet's vain struggle to balance conservation with human aspirations, the Ndoki has no villages whose needs must be met or colonists determined to build a new outpost of civilization. Fortunately, this last Eden has formidable barriers protecting its treasures. In all the world, it is perhaps the perfect place to make a stand for wild nature.

Observations

*I know these forests. I mean I have often navigated their
obscure waterways, rafting through the wilds on a map,
in my slippers, at night. Now these forests soon were to loom
on a veritable skyline. I should see them where they stood,
their roots in the unfrequented floods.*

—H. M. Tomlinson

*These are my jungles. I only hope that one day you may be
able to visit them, before they are all bulldozed or atomized, to
see for yourself their astonishing plants and animals and meet
their wonderful human inhabitants face to face.*

—Ivan T. Sanderson

Business and Pleasure in Brazil

By Ulick Ralph Burke (1882)

Little is known about the author of this selection except that Ulick Ralph Burke was an English businessman who visited Brazil in the years 1881–1882. It's not even clear from his account exactly what kind of business Burke was in, but he seemed to be looking for opportunity of most any kind and was prepared, to a degree, to suffer some discomfort in its pursuit. Like many bourgeois Europeans of his day, Burke was somewhat of a casual racist—not necessarily an outright bigot, but very aware of national and ethnic characteristics, as he perceived them. And he was prepared to state his feelings (especially in letters to his wife, which make up the text of his book), with a breezy lack of sensitivity.

Regardless, he certainly made a grand tour of the country. Burke hobnobbed with the local gentry, saw the sights, and even had an audience with the emperor and empress. In these letters to his wife back in England, he expresses his opinions about nearly everything. (MWC)

Petropolis, Sunday, July 16th—Yesterday, after doing a certain amount of work in Rio, I took the steamer at one o'clock, which carried me across the bay to the foot of the Organ mountains. I cannot attempt to give you an idea of the beauty of the scene. The bay is studded with islands, some very small, some merely heaps of loose boulders of granite; most, however, green and glittering, covered with dense and varied tropical vegetation. And one, as large as Guernsey, covered with mangoes; the whole surrounded by mountains, some over seven thousand feet high, all densely wooded. After an hour's steam, we disembarked and took the rail, the first railway built in South America, just thirty years ago; and were drawn by one of Fairbairn's engines, dated 1853, which has been running ever since. We got over ten miles in less than half an hour, through a dense tropical forest, varied by clearings where sugar and mandioca grow luxuriantly.

When the rail came to an end we found good carriages, drawn by five mules apiece, and "coached by a Switzer," or rather a Petropolitan German, which took us nine miles up the hill to Petropolis, 2,200 feet above the level of the sea. The ascent is very steep, and winds after the accustomed manner of good mountain roads. It was engineered by an Italian, thirty years ago; but the peculiar character of the scenery is that it runs through a virgin forest—tropical nature and Swiss art. And the views of and over the great and glorious bay of Rio, as each turn of the road brings one higher and higher above it, are infinitely striking.

I was introduced, as we started, to Mr. Robert Norton, head of the most important house of business in Rio; and he proved a most pleasant and interesting travelling companion. Unlike most people who live abroad, he had a great admiration of the beauties of the scenery amidst which he lived; and in this he is not singular as far as Rio is concerned, for Mrs. Ricketts, the wife of the consul, who visited Europe last year and saw Athens, Constantinople, and the most beautiful places in Italy and Switzerland, came back to Rio with the impression that its varied beauties were only increased with comparison with all she had seen elsewhere. I think the single view from the rest-house above Madhopore on the way to Dalhousie, from the Corniche road midway between Mentone and Monaco, the first sight of Italy from Domo d'Ossola on the road over the Simplon, and one or two other spots on the world's surface that I have already seen, may each be more beautiful than any one view of or from the Bay of Rio; but every point here presents new beauties, and that which fascinates me is not only the great size of the bay, the beauty of the surrounding mountains, some always near—some always distant, the picturesque tropical vegetation on the shores and islands, but the endless variety and combination of all, under the bright sun of the tropics. The gorgeous flowering shrubs and trees, and the still more gorgeous butterflies, also a characteristic feature in the landscape; and though I am disappointed at not yet having seen any humming-birds, the palms even surpass my expectation. Petropolis is, of course, something like an Indian Hill-station, but it is more of a town: the houses are chiefly built in the streets; it covers a comparatively small area of ground, and there are some good shops, grocers, chemists, and others, looking more like those of a country town in England than anything in India, still less in Rio. Indeed, the change from *Corte* to the hill suburb is even greater in this than in the air, which is saying a great deal. I feel quite braced up this morning, although the climate is not as cold as Murree, say in August, but it is far less dryer. This hotel, founded by a Scotchman, McDowell, is kept, and very well kept, by an Englishman, Mills. Petropolis itself is a German colony, which, together with the difference in climate, makes it a far more civilized place than Rio; for although it is on the top of a mountain, and can only draw its supplies from and through the capital—of which it is practically a suburb—there is not only more real, but even more apparent, comfort than in the city. I wonder how much is race and how much climate? But I feel sure that if the English had colonized Rio de Janeiro, it would have been one of the most prosperous cities in the world. Even the yellow fever is not indigenous, but has been created quite within the last few years by an accumulation of Portuguese filth.

There is a general complaint in Rio at present of "business being bad." It is a pretty general complaint at all times and all places; but it is to a great extent true in the present instance. The production of coffee has nearly doubled in Brazil in the last ten years, and the quality having deteriorated owing to careless cultivation, and the consumption not having kept pace with the production, prices have fallen immensely, and are still falling. Now, owing to the gradual enfranchisement of the slaves, who as soon as they are free cease to do any work at all, the cost of production is actually becoming greater as the price of the thing produced is falling; and considering that coffee is not only the greatest, but almost the only, export from Rio, you can easily understand that this part of Brazil is poor, and getting poorer. And the evil is intensified by the fact that although a great deal of first-rate coffee is grown in the country, none is exported, as the factors use it for mixing with the far greater quantity of inferior berries that are sent to them, and which they could not otherwise get off their hands at all.

I think you know that potatoes are largely exported to Brazil from both France and Portugal, and come into Rio, after the expense and risk of long sea voyage, charged with a heavy import duty. I naturally asked why potatoes will not grow in this country. I am told that they not only grow, but that three crops a year can be obtained, and the potatoes themselves are far finer than those imported, and that their cultivation would use up a good deal of the farmyard manure which is now allowed to go to waste. Yet potatoes are not planted. It has not been the custom to plant them; and a new agricultural department might possibly be productive of trouble. Besides, is not coffee the best thing for a Brazilian to cultivate? Yet the fact that coffee is to-day half the price it was ten years ago, and the inferior kinds do not even pay for their carriage, is nothing. And while the whole community is crying out about the fall in coffee, and the great falling off in national prosperity in consequence of its over-production in the country, every one still goes on planting coffee, and importing their potatoes from Bordeaux!

Let me add one local characteristic that I learned yesterday, and you will not be astonished that the country does not roll in wealth. The bay of Rio is full of fish; I cannot say that they are equal to those we are accustomed to in England or India, but they are excellent food. Now the fishermen finding that by fishing two days a week they can earn enough to keep themselves for the whole seven, resolutely refuse to catch fish during the odd five; and thus the price is kept up, the supply kept down, and the riches that God has brought to their very doors swims away from the inhabitants.

Coming up yesterday, Mr. Norton very kindly asked me to breakfast this morning; but I found on arrival at the hotel that Staples had already presented my letters of introduction and accepted an invitation to breakfast at the Embassy, and to dine with Mr. Leveson-Gower, the Secretary. However, I spent part of the morning to-day at Mr. N———'s very fine house, and met Mrs. N———, who is a very pleasant and culti-vated woman. Last night, on arriving, I was told there was but one other man staying in the house, an Englishman, and that Staples had arranged for him to dine with us. Judge of my astonishment when, at half-past six, in walked—John Ball! He has been going round South America botanizing and was, as he always is, a most charming compan-ion, and entertained us till late at night with an account of his travels. At half-past eleven to-day we all three breakfasted with the Minister; and I confess I did enjoy a really good meal, with fresh milk and butter, burnished silver, a French cook, a German *maître d'hôtel*, and an English footman. After all, it is a month since I dined at Hyde Park Gate, and with the exception of dinner on board the *Swiftsure*, I have not had a refined meal since.

After breakfast Mr. Corbett took us for a ride in the virgin forest; Staples got a mount from Mr. Leveson-Gower; but I had to put up with a hired animal, which for roughness and power of fatiguing its rider at a foot's pace, stands first—the rest being nowhere—of all the horses I have ever mounted. The path was too rough to admit of cantering, and the only other *allure* my beast knew was a sort of a jog, or indescribable amble, which no tactics known to me could change into a walk for ten yards during a three hour's ride. I would honestly go through it all again, however, for what I saw; and I do not write this when time has effaced the remembrance of the *amari aliquid*, but sore of flesh and aching in every bone and muscle; for nothing I had ever imagined of a tropical forest comes up to the reality, and I regret, even more than my shaking, my utter inability to give you any idea of it. On my way up yesterday, I thought that when one visits a country like this, one should learn something of its botany, as well as of its language, before coming. And to-day this feeling of admiring ignorance was intensified. Enormous trees, with smooth stems and leafy tops, from which long parasites hang down, themselves covered, as well as the trunks of the trees, with creeping plants of every kind. Then great tree-ferns, palms, and lower forest trees; then shrubs, with huge leaves and gay flowers; and on the ground a luxuriant mass of plants of all kinds, ferns, and mosses, and among these, from highest to lowest, nothing I had ever seen before. To bring home one specimen or a dozen specimens to you of all these riches would be like chipping a little bit of stone off the palace at Delhi, or the Alhambra at Granada, and bringing it back to give you some idea of the glories of the building; and for any one so ignorant of botany as I am to attempt to *describe* such things to you, would be like a Chinese traveler writing home an account to his wife of *The Huguenots* or *Guillaume Tell*. The one thing I missed was animal life. Not a bird, not a beast was seen or even heard; and as it is the winter here, there were comparatively few flowers. But the mere luxuriousness of nature, still, green, and grand, overwhelmed me.

The Durion

From The Malay Archipelago *(1869)*
By Alfred Russel Wallace

Insecure about his ability to write narrative, Alfred Russel Wallace hesitated for
seven years before publishing The Malay Archipelago, *the classic book on the*
region's nature. The delay did not cost this nineteenth-century British naturalist
much; the work was warmly received and, more than one hundred years later,
continues to be the standard on its subject.

What did cost Wallace, however, was his failure to promote his thoughts on
natural selection and the origins of new species. His work closely paralleled that
of his contemporary and colleague Charles Darwin, but it was Darwin who was
acclaimed as the creator of the theory of evolution. Wallace is known as the
father of zoogeography (the distribution of animals and their interactions with
the environment), a distinction that carries somewhat less panache.

Wallace spent the years 1854 through 1860 collecting, studying, and observ-
ing in the Malay Archipelago. During that time, he collected a whopping
125,660 species, mainly beetles, butterflies, and birds. He also chanced upon

the wonderful durion, which is, at the same time, the world's tastiest and smelliest fruit. His description of this rarity follows. (DRK)

I slept that night in the village of the Sebungow Dyaks, and the next day reached Saráwak, passing through a most beautiful country, where limestone mountains, with their fantastic forms and white precipices, shot up on every side, draped and festooned with a luxuriant vegetation. The banks of the Saráwak River are everywhere covered with fruit-trees, which supply the Dyaks with a great deal of their food. The mangosteen, lansat, rambutan, jack, jambou, and blimbing are all abundant; but most abundant and most esteemed is the durion, a fruit about which very little is known in England, but which both by natives and Europeans in the Malay Archipelago is reckoned superior to all others. The old traveller Linschott, writing in 1599, says: "It is of such an excellent taste that it surpasses in flavor all the other fruits of the world, according to those who have tasted it." And Doctor Paludanus adds: "This fruit is of a hot and humid nature. To those not used to it, it seems at first to smell like rotten onions, but immediately after they have tasted it they prefer it to all other food. The natives give it honorable titles, exalt it, and make verses on it." When brought into a house the smell is often so offensive that some persons can never bear to taste it. This was my own case when I first tried it in Malacca, but in Borneo I found a ripe fruit on the ground, and, eating it out-of-doors, I at once became a confirmed durion eater.

The durion grows on a large and lofty forest-tree, somewhat resembling an elm in its general character, but with a more smooth and scaly bark. The fruit is round or slightly oval, about the size of a large cocoa-nut, of a green color, and covered all over with short stout spines the bases of which touch each other, are consequently somewhat hexagonal, while the points are very strong and sharp. It is so completely armed that if the stalk is broken off it is a difficult matter to lift one from the ground. The outer rind is so thick and tough that from whatever height it may fall it is never broken. From the base to the apex five very faint lines may be traced, over which the spines arch a little; these are the sutures of the carpels, and show where the fruit may be divided with a heavy knife and a strong hand. The five cells are satiny-white within, and are each filled with an oval mass of cream-colored pulp, imbedded in which are two or three seeds about the size of chestnuts. This pulp is the eatable part, and its consistence and flavor are indescribable. A rich butter-like custard highly flavored with almonds gives the best general idea of it, but intermingled with it come wafts of flavor that call to mind cream-cheese, onion-sauce, brown-sherry, and other incongruities. Then there is a rich glutinous smoothness in the pulp which nothing else possesses, but which adds to its delicacy. It is neither acid, nor sweet, nor juicy, yet one feels the want of none of these qualities, for it is perfect as it is. It produces no nausea or other bad effect, and the more you eat of it the less you feel inclined to stop. In fact, to eat durions is a new sensation worth a voyage to the East to experience.

When the fruit is ripe it falls of itself, and the only way to eat durions in perfection is to get them as they fall, and the smell is then less overpowering. When unripe, it makes a very good vegetable if cooked, and it is also eaten by the Dyaks raw. In a good fruit season large quantities are preserved salted, in jars and bamboos, and kept the year round, when it acquires a most disgusting odor to Europeans; but the Dyaks appreciate it highly as a relish with their rice. There are in the forest two varieties of wild durions with much smaller fruits, one of them orange-colored inside; and these are probably the origin of the large and fine durions, which are never found wild. It would not, perhaps, be correct to say that the durion is the best of all fruits, because it can not supply the place of the subacid juicy kinds, such as the orange, grape, mango, and mangosteen, whose refreshing and cooling qualities are so wholesome and grateful; but as producing a food of the most exquisite flavor it is unsurpassed. If I had to fix on two only as representing the perfection of the two classes, I should certainly choose the durion and the orange as the king and queen of fruits.

The durion is, however, sometimes dangerous. When the fruit begins to ripen it falls daily and almost hourly, and accidents not unfrequently happen to persons walking or working under the trees. When the durion strikes a man in its fall, it produces a dreadful wound, the strong spines tearing open the flesh, while the blow itself is very heavy; but from this very circumstance death rarely ensues, the copious effusion of blood preventing the inflammation which might otherwise take place. A Dyak chief informed me that he had been struck down by a durion falling on his head, which he thought would certainly have caused his death, yet he recovered in a very short time.

Poets and moralists, judging from our English trees and fruits, have thought that small fruits always grew on lofty trees, so that their fall should be harmless to man, while the large ones trailed on the ground. Two of the largest and heaviest fruits known, however, the Brazil-nut fruit (Bertholletis) and durion, grow on lofty forest-trees, from which they fall as soon as they are ripe, and often wound or kill the native inhabitants. From this we may learn two things: first, not to draw general conclusions from a very partial view of nature, and secondly, that trees and fruits, no less than the varied productions of the animal kingdom, do not appear to be organized with exclusive reference to the use and convenience of man.

The Jívaro Heads

From Head Hunters of the Amazon *(1923)*
By F. W. UpdeGraff

In 1894, fresh out of Union College in Schenectady, New York, F. W. UpdeGraff received a letter from a classmate encouraging him to take an adventure through the unexplored Ecuadorian Amazon. The young student immediately packed his bags for what turned into a seven-year immersion in tropical culture. Twenty years after UpdeGraff returned from his exploration, he dusted off his travel notes and his letters to his mother and, with the help of a friend, recounted his experiences in his book Head Hunters of the Amazon.*

While UpdeGraff claims to be neither a naturalist nor an anthropologist, it's too bad he wasn't; the Jívaro Indians, a proud and independent Ecuadorian people, allowed him a once-in-a-lifetime opportunity to witness an event of infinite interest to those wishing to understand the ways in which different cultures work. UpdeGraff vividly recounts this remarkable experience, but his opinions, which now seem shallow and insensitive, color his retelling of this event.

Be forewarned. This excerpt contains a detailed account of how to shrink a head. Read on, if you dare. But with tongue very much in cheek we warn you: Do not try this at home! (DRK)

A victory on the battlefield is for these Upper Amazon Indians the signal for the most hideous, the most significant of all their rites to be begun. On that never-to-be-forgotten day the whole scene was enacted before our eyes, an experience which it has, perhaps, never been the lot of civilized beings to undergo before or since. That is a sweeping statement, and at best I am only assuming the probable, but I can only say that neither I nor my fellow explorers were ever able to discover, directly or by hearsay, that this ghastly performance was ever witnessed by any other white men. Certain it is that in all my conversations with prospectors and rubber-hunters, I have never heard of any but the most conflicting conjectures as to the mode of preparation of the Jívaro heads.

The comparatively little that has been written about the process through which they pass—and they are relics of war which are unique in all the world—has been invariably, as far as my study of the question goes, based on the hearsay evidence, often incorrect in essential details, of the white or half-caste planters or priests whose lives are spent at stations situated on the fringe of the real Jívaro head-hunters' country, the basins of the Marañon and Santiago within a radius of some three hundred miles from Borja.

It would seem that this rite is so closely guarded a secret, by reason of the inter-racial hatred between white man and brown man, and the obvious natural obstacles in the way of him who would explore these regions, that the ceremony is destined to be observed only by a very few. It must indeed be a strange set of circumstances, in which chance must play no small part, which will combine to show a white man what we were compelled to observe.

Thus my account of the events of that day constitutes, if I may presume to say so, an authentic description of a process which has baffled many a commentator on the subject.

Those of the Huambizas, then, who had been fortunate enough to escape from the spears of the raiders had fled to the shelter of the largest of the little group of houses which had been attacked. There cannot have been more than ten or fifteen of them shut up within its walls, but the Aguarunas had not the spirit to attack them now that they were aroused. That is the Jívaro way.

The enemy having left their dead and dying behind them in their flight, the victors dashed forward to seize the most highly treasured of the spoils of battle—the heads of the enemy slain. With stone-axes and split bamboo knives, sharpened clam-shells (rubbed to a keen edge on sand-stone), and *chonta*-wood machetes, they went from corpse to corpse, gathering and stringing their gruesome emblems of victory.

I must mention that no delicate considerations of sex are allowed to interfere with these rites; a woman who fights, or a woman who refuses to accompany the victorious war-party to their homes and serve a new master, exposes herself by the acknowledged code of warfare among these people to the risk of suffering the same fate as her men-folk. Indeed I myself happened to watch the fate of a Huambiza woman who had fallen in the fight wounded by three spears. Little did we imagine what the ultimate issue might prove to be, when we attacked that morning.

The woman lay where she had been borne down by the spear-thrusts. The Aguarunas, eager to collect her head, went to work while she was still alive, though powerless to protect herself. While one wrenched at her head another held her to the ground, and yet another hacked at her neck with his stone-axe. Finally I was called upon to lend my machete, a far better implement for the work in hand. This was truly an act of mercy, to put the poor creature out of her misery as soon as possible. It was a truly hideous spectacle. But it must be remembered that had we attempted interference, we were but five in a horde of fiends, crazed by blood and lust. When at last the head was severed, it was strung with the one other which had fallen to the lot of our party.

This stringing of the heads is in itself an art, the object of which is to facilitate their transportation. They are strung on thin lengths of pliable bark stripped from some nearby sapling, which make a first-rate substitute for the hempen cord of civilization. These bark-ropes are passed through the mouth and out at the neck.

The party then set to work to loot the houses from which the occupants had been driven. Nothing escaped the raiders. I was there in one of the houses with them, and well remember the motley collection of things that we found. There were Peruvian coins, china cups and saucers, a butcher's knife, a number of red bandanna handkerchiefs, all evidently looted from Barranca, a Jívaro hand-loom with a half-finished piece of cloth on it, an iron spear-head, and a number of small Jívaro house-hold objects which are to be found in any settlement. Nothing was too small to escape the Aguarunas' attention. They cleaned out the house from end to end, every man keeping for himself all he could lay hands on. Then they fired the roof, and in a moment the whole house was ablaze, the great heat roasting the decapitated body of the Huambiza woman.

It will be remembered that a party of Antipas had separated from the main body, as agreed between the Indians before the attack, to storm another group of hutments further up the creek. It was at this moment, then, that we decided among ourselves to push on after them and see how they had fared. We had not gone more than a few yards when we were met by the same party returning, laden with dripping heads. No less than nine they brought; some tied in pairs by their own hair and slung round the neck of one of their conquerors, others slung with bark-ropes. This gruesome procession was led by a short, fat savage; laden with his share of the spoils, grinning in triumph, with his teeth stained black and filed to a point, his thick-set shoulders spattered with the blood of his victims, he was a diabolical-looking creature.

In single file the whole party retreated through the forest to the mouth of the creek where the canoes had been left, hurling threats at the Huambizas and admonitions not to follow, as certain death at the hands of the rifle-bearing *Christianos* awaited them—all this the merest bluff, it must be said, for in reality they feared an onslaught by their infuriated enemies who were believed to possess some form of firearms stolen from Barranca. To strike further terror to the hearts of the Huambizas, each man of our party indulged in a series of imitations of the human voice guaranteed to give the impression that he was at least six men.

Arrived at our base, with the trophies and prisoners—three children—we settled down to the preparation of the gruesome spoils, destined to be displayed in the glass cases of some great museum or to pass into the collection of a curio hunter at the other end of the world. For, as it happened, they eventually fell to our lot.

While the warriors brought the heads from the canoes to the sand-spit on which they were to be prepared, the children sat round contentedly chewing bananas, all unconcerned at their parents' fate. With the empty canoes drawn up on the sand, outposts thrown out to guard against surprise attack, the sun blazing down on the whole scene, little groups of warriors formed themselves round the heads.

The ceremony commenced with the placing of the heads in the sand, face upwards; each naked warrior in turn seated himself on one of them and the medicine men, of which there were two with the party, commenced to chew tobacco (borrowed from me, I remember). Approaching from behind, one of them took a half-Nelson on the seated warrior, drew his head back, took his nostrils in his mouth, and forced a quantity of tobacco juice up his nose. This strange procedure is not without explanation; it is the local equivalent to an anti-toxin against the baneful influence of the enemy's medicine man, a form of protection which the natives firmly believe makes them immune from the disasters and plagues to which their foes can subject them. (I may mention that my firm resolution to take a personal part in the ceremonies faded before the nauseous picture of this, the first degree of that wild brotherhood. Jack aptly termed this performance "The Bull's Eye Degree.") The effect which this treatment had on the warriors was at once exhilarating and overwhelming—the former on account of their unshakable faith in its merits, the latter because of its natural physical results.

Recovered from their choking and gasping, the privileged few who had merited this nicotinous inoculation by reason of their having participated in the killing of the victims and dipped their spears in their blood, proceeded to peel the heads.

This is done by carefully parting the hair straight down from the crown to the base of the skull, slitting the skin down the line formed by the parting, hard on to the bone of the skull; turning it back on both sides, and peeling it from the bony structure just as a stocking is drawn from the foot. At the eyes, ears, and nose, some cutting is necessary, after which the flesh and muscles come off with the skin, leaving the skull clean and naked but for the eyes and teeth.

The incision or slit from the crown to the base of the neck, was then sewn together again, with a bamboo needle and palm-leaf fibre (the *chambira* from which the hammocks, ropes, fish-lines and nets are made), leaving untouched for the moment the opening at the neck. The lips were skewered with three bamboo splinters, each about two and a half inches long and lashed together with strands of cotton fibre, which held them tightly closed, in the same manner as the sheets of a sailing boat are fastened to the cleats on the deck; tassels being afterwards formed by the frayed ends of the fibre. The eyeholes were closed by drawing down the upper eyelashes. The eyebrows were held from falling by small pegs or props of bamboo, vertically set between the outer rim of the eyelashes (thus effectively holding them in place) and the shoulders of the corresponding eyebrows. The holes of the nose and ears were temporarily plugged with cotton.

The purpose of these several operations was to hold the features of the face in position and to seal the openings, so that the head could again be expanded to its normal proportions by filling it with hot sand and thus permit an even contraction of the whole in the further process of curing. The meat at the base of the neck was "basted" with *chambira*, to prevent its wearing and wasting away by handling in the succeeding operations.

In the meantime, several large fires had been kindled and numerous earthenware crocks filled with water were placed in readiness.

A description at this point of the ease with which the Jívaros start a fire by means of their primitive methods may be of interest.

A hard-wood stick is made to revolve at high speed by means of a bow whose string is wrapped about it, its lower end resting on a piece of pith. The necessary pressure on the stick is obtained by bearing on a flat stone which fits on the upper end of the stick, held in position by means of a small round hole which serves as a socket. The pressure of the stick on the pith sets up sufficient friction to cause the latter to smolder, when it is easily blown into a flame. This simple equipment is packed with every party as we carry matches. But also, on short trips, the Jívaros carry with them a smoldering hornet's nest, at the end of the branch on which it was originally built, which serves the double purpose of a kindler and of a protection against the swarming myriads of sand-flies and gnats which infest the shores of some rivers during the summer months.

The crocks which are used on these occasions have been made with the utmost care by the medicine men in person, far removed from all human eyes and under auspicious lunar conditions; they are brought carefully wrapped in palm-leaves to ensure the impossibility of their being either touched or seen by any unauthorized person until the moment for the ceremony arrives. For every head there is one of these red, baked clay, conical pots, some eighteen inches in diameter by eighteen inches deep; the apex of the cone rests on the earth, the sides being supported by stones; in this way the fire has ample access to the greatest possible surface.

The pots were filled with cold water, straight from the river, and the boneless heads filled with sand placed in them. Within half an hour, the water had been brought to a boiling-point. This was the critical moment. The heads must be removed before the water actually boils, to prevent the softening of the flesh and the scalding of the roots of the hair, which would cause it to drop out. The heads, on being removed, were found to have shrunk to about one-third of their original size. The water, I noticed, was covered with a yellow grease similar to that which forms when other meats are cooked.

The pots were cast away into the river, too holy to be put to any further use, and the fires were heaped up with fresh logs, to heat the sand on which they stood. For henceforth the sand played an important part in the proceedings.

Meanwhile, those who had been treated, or initiated by the medicine men, namely the participants in the actual kill, were privileged to hold a special ceremony of their own; the naked skulls were taken off, and each group retired a short distance to hold the sacred rites which follow the boiling of the flesh-heads. We were not allowed to participate, as is to be supposed, and furthermore, the temper of the Indians at that particular moment was not conducive to too close an observation of their doings on our part; we were, indeed, convinced by this time of the very real desire which shone through the eyes of our brothers-in-arms to add five more heads, as well as five rifles and a canoe-load of presents, to the day's booty. It would appear that some form of muttered parley took place, a serious business in comparison with the wild caper-ings which follow when the skulls are brought back to the main party. The interpretation of these rites was undiscoverable by reason of the fact that the Chief, the sole interpreter among the Jívaros, was far too busily occupied with an attempt to persuade me of the absolute necessity of our going down-stream not more than one white man in any single canoe! The childlike simplicity of these people's natures, the blatant transparency of their ruses, is only another proof of their close proximity to animals.

So the skulls were brought back and stuck on spear-heads, the spears standing upright in the ground, and around them took place a dance, celebrated by all and sundry with wild yells, and the throwing of spears across the skulls from one warrior to another. We had to play our part, leaping and shooting our rifles into the air—but not more than two of us at a time exposed ourselves to the obvious risk of some accidental spear-thrust! With all of us in the ring together, the Indians would have made short work of the party.

By now hot sand had been prepared in large quantities. This was poured into the heads at the neck-opening and while thus filled they were ironed with hot stones picked up with the aid of palm-leaves. This process, which began that day on the sand-bar, is continued in the ordinary way for some forty-eight hours until the skin is smooth and hard and as tough as tanned leather, the whole head gradually shrinking to the size of a large orange. The resemblance to the living man is extraordinary. Indeed, the reduced heads, when skillfully made, are exact miniatures of their former selves. Every feature, hair, and scar is retained intact, and even the expression is not always lost. When perfected, they are hung in the smoke of a fire to preserve them from the depredations of the multitudinous insects which would attack and demolish them. As I noticed that afternoon, however, the preservation of the features in their former shape is not always the object of those who prepare them; some of the Aguarunas were to be seen deliberately distorting them while they were still flexible, as if in mockery of their enemies. They took a particular pleasure in distending the mouth, which accounts for the expression to be seen on many Jívaro heads.

Into the late afternoon the careful preparation of the heads continued. By this time, all were working with a will to cure them, so that a start down-stream could be made that evening. Time and again the cool greasy sand was poured from the half-dried heads, giving out the odour of an evening meal, only to be refilled with a fresh hot supply. Flat stones were always in the fires, being heated for the constant ironing to which the faces were subjected; they slid easily over the skin, like a flat-iron on linen, due to the natural oil which exuded from the contracting pores.

Hot coarse pebbles were substituted for sand in the final process, the heads being constantly tilted from side to side to prevent them from burning the meat, as dice are shaken in a box. The small amount of oil still exuding on the face was now wiped away with fresh cotton as fast as it appeared and the operation continued until all the fat and grease was "fried out" of the head when it was considered "cured" or mummified; shrunk to the last diminutive size attainable.

Even the captive children were playing round the fires, innocent of the hideous import to them of this, the most tragic moment of their lives. Little did they realize that in a few years' time they would themselves be called upon to kill and behead their own kin. Already they were friends with their captors into whose family they had been merged forever.

Thus ended a day unique, I verily believe, in the history of exploration.

I will add a few remarks concerning the ultimate fate of the trophies whose early history I have told.

The Jívaros never take adult male prisoners, but the women and children who are caught in the periodical raids are given the same standing in the victorious tribe as those who are born into it. Polygamy is forced on the Jívaro peoples by the constant drain on the male population caused by the incessant inter-tribal warfare. But for polygamy they would soon become extinct.

What the scalp is to the North American Indian, the battle-standard to the civilized warrior, the heads are to the Jívaro. But the comparison is only true up to a point. For whereas the glory of the battle-standard and the scalp is undying, that of the Jívaro heads endures only to the end of the great Festival of Rejoicing with which they are honoured on the return of the war-party to their homes.

During the absence of the warriors their women have made ready vast quantities of *giamanchi*. This preparation contains just enough alcohol to inebriate when taken in enormous quantities, as the savages do on these occasions. Unlike civilized intoxicants its only action is stupefying. The tom-toms are brought out, and men and women throw themselves into the business of dancing and drinking themselves to sleep. The rhythmic beats of the drums resound through the woods for many a long hour. Only the soporific effect of the liquor suffices to bring the orgy to an end.

Afterwards the heads are shorn of their hair, which is converted into permanent trophies in the form of belts to be worn round the loin-cloths of their distinguished owners in battle or at the feast. The posses-sion of such a trophy singles a man out for special regard. But the heads themselves have now lost their value, as surely as pearls which have died. It is curious that the fanatical jealousy with which they are guarded up to the time of the festival should give place to that complete indiffer-ence which allows them to be thrown to the children as playthings and finally lost in river or swamp.

NOTE: It has come to the author's attention that there is in Panama a man who makes a business of preparing and shrinking heads, and who has even shrunken two entire bodies, one of an adult, the other evi-dently of a child; the body of the latter only ten by twelve inches. These heads, human or otherwise, are much more skillfully prepared than the legitimate work of the Jívaros. The slit in the legitimate Jívaro head is drawn together with a very coarse fibre, while the work of this expert is so neatly done that the incision can hardly be noticed. The heads are those of white men, negroes, Chinamen and natives, probably selected from unclaimed hospital dead. In Europe the author has also run across these heads which evidently must have come from the same source. In Panama, where tourists have created a brisk demand for these uncouth curios, heads, either human or monkey, are made to order or sold for $25 each.

Hammock Nights

From The Edge of the Jungle *(1921)*
By William Beebe

If you have never slept in a hammock, you haven't slept, claims William Beebe. Others, however, might say that if you have ever tried to sleep in a hammock, you haven't slept, but Beebe ought to know—as a first-rate naturalist for the New York Zoological Society in the 1920s and 1930s, he went everywhere, did everything, and met everybody. But he enjoyed few things more than the comforts of a hammock. (DRK)

There is a great gulf between pancakes and truffles: an eternal, fixed abysmal cañon. It is like the chasm between beds and hammocks. It is not be denied and not to be traversed; for if pancakes with syrup are a necessary of life, then truffles with anything must be, by the very nature of things, a supreme and undisputed luxury, a regal food for royalty and the chosen of the earth. There cannot be a shadow of a doubt that these two are divided; and it is not alone a mere arbitrary division of poverty and riches as it would appear on the surface. It is an alienation brought about by profound and fundamental differences; for the gulf between them is that gulf which separates the prosaic, the ordinary, the commonplace, from all that is colored and enlivened by romance.

The romance of truffles endows the very word itself with a halo, an aristocratic halo full of mystery and suggestion. One remembers the hunters who must track their quarry through marshy and treacherous lands, and one cannot forget their confiding catspaw, that desolated pig, created only to be betrayed and robbed of the fungi of his labors. He is one of the pathetic characters of history, born to secret sorrow, victimized by those superior tastes which do not become his lowly station. Born to labor and to suffer, but not to eat. To this day he commands my sympathy, his ghost—lean, bourgeois, reproachful— looks out at me from every marketplace in the world where the truffle proclaims his faithful service.

But the pancake is a pancake, nothing more. It is without inherent or artificial glamour; and this unfortunately, when you come right down to it, is true of food in general. For food, after all, is one of the lesser considerations; the connoisseur, the gourmet, even the gourmand, spends no more than four hours out of the day at his table. From the cycle, he may select four in which to eat; but whether he will or not, he must set aside seven of the twenty-four in which to sleep.

Sleeping, then, as opposed to eating, is of almost double importance, since it consumes nearly twice as much time—and time, in itself, is the most valuable thing in the world. Considered from this angle, it seems incredible that we have no connoisseurs of sleep. For we have none. Therefore it is with some temerity that I declare sleep to be one of the romances of existence, and not by any chance the simple necessary it is reputed to be.

However, this romance, in company with whatever is worthy, is not to be discovered without the proper labor. Life is not all truffles. Neither do they grow in modest back-yards to be picked of mornings by the maid-of-all-work. A mere bed, notwithstanding its magic camouflage of coverings, of canopy, of disguised pillows, of shining brass or fluted carven posts, is, pancake like, never surrounded by this aura of romance. No, it is hammock sleep which is the sweetest of all slumber. Not in the hideous, dyed affairs of our summer porches, with their miserable curved sticks to keep the strands apart, and their maddening creaks which grow in length and discord the higher one swings—but in a hammock woven by Carib Indians. An Indian hammock selected at random will not suffice; it must be a Carib and none other. For they, themselves, are part and parcel of the romance, since they are not alone a quaint and poetic people, but the direct descendants of those remote Americans who were the first to see the caravels of Columbus. Indeed, he paid the initial tribute to their skill, for in the diary of his first voyage he writes—

"A great many Indians in canoes came to the ship to-day for the purpose of bartering their cotton, and *hamacas* or nets in which they sleep."

It is supposed that this name owes its being to the hammock tree, from the bark of which they were woven. However that may be, the modern hammock of these tropical Red Men is so light and so delicate in texture that during the day one may wear it as a sash, while at night it forms an incomparable couch.

But one does not drop off to sleep in this before a just and proper preparation. This presents complexities. First, the hammock must be slung with just the right amount of tautness; then, the novice must master the knack of winding himself in his blanket that he may slide gently into his aerial bed and rest at right angles to the tied ends, thus permitting the free side-meshes to curl up naturally over his feet and head. This cannot be taught. It is an art; and any art is one-tenth technique, and nine-tenths natural talent. However, it is possible to acquire a certain virtuosity, which, after all is said, is but pure mechanical skill as opposed to sheer genius. One might, perhaps, get a hint by watching the living chrysalid of a potential moon-moth wriggle back into its cocoon—but little is to be learned from human teaching. However, if, night after night, one observes his Indians, a certain instinctive knowledge will arise to aid and abet him in his task. Then, after his patient apprenticeship, he may reap as he has sowed. If it is to be disaster, it is as immediate as it is ignominious; but if success is to be his portion, then he is destined to rest, wholly relaxed, upon a couch encushioned and resilient beyond belief. He finds himself exalted and supreme above all mundane disturbances, with the treetops and the stars for his canopy, and the earth a shadowy floor far beneath. This gentle aerial support is distributed throughout hundreds of fine meshes, and the sole contact with the earth is through twin living boles, pulsing with swift running sap, whose lichened bark and moonlit foliage excel any tapestry of man's devising.

Perhaps it is atavistic—this desire to rest and swing in a hamaca. For these are not unlike the treetop couches of our arboreal ancestors, such a one as I have seen an orang-utan weave in a few minutes in the swaying crotch of a tree. At any rate, the hammock is not dependent upon four walls, upon rooms and houses, and it partakes altogether of the wilderness. Its movement is æolian—yielding to every breath of air. It has even its own weird harmony—for I have often heard a low, whistling hum as the air rushed through the cordage mesh. In a sudden tropical gale every taut strand of my hamaca has seemed a separate, melodious, orchestral note, while I was buffeted to and fro, marking time to some rhythmic and reckless tune of the wind playing fortissimo on the woven strings about me. The climax of this musical outburst was not without a mild element of danger—sufficient to create that enviable state of mind wherein the sense of security and the knowledge that a minor catastrophe may perhaps be brought about are weighted against the other.

Special, unexpected, and interesting minor dangers are also the province of the hamaca. Once, in the tropics, a great fruit fell on the elastic strands and bounced upon my body. There was an ominous swish of the air in the sweeping arc which this missile described, also a goodly shower of leaves; and since the fusillade took place at midnight, it was, all in all, a somewhat alarming visitation. However, there were no honorable scars to mark its advent; and what is more important, from all my hundreds of hammock nights, I have no other memory of any actual or threatened danger which was not due to human carelessness or stupidity. It is true that once, in another continent, by the light of a campfire, I saw the long, liana-like body of a harmless tree-snake wind down from one of my fronded bed-posts and, like living woof following its shuttle, weave a passing pattern of emerald through the pale meshes. But this heralded no harm, for the poisonous reptiles of that region never climb; and so, since I was worn out by a hard day, I shut my eyes and slept neither better nor worse because of the transient confidence of a neighborly serpent.

As a matter of fact, the wilderness provides but few real perils, and in a hammock one is safely removed from these. One lies in a stratum above all damp and chill of the ground, beyond the reach of crawling tick and looping leech; and with an enveloping *mosquitaro*, or mosquito shirt, as the Venezuelans call it, one is fortified even in the worst haunts of these most disturbing of all pests.

Once my ring rope slipped and the hammock settled, but not enough to wake me up and force me to set it to rights. I was aware that something had gone wrong, but, half asleep, I preferred to leave the matter in the lap of the gods. Later as a result, I was awakened several times by the patting of tiny paws against my body, as small jungle-folk, standing on their hind-legs, essayed to solve the mystery of the swaying, silent, bulging affair directly overhead. I was unlike any tree or branch or liana which had come their way before; I do not doubt that they thought me some new kind of ant-nest, since these structures are alike only as their purpose in life is identical—for they express every possible variation in shape, size, color, design, and position. As for their curiosity, I could make no complaint, at best, my visitors could not be so inquisitive as I, inasmuch as I had crossed one ocean and two continents with no greater object than to pry into their personal and civic affairs as well as those of their neighbors. To say nothing of their environment and other matters.

That my rope slipped was the direct result of my own inefficiency. The hammock protects one from the dangers of the outside world, but like any man-made structure, it shows evidences of those imperfections which are part and parcel of human nature, and serve, no doubt, to make it interesting. But one may at least strive for perfection by being careful. Therefore tie the ropes of your hammock yourself, or examine and test the job done for you. The master of hammock makes a knot the name of which I do not know—I cannot so much as describe it. But I would like to twist it again—two quick turns, a push and a pull; then, the greater the strain put upon it, the greater its resistance.

This trustworthiness commands respect and admiration, but it is in the morning that one feels the glow of real gratitude; for, in striking camp at dawn, one has but to give a single jerk and the rope is straightened out, without so much as a second's delay. It is the tying, however, which must be well done—this I learned from bitter experience.

It was one morning, years ago, but the memory of it is with me still, vivid and painful. One of the party had left her hammock, which was tied securely since she was skilful in such matters, to sit down and rest in another, belonging to a servant. This was slung at one end of a high, tropical porch, which was without the railing that surrounds the more pretentious verandahs of civilization, so that the hammock swung free, first over the rough flooring, then a little out over the yard itself. A rope slipped, the faulty knot gave way, and she fell backward—a seven-foot fall with no support of any kind by which she might save herself. A broken wrist was the price she had to pay for another's carelessness—a broken wrist which, in civilization, is perhaps, one of the lesser tragedies; but this was in the very heart of the Guiana wilderness. Many hours from ether and surgical skill, such an accident assumes alarming proportions. Therefore, I repeat my warning: tie your knots or examine them.

It is true, that, when all is said and done, a dweller in hammock may bring upon himself any number of diverse dangers of a character never described in book or imagined in fiction. A fellow naturalist of mine never lost an opportunity to set innumerable traps for the lesser jungle-folk, such as mice and opossums, all of which he religiously measured and skinned, so that each, in its death, should add its mite to human knowledge. As a fisherman runs out set lines, so would he place his traps in a circle under his hammock, using a cord to tie each and every one to the meshes. This done, it was his custom to lie at ease and wait for the click below which would usher in a new specimen—perhaps a new species—to be lifted up, removed, and safely cached until morning.

This strategic method served a double purpose: it conserved natural energy, and it protected the catch. For if the traps were set in the jungle and trustfully confided to its care until the break of day, the ants would leave a beautifully cleaned skeleton, intact, all unnecessarily entrapped.

Now it happened that once, when he had set his nocturnal traps, he straightaway went to sleep in the midst of all the small jungle people who were calling for mates and new life, so that he did not hear the click which was to warn him that another little beast of fur had come unawares upon his death. But he heard, suddenly, a disturbance in the low ferns beneath his hammock. He reached over and caught hold of one of the cords, finding the attendant trap heavy with prey. He was on the point of feeling his way to the trap itself, when instead, by some subconscious prompting, he reached over and snapped on the flashlight. And there before him, hanging in mid-air, striking viciously at his fingers which were just beyond its reach, was a young fer-de-lance— one of the deadliest of tropical serpents. His nerves gave way, and with a crash the trap fell to the ground where he could hear it stirring and thrashing about among the dead leaves. This ominous rustling did not encourage sleep; he lay there for a long time listening—and every minute is longer in the darkness—while his hammock quivered and trembled with the reaction.

Guided by this, I might enter into a new field of naturalizing and say to those who might, in excitement, be tempted to do otherwise, "Look at your traps before lifting them." But my audience would be too limited; I will refrain from so doing.

It is true that this brief experience might be looked upon as one illustration of the perils of the wilderness, since it is not customary for the fer-de-lance to frequent the city and the town. But this would give rise to a footless argument, leading nowhere. For danger is everywhere—it lurks in every shadow and is hidden in the bright sunlight, it is the uninvited guest, the invisible pedestrian who walks beside you in the crowded street ceaselessly, without tiring. But even a fer-de-lance should rather add to the number of hammock devotees than diminish them; for the three feet or more of elevation is as good as many miles between the two of you. And three miles from any serpent is sufficient. . . .

And this brings us to the greatest joy of hammock life, admission to the secrets of the wilderness, initiation to new intimacies and subtleties of this kingdom, at once welcomed and delicately ignored as any honored guest should be. For this one must make unwonted demands upon one's nocturnal senses. From habit, perhaps, it is natural to lie with the eyes wide open, but with all the faculties concentrated on the two senses which bring impressions from the world of darkness—hearing and smell. In a jungle hut a loud cry from out of the black treetops now and then reaches the ear; in a tent the faint noises of the night outside are borne on the wind, and at times the silhouette of a passing animal moves slowly across the heavy cloth; but in a hamaca one is not thus set apart to be baffled by hidden mysteries—one is given the very point of view of the creatures who live and die in the open.

Through the meshes which press gently against one's face comes every sound which our human ears can distinguish and set apart from the silence—a silence which in itself is only a mirage of apparent soundlessness, a testimonial to the imperfection of our senses. The moaning and whining of some distant beast of prey is brought on the breeze to mingle with the silken swishing of the palm fronds overhead and the insistent chirping of many insects—a chirping so fine and shrill that it verges upon the very limits of our hearing. And these, combined, unified, are no more than the ground surge beneath the countless waves of sound. For the voice of the jungle is the voice of love, of hatred, of hope, of despair—and in the night-time, when the dominance of sense-activity shifts from eye to ear, from retina to nostril, it cries aloud its confidences to all the world. But the human mind is not equal to a true understanding of these; for in a tropical jungle the birds and the frogs, the beasts and the insects are sending out their messages so swiftly one upon the other, that the senses fail of their mission and only chaos and great confusion are carried to the brain. The whirring of invisible wings and the movement of the wind in the low branches become one and the same; it is an epic, told in some strange tongue, an epic filled to overflowing with tragedy, with poetry and mystery. The cloth of this drama is woven from many-colored threads, for Nature is lavish with her pigment, reckless with life and death. She is generous because there is no need for her to be miserly. And in the darkness, I have heard the working of her will, translating as best I could.

In the darkness, I have at times heard the tramping of many feet; in a land traversed only by Indian trails I have listened to an overloaded freight train toiling up a steep grade; I have heard the noise of distant battle and the cries of the victor and the vanquished. Hard by, among the trees, I have heard a woman seized, have heard her crying, pleading for mercy, have heard her choking and sobbing till the end came in a terrible gasping sigh; and then, in the sudden silence, there was a movement and thrashing about in the topmost branches, and the flutter and whirr of great wings moving swiftly away from me into the heart of the jungle—the only clue to the author of this vocal tragedy. Once, a Pan of the woods tuned up his pipes—striking a false note now and then, as if it were his whim to appear no more than the veriest amateur; then suddenly, with the full liquid sweetness of his reeds, bursting into a strain so wonderful, so silvery clear, that I lay with mouth open to still the beating of blood in my ears, hardly breathing, that I might catch every vibration of his song. When the last note died away, there was utter stillness about me for an instant—nothing stirred, nothing moved; the wind seemed to have forsaken the leaves. From a great distance, as if we were going deeper into the woods, I heard him once more tuning up his pipes; but he did not play again.

Beside me, I heard the low voice of one of my natives murmuring, *"Muerte ha pasado."* My mind took up this phrase, repeating it, giving it the rhythm of Pan's song—a rhythm delicate, sustained, full of color and meaning in itself. I was ashamed that one of my kind would translate such sweet and poignant music into a superstition, could believe that it was the song of death—the death that passes—and not the voice of life. But it may have been that he was wiser in such matters than I; superstitions are many times no more than truth in masquerade. For I could call it by no name—whether bird or beast, creature of fur or feather or scale. And not for one, but for a thousand creatures within my hearing, any obscure nocturnal sound may have heralded the end of life. Song and death may go hand in hand, and such a song may be a beautiful one, unsung, unuttered until this moment when nature demands the final payment for what she has given so lavishly. In the open, the dominant note is the call to a mate, and with it, that there may be color and form and contrast, there is that note of pure vocal exuberance which is beauty for beauty and for nothing else; but in this harmony there is sometimes the cry of a creature who has come upon death unawares, a creature who has perhaps been dumb all the days of his life, only to cry aloud this once for pity, for mercy, or for faith, in this hour of his extremity. Of all, the most terrible is the death-scream of a horse—a cry of frightful timbre—treasured, according to some secret law, until this dire instant when for him death indeed passes.

It was years ago that I heard the pipes of Pan; but one does not forget these mysteries of the jungle night: the sounds and scents and the dim, glimpsed ghosts which flit through the darkness and the deepest shadow mark a place for themselves in one's memory, which is not erased. I have lain in my hammock looking at a tapestry of green draped over a fallen tree, and then for a few minutes have turned to watch the bats flicker across a bit of sky through the dark branches. When I looked back again at the tapestry, although the dusk had only a moment before settled into the deeper blue of twilight, a score of great lustrous stars were shining there, making new patterns in the green drapery; for in this short time, the spectral blooms of the night had awakened and flooded my resting-place with their fragrance.

And these were but the first of the flowers; for when the brief tropic twilight is quenched, a new world is born. The leaves and blossoms of the day are at rest, and the birds and insects sleep. New blooms open, strange scents pour forth. Even our dull senses respond to these; for just as the eye is dimmed, so are the other senses quickened in the sudden night of the jungle. Nearby, so close that one can reach out and touch them, the pale Cereus moons expand, exhaling their sweetness, subtle breaths of fragrance calling for the very life of their race to the whirring hawkmoths. The tiny miller who, through the hours of glare, has crouched beneath a leaf, flutters upward, and the trail of her perfume summons her mate perhaps half a mile down wind. The civet cat, stimulated by love or war, fills the glade with an odor so pungent that it seems as if the other senses must mark it.

Although there may seem not a breath of air in motion, yet the tide of scent is never still. One's moistened finger may reveal no cool side, since there is not the vestige of a breeze; but faint odors arrive, become stronger, and die away, or are wholly dissipated by the onrush of others, so musky or so sweet that one can almost taste them. These have their secret purposes, since Nature is not wasteful. If she creates beautiful things, it is to serve some ultimate end; it is her whim to walk in obscure paths, but her goal is fixed and immutable. However, her designs are hidden and not easy to decipher; at best, one achieves, not knowledge, but a few isolated facts.

Sport in a hammock might, by the casual thinker, be considered as limited to dreams of the hunt and chase. Yet I have found at my disposal a score of amusements. When the dusk has just settled down, and the little bats fill every glade in the forest, a box of beetles or grasshoppers—or even bits of chopped meat—offers the possibility of a new and neglected sport, in effect the inversion of baiting a school of fish. Toss a grasshopper into the air and he has only time to spread his wings for a parachute to earth, when a bat swoops past so quickly that the eyes refuse to see any single effort—but the grasshopper has vanished. As for the piece of meat, it is drawn like a magnet to the fierce little face. Once I tried the experiment of a bit of blunted bent wire on a long piece of thread, and at the very first cast I entangled a flutter-mouse and pulled him in. I was aghast when I saw what I had captured. A body hardly as large as that of a mouse was topped with the head of a fiend incarnate. Between his red puffed lips his teeth showed needle-sharp and ivory-white; his eyes were as evil as a caricature from *Simplicissimus*, and set deep in his head, while his ears and nose were monstrous with fold upon fold of skinny flaps. It was not a living face, but a mask of frightful mobility.

I set him free, deeming anything so ugly well worthy of life, if such could find sustenance among his fellows and win a mate for himself somewhere in this world. But he, for all his hideousness and unseemly mien, is not the vampire; the blood-sucking bat has won a mantle of deceit from the hands of Nature—a garb that gives him a modest and not unpleasing appearance, and makes it a difficult matter to distinguish him from his guileless confrères of our summer evenings.

But in the tropics—the native land of the hammock—not only the mysteries of the night, but the affairs of the day may be legitimately investigated from this aerial point of view. It is a fetish of belief in hot countries that every unacclimatized white man must, sooner or later, succumb to that sacred custom, the siesta. In the cool of the day he may work vigorously, but this hour of rest is indispensable. To a healthful person, living a reasonable life, the siesta is sheer luxury. However, in camp, when the sun nears the zenith and the hush which settles over the jungle proclaims that most of the wild creatures are resting, one may swing one's hammock in the very heart of this primitive forest and straightway be admitted into a new province, where rare and unsuspected experiences are open to the wayfarer. This is not the province of sleep and dreams, where all things are possible and preëminently reasonable; for one does not go through sundry hardships and all manner of self-denial, only to be blindfolded on the very threshold of his ambition. No naturalist of a temperament which begrudges every unused hour will, for a moment, think of sleep under such conditions. It is not true that the rest and quiet are necessary to cool the Northern blood for active work in the afternoon, but the eye and the brain can combine relaxation with keenest attention.

In the northlands the difference in the temperature of the early dawn and high noon is so slight that the effect on birds and other creatures, as well as plants of all kinds, is not profound. But in the tropics a change takes place which is as pronounced as that brought about by day and night. Above all, the volume of sound becomes no more than a pianissimo melody; for the chorus of birds and insects dies away little by little with the increase of heat. There is something geometrical about this, something precise and fine in this working of a natural law—a law from which no living being is immune, for at length one unconsciously lies motionless, overcome by the warmth and this illusion of silence.

The swaying of the hammock sets in motion a cool breeze, and lying at full length, one is admitted at high noon to a new domain which has no other portal but this. At this hour, the jungle shows few evidences of life, not a chirp of bird nor song of insect, and not rustling of leaves in the heat which has descended so surely and so inevitably. But from hidden places and cool shadows come broken sounds and whisperings, which cover the gamut from insects to mammals and unite to make a drowsy and contented murmuring—a musical undertone of amity and goodwill. For pursuit and killing are the lowest ebb, the stifling heat being the flag of truce in the world-wide struggle for life and food and mate—a struggle which halts for naught else, day or night.

Lying quietly, the confidence of every unconventional and adventurous wanderer will include your couch, since courage is a natural virtue when the spirit of friendliness is abroad in the land. I felt that I had acquired merit that eventful day when a pair of hummingbirds—thimblefuls of fluff with flaming breastplates and caps of gold—looked upon me with such favor that they made the strands of my hamaca their boudoir. I was not conscious of their designs upon me until I saw them whirring toward me, two bright, swiftly moving atoms, glowing like tiny meteors, humming like a very battalion of bees. They betook themselves to two chosen cords and, close together, settled themselves with no further demands upon existence. A hundred of them could have rested upon the pair of strands; even the dragon-flies which dashed past had a wider spread of wing; but for these two there were a myriad glistening featherlets to be oiled and arranged, two pairs of slender wings to be whipped clean of every speck of dust, two delicate, sharp bills to be wiped again and again and cleared of microscopic drops of nectar. Then—like great eagles roosting high overhead in the clefts of the mountainside—these mites of birds must needs tuck their heads beneath their wings for sleep; thus we three rested in the violent heat.

On other days, in Borneo, weaver birds have brought dried grasses and woven them into the fabric of my hammock, making me indeed feel that my couch was a part of the wilderness. At times, some of the larger birds have crept close to my glade, to sleep in the shadows of the low jungle-growth. But these were, one and all, timid folk, politely incurious, with evident respect for the right of the individual. But once, some others of a ruder and more barbaric temperament advanced upon me unawares, and found me unprepared for their coming. I was dozing quietly, glad to escape for an instant the insistent screaming of a cicada which seemed to have gone mad in the heat, when a low rustling caught my ear—a sound of moving leaves without wind; the voice of a breeze in the midst of breathless heat. There was in it something sinister and foreboding. I leaned over the edge of my hammock, and saw coming toward me, in a broad irregular front, a great army of ants, battalion after battalion of them flying like a sea of living motes over twigs and leaves and stems. I knew the danger and I half sat up, prepared to roll out and walk to one side. Then I gauged my supporting strands, tested them until they vibrated and hummed, and lay back, watching to see what would come about. I knew that no creature in the world could stay in the path of this horde and live. To kill an insect or a great bird would require only a few minutes, and the death of a jaguar or a tapir would mean only a few more. Against this attack, claws, teeth, poison fangs would be idle weapons.

In the van fled a cloud of terrified insects—those gifted with flight to wing their way far off, while the humbler ones went running head-long, their legs, four, six or a hundred, making the swiftest pace vouch-safed them. There were foolish folk who climbed up low ferns, achieving the swaying topmost fronds only to be trailed by the savage ants and brought down to instant death.

Even the winged ones were not immune, for if they hesitated a second, an ant would seize upon them, and, although carried into the air, would not loosen his grip, but cling to them, obstruct their flight, and perhaps bring them to earth in the heart of the jungle, where, cut off from their kind, the single combat would be waged to the death. From where I watched, I saw massacres innumerable; terrible battles in which some creatures—a giant beside an ant—fought for his life, crushing to death scores of the enemy before giving up.

They were a merciless army and their number was countless, with host upon host following close on each other's heels. A horde of warriors found a bird in my game-bag, and left of it hardly a feather. I wondered whether they would discover me, and they did, though I think it was more by accident than by intention. Nevertheless a half-dozen ants appeared on the foot-strands, nervously twiddling their antennæ in my direction. Their appraisal was brief; with no more than a second's delay they started toward me. I waited until they were well on their way, then vigorously twanged the cords under them harpwise, sending all the scouts into mid-air and headlong down among their fellows. So far as I know, this was a revolutionary maneuver in military tactics, comparable only to the explosion of a set mine. But even so, when the last of their brigade had gone on their menacing, pitiless way, and the danger had passed to a new province, I could not help thinking of the certain, inexorable fate of a man who, unable to move from his hammock or to make any defense, should be thus exposed to their attack. There could be no help for him if but one of this great host should scent him out and carry the word back to the rank and file.

It was after this army had been lost in the black shadows of the forest floor, that I remembered those others who had come with them—those attendant birds of prey who profit by the evil work of this legion. For, hovering over them, sometimes a little in advance, there had been a flying squadron of ant-birds and others which had come to feed, not on the ants, but on the insects which had been frightened into flight. At one time, three of these dropped down to perch on my hammock, nervous, watchful, and alert, waiting but a moment before darting after some ill-fated moth or grasshopper which, in its great panic, had escaped one danger only to fall an easy victim to another. For a little while, the twittering and chirping of these camp-followers, these feathered profiteers, was brought back to me on the wind; and when it had died away, I took up my work again in a glade in which no voice of insect reached my ears. The hunting ants had done their work thoroughly.

And so it comes about that by day or by night the hammock carries with it its own reward to those who have learned but one thing—that there is a chasm between pancakes and truffles. It is an open door to a new land which does not fail of its promise, a land in which the prosaic, the ordinary, the everyday have no place, since they have been shouldered out, dethroned, by a new and competent perspective. The god of hammock is unfailingly kind, just, and generous to those who have found pancakes wanting and have discovered by inspiration, or what-not, that truffles do not grow in back-yards to be served at early breakfast by the maid-of-all-work. Which proves, I believe, that a mere bed may be a block in the path of philosophy, a commonplace, and that truffles and hammocks—hammocks unquestionably—are twin doors to the land of romance.

The swayer in hammocks may find amusement and may enrich science by his record of observations; his memory will be more vivid, his caste the worthier, for the intimacy with wild things achieved when swinging between earth and sky, unfettered by mattress or roof.

The Jungle of Ceylon

From Passions and Impressions *(1978)*
By Pablo Neruda

The following travel dispatch was first published in La Nación, *a Chilean newspaper, in 1927.*

Pablo Neruda is perhaps Latin America's greatest poet—and definitely my favorite. He was an undisputed master of the written word who so very clearly understood the intricate mechanisms of the human heart and soul.

This description of a visit to Ceylon, now Sri Lanka, is clear proof of the poet's gift. Neruda's words build a tropical island so authentic that readers find themselves there alongside him. Anyone wondering how this might be possible will be interested to know that Neruda considered his writing to be so closely tied to the earth that he always wrote in green ink. (DRK)

Felicitous shore! A coral reef stretches parallel to the beach; there the ocean interposes in its blues the perpetual white of a rippling ruff of feathers and foam; the triangular red sails of sampans; the unmarred line of the coast on which the straight trunks of the coconut palms rise like explosions, their brilliant green Spanish combs nearly touching the sky.

Crossing the island in an almost straight line in the direction of Trincomalee, the landscape becomes dense, earth-dominated; human beings and their belongings disappear; the immutable, impenetrable jungle replaces everything. Trees knot in clumps, aiding or destroying one another, and as they meld together they lose their contours, so one travels as if through a low, thick, vegetal tunnel, through a frightening world of chaotic and violent cabbages.

Herds of elephants cross the road one by one; small jungle rabbits leap frantically, fleeing from the automobile; perfect little wild hens and cocks are everywhere; fragile blue birds of paradise appear and flee.

By night, our vehicle travels silently through the perfumes and shadows of the jungle. All around us, the blazing eyes of surprised beasts, eyes like flames of alcohol; it is the night of the jungle, seething with insects, hungers, and desires. We shoot wild boar, beautiful leopards, and deer. They stop in their tracks before the headlights, making no attempt to flee, as if disoriented, and then fall, disappearing among the branches; the downed animal is dragged to the car, damp and magnificent with dew and blood, smelling of foliage and of death.

In the deep jungle, there is a silence like that of libraries: abstract and humid.

At times, we hear the trumpeting of wild elephants or the familiar howling of the jackal. At times, a shot from a hunter's gun rings out, then fades, swallowed by the silence as water swallows stone.

Also reposing in the middle of the jungle, and overrun by it, lie the ruins of mysterious Singhalese cities: Anuradhapura, Polonnaruwa, Mihintale, Sigiriya, Dambulla. The gray shells of narrow stone columns buried for twenty centuries peer through the vegetation, tumbled statues and stairways, enormous ponds and palaces that have returned to earth, to their progenitors long forgotten. Even so, beside those scattered stones in the shadow of the enormous pagodas of Anuradhapura, the moonlit night is filled with kneeling Buddhists, and the ancient prayers return to Singhalese lips.

The tragedy of the rock of Sigiriya comes to mind as I write. In the deep heart of the jungle rises an enormous and precipitous hill or rock, accessible only by insecure, risky gradins carved into the great stone; and on its heights, the ruins of a palace, and marvelous Sigiriyan frescoes still intact in spite of the centuries. Fifteen hundred years ago a King of Ceylon, a parricide, sought asylum from his avenging brother on the summit of this terrible mountain of stone. There, in his image and likeness, he constructed his isolated castle of remorse. With his queens and his warriors and his artists and his elephants, he climbed the rock and remained there for twenty years, until his implacable brother arrived to kill him.

On all the planet there is no site so desolate as Sigiriya. The gigantic rock with its tenuous, interminable, carved stairways and its sentry posts forever divested of sentinels; above, the remains of the palace, the audience chambers of the monarch with his throne of black stone, and, everywhere, ruins of what once had been, covered now in vegetation and oblivion; and, from the heights, nothing around us for leagues and leagues but the impenetrable jungle; nothing, no human being, not one hut, not one flicker of life, nothing but the dark, thick, oceanic jungle.

The Menkranoti

From The Rivers Amazon *(1978)*
By Alex Shoumatoff

In 1976, Alex Shoumatoff left the comforts of home to trace the footsteps of three famous nineteenth-century Amazonian naturalists. His quest to follow their tracks led him from the seaport of Belem at the mouth of the Amazon to the river's source in the Apurimac Valley of Peru.

Along the way, Alex received permission to visit a remote Cayapo (Kayapo) village several hundred miles northwest of the Xingu National Park. The village is home to the Menkranoti, whose name means "the people with black faces"; they paint themselves with the black juice of the genipape fruit. Incidentally, these once-remote Menkranoti are today vocal defenders of the rights of Indians throughout the Amazon. (DRK)

The next day I had diarrhea and just lay in my hammock, stewing. When an attack came I had to rush behind the hut and squat over a hole in which a large *Mygales* spider, the type that eats finches and is known in Portuguese as the *caranguejeira*, lived. After half a dozen trips I became profoundly apathetic and drifted into a nightmare of complete deterioration, of wandering around South America no longer caring where I was or what was happening. The jungle was beginning to get on my nerves. The steady hum of billions of tiny *pium* flies who lived in the village, feeding on excrement and banana peels, swarming around our ankles as we walked through the plaza and forming a palpable cloud six inches from the ground, was beginning to prey on my sanity. There were other painful and irritating insects: chiggers, ticks, scabietic mites, and *bichos de pe*, who lay their eggs in the soles of your feet, buttocks, or any other part of the body in contact with the ground, and whose egg-sacs have to be dug out with a needle. Certain things about the Indians were also wearing on me. The women were always pestering us for salt and needles, and some of the men had become complete beggars. If you said *árupke*, meaning that you didn't have any more of what they were asking for, they would just ask for something else. Gustaaf said that after you had run out of everything they stopped bothering you, but this did not alter the fact that many of the Menkranoti were highly materialistic people whose main interest in relating to you was to get the goods you had brought. Another thing that took a little getting used to was their habit of spitting wherever and whenever they wanted to. You would be sitting next to a nice old lady who was puffing away abstractedly on her *warikoko* when suddenly she would conjure up a juicy quid and deposit it several inches from your feet. I found that the best way of dealing with this situation was to conjure up an even bigger quid and to deposit it as close as possible to where the original had landed.

The jungle either accepts you or it doesn't, as someone once wrote. I was beginning to think that I was not one of the chosen. The countless *pium* bites on my legs, scratched by dirty fingernails, had begun to infect and swell; in another few days walking would become excruciatingly painful and long treks in the jungle impossible. I was getting stir-crazy. I was beginning to feel "the stupefying boredom that drives men to the brink of madness," as one explorer described the effect of being confined by the humid, claustrophobic rainforest. My feelings vacillated between thinking I had the privilege to be a witness of the life of some of the last humans to be living in a natural state, and listless, enervated withdrawal.

The two environments, village and jungle, offered escape from one another. But within a short time both became unbearable.

As I lay in my hammock, a day-flying *Uranea* moth, jet-black with swallowtails and opal bars, flew in and fluttered under the latticework of the ceiling. I pulled myself together. With such an exquisite sight in range of my hammock, think of what there would be to see if I got outside. I joined a crowd of women and children who were running to the other side of the village. Bepkum had come back from the forest with four tortoises—too small for the festival—and some tapir and peccary meat. His mother put her hand on her forehead and sobbed uncontrollably for all the days that he'd been gone. Several women comforted her. Everyone else crowded around Bepkum with outstretched hands as he distributed the meat.

That night the thunder boomed and lightning lit up the edges of the thunderheads that hung over the hills around the village. We could hear the chief telling stories to his family in the next hut. The Cayapo have some eighty myths. They call themselves "the people who came from a hole in the sky." Originally, according to them, the earth was uninhabited. Everyone lived in the sky. One day an old man was digging out an armadillo burrow when he broke through the undersurface of the sky and saw the earth far below. He summoned his fellow villagers who made a long rope out of vines. Half of them, led by a daring youth called "the son of the people," climbed down the rope, and we are all descended from them.

In the morning we went out with Bepkum and twelve others between the ages of ten and twenty-four. We walked for several hours, crossing creeks on logs, the young men cutting loose with full-throated yodels as they loped along with hundred-pound baskets of *farinha*. They were happy to become animal again, open to every sight and smell, away from the domesticating influence of the village.

Reaching a flat place near water, the young men set down their loads and without talking, set up camp. The youngest boys cleared the ground with machetes. Others ripped fresh long strips of bark from nearby trees, cut four poles with a fork at one end and a sharpened point at the other. They planted the sharpened point into the ground. Then they cut two long horizontal poles and lashed them to the crotches with the bark strips. Others returned with saplings about fifteen feet long, which they planted into the ground, bending them over the first horizontal pole, and lashing them to the second. A fourth party came back with trains of palm fronds which they tied to the wall of vertical saplings and threw in twos over the arching roof. The final product, a palm hut, was ready in fifteen minutes. It was six by thirty feet, fully waterproof, and could sleep twenty comfortably. The rest of the day was left for hunting.

Half a mile from the camp Kadiure suddenly stopped, rubbed a sapling several inches from its base, and smelled his hand. It had a strong, musky odor. *Kukrùt*, he said—tapir. We broke up into groups of two and three, keeping in contact with high, dove-like hoots, snapping twigs to retrace our way. I went with Bepkum and Wakontire. They led me to a huge tree with flaring buttresses, in the sheltered nook between two of which the tapir had last slept. We trailed the animal to a stream and saw his fresh, ungulate prints in the sand, then lost them in the water. Bepkum examined some holes in the riverbank which he said were inhabited by snakes. The dogs took off in a yelping frenzy after a deer. Looking up, Bepkum motioned for us to freeze. *Macaco*. A troop of monkeys was swinging through the trees, but the foliage was thick, and they were too high for him to pick off with his .22 rifle. We came upon some women who had cut down a Brazil-nut tree and were roasting the nuts. It must have taken them a day to fell the monarch, which was about eight feet in diameter; and it would take several more to gather all the nuts, roast them, and carry them back to the village. The fruit of the *Bertholetia excelsa* (Brazil-nut tree) is a woody ball or pixidium the size of a grapefruit, containing eighteen to twenty-five nuts. A good-sized tree may produce hundreds of balls. People have been killed by the falling fruit. After roasting the whole pixidium in an open fire, the women open it with their axes and pour the nuts into their baskets. The Menkranoti shell Brazil nuts with a single, well-placed bite. We sampled a handful. The nut has moist white meat, richer than coconut.

With Wakontire in the lead, we entered a *mata de cipó*, a wood consisting mostly of vines. I had the feeling that if I had not been there he wouldn't have been slashing down everything in our path, which I was sure was alerting every animal within earshot to our presence. But the Menkranoti are very protective of the *kuben*, the strangers who are living with them. They call them *noket*, no eyes; like children, the *kuben* cannot see, and they must be carefully supervised so they don't get into trouble.

We came across a bee's nest in a dead tree, and Bepkum pried it off with a pole, wrapped the honey capsules in a leaf and passed it around. We took turns squeezing the bittersweet nectar into our waiting mouths. Just as Eskimos recognize over sixty kinds of snow, the Cayapo have names for twenty-eight species of bees. Most of them, like these bees, do not sting, so you can raid their hives with impunity.

Suddenly a shotgun popped twice in the distance. Bepkum and Wakontire dropped the stake with which they had been reaming out a hole and ran toward the sound. Twenty minutes later we joined the rest of the party. Kadiure had shot the tapir. The others were butchering the animal—which weighed at least three hundred pounds—and carrying it back to the camp. You could see how well it was adapted to a close, sticky environment: its hair was short, sparse, and spiny; its ears, neck, legs and tail elongated—the better to pass off body heat.

A fire was made, and stones piled on it, and strips of the flesh laid to roast on the stones. The liver, heart, and other organs were boiled in a pot; two fish, an ibis, and a guan were suspended over the flames on a spit. Several plantains were deposited in the ashes. For the rest of the afternoon we lazed in camp, chewing on the tapir meat, smoking, and naming the birds that sang: the watery gurgles were a *wanamariket*, the piercing whistles a *tanokororina*. With vivid eyes and excited gestures, Kadiure told how he had shot the tapir. Kopran, fifteen, the youngest husband in the village, showed me how to make a *warikoko*: finding a certain tree, you carve out the goblet shape, hold it between your knees, and bore out the pith by rolling the stem of a tough grass back and forth quickly in your palms. Danny introduced the group to Wrigley's spearmint gum, clutching his throat with his hands to show that it was not to be swallowed. Hundreds of sweat bees swarmed over us, and to escape them we would periodically go and sit in the creek. Monekabo taught me how to count to ten:

1) *pudi*
2) *amaikrut*
3) *amaikrutikeke*
4) *amaikrutamaikrut*
5) *amaikrutamaikrutikeke*
6) *amaikrutamaikrutamaikrut*
7) *amaikrutamaikrutamaikrutikeke*
8) *amaikrutamaikrutamaikrutamaikrut*
9) *amaikrutamaikrutamaikrutamaikrutikeke*
10) *amaikrutamaikrutamaikrutamaikrutamaikrut*

Clearly the Cayapo have little use for numbers.

That night Danny and I slept in our hammocks, and the men and boys lay on the floor of the hut, sleeping against each other in a great curled-up ball of snoring bodies. Whenever one of them turned over, the others would all turn by chain reaction. At their feet smoldering faggots of dead-wood kept the animals away. Fire, which the Cayapo believe they got from the jaguar, is their protector at night in the woods. Cooking itself is regarded as a civilizing process, representing the transformation of raw, bloody meat into something palatable to humans. Their word for community, *tchet*, also means "baked" or "roasted." They are at a loss to explain why the word should have these two meanings.

In the middle of the night the rainy season began in earnest. We could hear the water pounding the leaves, but so dense was the canopy that for minutes we felt nothing. Then the rain broke through the saturated tree-tops and we scrambled into the lean-to, spending the rest of the night huddled among warm bodies. Bepiakoti, twenty-four, my right-hand neighbor, was fascinated with the hairs on my chest, and he pulled them and played with them while I struggled with my inhibitions at being touched so freely by a member of the same sex.

In the morning as I took down my soggy hammock it ripped down the middle. After two weeks in the jungle, the cloth was already rotten. The Indians broke camp, walked for three hours, and set up a new one exactly as they had done the previous morning. Krâtùk and Kàprõt left for the village with slabs of tapir meat and we went with them.

That night, at about two-thirty in the morning, a chorus of heartrending shrieks and wails went up in the village. An infant child had died of diarrhea. At dawn Karekra, the closest male relative, fired off two shots. Three shots would have meant a birth. The child who died was a twin. Her sister had been "allowed" to die some months before, probably clubbed to death by her mother, who was unmarried and in no position to bring up children. Karekra, the head male of her household and thus the person in charge of curing the child, had refused to go to FUNAI [Fundaçaõ Nacional do Indio, or the National Indigenous Agency of Brazil]; Guillerme would have given him lomotil tablets, which quickly stop diarrhea. Karekra also refused to let the child have water, in the belief that it would only be excreted—so that she probably died of dehydration. Her death was not seen as a great tragedy because there were already ten extra females in the adult population and an even greater surplus in her own generation. The mother went about work as usual that day except that her eyes seemed sad, and she spoke slowly, as if stunned, and in a low voice. In the afternoon, the child was buried at the edge of the village with her beaded armbands and necklaces, and a cone of sand was piled up on the spot. Afterwards the old women came to the mother and took all of her possessions from her. We debated why the woman should be subjected to further bereavement. Gustaaf's explanation seemed the most reasonable: if you lost a child, you lost everything, and had to start all over again.

We stayed away from the funeral and from Karekra's house; it was no time for *kuben* to be poking around. Tewet took me to his hut and played five songs for me on his bamboo flute, which only had four holes. The songs had a purity and a simplicity which western music could not command; I felt as if I were listening to a beautiful bird. Afterwards, Tewet tied a bark strap to his old Winchester repeater and set off to climb Kraenprekti, the high hill that overlooks the village. The vegetation was frothing over the summit cone, and we slashed for an hour through vines and saplings armed with thorns, until suddenly the land fell away on all sides, and

I realized we were at the top. A cool breeze blew up the leaves, and between them we could see the morning mist rising over hundreds of miles of jungle. Tewet fired up his pipe and smoked. His lashless almond eyes were shining, and as he looked my way his thick lips spread into an engaging smile that revealed his upper gum.

On the way down he spotted a *buriti* palm tree, built a makeshift ladder, stood it up to the trunk, climbed up, and hacked down the fruit cluster. Within minutes he had woven two baskets of palm fronds for us to take the nuts, which tasted like soapy apricots, back to the village. At the base of the mountain he carefully cleared a place among the dead leaves, and as he was planting one of the nuts in the earth he heard the faint drone of an engine. "*Màdu-ka,*" he said, looking up. Our plane had come.

Adventure Gone Bad: Things That Go Bump in the Night

﹏

If you don't wear a helmet you will probably be killed by the sun. If you are careless about your drinking-water you stand an excellent chance of getting typhoid. If you expose yourself to tsetse-flies you are quite likely to die of sleeping-sickness. You must be careful about your food if you are to avoid dysentery. To escape liver trouble you must take regular exercise. If you are to be kept reasonably free from fever you must guard against being bitten by mosquitos and take daily doses of quinine. You must wear stout boots while walking in the grass and bathe your feet several times a day if you do not court trouble from jiggers and hook-worms. Keep away from crowds of natives if you would avoid exposing yourself to leprosy and beriberi. Don't invite trouble by wandering about at night by yourself. And if you do not want to come down with venereal diseases you must leave the native girls alone. Disregard these rules, and you will probably be planted in a weed-grown cemetery.

—*E. Alexander Powell*

The Man-Eating Tree

By Carl Liche (1878?)

The following excerpt purports to be an eyewitness account of a human sacrifice to what must certainly qualify as the king of all carnivorous plants. The legend of the man-eating tree of Madagascar comes to us down a terrifically long, dark, and twisted road. Is this indeed part of a letter written, in 1878, from a certain German, Carl Liche, to his friend and inestimable Polish colleague Dr. Omelius Fredlowski? Is this a ruse first perpetrated upon an unsuspecting public by a bored group of missionaries in an 1881 magazine article and later quoted by one Chase Salmon Osborn, LL.D., in his 1924 book Madagascar, Land of the Man-Eating Tree? *Is this a rejected first draft of a treatment for the 1960 B picture* The Little Shop of Horrors?*

You be the judge. (MWC)*

The Mkodos, of Madagascar, are a very primitive race, going entirely naked, having only faint vestiges of tribal relations, and no religion beyond that of the awful reverence which they pay to the sacred tree. They dwell entirely in caves hollowed out of the limestone rocks in the hills, and are one of the smallest races, the men seldom exceeding fifty-six inches in height. At the bottom of a valley (I had no barometer, but should not think it over four hundred feet above the level of the sea), and near its eastern extremity, we came to a deep tarn-like lake about a mile in diameter, the sluggish oily water of which overflowed into a tortuous reedy canal that went unwillingly into the recesses of a black forest composed of jungle below and palms above. A path diverging from its southern side struck boldly for the heart of the forbidding and seemingly impenetrable forest. Hendrick led the way along this path, I following closely, and behind me a curious rabble of Mkodos, men, women and children. Suddenly, all the natives began to cry "Tepe! Tepe!" and Hendrick, stopping short, said, "Look!" The sluggish canal-like stream here wound slowly by, and in a bare spot in its bend was the most singular of trees. I have called it "Crinoida," because when its leaves are in action it bears a striking resemblance to that well-known fossil the crinoid lily-stone or St. Cuthbert's head. It was now at rest, however, and I will try to describe it to you. If you can imagine a pineapple eight feet high and thick in proportion resting upon its base and denuded of leaves, you will have a good idea of the trunk of the tree, which, however, was not the color of an anana, but a dark dingy brown, and apparently as hard as iron. From the apex of this truncated cone (at least two feet in diameter) eight leaves hung sheer to the ground, like doors swung back on their hinges. These leaves, which were joined at the top of the tree at regular intervals, were about eleven or twelve feet long, and shaped very much like the leaves of an American agave or century plant. They were two feet through at their thickest point and three feet wide, tapering to a sharp point that looked like a cow's horn, very convex at the outer (but now under) surface, and on the under (now upper) surface slightly concave. The concave face was thickly set with strong thorny hooks like those on the head of the teazle. These leaves hanging thus limp and lifeless, dead green in color, had in appearance the massive strength of oak fibre. The apex of the cone was a round white concave figure like the smaller plate set within a larger one. This was not a flower but a receptacle, and there extruded into it a clear treacly liquid, honey sweet, and possessed of violent intoxicating and soporific properties. From underneath the rim (so to speak) of the undermost plate a series of long hairy green tendrils stretched out in every direction towards the horizon. These were seven or eight feet long, tapered from four inches to half an inch in diameter, yet they stretched out stiffly as iron rods. Above these (from between the upper and under cup) six white almost transparent palpi reared themselves towards the sky, twirling and twisting with a marvelous incessant motion, yet constantly reaching upwards. Thin as reeds and frail as quills, apparently they were yet five or six feet tall, and were so constantly and vigorously in motion, with such a subtle, sinuous, silent throbbing against the air, that they made me shudder in spite of myself, with their suggestion of serpents flayed, yet dancing upon their tails. The description I am giving you now is partly made up from a subsequent careful inspection of the plant. My observations on this occasion were suddenly interrupted by the natives, who had been shrieking around the tree with their shrill voices, chanting what Hendrick told me were propitiatory hymns to the great tree devil. With still wilder shrieks and chants they now surrounded one of the women, and urged her with the points of their javelins, until slowly, and with despairing face, she climbed up the stalk of the tree and stood on the summit of the cone, the palpi swirling all about her. "Tsik! Tsik!" ("Drink, drink!") cried the men. Stooping, she drank of the viscous fluid in the cup, rising instantly again, with wild frenzy in her face and convulsive cords in her limbs. But she did not jump down, as she seemed to intend to do. Oh, no! The atrocious cannibal tree that had been so inert and dead came to sudden savage life. The slender delicate palpi, with the fury of starved serpents, quivered a moment over her head, then as if instinct with demoniac intelligence fastened upon her in sudden coils round and round her neck and arms; then while her awful screams and yet more awful laughter rose wildly to be instantly strangled down again into a gurgling moan, the tendrils one after, like green serpents, with brutal energy and infernal rapidity, rose, retracted themselves, and wrapped her about in fold after fold, ever tightening with cruel swiftness and the savage tenacity of anacondas fastening upon their prey. It was the barbarity of the Laocoön without its beauty—this strange horrible murder. And now the great leaves slowly rose and stiffly, like the arms of a derrick, erected themselves in the air, approached one another and closed the dead and hampered victim with the silent force of a hydraulic press and the ruthless purpose of a thumb screw. A moment more, and while I could see the bases of these great levers pressing more tightly towards each other, from their interstices there trickled down the stalk of the tree great streams of the viscid honey-like fluid mingled horribly with the blood and oozing viscera of the victim. At sight of this the savage hordes around me, yelling madly, bounded forward, crowded to the tree, clasped it, and with cups, leaves, hands and tongues each one obtained enough of the liquor to send him mad and frantic. Then ensued a grotesque and indescribably hideous orgy, from which even while its convulsive madness was turning rapidly into delirium and insensibility, Hendrick dragged me hurriedly away into the recesses of the forest, hiding me from the dangerous brutes.

The retracted leaves of the great tree kept their upright position during ten days, then when I came one morning they were prone again, the tendrils stretched, the palpi floating, and nothing but a white skull at the foot of the tree to remind me of the sacrifice that had taken place there. I climbed into a neighboring tree, and saw that all trace of the victim had disappeared and the cup was again supplied with the viscid fluid.

May I never see such a sight again.

A Swarm of Beetles

From What Led to the Discovery of the Source of the Nile *(1864)*
By John Hanning Speke

This horrifying selection comes from John Hanning Speke's book What Led
to the Discovery of the Source of the Nile, *the title of which is somewhat
misleading. There was great rivalry among African explorers of all nationalities
in the middle of the nineteenth century, and many reputations were made and
lost with claims of being the first white man to arrive at some particular place.
Speke's book notwithstanding, it was not until Alan Morehead's two volumes,*
The White Nile *(1960) and* The Blue Nile *(1962), that the complete story
of the Nile's exploration, and all of its white male "discoverers," was fully told.*

*Speke (1827–1864) was an adventurer of the old school—pith helmet,
swagger stick, camp bathtub—and a great friend of the explorer Sir Richard
Burton. Speke and Burton undertook two African journeys together, in 1854
and 1858, and then had a violent falling-out. They each published separate
accounts of their efforts, and their rivalry became front-page news in the tabloid
newspapers of the day. Speke died in a hunting accident just before a public*

debate between the two was to be held by the Royal Geographical Society in London. Whether Speke's death was a suicide or not is a matter still debated in some academic and literary circles. (MWC)

At night a violent storm of rain and wind beat on my tent with such fury that its nether parts were torn away from the pegs, and the tent itself was only kept upright by sheer force. On the wind's abating, a candle was lighted to rearrange the kit, and in a moment, as though by magic, the whole interior became covered with a host of small black beetles, evidently attracted by the glimmer of the candle. They were so annoyingly determined in their choice for peregrinating, that it seemed hopeless my trying to brush them off the clothes or the bedding, for as one was knocked aside another came on, and then another; till at last, worn out, I extinguished the candle, and with difficulty—trying to overcome the tickling annoyance occasioned by these intruders crawling up my sleeves and into my hair, or down my back and legs—fell off to sleep. Repose that night was not destined to be my lot. One of these horrid little insects awoke me in his struggles to penetrate my ear, but just too late: for my endeavor to extract him, I aided his immersion. He went his course, struggling up the narrow channel, until he got arrested by want of passage-room. This impediment evidently enraged him, for he began with exceeding vigour, like a rabbit in a hole, to dig violently away at my tympanum. The queer sensation this amusing measure excited in me is past description. I felt inclined to act as our donkeys once did, when beset by a swarm of bees, who buzzed about their ears and stung their heads and eyes until they were so irritated and confused that they galloped about in the most distracted order, trying to knock them off by treading on their heads, or by rushing under bushes, into houses, or through any jungle they could find. Indeed, I do not know who was worse off. The bees killed some of them, and this beetle nearly did for me. What to do I knew not. Neither tobacco, oil, nor salt could be found: I therefore tried melted butter; that failing, I applied the point of a penknife to his back, which did more harm than good; for though a few thrusts quieted him, the point also wounded my ear so badly that inflammation set in, severe suppuration took place, and all the facial glands extending from that point down to the point of the shoulder became contorted and drawn aside, and a string of boils decorated the whole length of that region. It was the most painful thing I ever remember to have endured; but, more annoying still, I could not masticate for several days and had to feed on broth alone. For many months the tumour made me almost deaf, and ate a hole between the ear and the nose, so that when I blew it, my ear whistled so audibly that those who heard it laughed. Six or seven months after this accident happened, bits of the beetle—a leg, a wing, or parts of its body—came away in the wax.

It was not altogether an unmixed evil, for the excitement occasioned by the beetle's operations acted towards my blindness as a counter-irritant, drawing the inflammation away from my eyes. Indeed, it operated far better than any other artificial appliance. To cure the blindness I once tried rubbing in some blistering liquor behind my ear, but this unfortunately had been injured by the journey, and had lost its stimulating properties. Finding it of no avail, I then caused my servant to rub the part with his finger until it was excoriated, which, though it proved insufficiently strong to cure me, was according to Dr. Bowman, whom I have since consulted, as good a substitute for a blister as could have been applied.

A Black Stream of Death

From The River of Singing Fish *(1951)*
By Arkady Fiedler

The following selection comes from a book that has the strangest provenance of any volume in this collection: It was discovered in Ireland, in the basement of the castle of the Marquess of Sligo, lying on a table in the gift shop. The author, Arkady Fiedler, was a Polish zoologist who was sent to Brazil in the 1940s to collect specimens for the Warsaw Zoo. Fiedler's other books, written mostly in German and Polish, include The Merry Drongo Bird *and* To-Morrow to Madagascar.

Nearly every firsthand account of Amazonian travel mentions ants. They are ubiquitous in tropical forests. If most of the animal life on the planet is insects, and so many of the insects are ants, and most of the ants live in the tropics, imagine how many different kinds of ants could spoil your picnic in the Amazon. After reading this account, you might just be grateful that it is killer bees, not killer ants, that are headed our way. (MWC)

One day, while hunting in the jungle not far from Cumaria, I came to a spot where all the living creatures appeared to be in an unnatural state of excitement. The birds, hopping madly from branch to branch, were screaming and squawking, and an armadillo, evidently just aroused from sleep, was blindly pushing its way through the undergrowth. Whole clouds of beetles, locusts, and other insects were buzzing among the trees; others, worn out, were snatching a brief rest on the leaves. But in their visible alarm they did not pause long, and soon resumed their flight. They were all coming from one direction. When a Mygale spider—the huge robber, usually fearless and the terror of all other creatures—tore past me frantically, I guessed some great danger must be at hand, menacing all the seething life of the jungle.

I gripped my rifle more firmly and hid behind a tree, curious as to what would happen next. The anxious screams of the birds and the terror of the insects affected me not a little. It is unnerving to await an unknown danger in a tropical forest. To be prepared for any eventuality I removed the fine shot from my gun and loaded one barrel with buckshot, the other with a bullet.

Soon the throng of insects vanished, but my ears caught a new sound—a muffled rustle as of paper being crumpled. It was difficult to determine whence the mysterious sound was coming. Simultaneously a repulsive, acrid smell began to pervade the air.

At last I saw and understood everything. Several paces away a broad black mass was advancing through the dense undergrowth. Ants!

A nomadic column of foraging ants, the Ecitons, a real scourge of God, which spells doom for every creature in its path; an advance which no living thing, neither man nor beast, can withstand. Anything that fails to escape must perish, torn to pieces by these tiny brigands.

Several sharp stabs on my legs reminded me that I must move quickly. Some of the ants had already succeeded in climbing on to me. I sprang to one side, but realized the escape was not so easy as that. Among the densely growing bushes it was difficult to jump clear of a solid, yard-wide column of ants. The insects, infuriated, began to cling to my feet. I ran in the other direction, with no better result; there also a black stream was moving along relentlessly. Meantime yet a third mighty column of Ecitons approached the tree under which I had been standing, and my position became somewhat unenviable. I was surrounded.

Without further delay I scanned the column for a weak spot and forced my way through. My escape was not an unqualified success, for while I had been hopping about, more and more ants had clung to me. Some of them had already crawled under my gaiters and were making hay where the sun shone. So persistent were they that even when torn in two they went biting my legs, and I had to crush their heads in order to get rid of them. They left a piercing pain, probably due to some poison. I swore under my breath, and stopped at a safe distance to watch the absorbing sight.

The file of ants was about fifty feet long, and was divided into several columns, like the parallel columns of marching troops. It was impossible to estimate how many there were. A million, perhaps, or more? Each column, one solid mass of ants, a yard or more wide, advanced at a rate of three to four paces a minute. As they moved, chiefly in a compact body, I was able to go quite close to them without much fear of being bitten again.

An entire ant colony seemed to be on the move. I saw ants of three sizes; the largest, half an inch long, marched at the sides of the columns and alternatively ran on in advance and fell behind, like officers maintaining discipline. These ants were agile and swift; they reconnoitred the vicinity and went on foraging expeditions. They climbed up bushes and trees, but never more than five or six feet above the ground. Then they returned to the columns.

In the center, medium- and smaller-sized ants were carrying their progeny, larvae, and white grubs.

This ravenous, invincible army spared nothing. Several caterpillars the size of a human finger were enjoying a peaceful existence on the branch of a nearby bush. One of the scouting ants discovered them and reported back to its comrades, and a good hundred of them fell on the prey. With scant ceremony they ripped the caterpillars into shreds and carried them off as provisions. The unfortunate victims were completely disposed of within a minute.

The pursuit of a spider was not so easy. Although thirty times as large as any of the ants, it fled in terror to the very end of a branch. But they got it even there. It seized two ants in its mandibles, stopped a third with its legs; but others were already on top, snipping up the hairy body and carving the thorax into pieces. Soon every particle of the spider was carried down to the ground, including its long legs. The operation was performed with amazing speed.

Next in the path was the rotten log of a fallen tree, a munificent treasure-trove for the Ecitons. Several dozen great fat grubs were hidden in the trunk. The ants drew them out into the light and, in a moment, they, too, were in a thousand tiny pieces. For some unknown reason the ants were becoming enraged, and they tore the prey from one another in savage fury, as if there were need for haste in the killing.

But some insects enjoyed the goodwill, even the friendship, of the little brigands. From my position quite close to one of the outer columns I could see every detail clearly, and from time to time, in the very middle of the column, I noticed red beetles belonging to quite a different family of insects, yet hurrying along with the same haste and in the same direction. These beetles were members of the numerous caste of ant-slaves and were jealously guarded by the Ecitons for the sake of their scented, tasty secretions.

Curious to see what would happen, I lifted up one of these beetles with a twig and set it down about a yard outside the column. An indescribable turmoil at once arose in the ranks of the black horde, and patrols ran off in all directions. When they found the beetle, three ants seized the deserter and dragged it back to the column, one of them biting off a leg in its fervor. Before the beetle even had a time to cherish the glimmering hope of freedom—though I doubt the idea ever entered its head—it was thrust back into the ranks and overwhelmed by an implacable torrent of bodies. The Ecitons carried out all their activities energetically, vigorously, without reflection or hesitation, and always with a clear sense of purpose.

Yet there was something rotten in the state of Denmark. Among the black mass I also noticed white insects moving along. They were surely not ants. I lifted one of them up and discovered that it was a fly grub. It was an extraordinary image, for on its own head it was wearing a cap formed from the head of an ant, eaten out from within. When I noticed scores of certain species of fly above the ants I understood the full significance of their presence. The flies were parasites which accompanied the ants in their wanderings. They were always on the watch for an opportunity of depositing their eggs on the ants' bodies. In a few days the grub would break out of the egg. It would slowly begin to consume the living ant, growing the while, until it last reached the head and emptied it from the inside. Thenceforth, equipped with this mask, it could crawl on insolently among the mass of ants until it was transformed into a larva.

I saw many such grubs among the Ecitons. Here was one of Nature's ironic tragedies: the rapacious ants, which had no mercy on any living creature, put up with these parasitic grubs in their midst, and were in turn devoured by them. They were oblivious to the enemy in their ranks, the traitor within the gates.

A more vivid allegory could hardly be found in Nature.

The Ecitons also served as food for whole flocks of birds which kept watch over the procession, among them the ant-thrushes. Their cries sounded everywhere in the jungle.

The advance guards of the ant columns startled a great Teju lizard, a giant, three feet long, which fled and hid in a burrow not far away. Thousands of Ecitons rushed down after him. The struggle underground did not last long. After a few minutes the lizard crawled out, its whole body black with ants clinging to it. Both its eyes were already eaten out, the sockets filled with insects. It only managed to creep a few yards. Then, paralysed, it halted and opened wide its jaws, armed with numerous sharp teeth. These teeth clashed desperately at the intangible enemy, but meantime hundreds of ants had crept into its mouth. It cast its head about convulsively and kept its jaws gaping, as though overwhelmed by some compulsion, while the Ecitons cut pieces off its body and dragged them away. Finally they began to dispose of the still living reptile's entrails.

When the ants' rearguard passed the spot some twenty minutes later there was nothing for them to carry off, all that was left of the lizard being a shapeless heap of bones and a few scales.

The ants passed on.

The black nightmare vanished in the depths of the jungle, the cries of the ant-thrushes died away. And the sun went on shining down on the forest, its rays penetrating the thicket.

Then a gaudy Heliconius butterfly with yellow spots and red bands on its black wings fluttered by and began assiduously to deposit eggs on the leaves of a bush near the lizard's remains. It performed this task with much love and care for the future progeny. In a fortnight small caterpillars would crawl out of the eggs, to bask in idyllic bliss in the warmth of the tropical sun.

"Colours are smiles of Nature," wrote Leigh Hunt. "When they are extremely smiling and break forth into other beauty beside, they are her laughs, as in flowers . . ." or butterflies. Whenever there was a smile or a laugh in the tropical jungle it could not be better expressed than in the jaunty flamboyant Heliconius. He was a chuckle—a hearty laugh in the face of all the black streams of death.

Yet a cynic might say it was a sardonic grin too.

Rumors of a Snake

From Natural Acts *(1985)*
By David Quammen

The readers of Outside *magazine are a lucky group, for they get to read a new piece by David Quammen every month. The rest of us have to wait until a collection of his unique essays is put together and published. At this point there are two: the one from which this piece comes, and the more recent collection,* The Flight of the Iguana. *There are also two spy novels and a collection of short fiction in his portfolio, and rumors about a forthcoming book-length work on the natural world. I hope the rumors are true, for there is no one writing about nature today with the insight, breadth of knowledge, and pure heart of David Quammen.*

The rumors in this piece are about snakes. There is probably more exaggeration by wilderness travelers about the size of snakes encountered in the wilds than about the size of any other animal in the world, with the possible exception of bears or the fisherman's "one that got away." Here, Quammen, a resident of Montana who knows a thing or two about both bears and large fish, explores this theme in his inimitable style and comes up with a masterful theory to explain why this may be so. (MWC)

What this world needs is a good vicious sixty-foot-long Amazon snake.

Don't look at me, it's not my private notion. There is a broader mandate of some murky sort, not biological but psychic, issuing from that delicately balanced ecosystem we call the human mind. *Give us a huge snake. A monster, a serpent out at the far fringe of imaginability. Let it inhabit the funkiest jungle. A horrific thing, slithering along in elegant menace, belly distended with pigs and missing children.* The evidence of this odd yearning is oblique but cogent: Lacking any such beast, we are eager to settle for rumors of one. Otherwise how to explain the breathless compoundment of hearsay, tall tale, and exaggeration that has always surrounded the anaconda?

A fair example appears in the memoirs of Major Percy Fawcett. In 1906 he was sent out from London by the Royal Geographical Society to make a survey along certain rivers in western Brazil. "The manager at Yorongas told me he killed an anaconda fifty-eight feet long in the Lower Amazon. I was inclined to look on this as an exaggeration at the time, but later, as I shall tell, we shot one even larger than that." The disclaimer is a cagey stroke. Major Fawcett would have us take him for a hard-headed British skeptic.

Later he tells: "We were drifting easily along in the sluggish current not far below the confluence of the Rio Negro when almost under the bow of the *igarité* there appeared a triangular head and several feet of undulating body. It was a giant anaconda. I sprang for my rifle as the creature began to make its way up the bank, and hardly waiting to aim smashed a .44 soft-nosed bullet into its spine, ten feet below the wicked head. . . . We stepped ashore and approached the reptile with caution. It was out of action, but shivers ran up and down the body like puffs of wind on a mountain tarn. As far as it was possible to measure, a length of forty-five feet lay out of the water, and seventeen in it, making a total length of sixty-two feet." The indisputable logic of good arithmetic. It might be true but most likely it isn't.

An adventurer of the 1920s named F. W. UpdeGraff offered a similar account, having observed his anaconda in shallow water. "It measured fifty feet for certainty, and probably nearer sixty. This I know from the position in which it lay. Our canoe was a twenty-four footer; the snake's head was ten or twelve feet beyond the bow; its tail was a good four feet beyond the stern; the center of its body was looped into a huge **S**, whose breadth was a good five feet." But size estimates made in a watery medium are notoriously unreliable—especially when that watery medium is the Amazon River.

Bernard Heuvelmans, in his feverish book about stalking mysterious animals, tells at third or fourth hand of another Brazilian specimen that was purportedly killed in 1948. "The snake, which was said to measure 115 feet in length, crawled ashore and hid in the old fortifications of Fort Tabatinga on the River Oiapoc in the Guaporé territory. It needed 500 machine-gun bullets to put paid to it. The speed with which bodies decompose in the tropics and the fact that its skin was of no commercial value may explain why it was pushed back into the stream at once." Always for the gigantic individuals there is this absence of physical evidence, and always a waterproof reason for the absence: no camera on hand, rotting meat, even the skin was too heavy to carry out. One photograph did exist that, during the 1950s, was sold all over Brazil as a postcard, its caption claiming a length of 131 feet for the snake pictured. Unfortunately, no object of reference appeared in the photo with it. That snake might as easily have been a robust but minuscule twenty-footer.

My own modest sighting comes not from Brazil but from northeastern Ecuador, along the Rio Aguarico, in a remote zone of lowland jungle that may be as favorable to the production and growth of anacondas as almost anywhere in the Amazon drainage. Like those other wide eyed witnesses Fawcett and UpdeGraff, I was in a dugout canoe. Our guide was an intrepid and jungle-smart young man named Randy Borman, who spotted the big snake on a log tangle near the river bank while the rest of us were gawking elsewhere. He steered the boat in for a closer look.

Dark gunmetal grey with sides mottled in reddish brown, the anaconda was sunning itself placidly. Barely above the water on a low-riding log; protectively colored and patterned so that, even from ten yards away, it was virtually invisible. Randy edged the canoe closer.

Do you see it now? Some of us did, several admitted they didn't. We moved closer. Here indeed was a formidable snake. Still motionless, still sunbathing dreamily. I was delighted with this glimpse of an anaconda in the wild but—amid the soft brushfire crackle of camera shutters—we had already ventured closer than I ever expected to get. Then closer still. A very tolerant and self possessed snake. Beautiful big head. Thick graceful coils of body. Sizable brown eye. Hello, Randy? Just when I thought our guide would back the canoe off, instead he dove over the gunnel to grab this creature around the neck.

A deeply startling act. But Randy came up again, deftly, with a great armload of anaconda wrapping itself onto him in surprise and anger, squeezing with the authority of a species that does its killing by constriction. My face bore the contemplative expression of two eggs sunnyside in a white Teflon skillet.

Randy smiled calmly. "We'll take him back to camp for the others to see." An hour later, having been much fawned over and photographed, the animal was gently released back into its river. A few fast pulses of undulant swimming, then a dive beneath the brown water, and it was gone. There was a convenient absence of physical evidence.

So in recounting the story afterward (which I have not hesitated to do often, cornering people at parties and hoping the talk might turn to giant reptiles) I could make that poor snake any damn size I pleased. A piddling ten feet? Maybe eleven? Roughly the same girth as a man's biceps? In fact (so I would say, with engaging dismissiveness) it was rather dainty as this species goes. Still, an impressive beast.

Very little is known about the biology of *Eunectes murinus*, the anaconda; even less about its life history in the wild; and a sad fact is that no one seems much to care. Not a single field-research project (one expert has told me) is currently being done on it. The species has not yet found its George Schaller, its Dian Fossey, its Jane Goodall.

We know that it is a nonvenomous constrictor of the boa family. We know that it is aquatic, preferring slow rivers and swamps. That it bears live young (as opposed to laying eggs) in litters of up to eighty. That it is native to tropical South America east of the Andes, and also to the island of Trinidad. That (unlike the other boas and pythons) it does poorly and dies soon in captivity. But as to the rest, its favored diet, its daily and seasonal rhythms, its mating and birthing behavior, physiology, growth rate, optimal longevity: almost a total blank. There is an absence of evidence.

Admittedly, the prospect of studying full-grown anacondas in their own habitat offers an array of uniquely forbidding logistical problems. For that reason or whatever others, scientific consideration of *Eunectes murinus* has been limited almost entirely to the simple question that so mesmerized those early explorers: *How big does it get?* Well, really quite big. Bigger than any other snake on earth. *But how big is that?*

A second sad fact about the anaconda: By scientific standards of verification, it just doesn't seem to be nearly so large as everyone seems to want to believe it is. Forget 131 feet. Forget 62 feet, even with faultless arithmetic. Discount the record-length skins, which generally have been stretched by a good 20 percent in the process of tanning. Scientists have their own unstretchable views on this matter.

One respected herpetologist, Afrânio do Amaral, has posited a maximum length for the anaconda of about forty-two feet. But then Afrânio do Amaral is a Brazilian, arguably with a vested patriotic interest. After him the figures only get stingier. James A. Oliver of the American Museum of Natural History was willing to grant 37½ feet, based on the measurement made by a petroleum geologist, with a surveyor's tape, of a snake shot along the Orinoco River. But again in this case there was the problem of physical evidence: "When they returned to skin it, the reptile was gone," we are told. "Evidently it had recovered enough to crawl away." Teddy Roosevelt is said to have offered $5,000 for a skin or skeleton thirty feet long, and the money was never claimed. Sherman and Madge Minton, authors of several reliable snake books, declare that "To the best of our knowledge, no anaconda over twenty-five feet long has ever reached a zoo or museum in the United States or Europe." And Raymond Ditmars, an eminent snake man at the Bronx Zoo early in this century, wouldn't believe anything over nineteen feet.

Can these people all be discussing the same animal? Can Ditmars' parsimonious nineteen feet be reconciled with the eyewitness account of Major Fawcett? Does Roosevelt's unclaimed cash square with Heuvelmans' 115 feet of worthless rotting meat? It seems impossible.

But new evidence has lately reached me that suggests an explanation for everything. The evidence is a small color photograph. The explanation is relativity.

Not Einstein's variety, but a similar sort, which I shall call *Amazonian relativity*. It's very simple: The *true genuine size* of an anaconda (this theory applies equally well to piranha and bird-eating spiders) is relative to three other factors: (1) whether or not the snake is alive; (2) how close you yourself are to it; and (3) how close both of you are, at that particular moment, to the Amazon heartland. A live snake is always bigger than a dead one, even allowing for posthumous stretch. And as the other two distances decrease—from you to the snake, from you to the Amazon—the snake varies inversely towards humongousness.

This small color photograph, of such crucial scientific significance, arrived in the mail from an affable Dutch-born engineer, a good fellow I met on that Rio Aguarico trip. Unlike me, he carried a camera; sending the print was meant as a favor. In its foreground can be seen the outline of my own dopey duck-billed hat. The background is a solid wall of green jungle. At the center of focus is Randy Borman, astride the stern of his dugout, holding an anaconda. Dark gunmetal grey with sides mottled in reddish brown.

The snake is almost as big around as his wrist. It might be five feet long. Possibly close to six. But photographs can be faked. I don't believe this one for a minute.

Jerry's Maggot

From Tropical Nature *(1984)*
By Adrian Forsyth and Kenneth Miyata

The first, and so far only, time I visited the Amazon was with a group of entertainment-industry people who were on a combination exotic vacation and fact-finding mission. Tom Lovejoy, a good friend as well as a distinguished scientist, had recommended Tropical Nature *as a general introduction to the local biota, and I was reading this chapter as we drove down the Atlantic Forest coastline to the beautiful colonial town of Paratì. As we passed Brazil's only nuclear power plant, I tossed the book to John Ritter, the actor, with a casual "check this out." About five minutes later I heard a groaning "Oh my God!!!!" emanating from the rear of the bus. John then marched up the aisle, picked up the tour guide's microphone, and read the entire chapter for us all. Needless to say, what with his talent and this amazing story, we were all doubled over with laughter. (MWC)*

For those of us who dwell in large cities, direct interactions with other species may be limited to encounters with dogs and cats (and even then we tend to treat them as conspecifics) and occasional battles with cockroaches. Modern urban life has pushed us to a distant final link in a disrupted ecosystem. We live our lives far removed from the food chains that support us, sitting atop a tropic pyramid we never really become a part of.

Our limited interactions with other species force on us a form of ecological myopia. The message of interconnectedness has never penetrated deeply into our society, and even those of us who accept it intellectually may fail to appreciate how complicated some of these relationships are. College biology texts often gloss over interspecific interactions, offering simplified discussions of predation, competition, mutualism, and little else. But there are still places and occasions when an urban North American can step back into a food chain and experience firsthand the ecological relationships between himself and other species. Our friend Jerry Coyne had such an experience on his first visit to the tropical forests of Central America.

Jerry is a biologist. At the time, he was a graduate student at Harvard's Museum of Comparative Zoology. Well versed in evolutionary logic, genetical theory, Ivy League ecology, and the use of biometrical tools, he was also aware that his actual experience with living creatures was "limited to unexciting fruit flies crawling feebly around food-filled glass tubes." Working in the Museum of Comparative Zoology has done little to change that. The museum was no longer what it had been in the days of its founder, the celebrated Swiss naturalist Louis Agassiz, whose constant exhortation to "study Nature, not books" was practiced by all. Jerry's biological interactions continued to be with fruit flies in a crowded, sterile lab, and the only animals he saw, aside from his fellow graduate students and the ubiquitous dogs of Cambridge, were the stuffed mammals that resided in the display cases between his office and the Pepsi machine. Finally, after a winter and spring of listening to some of us urge him to get out of the lab, he enrolled in a field course in tropical ecology. Soon he was jetting to Costa Rica, determined to experience for himself the riches of tropical nature.

Jerry's introduction to the tropics was a revelation. It not only confirmed his misgivings about his previous training but changed his entire approach to his science. No longer would he trust "the naive and simple generalizations about nature produced by so-called theoretical ecologists," as he put it, and no longer would he search for slick hypotheses while glossing over the rich natural historical details of life. But he came away with more than these intellectual revelations.

A few weeks before Jerry was due to return to the Museum, his head began to itch. This was hardly remarkable. Skin fungus, chigger and mosquito bites, and a wealth of other pruriginous rot are the lot of field biologists in the lowland tropics, as he and his fellow students were by then well aware. Their field station was next to a large marsh, and hordes of mosquitoes descended on them as they listened to lectures after dinner. At first, Jerry assumed that the itch on his scalp was a mosquito bite, as indeed it was. But unlike the usual mosquito bite, this one did not subside. It grew larger, forming a small mound, and besides scratching Jerry began to worry. After several days of private fretting he sought help. One of his fellow students, a medical entomologist, agreed to examine the wound. Her diagnosis sent a chill of fear through poor Jerry. Poking out of a tiny hole in his scalp was a wiggling insect spiracle. A hideous little botfly maggot was living inside the skin on his head and eating his flesh! This intimacy with nature was a little too much for Jerry, and he ran around in circles crying for the removal of the maggot.

Unfortunately, removal of a botfly maggot is no simple task. This botfly (*Dermatobia hominis*) has existed as an unwanted guest in the skins of mammals and birds for countless generations. Its larvae have evolved two anal hooks that hold them firmly in their meaty burrow. If you pull gently on the larva, these hooks dig in deeper and bind it tightly to your flesh. If you pull harder, the maggot will eventually burst, leaving part of its body inside the host, which can lead to an infection far more dangerous to the host than the original bot. Botfly larvae secrete an antibiotic into their burrow, a tactic that prevents competing bacteria and fungi from tainting their food. A single bot in a nonvital organ thus poses little danger to an adult human, aside from mild physical discomfort and possible psychological trauma.

Occasionally a bot sets up residence in a particularly tender or private patch of flesh that cries out for immediate removal. In Costa Rica the locals used to use a plant called the *matatorsalo* (bot-killer) to kill the embedded larva. The acrid white sap of this milkweed kills the larva, but the task of removing the corpse remains. The most appropriate course of action then is a deft slice of a sterile scalpel. But surgeons are few and scattered in most tropical forests, and under these conditions many unwilling botfly hosts choose the meat cure.

This treatment, which is far from perfect, takes advantage of the biology of the botfly larva. The maggots are air-breathers and must maintain contact with the air through their respiratory spiracle, a snorkel-like tube that they poke through the host's skin. If you sandwich a piece of soft, raw meat over this air hole tightly enough, the larva must eventually leave its hole and burrow up through the meat in search of fresh air. When this happens, both meat and botfly are discarded. One of the students in Jerry's course afflicted with a bot in the buttock did this successfully. But the dense mat of hair that was Jerry's pride and joy would have to be shaved off in order for this to work, and toiling in the sweaty tropical heat with a patch of raw meat strapped atop his head was not something he relished. Faced with such a choice, Jerry decided to live and let live for the time being, and to seek professional help when he returned to Harvard.

After his initial bout of hysterical revulsion, Jerry learned to accept his guest. It was relatively painless most of the time. Only when the larva twisted would it cause sharp twinges of pain. Swimming made the larva squirm, presumably a reaction to having its air supply cut off temporarily, and Jerry felt this as a grating against his skull. These inconveniences were not enough to blind him to the wonder of it all. The bot was taking Jerry's "own body substance" and rendering it into more botfly flesh. This transmogrification of one creature into another is a miracle easily observed, but difficult to experience. Sudden death at the jaws of a large carnivore or the brief bite of a flea do not provide one the opportunity to reflect on the transmutative nature of predation and parasitism. But for the minor expense of a few milligrams of flesh,

Jerry could both contemplate and feel the process at his leisure. He was inside a food chain, rather than at its end. Jerry grew fond of his bot and the bot grew fat on Jerry.

When Jerry returned to New England, his bot had produced a goose egg–sized swelling on his head. It hurt more and he immediately sought medical advice at the Harvard Health Services clinic. Although he was quickly surrounded by a crowd of physicians and nurses, none of them had seen a botfly before and they regarded Jerry more as a medical curiosity than a suffering patient. Chagrined, he abandoned thoughts of a medical solution and decided to let nature take its course. Despite the discomfort, the bot continued to provide some pleasure. Jerry took great delight in the looks of horror he could produce by telling acquaintances of his guest as he dramatically brushed aside his hair.

While sitting in the bleachers at Fenway Park one evening watching the Red Sox fall prey to the Yankees, Jerry felt the beginning of the end. Protruding from the goose egg atop his scalp was a quarter inch of botfly larva. Over the course of the evening this protrusion grew, and eventually the bristly, inch-long larva fell free. Jerry prepared a glass jar with sterilized sand to act as a nursery for his pupating bot, but despite his tender ministrations the larva dried out and died before it could encase itself in a pupal sheath.

The Snake Doctor

From Last Chance to See *(1990)*
By Douglas Adams and Mark Carwardine

In Last Chance to See, *Douglas Adams, whose bestsellers include* The Hitchiker's Guide to the Galaxy, *uses the whip of wit to strike back at the forces that drive the present-day extinction of wildlife. In this passage we find Adams and his cohort Mark Carwardine preparing for a potentially dangerous voyage. They are going to Komodo, a remote Indonesian island, in search of the rare and endangered Komodo dragon lizard, a true man-eater whose bite is indeed worse than its bark.*

Preparation for the trip includes a visit to a peculiar Australian doctor, from whom Adams and Carwardine hope to pick up some remedies for the dragon's fatal bite. They need a snakebite kit, too, because some of the world's deadliest snakes happen to be the Komodo dragon's nearby neighbors. (DRK)

There is in Melbourne a man who probably knows more about poisonous snakes than anyone else on earth. His name is Dr. Struan Sutherland, and he has devoted his entire life to a study of venom.

"And I'm bored with it," he said when we went along to see him the next morning. "Can't stand all these poisonous creatures, all these snakes and insects and fish and things. Stupid things, biting everybody. And then people expect me to tell them what to do about it. I'll tell them what to do. Don't get bitten in the first place. That's the answer. I've had enough of it. Hydroponics, now, that's interesting. Talk to you all you like about hydroponics. Fascinating stuff, growing plants artificially in water, very interesting technique. We'll need to know all about it if we're going to go to Mars and places. Where did you say you were going?"

"Komodo."

"Well, don't get bitten, that's all I can say. And don't come running to me if you do because you won't get here in time, and anyway I'll probably be out. Hate this office, look at it. Full of poisonous animals all over the place. Look at this tank, it's full of fire ants. Poisonous. Bored silly with them. Anyway, I got some little cakes in case you were hungry. Would you like some little cakes? I can't remember where I put them. There's some tea but it's not very good. Sit down for heaven's sake.

"So, you're going to Komodo. Well, I don't know why you want to do that, but I suppose you have your reasons. There are fifteen different types of snake on Komodo, and half of them are poisonous. The only potentially deadly ones are the Russell's viper, the bamboo viper, and the Indian cobra.

"The Indian cobra is the fifteenth deadliest snake in the world, and all the other fourteen are here in Australia. That's why it's so hard for me to find time to get on with my hydroponics, with all these snakes all over the place.

"And spiders. The most poisonous spider is the Sydney funnel web, which bites about five hundred people a year. A lot of them used to die, so I had to develop an antidote to stop people bothering me with it all the time. Took us years. Then we developed this snake-bite detector kit. Not that you need a kit to tell you when you've been bitten by a snake, you usually know, but the kit is something that will detect what you've been bitten by so you can treat it properly.

"Would you like to see a kit? I've got a couple in the venom fridge. Let's have a look. Ah. Look, the cakes are in here too. Quick, have one while they're still fresh. Fairy cakes, I baked 'em myself."

He handed around the snake-bite detector kits and the rock-hard fairy cakes and retreated back to his desk, where he beamed at us cheerfully from behind his curly beard and bow tie. We admired the kits more than the cakes and asked him how many of the snakes he had been bitten by himself.

"None of 'em," he said. "Another area of expertise I've developed is that of getting other people to handle the dangerous animals. Won't do it myself. Don't want to get bitten, do I? You know what it says in my entry in *Who's Who*? 'Hobbies: gardening—with gloves; fishing— with boots; traveling—with care.' That's the answer. Oh, and wear baggy trousers. When a snake strikes, it starts to inject venom as soon as it hits something. If you've got baggy trousers, most of the venom will just get squirted down the inside of your trousers, which is better than it being squirted down the inside of your leg. You're not eating your cakes. Come on, get them down you, there's plenty more in the fridge."

We asked, tentatively, if we could perhaps take a snake-bite detector kit with us to Komodo.

" 'Course you can, 'course you can. Take as many as you like. Won't do you a blind bit of good because they're only for Australian snakes."

"So what do we do if we get bitten by something deadly, then?" I asked.

He blinked at me as if I were stupid.

"Well, what do you think you do?" he said. "You die, of course. That's what deadly means."

"But what about cutting open the wound and sucking out the poison?" I asked.

"Rather you than me," he said. "I wouldn't want a mouthful of poison. All the blood vessels beneath the tongue are very close to the surface, so the poison goes straight into the bloodstream. That's assuming you could get much of the poison out, which you probably couldn't. And in a place like Komodo it means you'd quickly have a seriously infected wound to contend with as well as a leg full of poison. Septicemia, gangrene, you name it. It'll kill you."

"What about a tourniquet?"

"Fine if you don't mind having your leg off afterwards. You'd have to because it would be dead. And if you can find anyone in that part of Indonesia who you'd trust to take your leg off, then you're a braver man than me. No, I'll tell you: the only thing you can do is apply a pressure bandage direct to the wound and wrap the whole leg or what-ever bit of you it is you've been bitten in, lower than your heart and your head. Keep very, very still, breathe slowly, and get to a doctor immediately. If you're on Komodo, though, that means a couple of days, by which time you'll be well dead. The only answer, and I mean this quite seriously, is don't get bitten. There's no reason why you should. Any of the snakes there will get out of your way well before you even see them. You don't really need to worry about the snakes if you're careful. No, the things you really need to worry about are the marine creatures."

"What?"

"Scorpion fish, stonefish, sea snakes. Much more poisonous than anything on land. Get stung by a stonefish and the pain alone can kill you. People drown themselves just to stop the pain."

"Where are all these things?"

"Oh, just in the sea. Tons of them. I wouldn't go near it if I were you. Full of poisonous animals. Hate them."

"Is there anything you do like?"

"Hydroponics."

"No, I mean is there any venomous creature you're particularly fond of?"

He looked out of the window for a moment.

"There was," he said, "but she left me."

The Jungle in the Mind: The Forests in Fiction

This is the story of Opalina,
Who lived in the Tad,
Who became the Frog,
Who was eaten by the Fish,
Who was nourished by the Snake,
Who was caught by the Owl,
But fed the Vulture,
Who was shot by Me,
Who wrote this Tale,
Which the Editor Took,
And published it Here,
To be read by You,
The last in the Chain,
Of Life in the Tropical Jungle.

—*William Beebe*

The Head of the Ethiopian

From She *(1887)*
By H. Rider Haggard

Henry Rider Haggard was a man whose life and career spanned many glorious and romantic eras, from Victorian England to the Roaring Twenties. In his brief career as a lawyer and civil servant he spent time in South Africa during the Zulu uprising, and, later, during the Boer War. It is, however, as the author of the high-adventure tales King Solomon's Mines, Allan Quartermain, Nada the Lily, *and* She *that he is best known. To read Haggard today is to experience the roots of so much of what we take for granted in the action/adventure genre—and this is especially true for the cinema. Without H. Rider Haggard's dashing Victorian-era heroes, there would probably never have been an Indiana Jones for our own time.*

This piece comes from the 1887 bestseller She. *The story involves a quest across deepest, darkest Africa for a legendary "lost" tribe of natives who have discovered the secret of everlasting life. They are ruled by the forever young and*

*luscious woman known to her followers only as "She—who must be obeyed."
The narrator is one Ludwig Horace Holly—Cambridge don, erstwhile sportsman, and world traveler. He brings his ward, his "nephew," Leo Vincey,
whom he has raised since the age of five as his own son, into the wilds of East
Africa on a pilgrimage that he swore to Leo's father he would someday undertake
with the young man. Leo is now a strapping man of twenty-five. They are
accompanied by Job, Holly's faithful manservant from Cambridge and Leo's
"nanny" since he was first taken to live with Holly, and Mahomed, an Arab
slave with whom they have recently survived a shipwreck.*

*As we pick up the scene, the intrepid party is aboard a specially outfitted
small boat they have brought with them from England. They are paddling into
the heart of a fetid swamp, and are about to spend their first night in the
primeval surroundings.* (MWC)

About midday the sun grew intensely hot, and the stench drawn up by
it from the marshes which the river drains was something too awful, and
caused us instantly to swallow precautionary doses of quinine. Shortly
afterwards the breeze died away altogether, and as rowing our heavy
boat against stream in the heat was out of the question, we were thankful enough to get under the shade of a group of trees—a species of
willow—that grew by the edge of the river, and lie there and gasp till
at length the approach of sunset put a period to our miseries. Seeing
what appeared to be an open space of water straight ahead of us, we
determined to row there before settling what to do for the night. Just
as we were about to loosen the boat, however, a beautiful water-buck,
with great horns curving forward, and a white stripe across the rump,
came down to the river to drink, without perceiving us hidden away
within fifty yards under the willows. Leo was the first to catch sight of
it, and being an avid sportsman thirsting for the blood of big game,
about which he had been dreaming for months, he instantly stiffened
all over, and pointed like a setter dog. Seeing what was the matter, I
handed him his express rifle, at the same time taking my own.

"Now then," I whispered, "mind you don't miss."

"Miss!" he whispered back contemptuously; "I could not miss it if
I tried."

He lifted the rifle, and the roan-coloured buck, having drunk his fill, raised his head and looked out across the river. He was standing right against the sunset sky on a little eminence, or ridge of ground, which ran across the swamp, evidently a favourite path for game, and there was something very beautiful about him. Indeed, I do not think that if I live to be a hundred I shall ever forget that desolate and yet most fascinating scene: it is stamped upon my memory. To the right and left were wide stretches of lonely, death breeding swamp, unbroken and unrelieved so far as the eye could reach, except here and there by ponds of black and peaty water that, mirror-like, flashed up the red rays of the setting sun. Behind us and before us stretched the vista of the sluggish river, ending in glimpses of a reed-fringed lagoon, on the surface of which the long lights of the evening played as the faint breeze stirred the shadows. To the west loomed the huge red ball of the sinking sun, now vanishing down the vapoury horizon, and filling the great heaven, high across whose arch the cranes and wild fowl streamed in line, square, and triangle, with flashes of flying gold and the lurid stain of blood. And then ourselves—three modern Englishmen in a modern English boat—seeming to jar upon and looking out of tone with that measureless desolation; and in front of us the noble buck limned out upon a background of muddy sky.

Bang! Away he goes with a mighty bound. Leo has missed him. *Bang!* right under him again. Now for a shot. I must have one, though he is going like an arrow, and a hundred yards away and more. By Jove! over and over and over! "Well, I think I wiped your eye there, Master Leo," I say, struggling against the ungenerous exultation that in such a supreme moment of one's existence will rise in the best-mannered sportsman's breast.

"Confound you, yes," growled Leo; and then, with that quick smile that is one of his charms lighting up his handsome face like a ray of light, "I beg your pardon, old fellow. I congratulate you; it was a lovely shot, and mine were vile."

We got out of the boat and ran to the buck, which was shot through the spine and stone dead. It took us a quarter of an hour or more to clean it and cut off as much of the best meat as we could carry, and, having packed this away, we barely had enough time to row up into the lagoon-like space, into which, there being a hollow in the swamp, the river here expanded. Just as the light vanished we cast anchor about thirty fathoms from the edge of the lake. We did not dare to go ashore, not knowing if we should find dry ground to camp on, and greatly fearing the poisonous exhalations from the marsh, from which we thought we should be freer on the water. So we lighted a lantern, and made our evening meal off another potted tongue in the best fashion we could, and then prepared to go to sleep, only, however, to find that sleep was impossible. For, whether they were attracted by the lantern, or the unaccustomed smell of a white man, for which they had been waiting for the last thousand years or so, I know not; but certainly we were attacked by tens of thousands of the most bloodthirsty, pertinacious, and huge mosquitos that I ever saw or read of. In clouds they came, pinged and buzzed and bit till we were nearly mad. Tobacco smoke only seemed to stir them into a merrier and more active life, till at length we were driven to covering ourselves with blankets, head and all, and sitting slowly to stew and continually scratch and swear beneath them. And as we sat, suddenly rolling out like thunder through the silence came the deep roar of a lion, and then of a second lion, moving among the reeds within sixty yards of us.

"I say," said Leo, sticking his head out from under his blanket, "lucky we ain't on the bank, eh, Avuncular?" (Leo sometimes addressed me in this disrespectful way.) "Curse it! A mosquito has bitten me on the nose," and the head vanished again. Shortly after this the moon came up, and notwithstanding every variety of roar that echoed over the water to us from the lions on the banks, we began, thinking ourselves perfectly secure, to gradually doze off.

I do not quite know what it was that made me poke my head out of the friendly shelter of the blanket, perhaps because I found out the mosquitos were biting right through it. Anyhow, as I did so I heard Job whisper, in a frightened voice—

"Oh, my stars, look there!"

Instantly we all of us looked, and this was what we saw in the moonlight. Near the shore were two wide and ever-widening circles of concentric rings rippling away across the surface of the water, and in the heart and centre of the circles were two dark moving objects.

"What is it?" asked I.

"It's those damn lions, sir," answered Job, in a tone which was an odd mixture of a sense of personal injury, habitual respect, and acknowledged fear, "and they are swimming here to *h*eat us," he added, nervously picking up an "h" in his agitation.

I looked again, and there was no doubt about it; I could catch the glare of their ferocious eyes. Attracted either by the smell of the newly killed waterbuck meat or of ourselves, the hungry beasts were actually storming our position.

Leo already had his rifle in his hand. I called to him to wait till they were nearer, and meanwhile grabbed my own. Some fifteen feet from us the water shallowed on a bank to a depth of about fifteen inches, and presently the first of them—it was the lioness—got to it and shook herself and roared. At that moment Leo fired, and the bullet went right down her open mouth and out at the back of her neck, and down she dropped, with a splash, dead. The other lion—a full grown male—was some two paces behind her. At this second he got his forepaws on to the bank when a strange thing happened. There was a rush and disturbance of the water, such as one sees in a pond in England when a pike takes a little fish, only a thousand times fiercer and larger, and suddenly the lion gave a most terrific snarling roar and sprang forward on to the bank, dragging something black with him.

"Allah!" shouted Mahomed, "a crocodile has got him by the leg!" and sure enough he had. We could see the large snout with its gleaming lines of teeth and the reptile body behind it.

And then followed an extraordinary scene indeed. The lion managed to get well on to the bank, the crocodile half standing and half swimming, still nipping his hind leg. He roared till the air quivered with the sound, and then, with a savage snarl, turned round and clawed hold of the crocodile's head. The crocodile shifted his grip, having, as we afterwards discovered, had one of his eyes torn out, and slightly turned over, and instantly the lion got him by the throat and held on, and then over and over they rolled upon the bank struggling hideously. It was impossible to follow their movements, but when next we got a clear view the tables had turned, for the crocodile, whose head seemed to be a mass of gore, had got the lion's body in his iron jaws just above the hips, and was squeezing him and shaking him to and fro. For his part the tortured brute, roaring in agony, was clawing and biting madly at his enemy's scaly head, and fixing his great hind claws in the crocodile's, comparatively speaking, soft throat, ripping it open as one would rip a glove.

Then, all of a sudden, the end came. The lion's head fell forward on the crocodile's back, and with an awful groan he died, and the crocodile, after standing for a minute motionless, slowly rolled over on to his side, his jaws still fixed across the carcase of the lion, which we afterwards found he had bitten almost in halves.

This duel to the death was a wonderful and shocking sight, and one that I suppose few men have seen—and thus it ended.

The Elephant's Child

From Just So Stories *(1902)*
By Rudyard Kipling

⤬

How can you possibly have a book of jungle stories without including one by Rudyard Kipling? This avatar of the British Empire, Nobel Prize–winning author, and part-time resident of Brattleboro, Vermont, was justly famous for telling stories of high adventure in exotic locales. Gunga Din, Kim, Captain's Courageous, *and* The Jungle Book *are but a few titles in a career that included journalism, poetry, short stories, novels, and even plays. Kipling was born in Bombay, India, in 1865, educated in England, and spent the greater part of his years shuttling between the two countries. He cut his writer's teeth as a correspondent for the Allabad* Pioneer *in India, and he later covered the Boer war in South Africa for the London* Times, *but it is mostly his novels and short stories that endure. Many critics have accused Kipling of being mawkish and sentimental, but it must be noted that whether you identify with his Imperialist leanings or not, his writing has a simple clarity that appeals to a mass audience and which has kept the popularity of his work very high since his death in 1936.*

For this collection we have chosen a wonderful, whimsical piece from the Just So Stories, *a collection of short fables that has enchanted children and adults alike since its publication at the turn of the century. This piece,* The Elephant's Child, *may be better known by its more familiar title "How the Elephant Got Its Trunk."* (MWC)

In the High and Far-Off Times the Elephant, O Best Beloved, had no trunk. He had only a blackish, bulgy nose, as big as a boot, that he could wriggle about from side to side; but he couldn't pick up things with it. But there was one Elephant—a new Elephant—an Elephant's Child—who was full of 'satiable curtiosity, and that means he asked ever so many questions. *And* he lived in Africa, and he filled Africa with his 'satiable curtiosities. He asked his tall aunt, the Ostrich, why her tail-feathers grew just so, and his tall aunt the Ostrich spanked him with her hard, hard claw. He asked his tall uncle, the Giraffe, what made his skin spotty, and his tall uncle, the Giraffe, spanked him with his hard, hard hoof. And still he was full of 'satiable curtiosity! He asked his broad aunt, the Hippopotamus, why her eyes were red, and his broad aunt, the Hippopotamus, spanked him with her broad, broad hoof; he asked his hairy uncle, the Baboon, why melons tasted just so, and his hairy uncle, the Baboon, spanked him with his hairy, hairy paw. And *still* he was full of 'satiable curtiosity! He asked questions about everything that he saw, or heard, or felt, or smelt, or touched, and all his uncles and aunts spanked him. And still he was full of 'satiable curtiosity.

One fine morning in the middle of the Procession of the Equinoxes this 'satiable Elephant's Child asked a new fine question that he had never asked before. He asked, "What does the Crocodile have for dinner?" Then everybody said, "Hush!" in a loud and dretful tone, and they spanked him immediately and directly, without stopping, for a long time.

By and by, when that was finished, he came upon Kolokolo Bird sitting in the middle of a wait-a-bit thorn-bush, and he said, "My father has spanked me, and my mother has spanked me; all my aunts and uncles have spanked me for my 'satiable curtiosity; and I *still* want to know what the Crocodile has for dinner!"

Then Kolokolo Bird said, with a mournful cry, "Go to the banks of the great grey-green greasy Limpopo River, all set about with fever-trees, and find out."

That very next morning, when there was nothing left of the Equinoxes, because Procession had preceded according to precedent, this 'satiable Elephant's Child took a hundred pounds of bananas (the little short red kind), and a hundred pounds of sugar-cane (the long purple kind), and seventeen melons (the greeny-crackly kind), and said to all his dear families, "Good-bye. I am going to the great grey-green greasy Limpopo River, all set about with fever-trees, to find out what the crocodile has for dinner." And they all spanked him once more for luck, though he asked them most politely to stop.

Then he went away, a little warm, but not at all astonished, eating melons, and throwing the rind about, because he could not pick it up.

He went from Graham's Town to Kimberley, and from Kimberley to Khama's Country, and from Khama's Country he went east by north, eating melons all the time, till at last he came to the banks of the great grey-green greasy Limpopo River, all set about with fever-trees, precisely as Kolokolo Bird had said.

Now you must know and understand, O Best Beloved, that till that very week, and day, and hour, and minute, this 'satiable Elephant's Child had never seen a Crocodile, and did not know what one was like. It was all his 'satiable curtiosity.

The first thing that he found was a Bi-Coloured-Python-Rock-Snake curled around a rock.

" 'Scuse me," said the Elephant's Child most politely, "but have you seen such a thing as a Crocodile in these promiscuous parts?"

"*Have* I seen a Crocodile?" said the Bi-Coloured-Python-Rock-Snake, in a voice of dretful scorn. "What will you ask me next?"

" 'Scuse me," said the Elephant's Child, "but could you kindly tell me what he has for dinner?"

Then the Bi-Coloured-Python-Rock-Snake uncoiled himself very quickly from the rock, and spanked the Elephant's Child with his scale-some, flailsome tail.

"That is odd," said the Elephant's Child, "because my father, and my mother, and my uncle and my aunt, not to mention my other aunt, the Hippopotamus, and my other uncle, the Baboon, have all spanked me for my 'satiable curtiosity—and I suppose this is the same thing."

So he said good-bye very politely to the Bi-Coloured-Python-Rock-Snake, and helped to coil him up on the rock again, and went on, a little warm, but not at all astonished, eating melons, and throwing the rind about, because he could not pick it up, till he trod on what he thought was a log of wood at the very edge of the great grey-green greasy Limpopo River, all set about with fever-trees.

But it was really the Crocodile, O Best Beloved, and the Crocodile winked one eye—like this!

" 'Scuse me," said the Elephant's Child most politely, "but do you happen to have seen a Crocodile in these promiscuous parts?"

Then the Crocodile winked the other eye, and lifted his tail out of the mud; and the Elephant's Child stepped back most politely, because he did not wish to be spanked again.

"Come hither, Little One," said the Crocodile. "Why do you ask such things?"

" 'Scuse me," said the Elephant's Child most politely, "but my father has spanked me, my mother has spanked me, not to mention my tall aunt, the Ostrich, and my tall uncle, the Giraffe, who can kick ever so hard, as well as my broad aunt, the Hippopotamus, and my hairy uncle, the Baboon, *and* including the Bi-Coloured-Python-Rock-Snake, with the scalesome, flailsome tail, just up the bank, who spanks harder than any of them; and *so,* if it's quite all the same to you, I don't want to be spanked any more."

"Come hither, Little One," said the Crocodile, "for I am the Croco-dile," and he wept crocodile-tears to show it was quite true.

Then the Elephant's Child grew all breathless, and panted, and kneeled down on the bank and said, "You are the very person I have been looking for all these long days. Will you please tell me what you have for dinner?"

"Come hither, Little One," said the Crocodile, "and I'll whisper."

Then the Elephant's Child put his head down close to the Crocodile's musky, tusky mouth, and the crocodile caught him by his little nose, which up to that very week, day, hour, and minute, had been no bigger than a boot, though much more useful.

"I think," said the Crocodile—and he said it between his teeth, like this—"I think to-day I will begin with Elephant's Child!"

At this, O Best Beloved, the Elephant's Child was much annoyed, and he said, speaking through his nose, like this, "Led go! You are hurtig be!"

Then the Bi-Coloured-Python-Rock-Snake scuffled down from the bank and said, "My Young friend, if you do not now, immediately and instantly, pull as hard as ever you can, it is my opinion that your acquaintance in the large-pattern leather ulster" (and by this he meant the Crocodile) "will jerk you into yonder limpid stream before you can say Jack Robinson."

This is the way Bi-Colored-Python-Rock-Snakes always talk.

Then the Elephant's Child sat back on his little haunches, and pulled, and pulled, and pulled, and his nose began to stretch. And the Crocodile floundered into the water, making it all creamy with great sweeps of his tail, and *he* pulled, and pulled, and pulled.

And the Elephant's Child's nose kept on stretching; and the Elephant's Child spread all his little four legs and pulled, and pulled, and pulled, and his nose kept on stretching; and the Crocodile threshed his tail like an oar, and *he* pulled, and pulled, and pulled, and at each pull the Elephant Child's nose grew longer and longer—and it hurt him hijjus!

Then the Elephant's Child felt his legs slipping, and he said through his nose, which was now nearly five feet long, "This is too butch for be!"

Then the Bi-Coloured-Python-Rock-Snake came down from the bank, and knotted himself in a double-clove-hitch round the Elephant Child's hind legs, and said, "Rash and inexperienced traveller, we will now seriously devote ourselves to a little high tension, because if we do not, it is my impression that yonder self-propelling man-of-war with the armour-plated upper deck" (and by this, O Best Beloved, he meant the Crocodile), "will permanently vitiate your future career."

That is the way all Bi-Coloured-Python-Rock-Snakes always talk.

So he pulled, and the Elephant's Child pulled, and the Crocodile pulled; but the Elephant's Child and the Bi-Coloured-Python-Rock-Snake pulled hardest; and at last the Crocodile let go of the Elephant's Child's nose with a plop that you could hear all the way up and down the Limpopo.

Then the Elephant's Child sat down most hard and sudden; but first he was careful to say "Thank You" to the Bi-Coloured-Python-Rock-Snake; and next he was kind to his poor pulled nose, and wrapped it up in cool banana leaves, and hung it in the great grey-green greasy Limpopo to cool.

"What are you doing that for?" said the Bi-Coloured-Python-Rock-Snake.

" 'Scuse me," said the Elephant's Child, "but my nose is badly out of shape, and I am waiting for it to shrink."

"Then you will have to wait a long time," said the Bi-Coloured-Python-Rock-Snake. "Some People do not know what is good for them."

The Elephant's Child sat there for three days waiting for his nose to shrink. But it never grew any shorter, and, besides, it made him squint. For, O Best Beloved, you will see and understand that the Crocodile had pulled it out into a really truly trunk same as all Elephants have to-day.

At the end of the third day a fly came and stung him on the shoulder, and before he knew what he was doing he lifted up his trunk and hit that fly dead with the end of it.

" 'Vantage number one!" said the Bi-Coloured-Python-Rock-Snake. "You couldn't have done that with a mere-smear nose. Try and eat a little now."

Before he thought what he was doing the Elephant's Child put out his trunk and plucked a large bundle of grass, dusted it clean against his fore-legs, and stuffed it into his own mouth.

" 'Vantage number two!" said the Bi-Coloured-Python-Rock-Snake. "You couldn't have done that with a mere-smear nose. Don't you think the sun is very hot here?"

"It is," said the Elephant's Child, and before he thought what he was doing he schlooped up a schloop of mud from the banks of the great grey-green greasy Limpopo, and slapped it on his head, where it made a cool schloopy-sloshy mud-cap all trickly behind his ears.

" 'Vantage number three!" said the Bi-Coloured-Python-Rock-Snake. "You couldn't have done that with a mere-smear nose. Now how do you feel about being spanked again?"

" 'Scuse me," said the Elephant's Child, "but I should not like it at all."

"How would you like to spank somebody?" said the Bi-Coloured-Python-Rock-Snake.

"I should like it very much indeed," said the Elephant's Child.

"Well," said the Bi-Coloured-Python-Rock-Snake, "you will find that new nose of yours very useful to spank people with."

"Thank you," said the Elephant's Child, "I'll remember that; and now I think I'll go home to all my dear families and try."

So the Elephant's Child went home across Africa frisking and whisking his trunk. When he wanted fruit to eat he pulled fruit down from a tree, instead of waiting for it to fall as he used to do. When he wanted grass he plucked grass up from the ground, instead of going on his knees as he used to do. When the flies bit him he broke off the branch of a tree and used it as a fly-whisk; and made himself a new, cool, slushy-squshy mud-cap whenever the sun was hot. When he felt lonely walking through Africa he sang to himself down his trunk, and the noise was louder than several brass bands. He went especially out of his way to find a broad Hippopotamus (she was no relation of his), and he spanked her very hard, to make sure that the Bi-Coloured-Python-Rock-Snake had spoken the truth about his new trunk. The rest of the time he picked up the melon rinds he had dropped on his way to the Limpopo—for he was a Tidy Pachyderm.

One dark evening he came back to all his dear families, and he coiled up his trunk and said, "How do you do?" They were very glad to see him, and immediately said, "Come here and be spanked for your 'satiable curtiosity."

"Pooh," said the Elephant's Child. "I don't think you peoples know anything about spanking; but *I* do, and I'll show you."

Then he uncurled his trunk and knocked two of his dear brothers head over heels.

"O, Bananas!" said they, "where did you learn that trick, and what have you done to your nose?"

"I got a new one from the Crocodile on the banks of the great grey-green greasy Limpopo River," said the Elephant's Child. "I asked him what he had for dinner, and he gave me this to keep."

"It looks very ugly," said his hairy uncle, the Baboon.

"It does," said the Elephant's Child. "But it's very useful," and he picked up his hairy uncle, the Baboon, by one hairy leg, and hove him into a hornet's nest.

Then that bad Elephant's Child spanked all his dear families for a long time, till they were very warm and greatly astonished. He pulled out his tall Ostrich aunt's tail-feathers; and he caught his tall uncle, the Giraffe, by the hind-leg, and dragged him through a thorn-bush; and he shouted at his broad aunt, the Hippopotamus, and blew bubbles into her ear when she was sleeping in the water after meals; but he never let anyone touch Kolokolo Bird.

At last things grew so exciting that his dear families went off one by one in a hurry to the banks of the great grey-green greasy Limpopo River, all set about with fever-trees, to borrow new noses from the Crocodile. When they came back nobody spanked anybody any more; and ever since that day, O Best Beloved, all the Elephants you will ever see, besides all those that you won't, have trunks precisely like the trunk of the 'satiable Elephant's Child.

Wonderful Things Happened

From The Lost World *(1912)*
By Sir Arthur Conan Doyle

Sir Arthur Conan Doyle is, of course, best known for his detective stories starring the famous character Sherlock Holmes. The novel from which this excerpt comes is one of his few successful works outside of the Holmes canon.

To set the story of The Lost World: *The narrator is a cub reporter for a great metropolitan London newspaper who has accepted an assignment to accompany a party of three on an expedition to the remote tepui highlands; to one of those weird tabletop plateaux in southern Venezuela. They are traveling to this remote jungle area in the company of Professor George E. Challenger to ascertain if his claims are true: that he has seen living examples of "prehistoric" animals on a previous trip. This scene takes place on the expedition's second day on top of the tepui—they have already witnessed a flock of "iguanadons" (large reptiles that resemble a stegosaurus), and are investigating the strange doings just over the top of the next wee hill. (MWC)*

It was destined that on this very morning—our first in the new country—we were to find out what strange hazards lay around us. It was a loathsome adventure, and one of which I hate to think. If, as Lord John said, the glade of the iguanadons will remain with us as a dream, then surely the swamp of the pterodactyls will for ever be our nightmare.

We passed very slowly through the woods, partly because Lord John acted as scout before he let us advance, and partly because at every second step one or another of our professors would fall, with a cry of wonder, before some flower or insect which presented him with a new type. We may have travelled two or three miles in all, keeping to the right of the line of the stream, when we came upon a considerable opening in the trees. A belt of brushwood led up to a tangle of rocks—the whole plateau was strewn with boulders. We were walking slowly towards these rocks, among bushes which reached over our waists, when we became aware of a strange low gabbling and whistling sound, which filled the air with a constant clamour and appeared to come from some spot immediately before us. Lord John held up his hand as a signal to us to stop, and he made his way swiftly, stooping and running, to the line of rocks. We saw him peep over them and give a gesture of amazement. Then he stood staring as if forgetting us, so utterly entranced was he by what he saw. Finally he waved us to come on, holding up his hand as a signal for caution. His whole bearing made me feel that something wonderful but dangerous lay before us.

Creeping to his side, we looked over the rocks. The place into which we gazed was a pit, and may, in the early days, have been one of the smaller volcanic blow-holes of the plateau. It was bowl-shaped, and at the bottom, some hundreds of yards from where we lay, were pools of green-scummed, stagnant water, fringed with bullrushes. It was a weird place in itself, but its occupants made it seem like a scene from the Seven Circles of Dante. The place was a rookery of pterodactyls. There were hundreds of them congregated within view. All the bottom area round the water-edge was alive with their young ones, and with hideous mothers brooding upon their leathery, yellowish eggs. From this crawling flapping mass of obscene reptilian life came the shocking clamour which filled the air and the mephistic, horrible, musty odour which turned us sick. But above, perched each upon its own stone, tall, grey, and withered, more like dead and dried specimens than actual living creatures, sat the horrible males, absolutely motionless save for the rolling of their red eyes or an occasional snap of their rat-trap beaks as a dragon-fly went past them. Their huge, membranous wings were closed by folding their fore-arms, so that they sat like gigantic old women, wrapped in hideous web-coloured shawls, and with their ferocious heads protruding above them. Large and small, not less than a thousand of these filthy creatures lay in the hollow before us.

Our professors would gladly have stayed there all day, so entranced were they by this opportunity of studying the life of a prehistoric age. They pointed out the fish and dead birds lying about among the rocks as proving the nature of the food of these creatures, and I heard them congratulating each other on having cleared up the point why the bones of this flying dragon are found in such great numbers in certain well-defined areas, as in the Cambridge Green-sand, since it was now seen that, like penguins, they lived in a gregarious fashion.

Finally, however, Challenger, bent upon proving some point which Summerlee had contested, threw his head over the rock and nearly brought destruction upon us all. In an instant the nearest male gave a shrill, whistling cry, and flapped its twenty-foot span of leathery wings as it soared up into the air. The females and young ones huddled together beside the water, while the whole circle of sentinels rose one after another and sailed off into the sky. It was a wonderful sight to see at least a hundred creatures of such enormous size and hideous appearance all swooping like swallows with swift, shearing wingstrokes above us; but soon we realized that it was not one on which we could afford to linger. At first the great brutes flew round in a huge ring, as if to make sure what the exact extent of the danger might be. Then, the flight grew lower and the circle narrower, until they were whizzing round and round us, the dry, rustling flap of their huge slate-coloured wings filling the air with a volume of sound that made me think of Hendon aerodrome upon a race day.

"Make for the wood and keep together," cried Lord John, clubbing his rifle. "The brutes mean mischief."

The moment we attempted to retreat the circle closed in upon us, until the tips of the wings of those nearest to us nearly touched our faces. We beat at them with the stocks of our guns, but there was nothing solid or vulnerable to strike. Then suddenly out of the whizzing, slate-coloured circle a long neck shot out, and a fierce beak made a thrust at us. Another and another followed. Summerlee gave a cry and put his hand to his face, from which the blood was streaming. I felt a prod at the back of my neck, and turned dizzy with the shock. Challenger fell, and as I stooped to pick him up I was struck from behind and dropped on the top of him. At the same instant I heard the crash of Lord John's elephant-gun, and, looking up, saw one of the creatures with a broken wing struggling upon the ground, spitting and gurgling at us with a wide-opened beak and blood-shot, goggled eyes, like some devil in a mediæval picture. Its comrades had flown higher at the sudden sound, and were circling above our heads.

"Now," cried Lord John, "now for our lives!"

We staggered through the brushwood, and even as we reached the trees the harpies were on us again. Summerlee was knocked down, but we tore him up and rushed among the trunks. Once there we were safe, for those huge wings had no space for their sweep beneath the branches. As we limped homewards, sadly mauled and discomfited, we saw them for a long time flying at great height against the deep blue sky above our heads, soaring round and round, no bigger than woodpigeons, with their eyes no doubt still following our progress. At last, however, as we reached the thicker woods they gave up the chase, and we saw them no more.

"A most interesting and challenging experience," said Challenger, as we halted beside the brook and he bathed a swollen knee. "We are exceptionally well informed, Summerlee, as to the habits of the enraged pterodactyl."

The Call of the Primitive

From Tarzan of the Apes *(1914)*
By Edgar Rice Burroughs

I think I was about nine years old when I saw my first Tarzan movie. I had to wait until I was in my mid-thirties to read the book. What a wonder! If only the Hays Office in 1930s Hollywood had allowed as much sex in the films as there is in this passage from the original novel. Burroughs certainly hit a nerve with this work, the first of twenty-three Tarzan novels that he wrote himself. Since then, there have been countless other novels, comic books, movies, television programs, as well as ripoffs of this, the original "Lord of the Jungle" story. Truly, this character Tarzan has entered the pantheon of modern myth.

In case you are not familiar with the original story, let us say only that Tarzan is the son of Lord and Lady Greystoke, who were put ashore by vicious pirates on the untamed African coast. Raised by a tribe of apes after his parents' deaths, he has just relinquished what primatologists call the "alpha male" position within his tribe.

In this passage he battles a rival ape, Terkoz, for possession of the fair Jane Porter, who is visiting the same coast with her father and his party. (MWC)

From the time Tarzan had left the tribe of great anthropoids in which he had been raised, it was torn by continual strife and discord. Terkoz proved a cruel and capricious king, so that, one by one, many of the older and weaker apes, upon whom he was particularly prone to vent his brutish nature, took their families and sought the quiet and safety of the far interior.

But at last those who remained were driven to desperation by the continued truculence of Terkoz, and it so happened that one of them recalled the parting admonition of Tarzan:

"If you have a chief who is cruel, do not do as the other apes do, and attempt, any one of you, to pit yourself against him alone. But, instead, let two or three or four of you attack him together. Then, if you will do this, no chief will dare to be other than he should be, for four of you can kill any chief who may ever be over you."

And the ape who recalled this wise counsel repeated it to several of his fellows, so that when Terkoz returned to the tribe that day he found a warm reception awaiting him.

There were no formalities. As Terkoz reached the group, five huge, hairy beasts sprang upon him.

At heart he was an arrant coward, which is the way with bullies among apes as well as men; so he did not remain to fight and die, but tore himself away from them as quickly as he could and fled into the sheltering boughs of the forest.

Two more attempts he made to rejoin the tribe, but on each occasion he was set upon and driven away. At last he gave it up and turned, foaming with rage and hatred, into the jungle.

For several days he wandered aimlessly, nursing his spite and looking for some weak thing on which to vent his pent anger.

It was in this state of mind that the horrible, man-like beast, swinging from tree to tree, came suddenly upon two women in the jungle.

He was right above them when he discovered them. The first intimation Jane Porter had of his presence was when the great hairy body dropped to the earth beside her, and she saw the awful face and the snarling, hideous mouth thrust within a foot of her.

One piercing scream escaped her lips as the brute hand clutched her arm. Then she was dragged toward those awful fangs which yawned at her throat. But ere they touched that fair skin another mood claimed the anthropoid.

The tribe had kept his women. He must find others to replace them. This hairless white ape would be the first of his new household, and so he threw her roughly across his broad, hairy shoulders and leaped back into the trees, bearing Jane Porter away toward a fate a thousand times worse than death.

Esmeralda's scream of terror had mingled once with that of Jane Porter, and then, as was Esmeralda's manner under stress of emergency which required presence of mind, she swooned.

But Jane Porter did not once lose consciousness. It is true that awful face, pressing close to hers, and the stench of the foul breath beating upon her nostrils, paralyzed her with terror, but her brain was clear, and she comprehended all that transpired.

With what seemed to her marvelous rapidity the brute bore her through the forest, but still she did not cry out or struggle. The sudden advent of the ape had confused her to such an extent that she thought now that he was bearing her toward the beach.

For this reason she conserved her energies and her voice until she could see that they had approached near enough to the camp to attract the succor she craved.

Poor child! Could she but have known it, she was being borne farther and farther into the impenetrable jungle.

The scream that had brought Clayton and the two older men stumbling through the undergrowth had led Tarzan of the Apes straight to where Esmeralda lay, but it was not Esmeralda in whom his interest centered, though pausing over her he saw that she was unhurt.

For a moment he scrutinized the ground below and the trees above, until the ape that was in him by virtue of training and environment, combined with the intelligence that was his by right of birth, told his wondrous woodcraft the whole story as plainly as though he had seen the thing happen with his own eyes.

And then he was gone again into the swaying trees, following the high-flung spoor which no other human eye could have detected, much less translated.

At boughs' ends, where the anthropoid swings from one tree to another, there is most to mark the trail, but least to point the direction of the quarry, for there the pressure is downward always, toward the small end of the branch, whether the ape be leaving or entering a tree; but nearer the center of the tree, where the signs of passage are fainter, the direction is plainly marked.

Here on this branch, a caterpillar has been crushed by the fugitive's great foot, and Tarzan knows instinctively where that same foot would touch in the next stride. Here he looks to find a tiny particle of the demolished larva, oft-times not more than a speck of moisture.

Again, a minute bit of bark has been upturned by the scraping hand, and the direction of the break indicates the direction of the passage. Or some great limb, or the stem of the tree itself has been brushed by the hairy body, and a tiny shred of hair tells him by the direction from which it is wedged beneath the bark that he is on the right trail.

Nor does he need to check his speed to catch these seemingly faint records of the fleeing beast.

To Tarzan they stand out boldly against all the myriad of other scars and bruises and signs upon the leafy way. But strongest of all is the scent, for Tarzan is pursuing up the wind, and his trained nostrils are as sensitive as a hound's.

There are those who believe that the lower orders are specially endowed by nature with better olfactory nerves than man, but it is merely a matter of development.

Man's survival does not hinge so greatly upon the perfection of his senses. His power to reason has relieved them of many of their duties, and so they have, to some extent, atrophied, as have the muscles which move the ears and scalp, merely from disuse. The muscles are there, about your ears and beneath your scalp, and so are the nerves which transmit sensations to your brain, but they are under-developed in you because you do not need them.

Not so with Tarzan of the Apes. From early infancy his survival had depended upon acuteness of eyesight, hearing, smell, touch, and taste far more than upon the more slowly developed organ of reason.

The least developed of all, in Tarzan, was the sense of taste, for he could eat luscious fruits, or raw flesh, long buried, with almost equal appreciation; but in that he differed but slightly from more civilized epicures.

Almost silently the ape-man sped on in the track of Terkoz and his prey, but the sound of his approach reached the ears of the fleeing beast and spurred it on to greater speed.

Three miles were covered before Tarzan overtook them, and then Terkoz, seeing that further flight was futile, dropped to the ground in a small open glade, that he might turn and fight for his prize, or be free to escape unhampered if he saw that the pursuer was more than a match for him.

He still grasped Jane Porter in one great arm as Tarzan bounded like a leopard into the arena which nature had provided for this primeval-like battle.

When Terkoz saw that it was Tarzan who pursued him, he jumped to the conclusion that this was Tarzan's woman, since they were of the same kind—white and hairless—and so he rejoiced at this opportunity for double revenge upon his hated enemy.

To Jane Porter the strange apparition of this god-like man was as wine to sick nerves.

From the description which Clayton and her father and Mr. Philander had given her, she knew that it must be the same wonderful creature who had saved them, and she saw in him only a protector and a friend.

But as Terkoz pushed her roughly aside to meet Tarzan's charge, and she saw the great proportions of the ape and the mighty muscles and the fierce fangs, her heart quailed. How could any animal vanquish such a mighty antagonist?

Like two charging bulls they came together, and like two wolves sought each other's throat. Against the long canines of the ape was pitted the thin blade of a man's knife.

Jane Porter—her lithe, young form flattened against the trunk of a great tree, her hands tight pressed against her rising and falling bosom, and her eyes wide with mingled horror, fascination, fear, and admiration—watched the primordial ape battle with the primeval man for possession of a woman—for her.

As the great muscles of the man's back and shoulders knotted beneath the tension of his efforts, and the huge biceps and forearm held at bay those mighty tusks, the veil of centuries of civilization and culture was swept from the blurred vision of the Baltimore girl.

When the long knife drank deep a dozen times of Terkoz' heart's blood, and the great carcass rolled lifeless upon the ground, it was a primeval woman who sprang forward with outstretched arms toward the primeval man who had fought for her and won her.

And Tarzan?

He did what no red-blooded man needs lessons in doing. He took his woman in his arms and smothered her upturned, panting lips with kisses.

For a moment Jane Porter lay there with half-closed eyes. For a moment—the first in her young life—she knew the meaning of love.

But as suddenly as the veil had been withdrawn it dropped again, an outraged conscience suffused her face with its scarlet mantle, and a mortified woman thrust Tarzan of the Apes from her and buried her face in her hands.

Tarzan had been surprised when he had found the girl he had learned to love after a vague and abstract manner a willing prisoner in his arms. Now he was surprised that she repulsed him.

He came close to her once more and took hold of her arm. She turned upon him like a tigress, striking his great breast with her tiny hands.

Tarzan could not understand it.

A moment ago it had been his intention to hasten Jane Porter back to her people, but that little moment was lost now in the dim and distant past of things which were but can never be again, and with it the good intention had gone to join the impossible.

Since then Tarzan of the Apes had felt a warm, lithe form close pressed to his. Hot, sweet breath against his cheek and mouth had fanned a new flame to life within his breast, and perfect lips had clung to his in burning kisses that had seared a deep brand to his soul—a brand which marked a new Tarzan.

Again he laid his hand upon her arm. Again she repulsed him. And then Tarzan of the Apes did just what his first ancestor would have done.

He took his woman in his arms and carried her into the jungle.

From Into the Heart of Darkness

By Joseph Conrad (1902)

~~~

Well, here it is—arguably the granddaddy of all modern jungle stories. Joseph Conrad (né Józef Teodor Konrad Korzeniowski) wrote this short novel sometime during 1898–99, and it is probably his most famous work. It is striking how the themes of this work—humankind's atavistic terror in the face of primordial nature, and the fragile veneer of civilization that so easily gets stripped away when we stare at the unbridled competition for living space that is "the bush" and see ourselves staring back—ring true still, nearly a century later. And to think that English was not Conrad's first language!

In this excerpt, Marlow, captain of a ramshackle steamboat, is headed up an unnamed river in search of the mysterious and near-mythical Mr. Kurtz.

Conrad places an ironic frame around this tale, the device being that Marlow is relating his story, in flashback form, to a group of colleagues as they sit on the aft deck of a schooner. We don't meet Kurtz here, but we do get an idea of the journey upriver, and of the welcome Marlow's party receives. (MWC)

"Going up that river was like traveling back to the earliest beginnings of the world, when vegetation rioted on the earth and the big trees were kings. An empty stream, a great silence, an impenetrable forest. The air was warm, thick, heavy, sluggish. There was no joy in the brilliance of sunshine. The long stretches of the waterway ran on, deserted, into the gloom of the overshadowed distances. On silvery sandbanks hippos and alligators sunned themselves side by side. The broadening waters flowed through a mob of wooded islands; you lost your way on that river as you would in a desert, and butted all day long against shoals, trying to find the channel, till you thought yourself bewitched and cut off forever from everything you had known once—somewhere—far away—in another existence perhaps. There were moments when one's past came back to one, as it will sometimes when you have not had a moment to spare yourself; but it came in the shape of an unrestful and noisy dream, remembered with wonder amongst the overwhelming realities of this strange world of plants, and water, and silence. And this stillness of life did not in the least resemble a peace. It was a stillness of an implacable force brooding over an inscrutable intention. It looked at you with a vengeful aspect. I got used to it afterwards; I did not see it anymore; I had no time. I had to keep guessing at the channel; I had to discern, mostly by inspiration, the signs of hidden banks; I watched for hidden stones; I was learning to clap my teeth smartly before my heart flew out, when I shaved by a fluke some infernal sly old snag that would have ripped the life out of the tin-pot steamboat and drowned all the pilgrims; I had to keep a lookout for the signs of deadwood we would cut up in the night for the next day's steaming. When you have to attend to things of that sort, to the mere incidents of the surface, the reality—the reality I tell you—fades. The inner truth is hidden—luckily, luckily. But I felt it all the same; I felt often its mysterious stillness watching me at my monkey tricks, just as it watches you fellows performing on your respective tightropes for—what is it? a half crown to tumble—"

"Try to be civil, Marlow," growled a voice, and I knew there was at least one listener awake besides myself.

"I beg your pardon. I forgot the heartache which makes up the rest of the price. And indeed what does the price matter, if the trick be well done? You do your trick very well. And I didn't do badly either, since I managed not to sink that steamboat on my first trip. It's a wonder to me yet. I imagine a blindfolded man set to drive a van over a bad road. I sweated and shivered over that business considerably, I can tell you. After all, for a seaman, to scrape the bottom of the thing that's supposed to float all the time under his care is the unpardonable sin. No one may know of it, but you never forget the thump—eh? A blow to your very heart. You remember it, you dream of it, you wake up at night and think of it—years after—and go hot and cold all over. I don't pretend to say that steamboat floated all the time. More than once she had to wade for a bit, with twenty cannibals splashing around and pushing. We enlisted some of these chaps on the way for a crew. Fine fellows—cannibals—in their place. They were men one could work with, and I am grateful to them. And, after all, they did not eat each other before my face: they had brought along a provision of hippo meat which went rotten, and made the mystery of the wilderness stink in my nostrils. Phoo! I can sniff it now. I had the manager on board and three or four pilgrims with their staves—all complete. Sometimes we came upon a station close to the bank, clinging to the skirts of the unknown, and the white men rushing out of a tumbledown hovel, with great gestures of joy and surprise and welcome, seemed very strange—had the appearance of being held there captive by a spell. The word ivory would ring in the air for a while—and on we went again into the silence, along empty reaches round the still bends, between the high walls of our winding way, reverberating in hollow claps the ponderous beat of the stern wheel. Trees, trees, millions of trees, massive, immense, running up high; and at their foot, hugging the bank against the stream, crept the little begrimed steamboat, like a sluggish beetle crawling on the floor of a lofty portico. It made you feel very small, very lost, and yet it was not altogether depressing, that feeling. After all, if you were small, the grimy beetle crawled on—which was just what you wanted it to do. Where the pilgrims imagined it crawled to I don't know. To some place where they expected to get something, I bet! For me it crawled towards Kurtz—exclusively; but when the steam pipes started leaking we started crawling very slow. The reaches opened before us and closed behind, as if the forest had stepped leisurely across the water to bar the way for our return. We penetrated deeper and deeper into the heart of darkness. It was very quiet there. At night sometimes the roll of drums behind the curtain of trees would run up the river and remain sustained faintly, as if hovering in the air high over our heads, till the first break of day. Whether it meant war, peace, or prayer we could not tell. The dawns were heralded by the descent of a chill stillness; the woodcutters slept, their fires burned low; the snapping of a twig would make you start. We were wanderers on prehistoric earth, on an earth that wore the aspect of an unknown planet. We could have fancied ourselves the first of men taking possession of an accursed inheritance, to be subdued at the cost of profound anguish and of excessive toil. But suddenly, as we struggled round a bend, there would be a glimpse of rush walls, of peaked grass roofs, a burst of yells, a whirl of black limbs, a mass of hands clapping, of feet stamping, of bodies swaying, of eyes rolling, under the droop of heavy and motionless foliage. The steamer toiled along slowly on the edge of a black and incomprehensible frenzy. The prehistoric man was cursing us, praying to us, welcoming us—who could tell? We were cut off from the comprehension of our surroundings; we glided past like phantoms, wondering and secretly appalled, as sane men would be before an enthusiastic outbreak in a madhouse. We could not understand because we were too far and could not remember, because we were traveling in the night of first ages, of those ages that are gone, leaving hardly a sign—and no memories.

"The earth seemed unearthly. We are accustomed to look upon the shackled form of a conquered monster, but there—there you could look at a thing monstrous and free. It was unearthly, and the men were—No, they were not inhuman. Well, you know, that was the worst of it—this suspicion of their not being inhuman. It would come slowly to one. They howled and leaped, and spun, and made horrid faces; but what thrilled you was just the thought of their humanity—like yours—the thought of your remote kinship with this wild and passionate uproar. Ugly. Yes, it was ugly enough; but if you were man enough you would admit to yourself that there was in you just the faintest trace of a response to the terrible frankness of that noise, a dim suspicion of there being a meaning in it which you—you so remote from the night of first ages—could comprehend. And why not? The mind of man is capable of anything—because everything is in it, all the past as well as the future. What was there after all? Joy, fear, sorrow, devotion, valor, rage—who can tell?—but truth—truth stripped of its cloak of time. Let the fool gape and shudder—the man knows, and can look on without a wink. But he must at least be as much of a man as these on the shore. He must meet that truth with his own true stuff—with his own inborn strength. Principles won't do. Acquisitions, clothes, pretty rags—rags that would fly off at the first good shake. No; you want a deliberate belief. An appeal to me in this fiendish row—is there? Very well; I hear; I admit, but I have a voice, too, and for good or evil mine is the speech that cannot be silenced. Of course, a fool, what with sheer fright and fine sentiments, is always safe. Who's that grunting? You wonder I didn't go ashore for a howl and a dance? Well, no—I didn't. Fine sentiments, you say? Fine sentiments be hanged! I had no time. I had to mess about with white lead and strips of woolen blanket helping to put bandages on those leaky steam pipes—I tell you. I had to watch the steering, and circumvent those snags, and get the tin-pot along by hook or by crook. There was surface truth enough in these things to save a wiser man. And between whiles I had to look after the savage who was fireman. He was an improved specimen; he could fire up a vertical boiler. He was there below me, and, upon my word, to look upon him was as edifying as seeing a dog in a parody of breeches and a feather hat, walking on his hind legs. A few months of training had done for that really fine chap. He squinted at the steam gauge and at the water gauge with an evident effort of intrepidity—and he had filed teeth, too, the poor devil, and the wool of his pate shaved into queer patterns, and three ornamental scars on each of his cheeks. He ought to have been clapping his hands and stamping his feet on the bank, instead of which he was hard at work, a thrall to strange witchcraft, full of improving knowledge. He was useful because he had been instructed; and what he knew was this—that should the water in that transparent thing disappear, the evil spirit inside the boiler would get angry through the greatness of his thirst, and take a terrible vengeance. So he sweated and fired up, and watched the glass fearfully (with an impromptu charm, made of rags, tied to his arm, and a piece of polished bone, as big as a watch, stuck flatways through his lower lip), while the wooded banks slipped past us slowly, the short noise was left behind, the interminable miles of silence—and we crept on, towards Kurtz. But the snags were thick, the water was treacherous and shallow, the boiler seemed indeed to have a sulky devil in it, and thus neither fireman nor I had any time to peer into our creepy thoughts.

"Some fifty miles below the Inner Station we came upon a hut of reeds, an inclined and melancholy pole, with unrecognizable tatters of what had been a flag of some sort flying from it, and a neatly stacked wood pile. This was unexpected. We came to the bank, and on the stack of firewood found a flat piece of board with some faded pencil writing on it. When deciphered it said: 'Wood for you. Hurry up. Approach cautiously.' There was a signature, but it was illegible—not Kurtz—a much longer word. Hurry up. Where? Up the river? "Approach cautiously." We had not done so. But the warning could not have been meant for the place where it could be found only after approach. Something was wrong above. But what—and how much? That was the question. We commented adversely upon the imbecility of that telegraphic style. The bush around said nothing, and would not let us look very far, either. A torn curtain of red twill hung in the doorway of the hut, and flapped sadly in our faces. The dwelling was dismantled: but we could see a white man had lived there not very long ago. There remained a rude table—a plank on two posts; a heap of rubbish reposed in a dark corner, and by the door I picked up a book. It had lost its covers, and the pages had been thumbed into a state of extremely dirty softness; but the back had been lovingly stitched afresh with white cotton thread, which looked clean yet. It was an extraordinary find. Its title was, *An Inquiry into Some Points of Seamanship*, by a man named Tower, Towson—some such name—Master in his Majesty's Navy. The matter looked dreary reading enough, with illustrative diagrams and repulsive tables of figures, and the copy was sixty years old. I handled this amazing antiquity with the greatest possible tenderness, lest it should dissolve in my hands. Within, Towson or Tower was inquiring earnestly into the breaking strain of ships' chains and tackle, and other such matters. Not a very enthralling book; but at the first glance you could see there a singleness of intention, an honest concern for the right way of going to work, which made these humble pages, thought out so many years ago, luminous with another than a professional light. The simple old sailor, with his talk of chains and purchases, made me forget the jungle and the pilgrims in a delicious sensation of having come upon something unmistakably real. Such a book being there was wonderful enough; but still more astounding were the notes penciled in the margin, and plainly referring to the text. I couldn't believe my eyes! They were in cipher! Yes, it looked like cipher. Fancy a man lugging with him a book of that description into this nowhere and studying it—and making notes—in cipher at that! It was an extravagant mystery.

"I had been dimly aware for some time of worrying noise, and when I lifted my eyes I saw the wood pile was gone, and the manager, aided by all the pilgrims, was shouting at me from the river side. I slipped the book into my pocket. I assure you to leave off reading was like tearing myself away from the shelter of an old and solid friendship.

"I started the lame engine ahead. 'It must be this miserable trader—this intruder,' exclaimed the manager, looking back malevolently at the place we had left. 'He must be English,' I said. 'It will not save him from getting into trouble if he is not careful,' muttered the manager darkly. I observed with assumed innocence that no man was safe from trouble in this world.

"The current was more rapid now, the steamer seemed at her last gasp, the stern wheel flopped languidly, and I caught myself listening on tiptoe for the next beat of the boat, for in sober truth I expected the wretched thing to give up every moment. It was like watching the last flickers of a life. But still we crawled. Sometimes I would pick out a tree a little way ahead to measure our progress towards Kurtz by, but I lost it invariably before we got abreast. To keep the eyes so long on one thing was too much for human patience. The manager displayed a beautiful resignation. I fretted and fumed and took to arguing with myself whether or no I would talk openly with Kurtz; but before I could come to any conclusion it occurred to me that my speech or my silence, indeed any action of mine, would be a mere futility. What did it matter who was the manager? One gets sometimes such a flash of insight. The essentials of this affair lay deep under the surface, beyond my reach, and beyond my power of meddling.

"Towards the evening of the second day we judged ourselves about eight miles from Kurtz's station. I wanted to push on; but the manager looked grave, and told me the navigation up there was so dangerous that it would be advisable, the sun being very low already, to wait where we were till the next morning. Moreover, he pointed out that if the warning to approach cautiously were to be followed, we must approach in daylight—not at dusk, or in the dark. This was sensible enough. Eight miles meant nearly three hours' steaming for us, and I could also see suspicious ripples at the upper end of the reach. Nevertheless, I was annoyed beyond expression at the delay, and most unreasonably, too, since one night more could not matter so much after so many months. As we had plenty of wood, and caution was the word, I brought up in the middle of the stream. The reach was narrow, strait, with high sides like a railway cutting. The dusk came gliding into it long before the sun had set. The current ran smooth and swift, but a dumb immobility sat on the banks. The living trees, lashed together by the creepers and every living bush of the undergrowth, might have been changed into stone, even to the slenderest twig, to the lightest leaf. It was not sleep—it seemed unnatural, like a state of trance. Not the faintest sound of any kind could be heard. You looked on amazed, and began to suspect yourself of being deaf—then the night came suddenly, and struck you blind as well. About three in the morning some large fish leaped, and the loud splash made me jump as though a gun had been fired. When the sun rose there was a white fog, very warm and clammy, and more blinding than the night. It did not shift or drive; it was just there, standing all round you like something solid. At eight or nine, perhaps, it lifted as a shutter lifts. We had a glimpse of the towering multitude of trees, of the immense matted jungle, with the blazing little ball of the sun hanging over all—all perfectly still—and then the white shutter came down again, smoothly, as if sliding in greased grooves. I ordered the chain, which we had begun to heave in, to be paid out again. Before it stopped running with a muffled rattle, a cry, a very loud cry, as of infinite desolation, soared slowly in the opaque air. It ceased. A complaining clamor, modulated in savage discords, filled our ears. The sheer unexpectedness of it made my hair stir under my cap. I don't know how it struck the others: to me it seemed as though the mist itself had screamed, so suddenly, and apparently from all sides at once, did this tumultuous and mournful uproar arise. It culminated in a hurried outbreak of almost intolerably excessive shrieking, which stopped short, leaving us stiffened in a variety of silly attitudes, and obstinately listening to the nearly as appalling and excessive silence. 'Good God! What is the meaning—' stammered at my elbow one of the pilgrims, a little fat man, with sandy hair and red whiskers, who wore sidespring boots, and pink pajamas tucked into his socks. Two others remained openmouthed a whole minute, then dashed into the little cabin, to rush out incontinently and stand darting scared glances, with Winchesters at 'ready' in their hands. What we could see was just the steamer we were on, her outlines blurred as though she had been on the point of dissolving, and a misty strip of water, perhaps two feet broad, around her—and that was all. The rest of the world was nowhere, as far as our eyes and ears were concerned. Just nowhere. Gone, disappeared; swept off without leaving a whisper or a shadow behind.

"I went forward, and ordered the chain to be hauled in short, so as to be ready to trip the anchor and move the steamboat at once if necessary. 'Will they attack?' whispered an awed voice. 'We will all be butchered in this fog,' murmured another. The faces twitched with the strain, the hands trembled slightly, the eyes forgot to wink. It was very curious to see the contrast of expressions of the white men and of the black fellows of our crew, who were as much strangers to that part of the river as we, though their homes were only eight hundred miles away. The whites, of course greatly discomposed, had besides a curious look of being painfully shocked by such an outrageous row. The others had an alert, naturally interested expression; but their faces were essentially quiet, even those of the one or two who grinned as they hauled at the chain. Several exchanged short, grunting phrases, which seemed to settle the matter to their satisfaction. Their headman, a young, broadchested black, severely draped in dark-blue fringed cloths, with fierce nostrils and his hair all done up artfully in oily ringlets, stood near me. 'Aha!' I said, just for good fellowship's sake. 'Catch 'im,' he snapped, with a bloodshot widening of his eyes and a flash of sharp teeth—'catch 'im. Give 'im to us.' 'To you, eh?' I asked; 'what would you do with them?' 'Eat 'im!' he said, curtly, and, leaning his elbow on the rail, looked out into the fog in a dignified and profoundly pensive attitude. I would no doubt have been properly horrified, had it not occurred to me that he and his chaps must be very hungry: that they must have been growing increasingly hungry for at least this month past. They had been engaged for six months (I don't think a single one of them had any clear idea of time, as we at the end of countless ages have. They still belonged to the beginnings of time—had no inherited experience to teach them as it were), and of course, as long as there was a piece of paper written over in accordance with some farcical law or other made down the river, it didn't enter anybody's head to trouble how they would live. Certainly they had brought with them some rotten hippo meat, which couldn't have lasted very long, anyway, even if the pilgrims hadn't, in the midst of the shocking hullabaloo, thrown a considerable quantity of it overboard. It looked like a high-handed proceeding; but it was really a case of legitimate self-defense. You can't breathe dead hippo waking, sleeping, and eating, and at the same time keep your precarious grip on existence. Besides that, they had given them every week three pieces of brass wire, each about nine inches long; and the theory was they were to buy their provisions with that currency in river-side villages. You can see how *that* worked. There were either no villages, or the people were hostile, or the director, who like the rest of us fed out of tins, with an occasional old he-goat thrown in, didn't want to stop the steamer for some more or less recondite reasons. So, unless they swallowed the wire itself, or made loops of it to snare the fishes with, I don't see what good their extravagant salary could be to them. I must say it was paid with a regularity worthy of a large and honorable trading company. For the rest, the only thing to eat—though it didn't look eatable in the least—I saw in their possession was a few lumps of some stuff like half-cooked dough, of a dirty lavender color, they kept wrapped in leaves, and now and then swallowed a piece of, but so small it seemed done more for the looks of the thing than for any serious purpose of sustenance. Why in the name of all gnawing devils of hunger they didn't go for us—they were thirty to five—and have a good tuck in for once, amazes me now when I think of it. They were big powerful men, with not much capacity to weigh the consequences, with courage, with strength, even yet, though their skins were no longer glossy and their muscles no longer hard. And I saw that something restraining, one of those human secrets that baffle probability, had come into play there. I looked at them with a swift quickening of interest—not because it occurred to me I might be eaten by them before very long, though I owe it to you that just then I perceived—in a new light, as it were—how unwholesome the pilgrims looked, and I hoped, yes, I positively hoped, that my aspect was not so—what shall I say?—so unappetizing: a touch of fantastic vanity which fitted well with the dream-sensation that pervaded all my days at that time. Perhaps I had a little fever, too. One can't live with one's finger everlastingly on one's pulse. I had often 'a little fever,' or a little touch of other things—playful pawstrokes of the wilderness, the preliminary trifling before the more serious onslaught which came in due course. Yes; I looked at them as you would on any human being, with a curiosity of their impulses, motives, capacities, weaknesses, when brought to the test of an inexorable physical necessity. Restraint! What possible restraint? Was it superstition, disgust, patience, fear—or some kind of primitive honor? No fear can stand up to hunger, no patience can wear it out, disgust simply does not exist where hunger is; and as to superstition, beliefs, and what you may call principles, they are less than chaff in a breeze. Don't you know the deviltry of the lingering starvation, its exasperating torment, its black thoughts, its somber and brooding ferocity? Well, I do. It takes a man all his inborn strength to fight hunger properly. It's really easier to face bereavement, dishonor, and the perdition of one's soul—than this kind of reason for any kind of scruple. Sad, but true. And these chaps, too, had no earthly expected restraint from a hyena prowling amongst the corpses of a battlefield. But there was the fact facing me—the fact dazzling, to be seen, like the foam on the depths of the sea, like a ripple on an unfathomable enigma, a mystery greater—when I thought of it—than the curious inexplicable note of desperate grief in this savage clamor that had swept by us on the river bank, behind the blind whiteness of the fog.

"Two pilgrims were quarreling in hurried whispers as to which bank. 'Left.' 'No, no; how can you? Right, right, of course.' 'It is very serious,' said the manager's voice behind me; 'I would be desolated if anything should happen to Mr. Kurtz before we came up.' I looked at him, and had not the slightest doubt he was sincere. He was just the kind of man who would wish to preserve appearances. That was his restraint. But when he muttered something about going on at once, I did not even take the trouble to answer him. I knew, and he knew, that it was impossible. Were we to let go our hold of the bottom, we would be absolutely in the air—in space. We wouldn't be able to tell where we were going to—whether up or down-stream, or across—till we fetched against one bank or the other, and then we wouldn't know at first which it was. Of course I made no move. I had no mind for a smashup. You couldn't imagine a more deadly place for a shipwreck. Whether drowned at once or not, we were sure to perish speedily in one way or another. 'I authorize you to take all the risks,' he said, after a short silence. 'I refuse to take any,' I said shortly; which was just the answer he expected, though its tone might have surprised him. 'Well, I must defer to your judgement. You are captain,' he said, with marked civility. I turned my shoulder to him in sign of my appreciation, and looked into the fog. How long would it last? It was the most hopeless lookout. The approach to this Kurtz grubbing for ivory in the wretched bush was beset by as many dangers as though he had been an enchanted princess sleeping in a fabulous castle. 'Will they attack, do you think?' asked the manager, in a confidential tone.

"I did not think they would attack, for several obvious reasons. The thick fog was one. If they left the bank in their canoes they would get lost in it, as we would be if we attempted to move. Still, I had also judged the jungle of both banks impenetrable—and yet eyes were in it, eyes that had seen us. The riverside bushes were certainly very thick; but the undergrowth behind was evidently penetrable. However, during the short lift I had seen no canoes anywhere in the reach—certainly not abreast of the steamer. But what made the idea of attack inconceivable to me was the nature of the noise—of the cries we had heard. They had not the fierce character boding of immediate hostile intention. Unexpected, wild, and violent as they had been, they had given me an irresistible impression of sorrow. The glimpse of the steamboat had for some reason filled those savages with unrestrained grief. The danger, if any, I expounded, was from our proximity to a great human passion let loose. Even extreme grief may ultimately vent itself in violence—but more generally takes the form of apathy. . . .

"You should have seen the pilgrims stare! They had no heart to grin, or even to revile me: but I believe they thought me gone mad—with fright, maybe. I delivered a regular lecture. My dear boys, it was no good bothering. Keep a lookout? Well, you may guess I watched the fog for the signs of lifting as a cat watches a mouse; but for anything else our eyes were of no more use to us than if we had been buried miles deep in a heap of cotton-wool. It felt like it, too—choking, warm, stifling. Besides, all I said, though it sounded extravagant, it was absolutely true to fact. What we afterwards alluded to as an attack was really an attempt at repulse. The action was very far from being aggressive— it was not even defensive, in the usual sense: it was undertaken under the stress of desperation, and in its essence was purely protective.

"It developed itself, I should say, two hours after the fog lifted, and its commencement was at a spot, roughly speaking, about a mile and a half below Kurtz's station. We had just floundered and flopped around a bend, when I saw an islet, a mere grassy hummock of bright green, in the middle of the stream. It was the only thing of its kind; but as we opened the reach more, I perceived it was the head of a long sandbank, or rather a chain of shallow patches stretching down the middle of the river. They were discolored, just awash, and the whole lot was seen just under the water, exactly as a man's backbone is seen running down the middle of his back under the skin. Now, as far as I could see, I could go to the right or to the left of this. I didn't know either channel, of course. The banks looked pretty well alike, the depth appeared the same; but as I had been informed the station was on the west side, I naturally headed for the western passage.

"No sooner had we fairly entered it than I became aware it was much narrower than I had supposed. To the left of us there was a long uninterrupted shoal, and to the right a high, steep bank heavily over-grown with bushes. Above the bush the trees stood in serried ranks. The twigs overhung the current thickly, and from a distance a large limb of some tree projected rigidly over the stream. It was then well on in the afternoon, the face of the forest was gloomy, and a broad strip of shadow had already fallen on the water. In this shadow we steamed up—very slowly, as you may imagine. I sheered her well in-shore—the water being deepest near the bank, as the sounding pole informed me.

"One of my hungry and forbearing friends was sounding in the bows just below me. This steamboat was exactly like a decked scow. On the deck, there were two little teakwood houses, with doors and windows. The boiler was in the fore-end, and the machinery right astern. Over the whole there was a light roof, supported on stanchions. The funnel projected through that roof, and in front of the funnel a small cabin built of light planks served for a pilot house. It contained a couch, two campstools, a loaded Martini-Henry leaning in one corner, a tiny table, and the steering wheel. It had a wide door in front and a broad shutter at each side. All these were always thrown open, of course. I spent my days perched up there on the extreme fore-end of that roof, before the door. At night I slept, or tried to, on the couch. An athletic black belonging to some coast tribe, and educated by my poor predecessor, was the helmsman. He sported a pair of brass earrings, wore a blue cloth wrapper from the waist to the ankles, and thought all the world of himself. He was the most unstable kind of fool I had ever seen. He steered with no end of swagger while you were by; but if he lost sight of you, he became instantly the prey of an abject funk, and would let that cripple of a steamboat get the upper hand of him in a minute.

"I was looking down at the sounding pole, and feeling much annoyed to see at each try a little more of it stick out of that river, when I saw my poleman give up the business suddenly, and stretch himself flat on the deck, without even taking the trouble to haul his pole in. He kept hold on it though, and it trailed in the water. At the same time the fireman, whom I could also see below me, sat down abruptly before his furnace and ducked his head. I was amazed. Then I had to look at the river mighty quick, because there was a snag in the fairway. Sticks, little sticks, were flying about—thick: they were whizzing past my nose, dropping below me, striking behind me against my pilot house. All this time the river, the shore, the woods, were very quiet—perfectly quiet. I could only hear the heavy splashing thump of the stern wheel and the patter of these things. We cleared the snag clumsily. Arrows, by Jove! We were being shot at! I stepped in quickly to close the shutter on the land side. That fool helmsman, his hands on the spokes, was lifting his knees high, stamping his feet, champing his mouth, like a reined-in horse. Confound him! And we were staggering within ten feet of the bank. I had to lean right out to swing the heavy shutter, and I saw a face amongst the leaves on the level with my own, looking at me very fierce and steady; and then suddenly, as though a veil had been removed from my eyes, I made out, deep in the tangled gloom, naked breasts, arms, legs, glaring eyes—the bush was swarming with human limbs in movement, glistening, of bronze color. The twigs shook, swayed, and rustled, the arrows flew out of them, and then the shutter came to. 'Steer her straight,' I said to the helmsman. He held his head rigid, face forward; but his eyes rolled, he kept on, lifting and setting down his feet gently, his mouth foamed a little. 'Keep quiet!' I said in a fury. I might just as well ordered a tree not to sway in the wind. I darted out. Below me there was a great scuffle of feet on the iron deck; confused exclamations; a voice screamed, 'Can you turn back?' I caught sight of a V-shaped ripple on the water ahead. What? Another snag! A fusillade burst out under my feet. The pilgrims had opened with their Winchesters, and were simply squirting lead into that bush. A deuce of a lot of smoke came up and drove slowly forward. I swore at it. Now I couldn't see the ripple or the snag either. I stood in the doorway, peering, and the arrows came in swarms. They might have been poisoned, but they looked as though they wouldn't kill a cat. The bush began to howl. Our woodcutters raised a warlike whoop; the report of a rifle just at my back deafened me. I glanced over my shoulder, and the pilot house was yet full of noise and smoke when I made a dash at the wheel. The fool nigger had dropped everything, to throw the shutter open and let off that Martini-Henry. He stood before the wide opening, glaring, and I yelled at him to come back, while I straightened the sudden twist out of that steamboat. There was no room to turn even if I had wanted to, the snag was somewhere very near ahead in that confounded smoke, there was no time to lose, so I just crowded her into the bank—right into the bank, where I knew the water was deep.

"We tore slowly along the overhanging bushes in a whirl of broken twigs and flying leaves. The fusillade below stopped short, as I had foreseen it would when the squirts got empty. I threw my head back to a glinting whizz that traversed our pilot house, in at one shutter-hole and out at the other. Looking past that mad helmsman, who was shaking the empty rifle and yelling at the shore, I saw vague forms of men running bent double, leaping, gliding, distinct, incomplete, evanescent. Something big appeared in the air before the shutter, the rifle went overboard, and the man stepped back swiftly, looked at me over his shoulder in an extraordinary, profound, familiar manner, and fell upon my feet. The side of his head hit the wheel twice, and the end of what appeared a long cane clattered round and knocked over a little campstool. It looked as though after wrenching that thing from somebody ashore he had lost his balance in the effort. The thin smoke had blown away, we were clear of the snag, and looking ahead I could see that in another hundred yards or so I would be free to shear off, away from the bank; but my feet felt so very warm and wet that I had to look down. The man had rolled on his back and stared straight up at me; both his hands clutched that cane. It was the shaft of a spear that, either thrown or lunged through the opening, had caught him in the side just below the ribs; the blade had gone in out of sight, after making a frightful gash; my shoes were full; a pool of blood lay very still, gleaming dark-red under the wheel; his eyes shone with an amazing luster. The fusillade burst out again. He looked at me anxiously, gripping the spear like something precious, with an air of being afraid I would try to take it away from him. I had to make an effort to free my eyes from his gaze and attend to the steering. With one hand I felt above my head for the line of the steam whistle, and jerked out screech after screech hurriedly. The tumult of angry and warlike yells was checked instantly, and then from the depths of the woods went out such a tremulous and prolonged wail of mournful fear and utter despair as may be imagined to follow the flight of the last hope from the earth. There was a great commotion in the bush; the shower of arrows stopped, a few dropping shots rang out sharply—then silence, in which the languid beat of the stern wheel came plainly to my ears. I put the helm hard a-starboard at the moment when the pilgrim in pink pajamas, very hot and agitated, appeared in the doorway. 'The manager sends me—' he began in an official tone, and stopped short. 'Good God!' he said, glaring at the wounded man.

"We two whites stood over him, and his lustrous and inquiring glance enveloped us both. I declare it looked as though he would presently put to us some question in an understandable language; but he died without uttering a sound, without moving a limb, without twitching a muscle. Only in the very last moment, as though in response to some sign we could not see, to some whisper we could not hear, he frowned heavily, and that frown gave to his black death mask an inconceivably somber, brooding, and menacing expression. The luster of inquiring glance faded swiftly into vacant glassiness. 'Can you steer?' I asked the agent eagerly. He looked very dubious; but I made a grab at his arm, and he understood at once I meant him to steer whether or no. To tell you the truth, I was morbidly anxious to change my shoes and socks. 'He is dead,' murmured the fellow, immensely impressed. 'No doubt about it,' said I, tugging like mad at the shoelaces. 'And by the way, I suppose Mr. Kurtz is dead as well by this time.' "

The Mysterious Sound

From Green Mansions: A Romance of the Tropical Forest *(1904)*
By W.H. Hudson

W.H. Hudson was one of the early novelists to use tropical forests in a manner that might actually appear true to life. An avid naturalist, Hudson had North American parents but was born and raised in South America and grew up with firsthand knowledge of the forests.

Green Mansions, a classic young reader's novel that still sells well today, takes place in the jungles of Guyana and Venezuela. It is a love story filled with spirits, secrets, and fear.

It is perhaps the fear of not knowing that is the scariest element of the forest, since it is much easier to hear things in a jungle than to see them. In the following excerpt, our narrator is fixated on seeing the sound . . . if he can overcome his own fear of the unknown. (DRK)

I was not disappointed on my next visit to the forest, nor on several succeeding visits; and this seemed to show that if I was right in believing that these strange, melodious utterances proceeded from one individual, then the bird or being, although still refusing to show itself, was always on the watch for my appearance, and followed me wherever I went. This thought only served to increase my curiosity; I was constantly pondering over the subject, and at last concluded that it would be best to induce one of the Indians to go with me to the wood on the chance of his being able to explain the mystery.

One of the treasures I had managed to preserve in my sojourn with these children of nature, who were always anxious to become possessors of my belongings, was a small, prettily fashioned metal match-box, opening with a spring. Remembering that Kua-kó, among others, had looked at this trifle with covetous eyes—the covetous ways in which they all looked at it had given it a fictitious value in my own—I tried to bribe him with the offer of it to accompany me to my favourite haunt. The brave young hunter refused again and again; but on each occasion he offered to perform some other service or to give me something in exchange for the box. At last I told him that I would give it to the first person who should accompany me, and fearing that someone would be found valiant enough to win the prize, he at length plucked up a spirit, and on the next day, seeing me going out for a walk, he all at once offered to go with me. He cunningly tried to get the box before starting—his cunning, poor youth! was not very deep. I told him that the forest we were about to visit abounded with plants and birds unlike any I had seen elsewhere, that I wished to learn their names, and everything about them, and that when I had got the required information, the box would be his—not sooner. Finally we started, he, as usual, armed with his *zabatana,* with which, I imagined, he would procure more game than usually fell to his little poisoned arrows. When we reached the wood I could see that he was ill at ease; nothing could persuade him to go into the deeper parts; and even where it was very open and light he was constantly gazing into bushes and shadowy places, as if expecting to see some frightful creature lying in wait for him. This behavior might have had a disquieting effect on me had I not been thoroughly convinced that his fears were purely superstitious, and that there could be no dangerous animal in a spot I was accustomed to walk in every day. My plan was to ramble about with an unconcerned air, occasionally pointing out an uncommon tree or shrub or vine, or calling his attention to a distant bird cry and asking the bird's name, in the hope that the mysterious voice would make itself heard, and that he would be able to give me some explanation of it. But for upwards of two hours we moved about, hearing nothing except the usual bird-voices, and during all that time he never stirred a yard from my side nor made an attempt to capture anything. At length we sat down under a tree, in an open spot close to the border of the wood. He sat down very reluctantly, and seemed more troubled in his mind than ever, keeping his eyes continually roving about, while he listened intently to every sound. The sounds were not few, owing to the abundance of animal and especially of bird life in this favoured spot. I began to question my companion as to some of the cries we heard. There were notes and cries familiar to me as the crowing of the cock—parrot screams and yelping of toucans, the distant wailing calls of maam and duraquara; and shrill laughterlike notes of the large tree-climber as it passed from tree to tree; the quick whistle of cotingas; and strange throbbing and thrilling sounds, as of pigmies beating on metallic drums, of the skulking pitta-thrushes; and with these mingled other notes less well known. One came from the treetops, where it was perpetually wandering amid the foliage—a low note, repeated at intervals of a few seconds, so thin and mournful and full of mystery, that I half expected to hear that it proceeded from the restless ghost of some dead bird. But no; he only said it was uttered by a "little bird"—too little presumably to have a name. From the foliage of a neighbouring tree came a few tinkling chirps, as of a small mandolin, two or three strings of which had been carelessly struck by the player. He said that it came from a small green frog that lived in the trees; and in this way my rude Indian—vexed perhaps at being asked such trivial questions—brushed away the pretty fantasies my mind had woven in the woodland solitude. For I often listened to this tinkling music, and it had suggested the idea that the place was frequented by a tribe of fairylike troubadour monkeys, and that if I could only be quick-sighted enough I might one day be able to detect the minstrel sitting, in a green tunic perhaps, cross-legged on some high, swaying bough, carelessly touching his mandolin suspended from his neck by a yellow ribbon.

By-and-by a bird came with a low, swift flight, its great tail spread open fan-wise, and perched itself on an exposed bough not thirty yards from us. It was all of a chestnut-red colour, long-bodied, in size like a big pigeon; its actions showed that its curiosity had been greatly excited, for it jerked from side to side, eyeing us first with one eye, then the other, while its long tail rose and fell in a measured way.

"Look, Kua-kó," I said in a whisper, "there is a bird for you to kill."

But he only shook his head, still watchful.

"Give me the blow-pipe, then," I said, with a laugh, putting out my hand to take it. But he refused to let me take it, knowing that it would only be an arrow wasted if I attempted to shoot anything.

As I persisted in telling him to kill the bird, he at last bent his lips near me and said in a half-whisper, as if fearful of being overheard, "I can kill nothing here. If I shot at the bird the daughter of the Didi would catch the dart in her hand and throw it back and hit me here," touching his breast just over his heart.

I laughed again, saying to myself, with some amusement, that Kua-kó was not such a bad companion after all—that he was not without imagination. But in spite of my laughter his words roused my interest, and suggested the idea that the voice I was curious about had been heard by the Indians, and was as great a mystery to them as to me; since not being like that of any creature known to them, it would be attributed by their superstition somewhat, inventing a daughter of a water-spirit to be afraid of. My thought was that if their keen, practised eyes had never been able to see this fitting woodland creature with a musical soul, it was not likely that I would succeed in my quest.

I began to question him, but he now appeared less inclined to talk and more frightened than ever, and each time I attempted to speak he imposed silence, with a quick gesture of alarm, while he continued to stare about him with dilated eyes. All at once he sprang to his feet as if overcome with terror, and started running at full speed. His fear infected me, and, springing up, I followed as fast I could, but he was far ahead of me, running for dear life; and before I had gone forty yards my feet were caught in a creeper trailing along the surface, and I measured my length on the ground. The sudden, violent shock almost took away my senses for a moment, but when I jumped up and stared round to see no unspeakable monster—Curupitá or other—rushing on to slay and devour me there and then, I began to feel ashamed of my cowardice; and in the end I turned and walked back to the spot I had just quitted and sat down once more. I even tried to hum a tune, just to prove to myself that I had completely recovered from the panic caught from the miserable Indian; but it is never possible in such cases to get back one's serenity immediately, and a vague suspicion continued to trouble me for a time. After sitting there for half an hour or so, listening to distant bird sounds, I began to recover my old confidence, and even to feel inclined to penetrate farther into the wood. All at once, making me almost jump, so sudden it was, so much nearer and louder than I had ever heard it before, the mysterious melody began. Unmistakably it was uttered by the same being heard on former occasions; but today it was different in character. The utterance was far more rapid, with fewer silent intervals, and it had none of the usual tenderness in it, nor ever once sunk to that low, whisperlike talking, which had seemed to me as if the spirit of the wind had breathed its low sighs in syllables and speech. Now it was not only loud, rapid, and continuous, but, while still musical, there was an incisiveness in it, a sharp ring as of resentment, which made it strike painfully on the sense.

The impression of an intelligent unhuman being addressing me in anger took so firm a hold on my mind that the old fear returned, and, rising, I began to walk rapidly away, intending to escape from the wood. The voice continued violently rating me, as it seemed to my mind, moving with me, which caused me to accelerate my steps; and very soon I would have broken into a run, when its character began to change again. There were pauses now, intervals of silence, long or short, and after each one the voice came to my ear with a more subdued and dulcet sound—more of that melting, flutelike quality it had possessed at other times; and this softness of tone, coupled with the talking-like form of utterance, gave me the idea of a being no longer incensed, addressing me now in a peaceable spirit, reasoning away my unworthy tremors, and imploring me to remain with it in the wood. Strange as this voice without a body was, and always productive of a slightly uncomfortable feeling on account of its mystery, it seemed impossible to doubt that it came to me now in a spirit of pure friendliness; and when I had recovered my composure I found a new delight in listening to it—all the greater because of the fear so lately experienced, and of its seeming intelligence. For the third time I reseated myself on the same spot, and at intervals the voice talked to me there for some time, and to my fancy expressed satisfaction and pleasure at my presence. But later, without losing its friendly tone, it changed again. It seemed to move away and to be thrown back from a considerable distance; and, at long intervals, it would approach me again with a new sound, which I began to interpret as of command, or entreaty. Was it, I asked myself, inviting me to follow? And if I obeyed, to what delightful discoveries or frightful dangers might it lead? My curiosity, together with the belief that the being—I called it *being,* not *bird,* now—was friendly to me, overcame all timidity, and I rose and walked at random towards the interior of the wood. Very soon I had no doubt left that the being had desired me to follow; for there was now a new note of gladness in its voice, and it continued near me as I walked, at intervals approaching me so closely as to set me staring into the surrounding shadowy places like poor scared Kua-kó.

On this occasion, too, I began to have a new fancy, for fancy or illusion I was determined to regard it, that some swift-footed being was treading the ground near me; that I occasionally caught the faint rustle of a light footstep, and detected a motion in leaves and fronds and threadlike stems of creepers hanging near the surface, as if some passing body had touched and made them tremble; and once or twice that I even had a glimpse of a grey, misty object moving at no great distance in the deeper shadows.

Led by this wandering tricksy being, I came to a spot where the trees were very large and the damp dark ground almost free from under-growth; and here the voice ceased to be heard. After patiently waiting and listening for some time I began to look about me with a slight feeling of apprehension. It was still about two hours before sunset; only in this place the shade of the vast trees made a perpetual twilight; moreover, it was strangely silent here, the few bird cries that reached me coming from a long distance. I had flattered myself that the voice had become to some extent intelligible to me; its outburst of anger caused no doubt by my cowardly flight after the Indian; then its recovered friendliness which had induced me to return; and, finally, its desire to be followed. Now that it had led me to this place of shadow and profound silence, and had ceased to speak and to lead, I could not help thinking that this was my goal, that I had been brought to this spot with a purpose, that in this wild and solitary retreat some tremendous adventure was about to befall me.

As the silence continued unbroken there was time to dwell on this thought. I gazed before me and listened intently, scarcely breathing, until the suspense became painful—too painful at last, and I turned and took a step with the idea of going back to the border of the wood, when close by, clear as a silver bell, sounded the voice once more, but only for a moment—two or three syllables in response to my movement, then it was silent again.

Once more I was standing still, as if in obedience to command, in the same state of suspense; and whether the change was real or only imagined I know not, but the silence every minute grew more profound and the gloom deeper. Imaginary terrors began to assail me. Ancient fables of men allured by beautiful forms and melodious voices to destruction all at once acquired a fearful significance. I recalled some of the Indian beliefs, especially that of the mis-shapen, man-devouring monster who is said to beguile his victims into the dark forest by mimicking the human voice—the voice sometimes of a woman in distress—or by singing some strange and beautiful melody. I grew almost afraid to look round lest I should catch sight of him stealing towards me on his huge feet with toes pointing backwards, his mouth snarling horribly to display his great green fangs. It was distressing to have such fancies in this wild, solitary spot—hateful to feel their power over me when I knew that they were nothing but fancies and creations of the savage mind. But if these supernatural beings had no existence, there were other monsters, only too real, in these woods which it would be dreadful to encounter alone and unarmed, since against such adversaries a revolver would be as ineffectual as a popgun. Some huge camoodi, able to crush my bones like brittle twigs in its constricting coils, might lurk in these shadows, and approach me stealthily, unseen in its dark colour on the dark ground. Or some jaguar or black tiger might steal towards me, masked by a bush or tree-trunk, to spring upon me unawares. Or worse still, this way might suddenly come a pack of those swift-footed, unspeakably terrible hunting leopards, from which every living thing in the forest flies with shrieks of consternation or else falls paralysed in their path to be instantly torn to pieces and devoured.

A slight rustling sound in the foliage above me made me start and cast up my eyes. High up, where a pale gleam of tempered sunlight fell through the leaves, a grotesque humanlike face, black as ebony and adorned with a great red beard, appeared staring down upon me. In another moment it was gone. It was only a large araguato, or howling monkey, but I was so unnerved that I could not get rid of the idea that it was something more than a monkey. Once more I moved, and again, the instant I moved my foot, clear, and keen, and imperative, sounded the voice! It was no longer possible to doubt its meaning. It commanded me to stand still—to wait—to watch—to listen! Had it cried, "Listen! Do not move!" I could not have understood it better. Trying as the suspense was, I now felt powerless to escape. Something very terrible, I felt convinced, was about to happen, either to destroy or to release me from the spell that held me.

And while I stood thus rooted to the ground, the sweat standing in large drops on my forehead, all at once close to me sounded a cry, fine and clear at first, and rising at the end to a shriek so loud, piercing, and unearthly in character that the blood seemed to freeze in my veins, and a despairing cry to heaven escaped by lips, then, before that long shriek expired, a mighty chorus of thunderous voices burst forth around me; and in this awful tempest of sound I trembled like a leaf; and the leaves on the trees were agitated as if by a high wind, and the earth itself seemed to shake beneath my feet. Indescribably horrible were my sensations at that moment; I was deafened, and would possibly have been maddened had I not, as by a miracle, chanced to see a large araguato on a branch overhead, roaring with open mouth and inflated throat and chest.

It was simply a concert of howling monkeys which had so terrified me! But my extreme fear was not strange in the circumstances; since everything that had led up to the display, the gloom and silence, the period of suspense and my heated imagination, had raised my mind to the highest degree of excitement and expectancy. I had rightly conjectured, no doubt, that my unseen guide had led me to that spot for a purpose; and the purpose had been to set me in the midst of a congregation of araguatos to enable me for the first time fully to appreciate their unparalleled vocal powers. I had always heard them at a distance; here they were gathered in scores, possibly hundreds—the whole araguato population of the forest, I should think—close to me, and it may give some faint conception of the tremendous power and awful character of the sound thus produced by their combined voices when I say that this animal—miscalled "howler" in English—would outroar the mightiest lion that ever woke the echoes of an African wilderness.

This roaring concert, which lasted three or four minutes, having ended, I lingered a few minutes longer on the spot, and not hearing the voice again, went back to the edge of the wood, and then started on my way back to the village.

A Chance for Mr. Lever

By Graham Greene (1936)

*In the landscape of literature, there is a region that has come to be known as "Greene-land." It is a territory fraught with intrigue, moral ambiguity, usually some peril, mostly populated by a collection of dreamers. There is customarily a fair share of heat and filth in Greene-land, too, as much of it lies in equatorial nations. This territory may be found in Central or South America (*The Power and the Glory*), the Caribbean (*The Comedians*), or Africa (*The Heart of the Matter*).*

The following story, A Chance for Mr. Lever, *dates from the 1930s. The setting, the Republic of Liberia on West Africa's Gold Coast, is definitely located in Greene-land. The central character, Mr. Lever, is definitely a dreamer—one whose dreams have led him to where he is, and then abandoned him.* (MWC)

Mr. Lever knocked his head against the ceiling and swore. Rice was stored above, and in the dark the rats began to move. Grains of rice fell between the slats on to his Revelation suitcase, his bald head, his

cases of tinned food, the little square box in which he kept his medicines. His boy had already set up the camp-bed and mosquito-net, and
outside in the warm damp dark his folding table and chair. The thatched
pointed huts streamed away towards the forest and a woman went from
hut to hut carrying fire. The glow lit her old face, her sagging breasts,
her tattooed diseased body.

It was incredible to Mr. Lever that five years ago he had been in
London.

He couldn't stand upright; he went down on hands and knees in the
dust and opened his suitcase. He took out his wife's photograph and
stood it on the chop-box; he took out a writing-pad and an indelible
pencil: the pencil had softened in the heat and left mauve stains on
his pyjamas. Then, because the light of the hurricane lamp disclosed
cockroaches the size of black-beetles flattened against the mud wall, he
carefully closed the suitcase. Already in the ten days he had learnt that
they'd eat anything—socks, shirts, the laces of your shoes.

Mr. Lever went outside; moths beat against the lamp, but there were
no mosquitoes; he hadn't seen or heard one since he landed. He sat in
a circle of light carefully observed. The blacks squatted outside their
huts and watched him; they were friendly, interested, amused, but their
strict attention irritated Mr. Lever. He could feel the small waves of
interest flashing round him, when he began to write, when he stopped
writing, when he wiped his damp hands with a handkerchief. He
couldn't touch his pocket without a craning of necks.

Dearest Emily, he wrote, *I've really started now. I'll send this letter back
with a carrier when I've located Davidson. I'm very well. Of course everything's
a bit strange. Look after yourself, my dear, and don't worry.*

"Massa buy chicken," his cook said, appearing suddenly between the
huts. A small stringy fowl struggled in his hands.

"Well," Mr. Lever said, "I gave you a shilling, didn't I?"

"They no like," the cook said. "These low bush people."

"Why don't they like? It's good money."

"They want king's money," the cook said, handing back the Victorian shilling. Mr. Lever had to get up, go back into his hut, grope for

his money-box, search through twenty pounds of small change: there was no peace.

He had learnt that very quickly. He had to economize (the whole trip was a gamble which scared him); he couldn't afford hammock carriers. He would arrive tired out after seven hours of walking at a village of which he didn't know the name and not for a minute could he sit quietly and rest. He must shake hands with the chief, he must see about a hut, accept presents of palm wine he was afraid to drink, buy rice and palm oil for the carriers, give them salts and aspirin, paint their sores with iodine. They never left him alone for five minutes on end until he went to bed. And then the rats began, rushing down the walls like water when he put out the light, gambolling among the cases.

I'm too old, Mr. Lever told himself, I'm too old, writing damply, indelibly, *I hope to find Davidson tomorrow. If I do, I may be back almost as soon as this letter. Don't economize on the stout and milk, dear, and call in the doctor if you feel bad. I've got a premonition this trip's going to turn out well. We'll take a holiday, you need a holiday,* and staring ahead past the huts and the black faces and the banana trees towards the forest from which he had come, into which he should sink again next day, he thought, Eastbourne, Eastbourne would do her a world of good; and he continued to write the only kind of lies he had ever told Emily, the lies which comforted. *I ought to draw at least three hundred in commission and expenses.* But it wasn't the sort of place where he'd been accustomed to sell heavy machinery; thirty years of it, up and down Europe and in the States, but never anything like this. He could hear his filter dripping in the hut, and somewhere somebody was playing something (he was so lost he hadn't got the simplest terms to his hands), something monotonous, melancholy, superficial, a twanging of palm fibres which seemed to convey that you weren't happy, but it didn't matter, everything would always be the same.

Look after yourself, Emily, he repeated. It was almost the only thing he found himself capable of writing to her; he couldn't describe the narrow, steep, lost paths, the snakes sizzling away like flames, the rats, the dust, the naked diseased bodies. He was unbearably tired of naked-ness. *Don't forget*—It was like living with a lot of cows.

"The chief," his boy whispered, and between the huts under a wav-ing torch came an old stout man wearing a robe of native cloth and a battered bowler hat. Behind him his men carried six bowls of rice, a bowl of palm oil, two bowls of broken meat. "Chop for the labourers," the boy exclaimed, and Mr. Lever had to get up and smile and nod and try to convey without words that he was pleased, that the chop was excellent, that the chief would get a good dash in the morning. At first the smell had been almost too much for Mr. Lever.

"Ask him," he said to his boy, "if he's seen a white man come through here lately. Ask him if a white man's been digging around here. Damn it," Mr. Lever burst out, the sweat breaking on the backs of his hands and on his bald head, "ask him if he's seen Davidson."

"Davidson?"

"Oh, hell," Mr. Lever said, "you know what I mean. The white man I'm looking for."

"White man?"

"What do you imagine I'm here for, eh? White man? Of course white man. I'm not here for my health." A cow coughed, rubbed its horns against the hut and two goats broke through between the chief and him, upsetting the bowls of meat scraps; nobody cared, they picked the meat out of the dust and dung.

Mr. Lever sat down and put his hands over his face, fat white well-cared-for hands with wrinkles of flesh over the rings. He felt too old for this.

"Chief say no white man been here long time."

"How long?"

"Chief say not since he pay hut tax."

"How long's that?"

"Long long time."

"Ask him how far is it to Greh, tomorrow."

"Chief say too far."

"Nonsense," Mr. Lever said.

"Chief say too far. Better stay here. Fine town. No humbug."

Mr. Lever groaned. Every evening there was the same trouble. The next town was always too far. They would invent any excuse to delay him, to give themselves a rest.

"Ask chief how many hours—?"

"Plenty, plenty." They had no idea of time.

"This fine chief. Fine chop. Labourers tired. No humbug."

"We are going on," Mr. Lever said.

"This fine town. Chief say—"

He thought: if this wasn't the last chance I'd give up. They nagged him so, and suddenly he longed for another white man (not Davidson, he daren't say anything to Davidson) to whom he could explain the desperation of his lot. It wasn't fair that a man, after thirty years' commercial travelling, should need to go from door to door asking for a job. He had been a good traveller, he had made money for many people, his references were excellent, but the world had moved on since that day. He wasn't streamlined, he certainly wasn't streamlined. He had been ten years retired when he lost his money in the depression.

Mr. Lever walked up and down Victoria Street showing his references. Many of the men knew him, gave him cigars, laughed at him in a friendly way for wanting to take on a job at his age ("I can't somehow settle at home. The old warhorse, you know . . ."), cracked a joke or two in the passage, went back that night to Maidenhead silent in the first-class carriage, shut in with age and ruin and how bad things were and poor devil his wife's probably sick.

It was in the rather shabby little office off Leadenhall Street that Mr. Lever met his chance. It called itself an engineering firm, but there were only two rooms, a typewriter, a girl with gold teeth and Mr. Lucas, a thin narrow man with a tic in one eyelid. All through the interview the eyelid flickered at Mr. Lever. Mr. Lever had never before fallen so low as this.

But Mr. Lucas struck him as reasonably honest. He put "all his cards on the table." He hadn't got any money, but he had expectations; he had the handling of a patent. It was a new crusher. There was money in it. But you couldn't expect the big trusts to change over their machinery now. Things were too bad. You'd got to get in at the start, and that was where—why, that was where this chief, the bowls of chop, the nagging and the rats and the heat came in. They called themselves a republic, Mr. Lucas said, he didn't know anything about that, they were not as black as they were painted, he supposed (ha, ha, nervously, ha, ha); anyway, this company had slipped agents over the border and grabbed a concession: gold and diamonds. He could tell Mr. Lever in confidence that the trust was frightened of what they'd found. Now an enterprising man could just slip across (Mr. Lucas liked the word slip, it made everything sound easy and secret) and introduce this new crusher to them: it would save them thousands when they started work, there'd be a fat commission, and afterwards, with that start . . . there was a fortune for them all.

"But can't you fix it up in Europe?"

Tic, tic, went Mr. Lucas's eyelid. "A lot of Belgians; they are leaving all decisions to the men on the spot. An Englishman called Davidson."

"How about expenses?"

"That's the trouble," Mr. Lucas said. "We are only beginning. What we want is a partner. We can't afford to send a man. But if you like a gamble . . . twenty per cent commission."

"Chief say excuse him." The carriers squatted round the basins and scooped up the rice in their left hands. "Of course. Of course," Mr. Lever said absent-mindedly. "Very kind, I'm sure."

He was back out of the dust and dark, away from the stink of goats and palm oil and whelping bitches, back among the rotarians and lunch at Stone's, "the pint of old," and the trade papers; he was a good fellow again, finding his way back to Golders Green just a bit lit; his masonic emblem rattled on his watch-chain, and he bore with him from the tube station to his house in Finchley Road a sense of companionship, of broad stories and belches, a sense of bravery.

He needed all his bravery now; the last of his savings had gone into the trip. After thirty years he knew a good thing when he saw it, and he had no doubts about the new crusher. What he doubted was his ability to find Davidson. For one thing there weren't any maps; the way you travelled in the Republic was to write down a list of names and trust that someone in the villages you passed would understand and know the route. But they always said "Too far." Good fellowship wilted before the phrase.

"Quinine," Mr. Lever said. "Where's my quinine?"

His boy never remembered a thing; they just didn't care what happened to you; their smiles meant nothing, and Mr. Lever, who knew better than anyone else the value of a meaningless smile in business, resented their heartlessness, and turned towards the dilatory boy with an expression of disappointment and dislike.

"Chief say white man in bush five hours away."

"That's better," Mr. Lever said. "It must be Davidson. He's digging for gold?"

"Ya. White man dig for gold in bush."

"We'll be off early tomorrow," Mr. Lever said.

"Chief say better stop this town. Fever humbug white man."

"Too bad," Mr. Lever said, and he thought with pleasure: my luck's changed. He'll want help. He won't refuse me a thing. A friend in need is a friend indeed, and his heart warmed towards Davidson, seeing himself arrive like an answer to prayer out of the forest, feeling quite biblical and vox humana. He thought: Prayer. I'll pray tonight, that's the kind of thing a fellow gives up, but it pays, there's something in it, remembering the long agonizing prayer on his knees, when Emily went to hospital.

"Chief say white man dead."

Mr. Lever turned his back on them and went into his hut. His sleeve nearly overturned the hurricane lamp. He undressed quickly, stuffing his clothes into a suitcase away from the cockroaches. He wouldn't believe what he had been told; it wouldn't pay him to believe. If Davidson were dead, there was nothing he could do but return; he had spent more than he could afford; he would be a ruined man. He supposed that Emily might find a home with her brother, but he could hardly expect her brother—he began to cry, but he couldn't have told in the shadowy hut the difference between the sweat and tears. He knelt down beside his camp-bed and mosquito net and prayed on the dust of the earth floor. Up until now he had always been careful never to touch ground with his naked feet for fear of jiggers; there were jiggers everywhere, they only waited for an opportunity to dig themselves in under the toe-nails, lay their eggs and multiply.

"O God," Mr. Lever prayed, "don't let Davidson be dead; let him be just sick and glad to see me." He couldn't bear the idea that he might no longer be able to support Emily. "O God, there's nothing I wouldn't do." But that was an empty phrase; he had no real notion as yet of what he would do for Emily. They had been happy together for thirty-five years; he had never been more than momentarily unfaithful to her when he was lit after a rotarian dinner and egged on by the boys; whatever skirt he'd been with in his time, he had never for a moment imagined that he could be happy married to anyone else. It wasn't fair if, just when you were old and needed each other most, you lost your money and couldn't keep together.

But of course Davidson wasn't dead. What should he have died of? The blacks were friendly. People said the country was unhealthy but he hadn't so much as heard a mosquito. Besides, you didn't die of malaria; you just lay between the blankets and took quinine and felt like death and sweated it out of you. There was dysentery, but Davidson was an old campaigner; you were safe if you boiled and filtered the water. The water was poisoned even to touch; it was unsafe to wet your feet because of guinea worm, but you didn't die of guinea worm.

Mr. Lever lay in bed and his thoughts went around and around and he couldn't sleep. He thought: you didn't die of a thing like guinea worm. It makes a sore on your foot, and if you put your foot in water you can see the eggs dropping out. You have to find the end of the worm, like a thread of cotton, and wind it round a match and wind it out of your leg without breaking it; it stretches as high as the knee. I'm too old for this country, Mr. Lever thought.

Then his boy was beside him again. He whispered urgently to Mr. Lever through the mosquito-net. "Massa, the labourers say they go home."

"Go home?" Mr. Lever asked wearily; he had heard it so often before. "Why do they want to go home? What is it now?" but he didn't really want to hear the latest squabble: that the Bande men were never sent to carry water because the headman was a Bande, that someone had stolen an empty treacle tin and sold it in a village for a penny, that someone wasn't made to carry a proper load, that the next day's journey was "too far." He said, "Tell 'em they can go home. I'll pay them off in the morning. But they won't get any dash. They'd have got a good dash if they'd stayed." He was certain it was just another try-on; he wasn't as green as all that.

"Yes, Massa. They no want dash."

"What's that?"

"They frightened fever humbug them like white man."

"I'll get carriers in the village. They can go home."

"Me too, Massa."

"Get out," Mr. Lever said; it was the last straw; "get out and let me sleep." The boy went at once, obedient even though a deserter, and Mr. Lever thought: sleep, what a hope. He lifted the net and got out of bed (barefooted again: he didn't care a damn about the jiggers) and searched for his medicine box. It was locked, of course, and he had to open his suitcase and find the key in a trouser pocket. His nerves were more on edge than ever by the time he found the sleeping tablets and he took three of them. That made him sleep, heavily and dreamlessly, though when he woke he found something had made him fling out his arms and open the net. If there had been a single mosquito in the place, he'd have been bitten, but of course there wasn't one.

He could tell at once that the trouble hadn't blown over. The village—he didn't know its name—was perched on a hilltop; east and west the forest flowed out beneath the little plateau; to the west it was a dark unfeatured mass like water, but to the east you could already discern the unevenness, the great grey cotton trees lifted above the palms. Mr. Lever was always called before dawn, but no one had called him. A few of his carriers sat outside a hut sullenly talking; his boy was with them. Mr. Lever went back inside and dressed; he thought all the time, I must be firm, but he was scared, scared of being deserted, scared of being made to return.

When he came outside again the village was awake: the women were going down the hill to fetch water, winding silently past the carriers, past the flat stones where the chiefs were buried, the little grove of trees where the rice birds, like green canaries, nested. Mr. Lever sat down on a folding chair among the chickens and whelping bitches and cow dung and called his boy. He took a "strong line"; but he didn't know what was going to happen. "Tell the chief I want to speak to him," he said.

There was some delay; the chief wasn't up yet, but presently he appeared in his blue and white robe, setting his bowler straight. "Tell him," Mr. Lever said, "I want carriers to take me to the white man and back. Two days."

"Chief no agree," the boy said.

Mr. Lever said furiously, "Damn it, if he doesn't agree he won't get any dash from me, not a penny." It occurred to him immediately afterwards how hopelessly dependent he was on these people's honesty. There in the hut for all to see was the money-box; they had only to take it. This wasn't a British or French colony; the blacks on the coast wouldn't bother, could do nothing if they did bother, because a stray Englishman had been robbed in the interior.

"Chief say how many?"

"It's only for two days," Mr. Lever said. "I can do with six."

"Chief say how much?"

"Sixpence a day and chop."

"Chief no agree."

"Ninepence a day then."

"Chief say too far. A shilling."

"All right, all right," Mr. Lever said, "a shilling then. You others can go home if you want to. I'll pay you off now, but you won't get any dash, not a penny."

He had never really expected to be left, and it gave him a sad feeling of loneliness to watch them move sullenly away (they were ashamed of themselves) down the hill to the west. They hadn't any loads, but they weren't singing; they drooped silently out of sight, his boy with them, and he was alone with his pile of boxes and the chief who couldn't talk a word of English. Mr. Lever smiled tremulously.

It was ten o'clock before his new carriers were chosen; he could tell that none of them wanted to go, and they would have to walk through the heat of the middle day if they were to find Davidson before dark. He hoped the chief had explained properly where they were going; he couldn't tell; he was completely shut off from them, and when they started down the eastward slope, he might just as well have been alone.

They were immediately caught up in the forest. Forest conveys a sense of wildness and beauty, of an active natural force, but this Liberian forest was simply a dull green wilderness. You passed, on a path a foot or so wide, through an endless back garden of tangled weeds; it didn't seem to be growing round you so much as dying. There was no life at all, except for a few large birds whose wings creaked overhead through the invisible sky like an unoiled door. There was no view, no way out for the eyes, no change of scene. It wasn't the heat that tired, so much as the boredom; you had to think of things to think about; but even Emily failed to fill the mind for more than three minutes at a time. It was a relief, a distraction, when the path was flooded and Mr. Lever had to be carried on a man's back. At first he had disliked the strong bitter smell (it reminded him of a breakfast food he was made to eat as a child), but he soon got over that. Now he was unaware that they smelt at all; any more than he was aware that the great swallow-tailed butterflies, which clustered at the water's edge and rose in green clouds round his waist, were beautiful. His senses were dulled and registered very little except his boredom.

But they did register a distinct feeling of relief when his leading carrier pointed to a rectangular hole dug just off the path. Mr. Lever understood. Davidson had come this way. He stopped and looked at it. It was like a grave dug for a small man, but it went down deeper than graves usually do. About twelve feet below there was black water, and a few wooden props which held the sides from slipping were beginning to rot; the hole must have been dug since the rains. It didn't seem enough, that hole, to have brought out Mr. Lever with his high industrial concerns, the sight of pitheads, the smoke of chimneys, the dingy rows of cottages back to back, the leather armchair in the office, the good cigar, the masonic hand-grip, and again it seemed to him, as it had seemed in Mr. Lucas's office, that he had fallen very low. It was as if he was expected to do business beside a hole a child had dug in an overgrown and abandoned back garden; percentages wilted in the hot damp air. He shook his head; he mustn't be discouraged; this was an old hole. Davidson had probably done better since. It was only common sense to suppose that the gold rift which was mined at one end in Nigeria, at the other in Sierra Leone, would pass through the Republic. Even the biggest mines had to begin with a hole in the ground. The company (he had talked to the directors in Brussels) were quite confident: all they wanted was the approval of the man on the post that the crusher was suitable for local conditions. A signature, that was all he had to get, he told himself, staring down in the puddle of black water.

Five hours, the chief had said, but after five hours they were still walking. Mr. Lever had eaten nothing; he wanted to get Davidson first. All through the heat of the day he walked. The forest protected him from the direct sun, but it shut out the air, and the occasional clearings, shrivelled though they were in the vertical glare, seemed cooler than the shade because there was a little more air to breathe. At four o'clock the heat diminished, but he began to fear they wouldn't reach Davidson before dark. His foot pained him; he had caught a jigger the night before; it was as if someone were holding a lighted match to his toe. Then at five they came on a dead black.

Another rectangular hole in a small cleared space among the dusty greenery had caught Mr. Lever's eye. He peered down and was shocked to see a face return his stare, white eyeballs like phosphorus in the black water. The black had been bent almost double to fit in; the hole was really too small to be a grave, and he had swollen. His flesh was like a blister you could prick with a needle. Mr. Lever felt sick and tired; he might have been tempted to return if he could have reached the village before dark, but now there was nothing to do but to go on; the carriers luckily hadn't seen the boy. He waved them forward and stumbled after them among the roots, fighting his nausea. He fanned himself with his sun helmet; his wide fat face was damp and pale. He had never seen an uncared-for body before; his parents he had seen carefully laid out with closed eyes and washed faces; they "fell asleep" quite in accordance with their epitaphs, but you couldn't think of sleep in connexion with the white eyeballs and swollen face. Mr. Lever would have liked very much to say a prayer, but prayers were out of place in the dead drab forest; they simply didn't "come."

With the dusk a little life did waken: something lived in the dry weeds and brittle trees, if only monkeys. They chattered and screamed all round you, but it was too dark to see them; you were like a blind man in the centre of a frightened crowd who wouldn't say what scared them. The carriers too were frightened. They ran under their fifty-pound loads behind the dipping light of the hurricane lamp, their huge flat carriers' feet flapping in the dust like empty gloves. Mr. Lever listened nervously for mosquitoes; you would have expected them to be out by now, but they didn't hear one.

Then at the top of a rise above a small stream they came on Davidson. The ground had been cleared in a square of twelve feet and a small tent pitched; he had dug another hole; the scene came dimly into view as they climbed the path, the chop-boxes piled outside the tent, the syphon of soda water, the filter, the enamel basin. But there wasn't a light, there wasn't a sound, the flaps of the tent were not closed, and Mr. Lever had to face the possibility that after all the chief might have told the truth.

Mr. Lever took the lamp and stooped inside the tent. There was a body on the bed. At first Mr. Lever thought Davidson was covered with blood, but then he realized it was a black vomit which stained his shirt and khaki shorts, the fair stubble on his chin. He put out a hand and touched Davidson's face, and if he hadn't felt a slight breath on his palm he would have taken him for dead; his skin was so cold. He moved the lamp closer, and now the lemon-yellow face told him all he wanted to know; he hadn't thought of that when his boy said fever. It was quite true that a man didn't die of malaria, but an odd piece of news read in New York in '98 came back to mind: there had been an outbreak of yellow jack in Rio and ninety-four per cent of these cases had been fatal. It hadn't meant anything to him then, but it did now. While he watched, Davidson was sick, quite effortlessly; he was like a tap out of which something flowed.

It seemed at first to Mr. Lever to be the end of everything, of his journey, his hopes, his life with Emily. There was nothing he could do for Davidson, the man was unconscious, there were times when his pulse was so low and irregular that Mr. Lever thought that he was dead until another black stream spread from his mouth; it was no use even cleaning him. Mr. Lever laid his own blankets over the bed on top of Davidson's because he was so cold to the touch, but he had no idea whether he was doing the right, or even the fatally wrong, thing. The chance of survival, if there were any chance at all, depended on neither of them. Outside the carriers had built a fire and were cooking the rice they had brought with them. Mr. Lever opened his folding chair and sat by the bed. He wanted to keep awake: it seemed right to keep awake. He opened his case and found his unfinished letter to Emily. He sat by Davidson's side and tried to write, but he could think of nothing but what he had already written so often: *Look after yourself. Don't forget that stout and milk.*

He fell asleep over his pad and woke at two and thought that Davidson was dead. But he was wrong again. He was very thirsty and missed his boy. Always the first thing his boy did at the end of the march was to light a fire and put on a kettle; after that, by the time his table and chair were set up, there was water ready for the filter. Mr. Lever found half a cup of soda water left in Davidson's syphon; if it had only been his health at stake he would have gone down to the stream, but he had Emily to remember. There was a typewriter by the bed, and it occurred to Mr. Lever that he might just as well begin to write his report of failure now; it might keep him awake; it seemed disrespectful to the dying man to sleep. He found paper under some letters which had been typed and signed but not sealed. Davidson must have been taken ill very suddenly. Mr. Lever wondered whether it was he who had crammed the black into the hole; his boy perhaps, for there was no sign of a servant. He balanced the typewriter on his knee and headed the letter "In Camp near Greh."

It seemed to him unfair that he should have come so far, spent so much money, worn out a rather old body to meet his inevitable ruin in a dark tent beside a dying man, when he could have met it just as well at home with Emily in the plush parlour. The thought of the prayers he had uselessly uttered on his knees by the camp-bed among the jiggers, the rats and the cockroaches made him rebellious. A mosquito, the first he had heard, went humming round the tent. He slashed at it savagely; he wouldn't have recognized himself among the rotarians. He was lost and he was set free. Moralities were what enabled a man to live happily and successfully with his fellows, but Mr. Lever wasn't happy and he wasn't successful, and his only fellow in the little stuffy tent wouldn't be troubled with the Untruth in Advertising or by Mr. Lever coveting his neighbour's oxen. You couldn't keep your ideas intact when you discovered their geographical nature. The Solemnity of Death; death wasn't solemn; it was lemon-yellow skin and a black vomit. Honesty is the Best Policy: he saw quite suddenly how false that was. It was an anarchist who sat happily over the typewriter, an anarchist who recognized nothing but one personal relationship, his affection for Emily. Mr. Lever began to type: *I have examined the plans and estimates of the new Lucas crusher . . .*

Mr. Lever thought with savage happiness: I win. This letter would be the last the company would hear from Davidson. The junior partner would open it in the dapper Brussels office; he would tap his false teeth with a Waterman pen and go in to talk to M. Golz. *Taking all these factors into consideration I recommend acceptance . . .*

They would telegraph to Lucas. As for Davidson, that trusted agent of the company would have died of yellow fever at some never accurately determined date. Another agent would come out, and the crusher . . . Mr. Lever carefully copied Davidson's signature on a spare sheet of paper. He wasn't satisfied. He turned the original upside-down and copied it that way, so as not to be confused by his own idea of how a letter should be formed. That was better, but it didn't quite satisfy him. He searched until he found Davidson's pen and began again to copy and copy the signature. He fell asleep copying it and woke again an hour later to find the lamp was out; it had burnt up all the oil. He sat there beside Davidson's bed till daylight; once he was bitten by a mosquito in the ankle and clapped his hand to the place too late; the brute went humming out. With the light Mr. Lever saw that Davidson was dead. "Dear, dear," he said. "Poor fellow." He spat out with the words, quite delicately in a corner, the bad morning taste in his mouth. It was like a little sediment of his conventionality.

Mr. Lever got two of his carriers to cram Davidson tidily into his hole. He was no longer afraid of them or of failure or of separation. He tore up his letter to Emily. It no longer represented his mood in its timidity, its secret fear, its gentle fussing phrases, *Don't forget the stout. Look after yourself.* He would be home as soon as the letter, and they were going to do things together now they'd never dreamt of doing. The money for the crusher was only the beginning. His ideas stretched farther now than Eastbourne, they stretched as far as Switzerland; he had a feeling that, if he really let himself go, they'd stretch as far as the Riviera. How happy he was on what he thought of as "the trip home." He was freed from what had held him back through a long pedantic career, the fear of unconscious fate that notes the dishonesty, notes the skirt in Piccadilly, notes the glass too many of Stone's special. Now he had said Boo to that goose . . .

But you who are reading this, who know so much more than Mr. Lever, who can follow the mosquito's progress from the dead swollen black to Davidson's tent, to Mr. Lever's ankle, you may possibly believe in God, a kindly God tender towards human frailty, ready to give Mr. Lever three days of happiness, three days off the galling chain, as he carried back through the forest his amateurish forgeries and the infection of yellow fever in the blood. The story might very well have encouraged my faith in that loving omniscience if it had not been shaken by personal knowledge of the drab forest through which Mr. Lever now went so merrily, where it is impossible to believe in any spiritual life, in anything outside the nature dying around you, the shrivelling of the weeds. But of course, there are two opinions about everything; it was Mr. Lever's favourite expression, drinking beer in the Ruhr, Pernod in Lorraine, selling heavy machinery.

The Outstation

By W. Somerset Maugham (1930)

William Somerset Maugham (1874–1965) is widely recognized as a master of the short story form and well known as one of the most enigmatic English literary figures of the late nineteenth and early twentieth centuries. His life and career spanned a remarkable time in history, from the Victorian era through the nuclear age. Best known to the public for his novels Cakes and Ale, Of Human Bondage, The Razor's Edge, and The Moon and Sixpence, among others, and The Ashenden Stories, his World War I spy series, he was also celebrated during his lifetime as a playwright, travel writer, and essayist. Although England was his birthplace, and his nature and outlook English to the utmost, he spent the majority of his days away from the British Isles, traveling widely and settling finally, in 1926, in the luxurious Villa Mauresque on the French Riviera.

Much of Maugham's short fiction involved Englishmen and -women in exotic locales behaving, or trying to behave, much as if they were at home in Mayfair, or Lambeth, as the case may be. In "The Outstation," he contrasts two differing classes of Englishmen who wind up together at the end of the line—in this *story, the jungles of Malaysia. Warburton, the local Resident and constable, greets Cooper, his assistant and manager of the local rubber plantation, and the two of them don't quite hit it off. Their contrasting styles and markedly differing embodiments of what it means to be "civilized" in a raw land have tragic results.* (MWC)

The new assistant arrived in the afternoon. When the Resident, Mr. Warburton, was told that the prahu was in sight he put on his solar topee and went down to the landing-stage. The guard, eight little Dyak soldiers, stood to attention as he passed. He noted with satisfaction that their bearing was martial, their uniforms neat and clean, and their guns shining. They were a credit to him. From the landing-stage he watched the bend of the river round which in a moment the boat would sweep. He looked very smart in his spotless ducks and white shoes. He held under his arm a gold-headed Malacca cane which had been given him by the Sultan of Perak. He awaited the newcomer with mingled feelings. There was more work in the district than one man could properly do, and during his periodical tours of the country under his charge it had been inconvenient to leave the station in the hands of a native clerk, but he had been so long the only white man there that he could not face the arrival of another without misgiving. He was accustomed to loneliness. During the war he had not seen an English face for three years; and once when he was instructed to put up an afforestation officer he was seized with panic, so that when the stranger was due to arrive, having arranged everything for his reception, he wrote a note telling him he was obliged to go up-river, and fled; he remained away till he was informed by a messenger that his guest had left.

Now the prahu appeared in the broad reach. It was manned by prisoners, Dyaks under various sentences, and a couple of warders were waiting on the landing-stage to take them back to gaol. They were sturdy fellows, used to the river, and they rowed with a powerful stroke. As the boat reached the side a man got out from under the attap awning and stepped on shore. The guard presented arms.

"Here we are at last. By God, I'm as cramped as the devil. I've brought you your mail."

He spoke with exuberant joviality. Mr. Warburton politely held out his hand.

"Mr. Cooper, I presume?"

"That's right. Were you expecting anyone else?"

The question had a facetious intent, but the Resident did not smile.

"My name is Warburton. I'll show you your quarters. They'll bring your kit along."

He preceded Cooper along the narrow pathway and they entered a compound in which stood a small bungalow.

"I've had it made as habitable as I could, but of course no one has lived in it for a good many years."

It was built on piles. It consisted of a long living-room which opened on to a broad veranda, and behind, on each side of a passage, were two bedrooms.

"This'll do me all right," said Cooper.

"I dare say you want to have a bath and a change. I shall be very much pleased if you'll dine with me tonight. Will eight o'clock suit you?"

"Any old time will do for me."

The Resident gave a polite, but slightly disconcerted smile, and withdrew. He returned to the Fort where his own residence was. The impression which Allen Cooper had given him was not very favourable, but he was a fair man, and he knew that it was unjust to form an opinion on so brief a glimpse. Cooper seemed to be about thirty. He was a tall, thin fellow, with a sallow face in which there was not a spot of colour. It was a face all in one tone. He had a large, hooked nose and blue eyes. When, entering the bungalow, he had taken off his topee and flung it to a waiting boy, Mr. Warburton noticed that his large skull, covered with short, brown hair, contrasted somewhat oddly with a weak, small chin. He was dressed in khaki shorts and a khaki shirt, but they were shabby and soiled; and his battered topee had not been cleaned for days. Mr. Warburton reflected that the young man had spent a week on a coasting steamer and had passed the last forty-eight hours lying in the bottom of a prahu.

"We'll see what he looks like when he come in to dinner."

He went into his room, where his things were as neatly laid out as if he had an English valet, undressed, and, walking down the stairs to the bath-house, sluiced himself with cool water. The only concession he made to the climate was to wear a white dinner jacket; but otherwise, in a boiled shirt and a high collar, silk socks and patent-leather shoes, he dressed as formally as though he were dining at his club in Pall Mall. A careful host, he went into the dining-room to see that the table was properly laid. It was gay with orchids, and the silver shone brightly. The napkins were folded into elaborate shapes. Shaded candles in silver candlesticks shed a soft light. Mr. Warburton smiled his approval and returned to the sitting-room to await his guest. Presently he appeared. Cooper was wearing the khaki shorts, the khaki shirt, and the ragged jacket in which he had landed. Mr. Warburton's smile of greeting froze on his face.

"Hullo, you're all dressed up," said Cooper. "I didn't know you were going to do that. I very nearly put on a sarong."

"It doesn't matter at all. I dare say your boys were busy."

"You needn't have bothered to dress on my account, you know."

"I didn't. I always dress for dinner."

"Even when you're alone?"

"Especially when I'm alone," replied Mr. Warburton, with a frigid stare.

He saw a twinkle of amusement in Cooper's eyes, and he flushed an angry red. Mr. Warburton was a hot-tempered man; you might have guessed that from his red face with its pugnacious features and from his red hair now growing white; his blue eyes, cold as a rule and observing, could flash with sudden wrath; but he was a man of the world and he hoped a just one. He must do his best to get on with this fellow.

"When I lived in London I moved in circles in which it would have been just as eccentric not to dress for dinner every night as not to have a bath every morning. When I came to Borneo I saw no reason to discontinue so good a habit. For three years during the war I never saw a white man. I never omitted to dress on a single occasion on which I was well enough to come in to dinner. You have not been very long in this country; believe me, there is no better way to maintain the proper pride which you should have in yourself. When a white man surrenders in the slightest degree to the influences that surround him he very soon loses his self-respect, and when he loses his self-respect you may be quite sure the natives will soon cease to respect him."

"Well, if you expect me to put on a boiled shirt and a stiff collar in this heat I'm afraid you'll be disappointed."

"When you are dining in your own bungalow you will, of course, dress as you think fit, but when you do me the pleasure of dining with me, perhaps you will come to the conclusion that it is only polite to wear the costume usual in civilized society."

Two Malay boys, in sarongs and songkoks, with smart white coats and brass buttons, came in, one bearing gin pahits, and the other a tray on which were olives and anchovies. Then they went in to dinner. Mr. Warburton flattered himself that he had the best cook, a Chinese, in Borneo, and he took great trouble to have as good food as in the difficult circumstances was possible. He exercised much ingenuity in making the best of his materials.

"Would you care to look at the menu?" he said, handing it to Cooper.

It was written in French and the dishes had resounding names. They were waited on by the two boys. In opposite corners of the room two more waved immense fans, and so gave movement to the sultry air. The fare was sumptuous and the champagne excellent.

"Do you do yourself like this every day?" said Cooper.

Mr. Warburton gave the menu a careless glance.

"I have not noticed that the dinner is any different from usual," he said. "I eat very little myself, but I make a point of having a proper dinner served to me every night. It keeps the cook in practice and it's good discipline for the boys."

The conversation proceeded with effort. Mr. Warburton was elaborately courteous and, it may be, found a slightly malicious amusement in the embarrassment which he thereby occasioned in his companion. Cooper had not been more than a few months in Sembulu, and Mr. Warburton's inquiries about friends of his in Kuala Solor were soon exhausted.

"By the way," he said presently, "did you meet a lad called Hennerley? He's come out recently, I believe."

"Oh yes, he's in the police. A rotten bounder."

"I should hardly have expected him to be that. His uncle is my friend Lord Barraclough. I had a letter from Lady Barraclough only the other day asking me to look out for him."

"I heard he was related to somebody or other. I suppose that's how he got the job. He's been to Eton and Oxford and he doesn't forget to let you know it."

"You surprise me," said Mr. Warburton. "All his family have been at Eton and Oxford for a couple of hundred years. I should have expected him to take it as a matter of course."

"I thought him a damned prig."

"To what school did you go?"

"I was born in Barbados. I was educated there."

"Oh, I see."

Mr. Warburton managed to put so much offensiveness into his brief reply that Cooper flushed. For a moment he was silent. "I've had two or three letters from Kuala Solor," continued Mr. Warburton, "and my impression was that young Hennerley was a great success. They say he's a first-rate sportsman."

"Oh, yes, he's very popular. He's just the sort of fellow they would like in K.S. I haven't got much use for the first-rate sportsman myself. What does it amount to in the long run that a man can play golf and tennis better than other people? And who cares if he can make a break of seventy-five at billiards? They attach a damned sight too much importance to that sort of thing in England."

"Do you think so? I was under the impression that the first-rate sportsman had come out of the war certainly no worse than anyone else."

"Oh, if you're going to talk of the war then I do know what I'm talking about. I was in the same regiment as Hennerley and I can tell you that the men couldn't stick him at any price."

"How do you know?"

"Because I was one of the men."

"Oh, you hadn't got a commission."

"A fat chance I had of getting a commission. I was what was called a Colonial. I hadn't been to a public school and I had no influence. I was in the ranks the whole damned time."

Cooper frowned. He seemed to have difficulty in preventing himself from breaking out into violent invective. Mr. Warburton watched him, his little blue eyes narrowed, watched him and formed his opinion. Changing the conversation, he began to speak to Cooper about the work that would be required of him, and as the clock struck ten he rose.

"Well, I won't keep you any more. I dare say you're tired by your journey."

They shook hands.

"Oh, I say, look here," said Cooper, "I wonder if you can find me a boy. The boy I had before never turned up when I was starting from K.S. He took my kit on board and all that, and then disappeared. I didn't know he wasn't there till we were out of the river."

"I'll ask my head-boy. I have no doubt he can find you someone."

"All right. Just tell him to send the boy along and if I like the look of him I'll take him."

There was a moon, so that no lantern was needed. Cooper walked across from the Fort to his bungalow.

"I wonder why on earth they've sent me a fellow like that?" reflected Mr. Warburton. "If that's the kind of man they're going to get out now I don't think much of it."

He strolled down his garden. The Fort was built on the top of a little hill and the garden ran down to the river's edge; on the bank was an arbour, and hither it was his habit to come after dinner to smoke a cheroot. And often from the river that flowed below him a voice was heard, the voice of some Malay too timorous to venture into the light of day, and a complaint or an accusation was softly wafted to his ears, a piece of information was whispered to him or a useful hint, which otherwise would never have come into his official ken. He threw himself heavily into a long rattan chair. Cooper! An envious, ill-bred fellow, bumptious, self-assertive, and vain. But Mr. Warburton's irritation could not withstand the silent beauty of the night. The air was scented with the sweet-smelling flowers of a tree that grew at the entrance to the arbour, and the fire-flies, sparkling dimly, flew with their slow and silvery flight. The moon made a pathway on the broad river for the light feet of Sila's bride, and on the further bank a row of palm trees was delicately silhouetted against the sky. Peace stole into the soul of Mr. Warburton.

He was a queer creature and he had had a singular career. At the age of twenty-one he had inherited a considerable fortune, a hundred thousand pounds, and when he left Oxford he threw himself into the gay life, which in those days (now Mr. Warburton was a man of four-and-fifty) offered itself to the young man of good family. He had his flat in Mount Street, his private hansom, and his hunting box in Warwickshire. He went to all the places where the fashionable congregate. He was handsome, amusing, and generous. He was a figure in the society of London in the early nineties, and society then had not lost its exclusiveness nor its brilliance. The Boer War which shook it was unthought of; the Great War which destroyed it was prophesied only by the pessimists. It was no unpleasant thing to be a rich young man in those days, and Mr. Warburton's chimney-piece during the season was packed with cards for one great function after another. Mr. Warburton displayed them with complacency. For Mr. Warburton was a snob. He was not a timid snob, a little ashamed of being impressed by his betters, nor a snob who sought the intimacy of persons who had acquired celebrity in politics or notoriety in the arts, nor the snob who was dazzled by riches; he was the naked, unadulterated common snob who dearly loved a lord. He was touchy and quick-tempered, but he would much rather have been snubbed by a person of quality than flattered by a commoner. His name figured insignificantly in Burke's Peerage, and it was marvellous to watch the ingenuity he used to mention his distant relationship to the noble family he belonged to; but never a word did he say of the honest Liverpool manufacturer from whom, through his mother, a Miss Gubbins, he had come by his fortune. It was the terror of his fashionable life that at Cowes, maybe, or at Ascot, when he was with a duchess or even with a prince of the blood, one of these relatives would claim acquaintance with him.

His failing was too obvious not soon to become notorious, but its extravagance saved it from being merely despicable. The great whom he adored laughed at him, but in their hearts felt his adoration not unnatural. Poor Warburton was a dreadful snob, of course, but after all he was a good fellow. He was always ready to back a bill for an impecunious nobleman, and if you were in a tight corner you could safely count on him for a hundred pounds. He gave good dinners. He played whist badly, but never minded how much he lost if the company was select. He happened to be a gambler, an unlucky one, but he was a good loser, and it was impossible not to admire the coolness with which he lost five hundred pounds at a sitting. His passion for cards, almost as strong as his passion for titles, was the cause of his undoing. The life he led was expensive and his gambling losses were formidable. He began to plunge more heavily, first on horses, and then on the Stock Exchange. He had a certain simplicity of character, and the unscrupulous found him an ingenuous prey. I do not know if he ever realized that his smart friends laughed at him behind his back, but I think he had an obscure instinct that he could not afford to appear other than careless of his money. He got into the hands of moneylenders. At the age of thirty-four he was ruined.

He was too much imbued with the spirit of his class to hesitate in the choice of his next step. When a man in his set had run through his money, he went out to the colonies. No one heard Mr. Warburton repine. He made no complaint because a noble friend had advised a disastrous speculation, he pressed nobody to whom he had lent money to repay it, he paid his debts (if he had only known it, the despised blood of the Liverpool manufacturer came out in him there), sought help from no one, and, never having done a stroke of work in his life, looked for a means of livelihood. He remained cheerful, unconcerned, and full of humour. He had no wish to make anyone with whom he happened to be uncomfortable by the recital of his misfortune. Mr. Warburton was a snob, but he was also a gentleman.

The only favour he asked of any of the great friends in whose daily company he had lived for years was a recommendation. The able man who was at that time Sultan of Sembulu took him into his service. The night before he sailed he dined for the last time at his club.

"I hear you're going away, Warburton," the old Duke of Hereford said to him.

"Yes, I'm going to Borneo."

"Good God, what are you going there for?"

"Oh, I'm broke."

"Are you? I'm sorry. Well, let us know when you come back. I hope you have a good time."

"Oh yes. Lots of shooting, you know."

The Duke nodded and passed on. A few hours later Mr. Warburton watched the coast of England recede into the mist, and he left behind everything which to him made life worth living.

Twenty years had passed since then. He kept up a busy correspondence with various great ladies and his letters were amusing and chatty. He never lost his love for titled persons and paid careful attention to the announcement in *The Times* (which reached him six weeks after publication) of their comings and goings. He perused the column which records births, deaths, and marriages, and he was always ready with his letter of congratulation or condolence. The illustrated papers told him how people looked and on his periodical visits to England, able to take up the threads as though they had never been broken, he knew all about any new person who might have appeared on the social surface. His interest in the world of fashion was as vivid as when himself had been a figure in it. It still seemed to him the only thing that mattered.

But insensibly another interest had entered into his life. The position he found himself in flattered his vanity; he was no longer the sycophant craving the smiles of the great, he was the master whose word was law. He was gratified by the guard of Dyak soldiers who presented arms as he passed. He liked to sit in judgement on his fellow men. It pleased him to compose quarrels between rival chiefs. When the head-hunters were troublesome in the old days he set out to chastise them with a thrill of pride in his own behavior. He was too vain not to be of dauntless courage, and a pretty story was told of his coolness in adventuring single-handed into a stockaded village and demanding the surrender of a bloodthirsty pirate. He became a skillful administrator. He was strict, just, and honest.

And little by little he conceived a deep love for the Malays. He interested himself in their habits and customs. He was never tired of listening to their talk. He admired their virtues, and with a smile and a shrug of the shoulders condoned their vices.

"In my day," he would say, "I have been on intimate terms with some of the greatest gentlemen in England, but I have never known finer gentlemen than some well-born Malays whom I am proud to call my friends."

He liked their courtesy and their distinguished manners, their gentleness and their sudden passions. He knew by instinct exactly how to treat them. He had a genuine tenderness for them. But he never forgot that he was an English gentleman, and he had no patience with the white men who yielded to native customs. He made no surrenders. And he did not imitate so many of the white men in taking a native woman to wife, for an intrigue of this nature, however sanctified by custom, seemed to him not only shocking but undignified. A man who had been called George by Albert Edward, Prince of Wales, could hardly be expected to have any connexion with a native. And when he returned to Borneo from his visits to England it was now with something like relief. His friends, like himself, were no longer young, and there was a new generation which looked upon him as a tiresome old man. It seemed to him that the England of today had lost a good deal of what he had loved in the England of his youth. But Borneo remained the same. It was home to him now. He meant to remain in service as long as was possible, and the hope in his heart was that he would die before at last he was forced to retire. He had stated in his will that wherever he died he wished his body to be brought back to Sembulu, and buried among the people he loved within the sound of the softly flowing river.

But these emotions he kept hidden from the eyes of men; and no one, seeing this spruce, stout, well-set-up man, with his clean-shaven strong face and his whitening hair, would have dreamed that he cherished so profound a sentiment.

He knew how the work of the station should be done, and during the next few days he kept a suspicious eye on his assistant. He saw very soon that he was painstaking and competent. The only fault he had to find with him was that he was brusque with the natives.

"The Malays are shy and very sensitive," he said to him. "I think you will find that you will get much better results if you take care always to be polite, patient, and kindly."

Cooper gave a short, grating laugh.

"I was born in Barbados and I was in Africa in the war. I don't think there's much about niggers that I don't know."

"I know nothing," said Mr. Warburton acidly. "But we were not talking of them. We were talking of Malays."

"Aren't they niggers?"

"You are very ignorant," replied Mr. Warburton.

He said no more.

On the first Sunday after Cooper's arrival he asked him to dinner. He did everything ceremoniously, and though they had met on the previous day in the office and later, on the Fort veranda where they drank a gin and bitters together at six o'clock, he sent a polite note across to the bungalow by a boy. Cooper, however unwillingly, came in evening dress and Mr. Warburton, though gratified that his wish was respected, noticed with disdain that the young man's clothes were badly cut and his shirt ill-fitting. But Mr. Warburton was in a good temper that evening.

"By the way," he said to him, as he shook hands, "I've talked to my head-boy about finding you someone and he recommends his nephew. I've seen him and he seems a bright and willing lad. Would you like to see him?"

"I don't mind."

"He's waiting now."

Mr. Warburton called his boy and told him to send for his nephew. In a moment a tall, slender youth of twenty appeared. He had large dark eyes and a good profile. He was very neat in his sarong, a little white coat, and a fez, without a tassel, of plum-coloured velvet. He answered to the name of Abas. Mr. Warburton looked on him with approval, and his manner insensibly softened as he spoke to him in fluent and idiomatic Malay. He was inclined to be sarcastic with white people, but with the Malays he had a happy mixture of condescension and kindliness. He stood in the place of the Sultan. He knew perfectly how to preserve his own dignity and at the same time put a native at his ease.

"Will he do?" said Mr. Warburton, turning to Cooper.

"Yes, I dare say he's no more of a scoundrel than any of the rest of them."

Mr. Warburton informed the boy that he was engaged, and dismissed him.

"You're very lucky to get a boy like that," he told Cooper. "He belongs to a very good family. They came over from Malacca nearly a hundred years ago."

"I don't much mind if the boy who cleans my shoes and brings me a drink when I want it has blue blood in his veins or not. All I ask is that he should do what I tell him and look sharp about it."

Mr. Warburton pursed his lips, but made no reply.

They went in to dinner. It was excellent, and the wine was good. Its influence presently had its effect on them, and they talked not only without acrimony, but even with friendliness. Mr. Warburton liked to do himself well, and on Sunday night he made it a habit to do himself even a little better than usual. He began to think he was unfair to Cooper. Of course he was not a gentleman, but that was not his fault, and when you got to know him it might be that he would turn out a very good fellow. His faults, perhaps, were faults of manner. And he was certainly good at his work, quick, conscientious, and thorough. When they reached the dessert Mr. Warburton was feeling kindly disposed towards all mankind.

"This is your first Sunday, and I'm going to give you a very special glass of port. I've only got about two dozen of it left and I keep it for special occasions."

He gave his boy instructions and presently the bottle was brought. Mr. Warburton watched the boy open it.

"I got this port from my old friend Charles Hollington. He'd had it for forty years, and I've had it for a good many. He was well-known to have the best cellar in England."

"Is he a wine merchant?"

"Not exactly," smiled Mr. Warburton. "I was speaking of Lord Hollington of Castle Reagh. He's one of the richest peers in England. A very old friend of mine. I was at Eton with his brother."

This was an opportunity that Mr. Warburton could never resist, and he told a little anecdote of which the only point seemed to be that he knew an Earl. The port was certainly very good; he drank a glass and then a second. He lost all caution. He had not talked to a white man for months. He began to tell stories. He showed himself in the company of the great. Hearing him, you would have thought that at one time ministries were formed and policies decided on his suggestion whispered into the ear of a duchess or thrown over the dinner-table to be gratefully acted on by the confidential adviser of the Sovereign. The old days at Ascot, Goodwood, and Cowes lived again for him. Another glass of port. There were the great house-parties in Yorkshire and in Scotland to which he went every year.

"I had a man called Foreman then, the best valet I ever had, and why do you think he gave me notice? You know in the Housekeeper's Room the ladies' maids and the gentlemen's gentlemen sit according to the precedence of their masters. He told me he was sick of going to party after party at which I was the only commoner. It meant that he always had to sit at the bottom of the table, and all the best bits were taken before a dish reached him. I told the story to the old Duke of Hereford, and he roared. 'By God, sir,' he said, 'if I were King of England, I'd make you a viscount just to give your man a chance.' 'Take him yourself, Duke,' I said. 'He's the best valet I've ever had.' 'Well, Warburton,' he said, 'if he's good enough for you he's good enough for me. Send him along.'"

Then there was Monte Carlo, where Mr. Warburton and the Grand Duke Fyodor, playing in partnership, had broken the bank one evening; and there was Marienbad. At Marienbad Mr. Warburton had played baccarat with Edward VII.

"He was only Prince of Wales then, of course. I remember him

saying to me, 'George, if you draw on a five you'll lose your shirt.'
He was right; I don't think he ever said a truer word in his life. He
was a wonderful man. I always said he was the greatest diplomatist in
Europe. But I was a young fool in those days, I hadn't the sense to
take his advice. If I had, if I'd never drawn on a five, I dare say I
shouldn't be here today."

Cooper was watching him. His brown eyes, deep in their sockets,
were hard and supercilious, and on his lips was a mocking smile. He
had heard a good deal about Mr. Warburton in Kuala Solor, not a bad
sort, and he ran his district like clockwork, they said, but by heaven,
what a snob! They laughed at him good-naturedly, for it was impossible
to dislike a man who was so generous and so kindly, and Cooper had
already heard the story of the Prince of Wales and the game of baccarat.
But Cooper listened without indulgence. From the beginning he had
resented the Resident's manner. He was very sensitive, and he writhed
under Mr. Warburton's polite sarcasms. Mr. Warburton had a knack of
receiving a remark of which he disapproved with a devastating silence.
Cooper had lived little in England and he had a peculiar dislike of the
English. He resented especially the public-school boy since he always
feared that he was going to patronize him. He was so much afraid of
others putting on airs with him that, in order as it were to get in first, he
put on such airs as to make everyone think him insufferably conceited.

"Well, at all events the war has done one good thing for us," he
said at last. "It's smashed up the power of the aristocracy. The Boer
War started it, and 1914 put the lid on."

"The great families of England are doomed," said Mr. Warburton
with the complacent melancholy of an *émigré* who remembered the
court of Louis XV. "They cannot afford any longer to live in their
splendid palaces and their princely hospitality will soon be nothing but
a memory."

"And a damned good job too in my opinion."

"My poor Cooper, what can you know of the glory that was Greece
and the grandeur that was Rome?"

Mr. Warburton made an ample gesture. His eyes for an instant grew
dreamy with a vision of the past.

"Well, believe me, we're fed up with all that rot. What we want is a business government by business men. I was born in a Crown Colony, and I've lived practically all my life in the colonies. I don't give a row of pins for a lord. What's wrong with England is snobbishness. And if there's anything that gets my goat it's a snob."

A snob! Mr. Warburton's face grew purple and his eyes blazed with anger. That was a word that had pursued him all his life. The great ladies whose society he had enjoyed in his youth were not inclined to look upon his appreciation of themselves as unworthy, but even great ladies are sometimes out of temper and more than once Mr. Warburton had had the dreadful word flung in his teeth. He knew, he could not help knowing, that there were odious people who called him a snob. How unfair it was! Why, there was no vice he found so detestable as snobbishness. After all, he liked to mix with people of his own class, he was only at home in their company, and how in heaven's name could anyone say that was snobbish? Birds of a feather.

"I quite agree with you," he answered. "A snob is a man who admires or despises another because he is of a higher social rank than his own. It is the most vulgar failing of our English middle-class."

He saw a flicker of amusement in Cooper's eyes. Cooper put up his hand to hide the broad smile that rose to his lips, and so made it more noticeable. Mr. Warburton's hands trembled a little.

Probably Cooper never knew how greatly he had offended his chief. A sensitive man himself, he was strangely insensitive to the feelings of others.

Their work forced them to see one another for a few minutes now and then during the day, and they met at six to have a drink on Mr. Warburton's veranda. This was an old-established custom of the country which Mr. Warburton would not for the world have broken. But they ate their meals separately, Cooper in his bungalow and Mr. Warburton at the Fort. After the office work was over they walked till dusk fell, but they walked apart. There were but few paths in this country where the jungle pressed close upon the plantations of the village, and when Mr. Warburton caught sight of his assistant passing along with his loose stride, he would make a circuit in order to avoid him. Cooper, with his bad manners, his conceit in his own judgement, and his intolerance, had already got on his nerves; but it was not till Cooper had been on the station for a couple of months that an incident happened which turned the Resident's dislike into bitter hatred.

Mr. Warburton was obliged to go up-country on a tour of inspection, and he left the station in Cooper's charge with more confidence, since he had definitely come to the conclusion that he was a capable fellow. The only thing he did not like was that he had no indulgence. He was honest, just, and painstaking, but he had no sympathy for the natives. It bitterly amused Mr. Warburton to observe that this man who looked upon himself as every man's equal should look upon so many men as his own inferiors. He was hard, he had no patience with the native mind, and he was a bully. Mr. Warburton very quickly realized that the Malays disliked and feared him. He was not altogether displeased. He would not have liked it very much if his assistant had enjoyed a popularity which might rival his own. Mr. Warburton made his elaborate preparations, set out on his expedition, and in three weeks returned. Meanwhile the mail had arrived. The first thing that struck his eyes when he entered his sitting-room was a great pile of open newspapers. Cooper had met him, and they went into the room together. Mr. Warburton turned to one of the servants who had been left behind, and sternly asked him what was the meaning of those open papers. Cooper hastened to explain.

"I wanted to read all about the Wolverhampton murder, and so I borrowed your *Times*. I brought them back again. I knew you wouldn't mind."

Mr. Warburton turned on him, white with anger.

"But I do mind. I mind very much."

"I'm sorry," said Cooper, with composure. "The fact is, I simply couldn't wait till you came back."

"I wonder you didn't open my letters as well."

Cooper, unmoved, smiled at his chief's exasperation.

"Oh, that's not quite the same thing. After all, I couldn't imagine you'd mind my looking at your newspapers. There's nothing private in them."

"I very much object to anyone reading my paper before me." He went up to the pile. There were nearly thirty numbers there. "I think it extremely impertinent of you. They're all mixed up."

"We can easily put them in order," said Cooper, joining him at the table.

"Don't touch them," cried Mr. Warburton.

"I say, it's childish to make a scene about a little thing like that."

"How dare you speak to me like that?"

"Oh, go to hell," said Cooper, and he flung out of the room.

Mr. Warburton, trembling with passion, was left contemplating his papers. His greatest pleasure in life had been destroyed by those callous, brutal hands. Most people living in out-of-the-way places when the mail comes tear open impatiently their papers and taking the last ones first glance at the latest news from home. Not so Mr. Warburton. His newsagent had instructions to write on the outside of the wrapper the date of each paper he dispatched, and when the great bundle arrived Mr. Warburton looked at these dates and with his blue pencil numbered them. His head-boy's orders were to place one on the table every morning in the veranda with the early cup of tea and it was Mr. Warburton's especial delight to break the wrapper as he sipped his tea, and read the morning paper. It gave him the illusion of living at home. Every Monday morning he read the Monday *Times* of six weeks back, and so went through the week. On Sunday he read the *Observer*. Like his habit of dressing for dinner it was a tie to civilization. And it was his pride that no matter how exciting the news was he had never yielded to the temptation of opening a paper before its allotted time. During the war the suspense sometimes had been intolerable, and when he read one day that a push was begun he had undergone agonies of suspense which he might have saved himself by the simple expedient of opening a later paper which lay waiting for him on a shelf. It had been the severest trial to which he had ever exposed himself, but he victoriously surmounted it. And that clumsy fool had broken open those neat tight packages because he wanted to know whether some horrid woman had murdered her odious husband.

Mr. Warburton sent for his boy and told him to bring wrappers. He folded up the papers as neatly as he could, placed a wrapper round each and numbered it. But it was a melancholy task.

"I shall never forgive him," he said. "Never."

Of course his boy had been with him on his expedition; he never travelled without him, for his boy knew exactly how he liked things, and Mr. Warburton was not the kind of jungle traveller who was prepared to dispense with his comforts; but in the interval since their arrival he had been gossiping in the servants' quarters. He had learnt that Cooper had had trouble with his boys. All but the youth Abas had left him. Abas had desired to go too, but his uncle had placed him there on the instructions of the Resident, and he was afraid to leave without his uncle's permission.

"I told him he had done well, Tuan," said the boy. "But he is unhappy. He says it is not a good house, and he wishes to know if he may go as the others have gone."

"No, he must stay. The Tuan must have servants. Have those who went been replaced?"

"No, Tuan, no one will go."

Mr. Warburton frowned. Cooper was an insolent fool, but he had an official position and must be suitably provided with servants. It was not seemly that his house should be improperly conducted.

"Where are the boys who ran away?"

"They are in the kampong, Tuan."

"Go and see them tonight, and tell them that I expect them to be back in Tuan Cooper's house at dawn tomorrow."

"They say they will not go, Tuan."

"On my order?"

The boy had been with Mr. Warburton for fifteen years, and he knew every intonation of his master's voice. He was not afraid of him, they had gone through too much together, once in the jungle the Resident had saved his life, and once, upset in some rapids, but for him the Resident would have been drowned; but he knew when the Resident must be obeyed without question.

"I will go to the kampong," he said.

Mr. Warburton expected that his subordinate would take the first opportunity to apologize for his rudeness, but Cooper had the ill-bred man's inability to express regret; and when they met next morning in the office he ignored the incident. Since Mr. Warburton had been away for three weeks it was necessary for them to have a somewhat prolonged interview. At the end of it, Mr. Warburton dismissed him.

"I don't think there's anything else, thank you." Cooper turned to go, but Mr. Warburton stopped him. "I understand you've been having some trouble with your boys."

Cooper gave a harsh laugh.

"They tried to blackmail me. They had the damned cheek to run away, all except that incompetent fellow Abas—he knew when he was well off—but I just sat tight. They've all come to heel again."

"What do you mean by that?"

"This morning they were all back on their jobs, the Chinese cook and all. There they were, as cool as cucumbers; you would have thought they owned the place. I suppose they'd come to the conclusion that I wasn't such a fool as I looked."

"By no means. They came back on my express order."

Cooper flushed slightly.

"I should be obliged if you wouldn't interfere with my private concerns."

"They're not your private concerns. When your servants run away it makes you ridiculous. You are perfectly free to make a fool of yourself, but I cannot allow you to be made a fool of. It is unseemly that your house should not be properly staffed. As soon as I heard that your boys had left you, I had them told to be back in their places at dawn. That'll do."

Mr. Warburton nodded to signify that the interview was at an end. Cooper took no notice.

"Shall I tell you what I did? I called them and gave the whole bally lot the sack. I gave them ten minutes to get out of the compound."

Mr. Warburton shrugged his shoulders.

"What makes you think you can get others?"

"I've told my own clerk to see about it."

Mr. Warburton reflected for a moment.

"I think you behaved very foolishly. You will do well to remember in future that good masters make good servants."

"Is there anything else you want to teach me?"

"I should like to teach you manners, but it would be an arduous task, and I have not the time to waste. I will see that you get boys."

"Please don't put yourself to any trouble on my account. I'm quite capable of getting them for myself."

Mr. Warburton smiled acidly. He had an inkling that Cooper disliked him as much as he disliked Cooper, and he knew that nothing is more galling than to be forced to accept the favours of a man you detest.

"Allow me to tell you that you have no more chance of getting Malay or Chinese servants here now than you have of getting an English butler or a French chef. No one will come to you except on an order from me. Would you like me to give it?"

"No."

"As you please. Good morning."

Mr. Warburton watched the development of the situation with acrid humour. Cooper's clerk was unable to persuade Malay, Dyak, or Chinese to enter the house of such a master. Abas, the boy who remained faithful to him, knew how to cook only native food, and Cooper, a coarse feeder, found his gorge rise against the everlasting rice. There was no water-carrier, and in that great heat he needed several baths a day. He cursed Abas, but Abas opposed him with sullen resistance and would not do more than he chose. It was galling to know that the lad stayed with him only because the Resident insisted. This went on for a fortnight and then, one morning, he found in his house the very servants whom he had previously dismissed. He fell into a violent rage, but he had learnt a little sense, and this time, without a word, he let them stay. He swallowed his humiliation, but the impatient contempt he had felt for Mr. Warburton's idiosyncrasies changed into a sullen hatred: the Resident with this malicious stroke had made him the laughing-stock of all the natives.

The two men now held no communication with one another. They broke the time-honoured custom of sharing, notwithstanding personal dislike, a drink at six o'clock with any white man who happened to be at the station. Each lived in his own house as though the other did not exist. Now that Cooper had fallen into the work, it was necessary for them to have little to do with one another in the office. Mr. Warburton used his orderly to send any message he had to give his assistant, and his instructions he sent by formal letter. They saw one another constantly, that was inevitable, but did not exchange half a dozen words in a week. The fact that they could not avoid catching sight of one another got on their nerves. They brooded over their antagonism, and Mr. Warburton, taking his daily walk, could think of nothing but how much he detested his assistant.

And the dreadful thing was that in all probability they would remain thus, facing each other in deadly enmity, till Mr. Warburton went on leave. It might be three years. He had no reason to send in a complaint to headquarters: Cooper did his work very well, and at that time men were hard to get. True, vague complaints reached him and hints that the natives found Cooper harsh. There was certainly a feeling of dissatisfaction among them. But when Mr. Warburton looked into specific cases, all he could say was that Cooper had shown severity where mildness would not have been misplaced, and had been unfeeling when himself would have been sympathetic. He had done nothing for which he could be taken to task. But Mr. Warburton watched him. Hatred will often make a man clear-sighted, and he had a suspicion that Cooper was using the natives without consideration, yet keeping within the law, because he felt that thus he could exasperate his chief. One day perhaps he would go too far. None knew better than Mr. Warburton how irritable the incessant heat could make a man and how difficult it was to keep one's self-control after a sleepless night. He smiled softly to himself. Sooner or later Cooper would deliver himself into his hand.

When at last the opportunity came, Mr. Warburton laughed aloud. Cooper had charge of the prisoners; they made roads, built sheds, rowed when it was necessary to send the prahu up or down stream, kept the town clean, and otherwise usefully employed themselves. If well-behaved they even on occasion served as house-boys. Cooper kept them hard at it. He liked to see them work. He took pleasure in devising tasks for them; and seeing quickly enough that they were being made to do useless things the prisoners worked badly. He punished them by lengthening their hours. This was contrary to the regulations, and as soon as it was brought to the attention of Mr. Warburton, without referring the matter back to his subordinate, he gave instructions that the old hours should be kept; Cooper, going out for his walk, was astounded to see the prisoners strolling back to the gaol; he had given instructions that they were not to knock off till dusk. When he asked the warder in charge why they had left off work he was told that it was the Resident's bidding.

White with rage he strode to the Fort. Mr. Warburton, in his spotless white ducks and his neat topee, with a walking-stick in his hand, followed by his dogs, was on the point of starting out on his afternoon stroll. He had watched Cooper go, and knew that he had taken the road by the river. Cooper jumped up the steps and went straight up to the Resident.

"I want to know what the hell you mean by countermanding my order that the prisoners were to work till six," he burst out, beside himself with fury.

Mr. Warburton opened his cold blue eyes very wide and assumed an expression of great surprise.

"Are you out of your mind? Are you so ignorant that you do not know that that is not the way to speak to your official superior?"

"Oh, go to hell. The prisoners are my pidgin, and you've got no right to interfere. You mind your business and I'll mind mine. I want to know what the devil you mean by making a damned fool of me. Everyone in the place will know that you've countermanded my order."

Mr. Warburton kept very cool.

"You had no power to give the order you did. I countermanded it because it was harsh and tyrannical. Believe me, I have not made half such a damned fool of you as you have made of yourself."

"You disliked me from the first moment I came here. You've done everything you could to make the place impossible for me because I wouldn't lick your boots for you. You got your knife into me because I wouldn't flatter you."

Cooper, spluttering with rage, was nearing dangerous ground, and Mr. Warburton's eyes grew on a sudden colder and more piercing.

"You are wrong, I thought you were a cad, but I was perfectly satisfied with the way you did your work."

"You snob. You damned snob. You thought me a cad because I hadn't been to Eton. Oh, they told me in K.S. what to expect. Why, don't you know that you're the laughing-stock of the whole country? I could hardly help bursting into a roar of laughter when you told your celebrated story about the Prince of Wales. My God, how they shouted at the club when they told it. By God, I'd rather be the cad I am than the snob you are."

He got Mr. Warburton on the raw.

"If you don't get out of my house this minute I shall knock you down," he cried.

The other came a little closer to him and put his face in his.

"Touch me, touch me," he said. "By God, I'd like to see you hit me. Do you want me to say it again? Snob. Snob."

Cooper was three inches taller than Mr. Warburton, a strong, muscular young man. Mr. Warburton was fat and fifty-four. His clenched fist shot out. Cooper caught him by the arm and pushed him back.

"Don't be a damned fool. Remember I'm not a gentleman. I know how to use my hands."

He gave a sort of hoot, and grinning all over his pale, sharp face jumped down the veranda steps. Mr. Warburton, his heart in his anger pounding against his ribs, sank exhausted into a chair. His body tingled as though he had prickly heat. For one horrible moment he thought he was going to cry. But suddenly he was conscious that his head-boy was on the veranda and instinctively regained control of himself. The boy came forward and filled him a glass of whisky and soda. Without a word Mr. Warburton took it and drank it to the dregs.

"What do you want to say to me?" asked Mr. Warburton, trying to force a smile on to his strained lips.

"Tuan, the assistant Tuan is a bad man. Abas wishes again to leave him."

"Let him wait a little. I shall write to Kuala Solor and ask that Tuan Cooper should go elsewhere."

"Tuan Cooper is not good with the Malays."

"Leave me."

The boy silently withdrew. Mr. Warburton was left alone with his thoughts. He saw the club at Kuala Solor, the men sitting round the table in the window in their flannels, when the night had driven them in from golf and tennis, drinking whiskies and gin pahits, and laughing when they told the celebrated story of the Prince of Wales and himself at Marienbad. He was hot with shame and misery. A snob! They all thought him a snob. And he had always thought them very good fellows, he had always been gentleman enough to let it make no difference to him that they were of very second-rate position. He hated them now. But his hatred for them was nothing compared with his hatred for Cooper. And if it had come to blows Cooper could have thrashed him. Tears of mortification ran down his red, fat face. He sat there for a couple of hours smoking cigarette after cigarette and he wished he were dead.

At last the boy came back and asked him if he would dress for dinner. Of course! He always dressed for dinner. He rose wearily from his chair and put on his stiff shirt and the high collar. He sat down at the prettily decorated table, and was waited on as usual by the two boys while two others waved their great fans. Over there in the bungalow, two hundred yards away, Cooper was eating a filthy meal clad only in a sarong and a baju. His feet were bare and while he ate he probably read a detective story. After dinner Mr. Warburton sat down to write a letter. The Sultan was away, but he wrote, privately and confidentially, to his representative. Cooper did his work very well, he said, but the fact was that he couldn't get on with him. They were getting dreadfully on each other's nerves and he would look upon it as a very great favour if Cooper could be transferred to another post.

He dispatched the letter the next morning by special messenger. The answer came a fortnight later with the month's mail. It was a private note, and ran as follows:

My dear Warburton,

I do not want to answer your letter officially, and so I am
writing you a few lines myself. Of course if you insist I will
put the matter up to the Sultan, but I think you would be
much wiser to drop it. I know Cooper is a rough diamond,
but he is capable, and he had a pretty thin time in the war, and
I think he should be given every chance. I think you are a
little too much inclined to attach importance to a man's social
position. You must remember that times have changed. Of
course it's a very good thing for a man to be a gentleman, but
it's better that he should be competent and hard-working.
I think if you'll exercise a little tolerance you'll get on very
well with Cooper.

Yours very sincerely,
Richard Temple

The letter dropped from Mr. Warburton's hand. It was easy to read
between the lines. Dick Temple, whom he had known for twenty years,
Dick Temple who came from quite a good country family, thought him
a snob, and for that reason had no patience with his request. Mr.
Warburton felt on a sudden discouraged with life. The world of which
he was a part had passed away and the future belonged to a meaner
generation. Cooper represented it and Cooper he hated with all his
heart. He stretched out his hand to fill his glass, and at the gesture his
head-boy stepped forward.

"I didn't know you were there."

The boy picked up the official letter. Ah, that was why he was
waiting.

"Does Tuan Cooper go, Tuan?"

"No."

"There will be misfortune."

For a moment the words conveyed nothing to his lassitude. But only
for a moment. He sat up in his chair and looked at the boy. He was
all attention.

"What do you mean by that?"

"Tuan Cooper is not behaving rightly with Abas."

Mr. Warburton shrugged his shoulders. How should a man like Cooper know how to treat servants? Mr. Warburton knew the type: he would be grossly familiar with them one moment and rude and inconsiderate the next.

"Let Abas go back to his family."

"Tuan Cooper holds back his wages so that he may not run away. He has paid him nothing for three months. I tell him to be patient. But he is angry, he will not listen to reason. If the Tuan continues to use him ill there will be a misfortune."

"You were right to tell me."

The fool! Did he know so little of the Malays as to think he could safely injure them? It would serve him damned well right if he got a kris in his back. A kris. Mr. Warburton's heart seemed on a sudden to miss a beat. He had only to let things take their course and one fine day he would be rid of Cooper. He smiled faintly as the phrase, a masterly inactivity, crossed his mind. And now his heart beat a little quicker, for he saw the man he hated lying on his face in a pathway of the jungle with a knife in his back. A fit end for the cad and the bully. Mr. Warburton sighed. It was his duty to warn him, and of course he must do it. He wrote a brief and formal note to Cooper asking him to come to the Fort at once.

In ten minutes Cooper stood before him. They had not spoken to one another since the day when Mr. Warburton had nearly struck him. He did not now ask him to sit down.

"Did you wish to see me?" asked Cooper.

He was untidy and none too clean. His face and hands were covered with little red blotches where mosquitoes had bitten him and he had scratched himself till the blood came. His long, thin face bore a sullen look.

"I understand that you are again having trouble with your servants. Abas, my head-boy's nephew, complains that you have held back his wages for three months. I consider it a most arbitrary proceeding. The lad wishes to leave you, and I certainly do not blame him. I must insist on your paying what is due to him."

"I don't choose that he should leave me. I am holding back his wages as a pledge of his good behavior."

"You do not know the Malay character. The Malays are very sensitive to injury and ridicule. They are passionate and revengeful. It is my duty to warn you that if you drive this boy beyond a certain point you run a great risk."

Cooper gave a contemptuous chuckle.

"What do you think he'll do?"

"I think he'll kill you."

"Why should you mind?"

"Oh, I wouldn't," replied Mr. Warburton, with a faint laugh. "I should bear it with the utmost fortitude. But I feel the official obligation to give you a proper warning."

"Do you think I'm afraid of a damned nigger?"

"It's a matter of entire indifference to me."

"Well, let me tell you this, I know how to take care of myself; that boy Abas is a dirty, thieving rascal, and if he tries any monkey tricks on me, by God, I'll wring his bloody neck."

"That was all I wished to say to you," said Mr. Warburton. "Good evening."

Mr. Warburton gave him a little nod of dismissal. Cooper flushed, did not for a moment know what to say or do, turned on his heel, and stumbled out of the room. Mr. Warburton watched him go with an icy smile on his lips. He had done his duty. But what would he have thought had he known that when Cooper got back to his bungalow, so silent and cheerless, he threw himself down on his bed and in his bitter loneliness on a sudden lost all control of himself? Painful sobs tore his chest and heavy tears rolled down his cheeks.

After this Mr. Warburton seldom saw Cooper, and never spoke to him. He read his *Times* every morning, did his work at the office, took his exercise, dressed for dinner, dined, and sat by the river smoking his cheroot. If by chance he ran across Cooper he cut him dead. Each, though never for a moment unconscious of the propinquity, acted as though the other did not exist. Time did nothing to assuage their animosity. They watched one another's actions and each knew what the other did. Though Mr. Warburton had been a keen shot in his youth, with age he had acquired a distaste for killing the wild things of the jungle, but on Sundays and holidays Cooper went out with his gun: if he got something it was a triumph over Mr. Warburton; if not, Mr. Warburton shrugged his shoulders and chuckled. These counter-jumpers trying to be sportsmen! Christmas was a bad time for both of them: they ate their dinners alone, each in his own quarters, and they got deliberately drunk. They were the only white men within two hundred miles and they lived within shouting distance of each other. At the beginning of the year Cooper went down with fever, and when Mr. Warburton caught sight of him again he was surprised to see how thin he had grown. He looked ill and worn. The solitude, so much more unnatural because it was due to no necessity, was getting on his nerves. It was getting on Mr. Warburton's too, and often he could not sleep at night. He lay awake brooding. Cooper was drinking heavily and surely the breaking point was near; but in his dealings with the natives he took care to do nothing that might expose him to his chief's rebuke. They fought a grim and silent battle with one another. It was a test of endurance. The months passed, and neither gave sign of weakening. They were like men dwelling in regions of eternal night, and their souls were oppressed with the knowledge that never would the day dawn for them. It looked as though their lives would continue for ever in this dull and hideous monotony of hatred.

And when at last the inevitable happened it came upon Mr. Warburton with all the shock of the unexpected. Cooper accused the boy Abas of stealing some of his clothes, and when the boy denied the theft took him by the scruff of the neck and kicked him down the steps of the bungalow. The boy demanded his wages and Cooper flung at his head every word of abuse he knew. If he saw him in the compound in an hour he would hand him over to the police. Next morning the boy waylaid him outside the Fort when he was walking over to his office, and again demanded his wages. Cooper struck him in the face with his clenched fist. The boy fell to the ground and got up with blood streaming from his nose.

Cooper walked on and set about his work. But he could not attend to it. The blow had calmed his irritation, and he knew that he had gone too far. He was worried. He felt ill, miserable, and discouraged. In the adjoining office sat Mr. Warburton, and his impulse was to go and tell him what he had done; he made a movement in his chair, but he knew with what icy scorn he would listen to the story. He could see his patronizing smile. For a moment he had an uneasy fear of what Abas might do. Warburton had warned him all right. He sighed. What a fool he had been! But he shrugged his shoulders impatiently. He did not care; a fat lot he had to live for. It was all Warburton's fault; if he hadn't put his back up nothing like this would have happened. Warburton had made life a hell for him from the start. The snob. But they were all like that: it was because he was a Colonial. It was a damned shame that he had never got his commission in the war; he was as good as anyone else. They were a lot of dirty snobs. He was damned if he was going to knuckle under now. Of course Warburton would hear of what had happened; the old devil knew everything. He wasn't afraid. He wasn't afraid of any Malay in Borneo, and Warburton could go to blazes.

He was right in thinking that Mr. Warburton would know what had happened. His head-boy told him when he went in to tiffin.

"Where is your nephew now?"

"I do not know, Tuan. He has gone."

Mr. Warburton remained silent. After luncheon as a rule he slept a little, but today he found himself very wide awake. His eyes involuntarily sought the bungalow where Cooper was not resting.

The idiot! Hesitation for a little was in Mr. Warburton's mind. Did the man know in what peril he was? He supposed he ought to send for him. But each time he had tried to reason with Cooper, Cooper had insulted him. Anger, furious anger welled up suddenly in Mr. Warburton's heart, so that the veins on his temples stood out and he clenched his fists. The cad had had his warning. Now let him take what was coming to him. It was no business of his, and if anything happened it was not his fault. But perhaps they would wish in Kuala Solor that they had taken his advice and transferred Cooper to another station.

He was strangely restless that night. After dinner he walked up and down the veranda. When the boy went away to his own quarters, Mr. Warburton asked him whether anything had been seen of Abas.

"No, Tuan, I think maybe he has gone to the village of his mother's brother."

Mr. Warburton gave him a sharp glance, but the boy was looking down, and their eyes did not meet. Mr. Warburton went down to the river and sat in his arbour. But peace was denied him. The river flowed ominously silent. It was like a great serpent gliding with sluggish movement towards the sea. And the trees of the jungle over the water were heavy with a breathless menace. No bird sang. No breeze ruffled the leaves of the cassias. All around him it seemed as though something waited.

He walked across the garden to the road. He had Cooper's bungalow in full view from there. There was a light in his sitting-room, and across the road floated the sound of rag-time. Cooper was playing his gramophone. Mr. Warburton shuddered; he had never got over his instinctive dislike of that instrument. But for that he would have gone over and spoken to Cooper. He turned and went back to his own house. He read late into the night, and at last he slept. But he did not sleep very long, he had terrible dreams, and he seemed to be awakened by a cry. Of course that was a dream too, for no cry—from the bungalow for instance—could be heard in his room. He lay awake till dawn. Then he heard hurried steps and the sound of voices, his head-boy burst suddenly into the room without his fez, and Mr. Warburton's heart stood still.

"Tuan, Tuan."

Mr. Warburton jumped out of bed.

"I'll come at once."

He put on his slippers, and in his sarong and pyjama-jacket walked across his compound and into Cooper's. Cooper was lying in bed, with his mouth open, and a kris sticking in his heart. He had been killed in his sleep. Mr. Warburton started, but not because he had not expected to see just such a sight, he started because he felt in himself a sudden glow of exultation. A great burden had been lifted from his shoulders.

Cooper was quite cold. Mr. Warburton took the kris out of the wound, it had been thrust in with such force that he had to use an effort to get it out, and looked at it. He recognized it. It was a kris that a dealer had offered him some weeks before, and which he knew Cooper had bought.

"Where is Abas?" he asked sternly.

"Abas is at the village of his mother's brother."

The sergeant of the native police was standing at the foot of the bed.

"Take two men and go to the village and arrest him."

Mr. Warburton did what was immediately necessary. With set face he gave orders. His words were short and peremptory. Then he went back to the Fort. He shaved and had his bath, dressed and went into the dining-room. By the side of his place *The Times* in its wrapper lay waiting for him. He helped himself to some fruit. The head-boy poured out his tea while the second handed him a dish of eggs. Mr. Warburton ate with a good appetite. The head-boy waited.

"What is it?" asked Mr. Warburton.

"Tuan, Abas, my nephew, was in the house of his mother's brother all night. It can be proved. His uncle will swear that he did not leave the kampong."

Mr. Warburton turned upon him with a frown.

"Tuan Cooper was killed by Abas. You know it as well as I know it. Justice must be done."

"Tuan, you would not hang him?"

Mr. Warburton hesitated an instant, and though his voice remained set and stern a change came into his eyes. It was a flicker which the Malay was quick to notice and across his own eyes flashed an answering look of understanding.

"The provocation was very great. Abas will be sentenced to a term of imprisonment." There was a pause while Mr. Warburton helped himself to marmalade. "When he has served a part of his sentence in prison I will take him into this house as a boy. You can train him in his duties. I have no doubt that in the house of Tuan Cooper he got into bad habits."

"Shall Abas give himself up, Tuan?"

"It would be wise of him."

The boy withdrew. Mr. Warburton took his *Times* and neatly slit the wrapper. He loved to unfold the heavy, rustling pages. The morning, so fresh and cool, was delicious and for a moment his eyes wandered out over the garden with a friendly glance. A great weight had been lifted from his mind. He turned to the columns in which were announced the births, deaths, and marriages. That was what he always looked at first. A name he knew caught his attention. Lady Ormskirk had had a son at last. By George, how pleased the old dowager must be! He would write her a note of congratulation by the next mail.

Abas would make a very good house-boy.

That fool Cooper!

From At Play in the Fields of the Lord

By Peter Matthiessen (1965)

Peter Matthiessen is one of the most respected writers of our day. He has been nominated for the National Book Award three times, for this novel, for the nonfiction work The Tree Where Man Was Born *(with Eliot Porter), and when he received it for the 1978 nonfiction book* The Snow Leopard. *A founder of* The Paris Review, *he has published twenty books in a career that started while he was still an undergraduate at Yale University. Matthiessen was the recipient of the Rainforest Alliance's 1994 Rainforest Champion award.*

    At Play in the Fields of the Lord *sets up a conflict that encompasses many of today's rainforest issues. The powerful novel, which takes place mostly in the isolated South American town of Madre de Dios, sets the "civilized" world, as represented by the characters in town (especially the missionary population), against the interests of a primitive tribe, the Niaruna, that inhabits the surrounding jungle. The interests of the outside world are pressing in on the*

Niaruna, and their time is running out: the local constabulary wants them exterminated, while the religious community wishes to convert them. The spiritual forces are represented by the local Catholic priest and the American missionaries: Leslie Huben, who has been living in an upriver station with his beautiful young wife, Andy, and the newly arrived Quarrier family, who are meant to take over the mission.

To add a leavening agent to the story, Matthiessen introduces two soldiers-of-fortune: Lewis Moon, a half-breed Native American, and his partner, Wolfie. This pair of rowdies have flown into Madre de Dios in their rattletrap airplane and are stuck there until they can raise enough money to move on. Lewis Moon, who is the central figure in the story, grew up on an Indian reservation in the States and is familiar with the missionaries' come-on. He distrusts everyone, especially the Americans, as he was once falsely accused of stealing money from the missionaries on his reservation and has been living a nomadic existence since then. He and Wolfie have been offered free passage out if they agree to drop some explosive devices on the Niaruna at the behest of the local Commandante. As we pick up the story Moon is terribly conflicted, to put it mildly. He has been drinking ayahuasca, a powerful hallucinogen extracted from jungle plants, seeking an answer to his own problems as well as those of the Niaruna, with whom he identifies. Wolfie has been doing some drinking of his own, and is sleeping it off in the hotel where all the Americans are living. Moon is too wired to sleep, and has been hallucinating. Their plane is gassed up and loaded with bombs, ready to fly, as this chapter begins. (MWC)

At the end of his long night of uproar and hallucinations, Lewis Moon had a dream. He dreamed that he walked homeward up the bed of an empty river and out onto a blasted land of rusted earth and bones and blackened stumps and stunted metal, a countryside of war. In the sky of a far distance he saw a bird appear and vanish; but no matter how far he walked, the world was one mighty industrial ruin, a maze of gutted factories and poisoned ground under the grey sky. He came finally to a signpost, and the signpost had caught a fragile ray of rising sun. He ran toward it, stumbled, fell, and ran again. The signpost pointed eastward, back toward the sun, and it read:

NOWHERE

Very tired, he turned back along his road, crossing the dead prairie. Though he had not noticed them on his outward journey, he now passed a series of signs all pointing eastward. Each was illuminated by a ray of sun, and each bore the same inscription:

NOWHERE

The terrible silence of the world made him move faster, and soon he saw, on the eastern horizon, the dark blur of a forest. He ran and trotted weakly, bewildered by the crashing of his feet upon the cinders. Another sign, and then another, pointed toward the wood.

As he drew near, the wood became a jungle, a maelstrom of pale boles and thickened fleshy leaves, shining and rubbery, of high dark passages and hanging forms, of parasites and strangler figs and obscene fruited shapes. But even here there was no sound, no sign of movement, not even a wind to stir the heavy leaves, sway the lianas; there was only the mighty hush of a dead universe.

He started forward, stopped, started again. Too frightened to go on, he turned around and saw what lay behind him; then he sat down on the road, and this time he wept.

When at last he lifted his eyes, he saw a signpost at the jungle edge; it was obscured by weeds and leaves and the tentacle of a liana, and at first he thought that its inscription was identical to all the rest. But this sign did not point to anywhere, and as he drew near and stared at it he saw that its inscription was quite different. It read:

NOWHERE

Astonished, he ventured on into the darkness of the jungle. Soon he came to a kind of clearing cut off from the sky by a canopy of trees, a soft round space like an amphitheater, diffused with sepia light. Everything was soft and brownish, and the ground itself quaked beneath his feet, giving off a smell of fungus and decay. In the center of the clearing he strayed into a quagmire; very quickly he sank, too tired to struggle. But as he passed into the earth and the warm smells of its darkness, he was still breathing without effort, and soon he dropped gently into a kind of earthen vault. Though closed off from the sky, this cave was suffused by the same soft brownish light as in the clearing far above. Here was a second sign, which read:

NOWHERE

The passage through the soil had cleaned him of his clothes, and he was naked; as soon as he stood there, small black spots appeared in pairs upon his skin. He pressed at them and discovered to his horror that the black spots were the tips of snail horns; at each touch a naked snail slid out through his skin and dropped to the cave floor. His hands flew wildly about his body, and the snails slid out and fell, until finally the earth at his bare feet was strewn with slimy writhings. Now, from the darkness near the wall, numbers of salamanders crept forward; each salamander grasped a snail behind its head and writhed with silent struggle with it, the soft bodies twitching back and forth in rhythm.

He backed toward one side of the room and fell into a tunnel. He ran along the tunnel, no longer afraid, for there was light ahead. He ran like a boy.

The tunnel emerged like a swallow's nest from the side of a high bank. Far below he saw a jungle clearing in a huge sunlight of the world's first morning, and in the clearing the Indians awaited him. Naked, he leaped into the radiant air, and fell towards them.

Moon awoke. He lay in the half-world between the dream and his narcosis, growing gradually aware of where he was. Though the room was dark, he could see the moth's white eyes above the door, and the glint of the bottle on the window sill. The man on the next bed was missing. In the background he heard singsong voices, a wailing and keening like a ringing in his ears.

The night air of Madre de Dios was fragmented by insect-singing and far barking, by the tocking of frogs in the puddles and ditches, the murmur of voices behind walls, by sounds of breaking. But the street below was rigid in its silence, and he wondered if he was not still in the dream. He rose slowly; though his head was light, he felt intensely strong and sure.

There was no question in his mind about what he was going to do. He would not wait until it was light; he would go now. He lifted his watch to his ear; its tick was murderous. The numerals of the watch face, reading five-fifteen, glowed with chinks of light, as if time burning had been forced into the casing; its metal swelled and shimmered with constraint. At this, his chest began to tighten, and his breathing hurt the cold wound in his heart; he removed the watch, and holding it by one end of the strap, rapped it sharply on the sink until it broke. Then he dropped it out the window.

He moved quickly without turning on the light. From his knapsack he took the last of the river diamonds, holding them a moment in his hands. He had found these on the upper Paragua, in Venezuela, bright alluvial diamonds, burnished clean by mountain torrents, green and blue and yellow and red. In the darkness, he could feel them burning, like fire and water of the universe, distilled.

He put one diamond in his pocket and slid the rest under Wolfie's pillow. His revolver, in its shoulder holster, he put on beneath his shirt. An instinct nagged at him to leave the gun behind, to go forth unarmed and clean; he slung it into a corner of the room. But after looking at it for a moment, his instinct weakened and he retrieved it.

He went out of his room and down the hall to where the missionaries slept; he opened the first door he came to, quietly but without hesitation. In the bed, his back to him, lay Leslie Huben. Beside Huben was the girl. He crossed the room and looked at her, the long hair on the pillow and soft mouth; he could smell the warmth of her. When he reached down and ran his fingertips from the corner of her eye along her temple, her eyes opened, widened. Slowly her hands reached for the sheet and drew it to her chin.

"Come with me," he told her, neither softly nor loudly.

She cried out faintly, like a child, which made him smile. She turned her head toward her husband, turned it back again.

"No," she whispered, "no, no, no."

He went out the door again and closed it. The next room was Martin Quarrier's, and he found what he was looking for in the hip pocket of the missionary's pants. Quarrier awoke and followed him out into the hall. The man talked on and on, and at the end he heard his own voice say, "No, not now."

He glanced back once as he turned down the stairs; the girl was watching through the door crack. When she closed the door, he kept on going.

He walked down the center of the empty street. On its last corner leaned a solitary man, a drunkard, attended by a dog. The drunkard was singing a sad slow mountain song, gasping for breath, lungs cracking. When Moon crossed his line of vision, he croaked, *"Dónde vas, amigo?"*

He kept on singing while Moon stopped, swaying, and regarded him. The drunkard's face waxed and waned, in caricature of idiocy, of rage and misery and innocence, of sensibility and soul. He sang softly out of his great mouth, his staring eyes and tear-eroded cheeks, his skull:

> *"Qué buen de bailar*
> *Qué buen de cantar."*

Was this man the solitary figure coming at him down the street? Moon said, *"Yo voy a otro mundo."*

"Sí." The man paused again, contemplating Moon. *"Sí, quieres venir?"*

"No, gracias." And then the man said gently, *"Una copita, sí—ayahuasca, no. Buen viaje."*

Moon emptied his pockets of his change and gave it to the singer. The man demurred: it was not Moon but the *ayahuasca* that made the gift. Moon said, "No, I no longer have need of it." The man took it. "God will repay you," he said; he looked uncertain.

Si, si. Dios le pagará.

Moon walked on, his enlarged pupils drawing in the faintest light; every sound and every smell enlivened him. In the nostrils of a lunatic, he thought, the night air is just as strong . . . In this moment he could scent, hunt out, run down and kill the swiftest creature on earth. Stalking the plane, he knew every sinew and muscle in his body, how each coiled and moved; in the darkness of the jungle night, he played cat, nerves taut, listening. He heard a small night animal and sprang for it, and was astonished when he missed it. An instant later he stopped breathing; something was hunting him in turn. He drew the revolver and ducked under the plane, rising silently behind the intruder.

The girl stood beside the wing. "Where are you going?" her voice said. "Are you going to bomb the Niaruna?"

"No."

"You must not."

"No." He laughed. He had not felt happy since—since when?

"Are you sick? You look so strange! I suppose you're very drunk."

"No."

"What is it then? What are you doing out here in the middle of the night? Why did you break into our room?"

"To say good-bye."

"But we haven't even said hello yet!"

"Let's say it then: hello."

Look, look, she's smiling!

She said, "Your name is Lewis Moon."

"Yes. Your name is Andy. What were you christened?"

"Agnes. Agnes Carr."

"That's much better than Andy Huben."

"I tried for days to place your name; then I remembered."

She had been running, and she paused for breath; gazing at him, her eyes filled with tears. "Your people, and the mission—they were all so *proud* of you!"

"Yes, they were."

"Yet you disgraced them!"

"That's what they said."

"May God forgive you!"

"Why should He, when I haven't forgiven Him?" He laughed.

She looked disgusted. "You're not the least repentant, are you?"

"No. Suppose I told you that I didn't steal that money, that it was given to me."

"Why didn't you tell the truth, then?"

"Because the truth looked worse than what was being said. A thief is one thing, but a betrayer—do you always talk like this?"

"Like what, Mr. Moon?"

"Like a missionary's wife."

"I *am* a missionary's wife."

"Then why did you follow me out here, with your hair still wild? Agnes Carr! Maybe you were never meant to be a missionary's wife."

"Mr. Moon, I came to beg you not to attack the Niaruna."

"All right."

"All right what?"

"All right, beg me."

"Oh please! You mustn't attack them—"

"I won't attack them; I'm just heading eastward." And he told her eagerly about his dream, about how all the signs had pointed eastward; that Indians said the Source of Life, the Sun, lay in the East, and that in the West, where the Sun touched the Darkness, was the Land of the Dead.

She nodded: The Tiros believed that because the white man came to them from the far side of the Andes, he was the Spirit of the Dead. As she spoke she gazed at him, and her face changed. This made him happy; he awaited her, saying nothing. "How strange you look—your eyes, I mean! And your voice, when you talk about these things, it's so quiet, so gentle. I don't understand you! Why do you do . . . And just now, coming here, I saw you crouched on all fours, like an animal! You looked like a cat! Really, you frightened me! What were you doing?"

He felt removed again and would not answer her.

She said, "You must listen to me. There's nothing east of here but jungle. For two thousand miles! You can't just *go* there!"

"That's the only way to do it—*go*. When there's a jungle waiting, you go through it and come out clean on the far side. Because if you struggle to back out, you get all snarled, and afterwards the jungle is still there, still waiting."

"I don't understand you." She looked annoyed; he was trying to see her body through her bathrobe. "You promise then?"

"I'll promise if you like."

She got down on her knees. "O Praise the Lord!" she said, and began to pray.

He too got down upon his knees, to see her face better. "What are you doing?" he inquired.

"Saying a prayer for you."

He took her hands and raised her to her feet. "Don't," he said. "Please don't do that. I knew yesterday that I would not attack them. Listen—I *know* something, Andy . . ." But he had forgotten what he wanted to say. He reached out to her and touched her face; her face implored him. "Agnes Carr," he murmured. He took from his pocket the wild diamond, the clear drop of river fire and mountain rain, and squeezed it hard into her hand. She ran. "Good-bye," he called.

Good-bye, good-bye.

It was still dark, dark and starless, when he turned the plane at the far end of the runway; he could scarcely make out the wall of trees at the far end or where earth merged with sky. His hands on the controls moved swiftly and precisely but he was breathing urgently, and he did not wait for break of day as he had planned. He roared away into the darkness, veering wildly from side to side; when he thought he was running out of ground he sighed, hauling back on the wheel, and the plane bounded aloft. The black wall was much too close, and jumped at him; he rolled his wing to miss a treetop, hooting, and then he was high and clear. Already, off to the east, the horizon was fire-black against the glow of the morning sun rolling toward him across Amazonas. A lone black palm, bent sadly on the sky of dawn, sank away into the darkness as he rose.

He flew boldly, straight into the sun. He was sailing eastward into all the mornings of the world, as the cloud forest and dark mountain range, the night and the dank river mists fell far behind. There had never been a day so brilliant. The dawn light caused the swamps to glitter, and pierced the muddy floods with life. It sparkled on the canopy, and illuminated from within the wings of birds; a flight of parakeets shimmered downriver like a windburst of bright petals, and an alabaster egret burned his eye. He laughed with joy and sang.

The cabin of the plane confined him; he would burst the plane apart. He was oriented to the sun, as if he had soared into its field of gravitation. He was the sun in the sun-flecked wings of a golden insect, crawling across the dome of sky inside his windshield; he was the sun in the white wings below, the sun in the huge voice of the bird morning. All air and light and sound poured through him, swelling the universe.

To meet the sun he wandered from his course, and now he whirled off northward; today, without effort, he could feel his bearings like a bird. Remate was in the distance; he was headed straight for it, though he had not checked his compass. He *knew*. He could trust his eyes and hand to take him by dead reckoning.

At Remate the inhabitants rushed like chickens to the center of the clearing; he passed overhead, up the Espíritù. It was not until he crossed a Tiro village that he felt a burst of somber dread. Realizing where he was, not sure why he had come, his hands grew cold.

He checked his gauges. His journey to the sun had consumed too much fuel; he must turn back now if he was to reach Madre de Dios. But Madre de Dios was the past, he had come across into the present, and in the next moment the dread left him and his mind soared once again. He switched on his radio set, wishing to sing something to the world; he sang "Shenandoah" and "Columbus Stockade" and "All My Trials," and the Portuguese words of "Jesus Wants Me for a Sunbeam": *"Brilhan-do, brilhan-do . . ."*

He flew onward. Because he did not know yet how he would do what he must do, he swung wide of the Niaruna village, circling at a distance; all the while he talked and sang.

Another voice crackled thinly over the radio; it had been crackling for some time. He put the earphones on and listened.

"This is Les Huben at Madre de Dios. Do you read me? Over."

Moon pressed the button on his transmitter. "This is Jesus, up in Heaven," he said affably. "How do you read me? Over."

But Huben ranted on. Offers of help and prayers for Moon's safety were interspersed with flight talk: *"By my estimate,"* Huben's voice said, *"fuel-range ratio of your aircraft is very critical. Can I assist you? Over."*

"How about some last rites?" Moon responded. "Over."

But he realized with annoyance that he had neglected to press his transmitter button.

Huben came back again: *"You are under the effects of a powerful drug; repeat, you are under the effects of a powerful drug. You must try to concentrate, you are in an emergency; repeat, you are in an emergency. May the Lord forgive you and keep you. Amen. Over."*

"Thus spake the Lord to Leslie Huben, His false witness: *I call heaven and earth to record this day against you, that I have set before you life and death, blessing and cursing.*" In the silence that followed he bellowed, "Deuteronomy, 30:16."

Huben's voice said, *"30:19. For the last time, fella, you are in emergency, repeat, you are in emergency. Where are you proceeding; repeat, where are you proceeding? Over."*

Moon looked a last time at his gauges.

"What is your exact location; repeat, what is your exact location? Over."

"I'm at play in the fields of the Lord," Moon said; he removed his earphones. "Repeat, at play in the fields of the Lord."

According to his own estimate, he would run out of fuel in a few more minutes. The girl had said that to these Indians the white man was a wild creature from the west; he circled wide and came in upon the Niaruna from the east, out of the sun. They spread like ants. A few stood still. They awaited him, just as they had awaited in his vision. But of course he could not land, not even a crash landing; flyers who pancaked their small planes onto the canopy had starved to death, for there was no means of descent from the monstrous trees. As for the river, it was too narrow and overgrown for an approach, and there were no sand bars.

In the vision he had leaped into the air, and he would do that here;

there was no wind, and if he timed it right and used his shrouds, he might drop into the clearing. He reached back across the crate of bombs and dragged the parachute up front, then began his climb in a widening circle, higher and higher, with the sun, until the canopy stretched away so far on every side that the whole jungle lay beneath him.

The climb had burned up the last of his fuel. The gauge was lifeless, and he knew he might stall at any time. His breath was short; the altimeter read 9600. He leveled off for his approach, so intent on his work that only when he braced the door open and the cold air seared his hand did his fear verge upon panic. But his breath came again, and with it a new exaltation; on such a morning, all light and purity and color, even death must be magnificent.

He tried to work himself into his parachute. But his vast solar energy was instantly exhausted; he sat there gasping. "Hoo, boy," he said, trying in vain to cheer himself. He bound his arm in the straps of the chute, and grasping the strut, inched out onto the wing; how cold it was, in this cold light of heaven! He was afraid again. He clutched the parachute to his chest, and with his other arm—the one run through the strap—he hugged the strut. Now he pulled the cord and the silk bulged at the crack.

Now you've done it. This time you've *really* done it.

The wind tore at his face, and his arms ached. Short of the clearing, a mile and a half above the trees, he kicked himself forward and away. Shoving his free arm among the straps, then clasping both arms tight to his chest, he closed his eyes against the gut-sucking suspense, and the blow of the silk snapped open; he fell the length of a long howl before the impact all but wrenched his arms out of their sockets. He blinked, in tears; he was alive again, laughing idiotically in the clean sunlight of the upper air, legs dangling and swaying like the legs of a rag doll, drifting, drifting down through the great morning, in a wild silence like the wake of bells.

The Fate of the Forests: The Future

There is so much smoke all the animals are being killed. The rivers as well. That is why I am very worried about my people. My spirit is always warning me that when the forest is destroyed there will be no more shade. There will be very strong winds. The sun will get very hot. And it will be difficult to breathe. Then everybody will die. Not just the Indians. Everybody will die. This is my concern. I am warning you. You have to think. You have to change your ideas. Leave the jungle alone.

—Chief Raoni

*I want to tell what the forests
were like*

*I will have to speak
in a forgotten language*

—W. S. Merwin, "Witness"

"I Don't Want Flowers at My Funeral"

From The Burning Season (1990)
By Andrew Revkin

In December 1988, the growing global movement to conserve tropical forests was galvanized by its own "shot heard round the world." The brutal assassination of Chico Mendes, a Brazilian rubber tapper who was president of his local rural workers' union, created an international uproar and sparked a new flame in the fight to conserve disappearing forests.

As the death of Mendes exploded into a huge media event, the attention took everyone by surprise. Already that year, several rubber tappers and four rural union presidents had been killed in Brazil. Who would have thought that the murder of yet another rubber tapper could make a difference? Who would have believed that scores of journalists and moviemakers would venture into a remote jungle town to try and find out who had killed Mendes?

An astute few looked at the larger implications of the event. Andy Revkin, a soft-spoken journalist, was one. He went to Brazil to find out the truth about

what had happened and why other murders were still taking place. He wanted
to know not only why Mendes had died but also why people were still killing
one another over tropical forests. (DRK)

At six-thirty on a Thursday evening in the Amazon town of Xapuri, the bell in the spire of the yellow stucco church on the town square began to ring. It was three days before Christmas, 1988, and the bell was the first call to a special mass for the children who were graduating from elementary school. The cicadas began their nightly drone, enfolding the town and the surrounding rainforest in a blanket of sound that resembled an orchestra of sitar players tuning their instruments. Although it was well into the rainy season, the regular torrential downpours had held off for a day. Bicycles and pickup trucks rattled along the uneven, cobbled brick lanes. In the darkness, bats began to feast around the streetlights, swooping in time and again, sending out shrill, curt chirps of sonar and snatching moths and winged ants from the whirling clouds drawn to the bulbs. An occasional dugout canoe passed the shabby bars and shops that overhung the muddy, crumbling embankment of the Acre River. The staccato popping of the boats' single-cylinder diesel motors echoed against the steep sandstone cliff on the opposite shore.

Until the night of December 22, there was little to distinguish Xapuri from many of the other river towns of the Amazon. Xapuri (pronounced shah-poo-*ree*) is a sleepy rubber trading outpost of five thousand people in the state of Acre (*ah*-cray), the westernmost part of Brazil, deep in the tropical belly of the South American continent. The town perches at the spot where the Xapuri River makes its small contribution to the Acre River, which pours into the Purus, which in turn empties into the milky Solimões, one of the two great arms of the Amazon River. Some 2,000 miles downstream, the effluent from the Xapuri, combined with that of the rest of the ten thousand tributaries that lace the Amazon basin, flows into the Atlantic Ocean.

The town is quiet and orderly, the kind of place where the elderly streetsweepers come out every morning at dawn to clear leaves and litter from the shady lanes, where no one cares that the newspaper does not arrive until the noon bus pulls in from the state capital, raising a cloud of orange dust. The town is much quieter now than it was when the brick paving was laid at the turn of the century. (A curious geological fact about the Amazon is that there is no usable stone in most of the region—thus the bricks.) Back then, Acre was the center of a rich rubber boom that flourished as the industrial world's appetite for rubber exploded and thousands of men were lured into the jungle to tap latex from the rubber trees. Seven decades have passed since the rubber boom went bust, but the market for natural rubber persists—albeit subsidized by the government—so hunched laborers still haul hundred-pound slabs and balls of cured latex up the steep riverbank to the dark warehouses of the wealthy merchants who control the rubber trade.

On this night, in the fifteen minutes after the call to mass, Xapuri would forever change, all because of a man who now sat in the kitchen of his four-room cottage, playing dominoes. The small house was nestled in a row of similar shacks along Dr. Batista de Moraes Street, a five-minute walk from the bars and warehouses along the waterfront, across the treeless square that was always 10 degrees hotter in the daytime than the surrounding forest. The cottage was little bigger than a single-car garage, raised on stilts 2 feet off the tamped, grassless soil. It had a steeply pitched roof covered in terra cotta tile, baked of the same red earth as the bricks of the streets. The siding was painted pale blue with pink trim. As with most of the houses in town, the only running water was in the outhouse in the back yard.

The man sitting on one of the five small stools around the kitchen table was Francisco Alves Mendes Filho, known to everyone as Chico Mendes. He was a rubber tapper and the president of the local rural workers' union, which was fighting to save the rain forest for the thousands of rubber tappers and Indians who lived and worked in it. Mendes had just returned home after a busy month that included visits to Rio de Janeiro and São Paulo, two of the great cities in the south of Brazil—rich, industrial cities that are separated from the impoverished Amazon by much more than distance. There he had stayed in the plush apartments of environmental activists who were helping the rubber tappers with their struggle. In recent years, he had traveled increasingly between these two different Brazils. But now, with Christmas approaching, Mendes planned to stop and relax at home with his family for a few days.

Relaxing did not come easy to him. That was clear from Mendes's face, a round face dominated by puffy, owlish eyes. It was a face that usually smiled but had recently begun to show signs of stress. He had turned forty-four one week earlier, but only this year had he started to look his age. A graying mustache broadened his grin and a deep dimple appeared in his right cheek every time he smiled. His perpetually tousled black and silver curls gave him a distracted look. His thin legs sprouted beneath a firm potbelly that he displayed with a certain sense of pride. Mendes was playing dominoes with two bodyguards provided by the Military Police. Although they were not in uniform and both were neighbors—one had done typing for the union when he was a teenager—they were nonetheless an unnerving presence. Mendes had resolved to ask the police to withdraw the security.

Now that it was dark, one of the guards got up from the game and, despite the muggy heat, closed the wooden shutters over the glassless windows and slid home the bolts. The guards had been assigned to Mendes because persistent death threats had been made against him. Xapuri was peaceful on the surface, but the underlying tension was palpable and had been rising steadily all year. Mendes's union, consisting of rubber tappers and small farmers, had scored a series of victories in its war against encroaching cattle ranchers, who were incinerating the rain forest to create pasture and to profit from tax breaks and booming real estate prices.

Starting in March, the tappers had staged a series of *empates* (em-*pah*-tays), forceful demonstrations in which chainsaw crews were confronted and driven from the forest. And, in October, they had convinced the government to declare a 61,000-acre tract of traditional rubber tapper territory near Xapuri, called Seringal Cachoeira, an "extractive reserve." Cachoeira was where Mendes had grown up and first worked as a tapper; the forest there had been his only school. The new designation meant that the forest could not be cut and must be used only in sustainable ways—for the harvest of rubber, Brazil nuts, and the like. The concept of the extractive reserve had been invented by Mendes and the tappers, then refined with some help from environmentalists and anthropologists. With the establishment of this and three other extractive reserves, Mendes had pulled off one of the most significant feats in the history of grass-roots environmental activism—and he had only known the word "environment" for three years.

His wife, Ilzamar, told the domino players to stop so that she could set the table for dinner. There was fresh fish waiting to be fried. Ilzamar, twenty years younger than Mendes, had a classic Amazonian beauty that hinted at both Indian and European features. The overall effect was remarkably Polynesian: full lips and huge black eyes framed by a long, thick mane of black hair.

"In a few minutes," Mendes said. "Let us finish this game." He was competitive and very good, and he liked to play the game to the end. Mendes and the guards were playing a difficult version, called *domino pontó,* which involved some mental arithmetic. He liked to make a point of triumphantly slapping his tile down when he had finished contemplating a move. The clacking of the bone tiles on the Formica tabletop carried through the thin walls of the house and into the darkness.

Mendes's five-year marriage to Ilzamar had faltered recently, as he traveled more and more and earned less and less. (A previous brief marriage had failed as well.) In 1986, he had crisscrossed Acre in a futile campaign for the state legislature. He had been a candidate of the leftist Workers party, PT, in a state that never swayed from center-right. In 1987 and 1988, he continued to hike through the forest, seeking rubber tappers for his union, and traveled to the south, recruiting allies from Brazil's burgeoning environmental movement. In 1986, Ilzamar almost died giving birth to twins, one of whom was stillborn. Mendes could not pay the hospital bill. Ilzamar was never allowed to go with her husband on his trips. "My work is not play," he would say, as their arguments echoed through the neighbors' yards. "This is business and you can't keep a secret." It was only in March that they had moved into a house of their own—and only because Mendes's environmentalist friends had chipped in to buy it for him. Ilzamar once said that she had not spent more than eight days with Mendes from 1986 to 1988.

His work so dominated his life that it was even reflected in the names he chose for his children. As the men finished their game, the two children played on the floor in the front room of the house, where Ilzamar had returned to watch the soap opera *Anything Goes,* which both lampooned and glorified the lives of Brazil's rich. The surviving twin, now a beautiful two-year-old boy, was named Sandino, after Augusto Cesar Sandino, the leader of the 1927 guerrilla war against American marines in the mountains of Nicaragua (and the man for whom the Sandinistas were named). Mendes had named his four-year-old daughter Elenira, after a legendary female guerrilla who stalked both police and soldiers in the Amazon state of Pará in the early 1970s, at the height of the military dictatorship. Elenira was famous for her marksmanship; she invariably killed her target with a rifle shot between the eyes. Mendes had always been attracted to radical social history, although his own activism was generally less extreme than that of his idols. As one of Brazil's leaders in the fight to save the rain forest, he insisted on a nonviolent approach.

But his opponents were not so civil. In May of 1988, two teenage rubber tappers participating in a peaceful demonstration were shot by a pair of hired gunmen. In June, Ivair Higino de Almeida, a member of Mendes's union and fellow PT politician, was shot dead. In September, another tapper fell. And now, as Mendes sat slapping dominoes on the table with his guards—he was winning, as usual—two men were slowly creeping into the flimsily fenced back yard. They had slipped through the thick underbrush behind the house, following an eroded gully cut by a small stream. They wore dark jeans and, because of the sticky heat, had tied their shirts at their waists. One had a white handkerchief covering his mouth and nose; the cloth fluttered in and out with his breathing. They had heard the church bell; now they heard the laughter and the domino game and the sound of the soap opera, which echoed eerily from television sets up and down the street. It was one of Brazil's most popular shows, and everyone was watching to find out who had murdered a key character.

This was not their first visit to that yard. Hidden in the bushes near where the river curled around this side of town, two small areas of grass had been crushed where they had been camping on and off for days, patiently watching. Cigarette butts and spilled *farinha*—a baked flour of ground manioc root that is a staple starch in the Amazon—littered the *tocaia,* ambush. Five moldy tins of Bordon sausage lay in the grass, swamped with ants, and two wine bottles with water in them lay nearby. Now the men settled down to wait once more, crouching on a pile of bricks behind a palm tree 30 feet from Mendes's back door. They were adept at being quiet, perhaps from their experience stalking game in the forest. No chickens clucked, and the many dogs in the neighborhood did not so much as growl.

In the rainforests of the western Amazon, the threat of violent death hangs in the air like mist after a tropical rain. It is simply a part of the ecosystem, just like the scorpions and snakes cached in the leafy canopy that floats over the forest floor like a seamless green circus tent. People from the Amazon say that the trouble always starts during the burning season, a period of two months or so between the two natural climatic seasons of the region—the dry and the wet. By then, the equatorial sun has baked the last moisture out of the brush, grass, and felled trees, and the people of the Amazon—sometimes Indians and rubber tappers, but most often wealthy ranchers and small farmers—set their world on fire. The fires clear the clogged fields or freshly deforested land and, in disintegrating vegetation, put a few of the nutrients essential for plant growth back into the impoverished soil. The burning season is the time before the return of the daily downpours that give the rainforest its name.

The trouble arises when one man's fires threaten another man's livelihood. Most often, that happens when one of the hundreds of ranchers or speculators who have been drawn to the region's cheap land acquires the title to property that already is the home of people who have squatted there legally—sometimes for decades. Often the new titles are acquired through fraud or coercion. And because the most efficient way to reinforce a claim to land in the Amazon is to cut down the forest and burn it, the new landlords do just that. Or they loose their cattle, which make quick work of the settlers' crops. If that does not work, they send out their *pistoleiros* to burn the families out of their shacks or, if they resist, to shoot them down.

The only thing that has prevented the Amazon River basin and its peoples from being totally overrun is its sheer size and daunting character. It is a shallow bowl covering 3.6 million square miles, twice the expanse of India. An average of 8 feet of rain falls here each year, inundating great stretches of forest, turning roads into bogs, and providing vast breeding grounds for malarial mosquitoes. The water drains eastward through a fanlike network of streams and rivers that together disgorge 170 billion gallons of water each hour into the Atlantic—eleven times the flow of the Mississippi. Besides producing this riverine sea, the deluge also nourishes the largest stretch of rain forest left on Earth. Rising from a dank forest floor—a seething mat of decomposition and decay—dense stands of trees support a verdant canopy of foliage, fruits, and flowers. Innumerable species of animal and microbial life have found niches in which to flourish, all intricately interdependent.

One of the tens of thousands of plant species in the forest is a tree with a smooth trunk that produces a white fluid in a reticulation of tubules beneath its bark. Its local name is *seringueira;* botanists call it *Hevea brasiliensis.* Its common name is the rubber tree. The fluid is thought to protect the tree from invasions of boring pests by gumming up the insects' mouth parts. This same fluid, congealed and properly processed, has remarkable qualities of resilience, water resistance, and insulation to the flow of electricity—all of which made it one of the most sought after raw materials of the industrial revolution.

It was this substance, called latex, that lured the grandfather of Chico Mendes and tens of thousands of other men to the Amazon rainforest in two waves over the past hundred and twenty years. Called *seringueiros,* these men settled in the forests around ports like Xapuri and worked in solitude, fighting to make a life from the living forest—and fighting to free themselves from bosses who saw to it that they remained enslaved by their debts. Recently, as outsiders intent on destroying the forest began to invade the Amazon, the *seringueiros* had to fight once again. This time, they were fighting to save their homes, their livelihood, and the rainforest around them.

In leading this struggle to preserve the Amazon, Chico Mendes had made a lot of trouble for a lot of powerful people. He was to the ranchers of the Amazon what César Chavez was to the citrus kings of California, what Lech Walesa was to the shipyard managers of Gdansk. The Xapuri Rural Workers' Union, which Mendes helped found in 1977, regularly sent swarms of demonstrators to thwart the ranchers' chainsaw crews. The rural workers had driven two of Brazil's biggest ranchers clear out of Acre—a man nicknamed Rei do Nelore (King of Cattle) and Geraldo Bordon, the owner of one of Brazil's biggest meat-packing corporations. With his aggressive tactics and affable, plain-talking style, Mendes had then attracted the attention of American environmentalists, who invited him to Washington and Miami to help them convince the international development banks to suspend loans that were allowing Brazil to pave the roads leading into the Amazon. Mendes made friends abroad, but he made more enemies at home.

One of his most dangerous foes was Darly Alves da Silva, a rancher who had come north to Acre from the state of Paraná in 1974. Alves lived on a 10,000-acre ranch with his wife, three mistresses, thirty children, and a dozen or so cowboys, most of whom the tappers considered little more than hired killers. Alves and his family had established a tradition of murder as they moved from state to state, starting in the 1950s. When somebody bothered the Alves family, somebody usually turned up dead—if he ever turned up again at all. Darly's scrappy father, Sebastião, once spent four and a half years in jail in the south for the murder of a neighbor. He only served time because he had a vision from God that told him to confess his crime. There were many other, unsolved murders that were allegedly his work.

A fourteen-year-old boy named Genézio, who lived at Alves's ranch, later testified in court about fourteen murders that had been committed on the ranch or by the family. For instance, one day he saw some *urubu*, vultures, circling over a little-used pasture. He waded into the weeds and saw a charred corpse. A wooden post, still smoldering, was embedded in the smashed rib cage. Two weeks earlier, a workman named Valdir had disappeared after arguing with one of Darly's sons, Oloci. Another time Raimundo Ferreira, a worker at the ranch, asked to marry Darly's nine-year-old daughter, Vera. Oloci told his father that Raimundo was "trying to joke with Darly's face." Later, Oloci and his half brother Darci asked Ferreira to go with them into the jungle. After a few days, word got around that the brothers had cut off Ferreira's ear and nose and then shot and stabbed him to death.

The Alves clan had threatened Mendes many times, and more than one attempt had been made on his life. But this time was different. With his *empates,* Mendes had prevented the Alveses from taking possession of a tract of forest that Darly wanted to add to his holdings and convert to pasture. The *empates* were a frustration, but what really infuriated Darly was that Mendes had forced him and his brother Alvarino into hiding back in September, after a lawyer working with the tappers found a fifteen-year-old arrest warrant from the family's days in the south.

Darly did not look dangerous. His eyes swam behind the thick lenses of bulky bifocals that overwhelmed his narrow face. Bony legs and arms dangled from thin shoulders and hips, as if someone had cut the strings of a marionette. His ill-fitting black mustache seemed pasted on. It was his voice, a thin, wispy voice, that hinted that this was a man to handle with care. Quick streams of words had to slip out around teeth that were always clenched. Darly swore that this was the last time Mendes would ever bother him. "No one has ever bested me," he told a friend. "And Chico wants to do that."

Darly was confident he could act with impunity. His brother worked in the Xapuri sheriff's office, just forty paces from Mendes's front door, and the sheriff was a good friend of the family. The main reason Darly had moved to the Amazon was that it was one of the last places where might still made right. In that sense, it differed little from the American West of the nineteenth century as described in 1872 by Mark Twain in *Roughing It*: "the very paradise of outlaws and desperadoes." In the Amazon, when you ask people about *justiça,* justice, they simply chuckle in a sad kind of way; most of the men in the prison cells are sleeping off a drunk, having had several too many slugs of the blazing, strong sugarcane rum called *cachaça,* which is sold for pennies a glass. In fact, more than a thousand people have been murdered in land disputes in rural Brazil since 1980, and Amnesty International estimates that fewer than ten of the killers have been convicted and sent to jail. (And not one *mandante,* mastermind, of a murder has ever been tried.) Sometimes the gunmen meet resistance; there is hardly a rubber tapper's shack that does not have an oil-stained spot on the wall where the shotgun is hung. But usually the professionals prevail. In this anarchic atmosphere, the *pistoleiros* often assume the look of their imagined Wild West predecessors, strutting through town with a revolver stuck in the waist of tight jeans, boot heels raising red dust.

Thus it was that in the latter half of December, the threats against Mendes had been replaced with death pronouncements. "Threat" implies that death is only a possibility; in Mendes's case, imminent death was a near inevitability. Mendes told his brother Zuza about a series of ominous telephone calls to the union hall and his neighbor's house (Mendes did not have his own telephone). "Zuza," he said, "you watch out because things are getting very hot. I have a feeling I'm not going to make it to Christmas."

Mendes and his guards finished their domino game and moved to the front room to catch the end of *Anything Goes.* Everyone jumped slightly each time a seed pod dropped onto the tile roof from the huge *benjamin* tree that took up most of the small front yard and overhung the house. Finally, dinner was ready. Ilzamar set out a platter of fish and pots of beans and rice. When the table was ready, the two guards sat down on the small wooden stools, along with the wife of one of Mendes's friends, who had stopped by to chat. The guards were not required to stay with Mendes after dark, but they were friends of the family—and they enjoyed dominoes and home cooking. Normally they ate in the Military Police barracks, several blocks away.

By now, the insect symphony outside had reached *fortissimo,* a layered blend of high-pitched hums and creaks and rattles that muffled human speech. Ilzamar took her plate to the front room to eat with the children. Even though he was wearing only a pair of white shorts, Mendes was hot and uncomfortable. Telling everyone else to eat, he threw a towel over his shoulder and opened the back door to head to the outhouse to splash down with cold water. The powder blue towel, decorated with a rainbow and musical notes, had been a birthday present.

As he had many times before, Mendes muttered about how dark it was in back. He had talked to friends about stringing a new wire for an outdoor light bulb; someone had cut the wire the last time they tried it. They had agreed to do it *amanhã,* tomorrow—a word that is heard often in the draining heat of the Amazon. Grumbling as he shut the door, he went into the bedroom and picked up the small black flashlight with the high–intensity beam that had been a gift from Mary Allegretti, an anthropologist from the south who had worked with him for years, trying to help the rubber tappers.

Opening the door once again, Mendes flicked on the flashlight. The narrow beam swept the darkness. It is possible that he saw the two figures crouched by the palm tree in the corner opposite the outhouse. But no one will ever know, because in that instant one of the men pulled the trigger on a .20-gauge shotgun.

In the darkness, the light blue towel must have made a good target. That is exactly where the load of buckshot struck. A tight pattern of sixty pellets buried themselves in Mendes's right shoulder and chest and sent him tottering back into the kitchen. He screamed once and said no more. Trailing blood, he staggered toward the bedroom, possibly in an attempt to reach his revolver; he had kept the weapon even though the police, who had openly sided with the Alveses, had taken away his permit early in December. But his body suddenly went limp, and Mendes fell into the arms of one of the guards, Roldão Roseno de Souza, who had been with him since late October. Mendes crumpled to the floor on the threshold of the bedroom door.

He took very little time to bleed to death; later, forensic analysis showed that eleven pieces of lead had found a lung. His blood spread a dark stain across the rough plank floor and dripped through the cracks onto the earth below. The towel, riddled with holes, lay beside him.

Now all the dogs in the neighborhood were barking. Roseno cradled Mendes's head. No one dared open the back door a second time. The other guard, who had only a five-shot revolver, jumped through a window facing the street and sprinted to the military barracks to get help and grab a machine gun. Friends came running with weapons of their own, knowing as soon as they heard the shot what had happened.

Ilzamar bolted into the street, screaming, "They've killed Chico!" But the regular gaggle of policemen and hangers-on sitting outside the sheriff's office just yards away did not stir.

The funeral of Chico Mendes was held on Christmas Day. Through what the tappers call *radio cipó*—vine radio, the rain forest version of the grapevine—word of the murder quickly spread. Hundreds of rubber tappers hiked for many hours through the forest to attend the wake and funeral. On Saturday night the church bell again rang a call to mass; one by one, the rubber tappers filed past Mendes's body and spoke of how he had changed their lives. Hour after hour they shuffled by, and the singing of hymns went on into the evening.

By Christmas morning, more than a thousand people had crowded around the church. The rains had returned in force, drenching the mourners who followed the casket to the cemetery on the road leading out of town. At the head of the cortege, a young man studying for the priesthood held aloft a wooden cross with a painted portrait of Mendes fastened to the middle. The painting had been done in 1987 by an artist named Jorge Rivas Plata da Cruz. That was the year Mendes first traveled abroad and began to make headlines for his environmental work. In the painting, his mustache and hair are carefully coiffed and pure black. There are no worry lines around his smiling eyes. He is wearing the first suit he ever owned, the one he wore on his first trip abroad. It had been in a batch of clothing sent from Italy for the poor of Xapuri.

Along with the hundreds of rubber tappers and small farmers in the procession were dozens of Mendes's friends from the other Brazil. The funeral brought together the two sides of his life—the people from the forest and those from the outside, who had found in this simple rubber tapper an indispensable ally. Mary Allegretti, Mendes's first friend from the world outside the forest, had flown down from New York City, forcing her way onto a booked flight to get to Xapuri on time. Now she stood holding her umbrella over Ilzamar and the children, although it had little effect in the driving downpour. A contingent of labor leaders, celebrities, and leftist politicians from São Paulo and Rio had flown up for the funeral, headed by Luis Inácio da Silva, better known as Lula, the gravel voiced socialist who later came close to gaining the presidency of Brazil. Surrounding the crowd were dozens of journalists, many from overseas. An international version of vine radio had efficiently disseminated the news of the killing.

Luis Ceppi, Xapuri's priest, presided over the service. Ceppi, who was Italian and a member of Italy's Communist party, had helped the rubber tappers' movement get European support. As he gave the benediction, rain and tears streamed down his cheeks and soaked his white robe. The casket was placed in a brick crypt next to that of Ivair Higino de Almeida, the union member who had been brutally murdered in June—allegedly by Darly Alves's sons and hired gunmen. A mason closed the crypt and troweled the cement flat. White porcelain tiles were then applied over the bricks. Mendes had told friends, "I don't want flowers at my funeral, because I know that they would be taken from the forest." Nevertheless, someone piled freshly picked blossoms on his grave that day.

The murder of Chico Mendes might well have been an unremarkable event. He was the fifth rural union president murdered in Brazil that year, and just a week later another president of a rural union, in eastern Brazil, was blasted in the face with a shotgun in front of his family. But over the previous three years, Mendes's close relationships with environmentalists, labor organizers, and human rights advocates from Brazil, the United States, and Europe had focused increased attention on the struggle of the rubber tappers. His *empates* and organizing skills had brought him awards from the United Nations Environment Program, the Gaia Foundation, and other groups. As a result, this murder deep in the Amazon rain forest—where it once took three weeks for news to travel down the river—instantly became an international story, making the front page of newspapers around the world.

The significance of his murder was further amplified by the disturbing environmental anomalies of 1988. The scorching summer in the United States that year had motivated politicians and the media for the first time to pay serious attention to the greenhouse effect: the theory that billions of tons of gases released each year by the burning of fossil fuels and forests are trapping solar energy in the atmosphere and disastrously warming the planet. And just as the heat was breaking records and fires were ravaging Yellowstone National Park, the television networks got detailed satellite photographs of the Amazon burning season—thousands of fires burning simultaneously. It almost felt as if the heat and smoke generated in the forests were being inhaled on the baking streets of Los Angeles, Washington, and New York.

Then came the slaying of Chico Mendes. In the months that followed, dozens of television crews, photographers, and reporters from around the world would take the six-hour, four-stop flight from São Paulo to Rio Branco, the capital of Acre, then bounce for four more hours along the rutted, dusty, partly paved road to Xapuri. The Hotel Veneza, the only hostelry in town with a bathroom for each room, quickly filled up. Those turned away had to walk down the block to Hospedaria Souza, where an oversexed rooster liked to start crowing at 3:00 A.M. and one of his hens had a habit of laying eggs on the floor of the outhouse, then roosting behind the toilet.

The citizens of Xapuri gradually adjusted to all the attention. After a while, the woman who ran the Veneza learned that Americans do not like heaps of sugar brewed directly into their coffee, as is usual in the Amazon. So many journalists wanted to be taken to Seringal Cachoeira, the rubber tapping area where Mendes and the tappers had their showdown with the Alves family, that the tappers started charging $200 to truck the visitors in and put them up for a day or two in tappers' homes. Mendes's house was turned into a small museum, and the guest book filled with a thousand, then two thousand, then—by the end of the dry season of 1989—four thousand names.

Visitors who stayed long enough to walk for a time in the surrounding forest discovered the bounty of the ecosystem that Mendes had died defending. It was a place of spectacular diversity and vitality. Turn over a log and find 50 species of beetle. Survey an acre and find 100 species of butterfly. In the Amazon, one type of rubber tree has exploding fruit that flings seeds 20 yards; three-toed sloths harbor dozens of species of insects and algae in their matted fur; river porpoises are cotton-candy pink. It was a living pharmacy that scientists had only just begun to explore. A fourth of all prescription drugs contain ingredients derived from plants—malaria drugs and anesthetics and antibiotics and more—and less than 1 percent of the Amazon's plants had been studied.

It became clear to outsiders that the murder was a microcosm of the larger crime: the unbridled destruction of the last great reservoir of biological diversity on Earth. Just a few centuries ago, the planet had 15 million square miles of rainforest, an area five times that of the contiguous United States. Now three Americas' worth of forest were gone, with just 6.2 million square miles left. A third of the remaining rainforest was in the Amazon basin, and over the past decade alone, chainsaws and fires had consumed about 10 percent of it—an area twice the size of California.

The aggression against the forest was therefore a many-layered tragedy, causing human deaths, killing millions of trees and other organisms, and resulting in the extinction of several species of plant and animal life each day—most of which had not even been noticed, let alone catalogued or studied. In some ways, Chico Mendes and the rubber tappers were simply another endangered species, as much a part of the ecosystem as the trees they tapped, the birds in the branches, or the ants underfoot.

Gorillas and Their People

From No Man's Land *(1982)*
by John Heminway

We knew we had to have something about gorillas in this collection, as the great apes have always fascinated us humans. It is a great pity and an outrageous circumstance, then, when the world's dwindling wild population of mountain gorillas is consigned to an ever-diminishing habitat in the high country of the Virunga Mountains, while the chaos that is modern Africa churns about below—almost every piece of contemporary writing about gorillas contains a large component of politics. We have chosen this piece by John Heminway because while it does give some necessary political background to the story, it is not a polemic.

John Heminway is familiar to public television audiences as the host and executive producer of the PBS series Travels; *he was before that the producer for much of the acclaimed PBS series* The Brain *and* The Mind. *He is also chairman of the African Wildlife Foundation and has done much work for the conservation not only of gorillas, but of many of the other "charismatic mega-fauna" of Africa.* (MWC)

As long as I can remember, I had a dream of gorillas. They were horrific and strong—mutilated humans, in fact—while at the same time being alarmingly familiar. Best of all, they lived in jungles, the fantasy world of boys born and raised in big cities. Alan Morehead, in *No Room in the Ark*, evoked an atavistic memory of them for me. After tracking them on the Virunga volcanoes of southwest Uganda for several days, he recounted how he finally sighted a troop. He admitted then that he felt like a Peeping Tom. "Of course he would have," I thought to myself, "and so must I." From that minute I was determined to see gorillas. I convinced myself that no encounter with a lion, elephant or rhino could possibly match a sighting of a gorilla. Alan Morehead had shown me that to be a complete person I must let a gorilla into my life. The year was 1961 and I was all of seventeen years old.

During the summer of that year I signed on with school friends and a would-be explorer to look for gorillas in the same area where Morehead once had been. The crossing of Central and East Africa took us nearly two months and when we reached Kisoro, straddling the border of Uganda and the Congo, we were scrawny, sunbleached and filthy.

Unlike other Ugandan villages of a similar size, this one possessed both a white man and a hotel. The white man was Walter Baumgartel, an Austrian, who a few years before had proclaimed himself "the king of gorillaland." The hotel, euphemistically called Travellers' Rest, belonged to him and evoked his rough and quirky nature. For a ratpack of schoolboys, it was as good as its name. The shower was almost hot, the sheets real sheets, although not clean, and the food available in large quantities. For other travelers it was no such luxury. The guest book was punctuated with such remarks as: "The food would not be so tasty if the kitchen wasn't so close to the loo," and "I'd rather live under canvas than stay here again," and "Don't sit at Baumgartel's table if you value your sanity."

We had already been warned in Kampala that Walter Baumgartel was manic-depressive (I was too shy to ask what that meant), and that neither one of his extremes of temperament was much of a diversion for a guest. On the other hand, his hotel was said to be an experience we would never forget; its location one of the most breathtaking sites in all the world.

The grounds of Travellers' Rest were well-clipped lawns, shimmeringly green, and beds of succulents, posing as flowers. The hotel was on the brow of a low hill. In three directions, small farms climbed toward mountain walls, obscured by clouds most of the day. The walls of the hotel buildings were wood and bougainvillea, each one supporting the other; Baumgartel's major worry, so I found, was keeping the jungle at bay. Flowers bloomed overnight, moths were mutating from pupa to chrysalis in the blink of an eye, and the damp and rot seemed to turn even the newest object into something flaccid and familiar after a day or two.

But Travellers' Rest was nonetheless an invigorating place. The evenings, despite the rain, were full of cozy charm with the machine-gun rattle of rain on the iron roof and the popping of green wood in the lounge fireplace. The mighty cloudbursts unfailingly scrubbed the sky clean of clouds just in time for the mornings. For all Travellers' Rest's singularities, the one I recall with the most nostalgia was its tomatoes. No matter how appalling the dinners, the tomatoes were always a tour de force. Their color verged on purple, deep enough to make one's eyes smart. Grown wild in black volcanic soil, they needed no dressing, no salt, no pepper. They were already pungent and sweet, seasoned in the rain forest, so it seemed, with chicory and garlic.

Walter Baumgartel was beside himself with the pleasure of being host to this vanguard from the Children's Crusade. He was foremost a storyteller and in us he found the perfect audience—attentive, enthusiastic and thoroughly gullible. His waving arms told half his stories, evoking the looming volcanoes, girded by clouds. He spoke of them as the haunt of the mountain gorilla, an animal whose ferocity was only matched by a black leopard—the gorilla's natural enemy. It was clear that Walter Baumgartel planned to use the leopard as his alibi in the event we never saw gorillas. "I make no promises," he said more than once. And all the time he tortured our adolescent minds with intrigue of pygmies, gorillas, swirling mists and the occasional cannibal. Each morning he was a different person. Bleary-eyed from too many steins of brandy and looking uncomfortably fat, he would stand by the bar in silence, rubbing out stains on the counter with his elbow. One moment he would berate one of his African staff, the next he would deliver bear hugs to his cook, his waiters, the puzzled chambermaids. "You know," he said to his bartender after one of these sweet and sour outbursts, "I luff you like mein own childt."

By the time we set forth into the volcanoes I was prepared for disappointment. Our retinue consisted of seven barefoot porters and a fifty-two-year-old guide called Reuben Rwanzagire, who was then the éminence grise of gorilla country. His feet were hard as pine boards and sinewy enough to wrap around a taproot. Like Baumgartel, he had a vivid narrative style. One of his stories was about a randy female gorilla who had fought him to the ground. By sheer cunning and sinew, Reuben had been able to slip out from under her and thwart her amorous advances. In telling the story Reuben required both an inter-preter and a large clearing, for there was much coming and going, charges and cartwheels. He fell to the ground, fought his gorilla, growled through a toothless mouth and finally, after frantic bicycling of his legs, secured his escape. The performance drew a burst of applause from the porters, and a big grin from Reuben. He was definitely the caretaker of these mountains. When he smiled so did his men; when he moved they followed. Even Alan Morehead had quoted him as a major source of information about gorilla behavior.

The final staging post with the cars was at six thousand feet above sea level. From here on the first day we climbed to twelve thousand feet through slippery, tangled ground cover. On several occasions I was sure I would be unable to advance another foot. But the sight of Reuben, bounding without effort as his lungs reprocessed the smoke from the rawest of African cigarettes, gave me bravado. At last, near the top, in the densest of jungles and on a slippery slope, Reuben gave us the alarm signal. There were gorillas ahead, he announced in a whisper. He had heard them feeding. Now we must advance with the greatest caution. We crept on our stomachs, collecting mud in our pants pockets, until Reuben indicated we were but a few feet from the gorillas. We waited. Reuben smiled, delighted to accommodate us on the first day of our quest. Suddenly there was a deafening crash of falling trees as three mammoth shadows plunged down the mountain a few feet from where we lay. For elephants they were small. Still, at two tons an animal, they little resembled gorillas. I looked at Reuben. For a so-called naturalist who had just made a giant gaffe, he showed little embarrassment. He began to laugh, pointing to where the elephants had been, then holding his stomach to contain all the absurdity. He was beside himself: All the way down to our camp just the mention of the word *ndofu* ("elephant") was enough to make him explode all over again.

We slept that night in metal huts on the saddle bridging the two volcanoes of M'gahinga and Muhavura. The next morning when I awoke, the door of my hut would not budge. I pushed several times with no effect. Finally, imagining that one of my school friends was playing a practical joke, I gave the door one violent shove. There was a sudden explosion of big hooves on wet mud, and as I opened the door, I was just in time to see a Cape buffalo beating his way down the mountain.

Reuben and the porters had been out looking for gorillas since before dawn. Now they were back, whistling to us from across the clearing, telling us in hushed voices to follow. We kept to their footsteps and within ten minutes we reached a copse where Reuben showed us the beds of gorillas from the previous night. These were fashioned out of willowy bamboo and the "sheets" were made from layers of leaves. To prove the Posturepedic comfort of these beds Reuben reclined in one, curled himself into the umbilical position, yawned and gave us a demonstration of falling asleep. Once again the performance was too much for the guides, who howled with laughter and only stopped when one of their members pointed to the far side of a gorge where a strand of heavy moss, suspended from the branch of a tree, was waving much too vigorously for the breeze. Five pairs of field glasses were immediately pressed into service as five schoolboys waited for this, the rarest of wildlife sightings. At last, after ten minutes, a large black cylindrical sphere, the shape of a bullet, emerged from the foliage. A gorilla's head,

Reuben assured us. Female too, he added with a leer. But from a distance of some hundred yards we could not even see its eyes. I then volunteered to accompany Reuben for a closer look while the others, well positioned, could film the first known instance of a white man being savaged by a gorilla.

The approach was on all fours, through stinging nettle that left large welts across forearms and face. When Reuben stopped, I stopped, and counted the drops of sweat splashing onto the leaves beneath my face. After twenty-five minutes I was not sure where we were. Above us, the sun was totally obscured by the mantle of high branches, and even the slope, which had been steep in one direction for the first ten minutes and now steep in another, was disorienting. Surely, I thought, we now must be near that bullet head.

I stopped to look back and as I turned there was a furious bark, nearly on top of me. No more than fifteen feet ahead of us a gorilla burst out of the leaves. She stood nearly my height, her head surely twice the size of mine, hers beveled by dark blazing eyes. True to the legend, she rattled on her chest with her fingertips, creating a sound both deep and hollow, like a bongo drum. Fear, bluff, anger—she ran the gamut in about fifteen seconds. She might easily have charged us, broken us as if we were matchwood, but she only seemed to want to be left alone. In looking back on that high-speed moment, I would willingly say I was scared. She was indeed frightening, but somehow my instinct was not to run. I was alarmed, too amazed in fact to take a picture, or, if I had held a gun, to take aim. Her eyes demobilized me. If anything, I felt awkward, apologetic. Then she melted into the foliage—some four hundred pounds of primate gliding into the greenery. Hers was not a disappearance. It was a dematerialization, and the sudden calm after her going left me unable to do much more than giggle ridiculously like an adolescent.

One second becomes an hour. A memory evolves into a plateau. My gorilla soon assumed giant dimensions, but even after a year the story remained incomplete. In my mind I would start from the beginning, proceed from one instant to another, only to discover at the end that a component was lacking, as effectively in the story as in my understanding of gorillas. I had had merely a flash of the animal: one freeze-frame. Both of us had been startled, and when the smoke of the moment had cleared I knew little more of gorillas than someone who had read about them in an encyclopedia or seen them in a zoo. Mine was like a hunting story—one brief unnatural moment.

Three years later I returned to the Virunga volcanoes. I had enticed a friend from university to join me, and after I had raised the costs of my trip by working for two months in South Africa, he and I left for southwest Uganda.

When we reached Travellers' Rest, Walter Baumgartel was at pains to recognize me. He had grown slightly heavier, and his hair had changed from black to white without an intervening stage of silver. Where once he had been compulsively conversational, now he seemed dazed. There were many guests at the hotel, all of them refugees from the Congo. They had reached the hotel that morning, and some of the Belgian families were camped on the lawn, their pots and pans and boxes of diapers under groundsheets as protection from the rain. At dinner that night Baumgartel assumed his usual seat at the head of the largest table, but he said very little. He listened gravely to the refugees' accounts of the siege of Stanleyville. He shook his head morosely when he heard how nuns had been raped, housewives' eyes plucked out. He muttered only one remark about World War II and the Anschluss, and then he continued to shake his head with disgust. When dinner was finished, he abandoned us all at the table to retire to a corner where he listened to a wireless for more tales of cannibalism, just across the range of volcanoes. The crackling news, broadcast by the BBC World Service, seemed to lend even more strength to his private convictions, for he often nodded his head, sighed and once even slammed his brandy down onto the side table as if he had just arrived at a decision. The hotel walls were only just standing. The rot had penetrated everything and the staff were brazenly taking advantage of Walter Baumgartel. Now, absolutely nothing—neither the generator, the kitchen nor the mosquito nets—worked. But Baumgartel was no longer concerned about niceties. Not even the gorillas mattered. The next morning when Reuben arrived to collect us, Baumgartel dismissed us all as if we were irrelevant.

Reuben was now wearing boots, and as soon as we began climbing—this time up the volcano M'gahinga—I noticed his limp. The higher we climbed, the more he suffered. The laughing and buffoonery which had accompanied my first ascent was no more, and his breathing was strained and aching. I asked him once whether he wished to pause on the trail. From the way he glared I knew I had paid him an insult. He never replied and continued to climb the near-vertical slope, pedaling in the mud. We followed an elephant path that traveled straight up the fall line and at ten thousand feet we stopped beside a gorilla's bed, similar to the one we had seen three years before. This time, however, Reuben treated it with contempt: It was old, maybe even last year's. Coughing and fighting for breath, he stabbed his fingers at the dried shit and kicked all that remained with his boot. He picked up a few branches and broke them. No, he was not going to lie down in the bed. These gorillas had been here too long before. This was history.

We continued our climb, but it was clear from the way Reuben moved that he had no intention of finding gorillas, whether or not any remained on this volcano. Soon the light turned blue and Reuben swung his gnarled head in the direction from where we had come. He wanted us to believe that his limp was of little consequence, but as he slipped and fell along the muddy path returning to the hotel in the valley below, I thought that he would never again see another gorilla. Of all the Africans I had known, he was taking old age the worst. When he fell, he grew angry with himself, and even when he was making good progress his hands shook. We were still traveling when night overtook us. Now we could only follow the path by the sound of Reuben's voice. That business about black leopards eating the gorillas and scaring them from one border to the next, he said, was all nonsense, offered up to guests at the hotel. The real culprits were poachers—pygmies starving in the Congo. And who was to blame them? They pressed the gorillas from one side; Ugandan farmers, hacking down the primary forest, were pressing them on the other. Much of Reuben's monologue was punctuated by coughs. At the end, he added that there was no one left on these mountains to stop poachers, to stop farmers, to stop war. By now the air had grown cold, and our sweaters were steaming as we skated down the narrow path to the hotel. Reuben was repeating himself. "The gorillas," he chanted, "they've gone for good."

The mountain gorilla has had the bad sense to inhabit three politically unstable African countries—Zaire (formerly the Congo), Uganda and Rwanda. What has traditionally saved this subspecies from extinction has not been its size or fierceness, but its nearly impenetrable habitat. Shrouded by mountain mists, dense ferns, thick stands of bamboo, it possesses very little needed by us bipeds. Its meat is an acquired taste (so I hear), and the land it inhabited farmers would clear only if there was no other land available. So the gorilla managed to endure, more or less, until about a decade ago. In these last years, however, war and overpopulation have upset the old truths.

The Congo revolution, in particular, drew a veil of secrecy over its well-being. Shortly after we left Travellers' Rest, I learned that Walter Baumgartel returned to Austria, abandoning his hotel. A year later, Reuben was dead. From then on, few outsiders dared look for gorillas on the Virunga volcanoes. Within a year of the publication of George Schaller's gorilla monograph and his popular account, *The Year of the Gorilla*, close observations of the animal, such as his, were more or less impossible in both Uganda and Zaire. Conservation authorities reported that gorillas were being shot to feed both soldiers and rebels, and for nearly four years there were no sightings of them by outsiders.

There was one insider, however, who, during this period, had much to do with gorillas. Dr. Jacques Verschuren was then the head of the national park system in the Congo. While Dian Fossey, a towering occupational therapist from California, was getting all sorts of kudos for her coziness with the gorillas in Rwanda, Jacques Verschuren lost twenty-three of his game guards to poachers' bullets, while they attempted to protect the game. It was a quiet, unpublicized campaign, but those who were familiar with the Congo during those years had persistently told me of Verschuren's bravery and the selflessness of the national park employees working under him.

In 1971 I had occasion to meet Verschuren in Kinshasa, the capital of Zaire. He was now said to live permanently in Room 816 at the Intercontinental Hotel. I thought to myself as I walked to his room for our appointment that if Jacques Verschuren spoke English, smoked a pipe, wore knee socks and knew how to work the cocktail party set in New York and Los Angeles he surely could be in the public eye. (Gorillas, after all, were a natural for a fund-raising campaign.) But when Dr. Verschuren opened the door I realized just how private a man can be. He had none of the qualities ascribed to game wardens—certainly none of the flamboyance that would have brought to the attention of the West the very dramatic and romantic war he had just won.

Jacques Verschuren spoke only a few words of English. He was pale and sickly, and for the first few minutes of our meeting, he seemed excruciatingly timid. For a man devoted to the out-of-doors, he could not have selected a more confined environment for living. He kept the windows sealed, the air conditioner turned off and, even in the middle of the day, the curtains closed. The humid atmosphere was sweet with the smell of old banana, which was, he claimed, the sole item in his diet. I could see the depression on the bed covers where he had just been lying.

Dr. Verschuren seemed a hunted man. When he looked out the window he pulled the curtains back only a few inches. He explained that although he had an office at the Wildlife Ministry (since he now worked in the capacity of adviser to the new government), he rarely went there. Instead, he conducted his business over the telephone from this hotel room. For the last week, he had not even ventured into the corridor.

Dr. Verschuren came to life when we talked of the war. He boasted of the heroism of his men. He told me of the problems—lack of communications, no paychecks, spies in every camp—yet his men had never failed him. For him, war had clearly brought out the best in human nature. For a moment as he talked, his voice faltered and his eyes clouded. "Yes," he said, "that was heroism." He rose from where he had been sitting and walked again to the window, stealing a quick look at the parking lot, glaring with sunshine and heat. "Since the war," he explained, "the number of people working for the national parks has increased more than ten times. The game was saved during the war with a handful of men. Now we need ten times more men to save them during peacetime. The point of national parks therefore is to give your cousin a job, not to save animals. Now we save fewer animals. *La verité, monsieur.* These people don't care anymore about the game." Verschuren pointed at his stomach. "They care about this alone. And . . ." He drew me by the arm, urgently, so that my face was nearly pressed against the window. "Look, look: Mercedes-Benz—that's the other problem. Everybody in the national parks must have one. You don't work for the parks unless you do."

Verschuren drew back the curtains and slipped exhausted into a chair. "The man you must meet is Adrien Deschriever. One of the great ones still living. He is always thin and he does not own a Mercedes-Benz. Those gorillas you like so much exist today because of Monsieur Deschriever. You must meet him. But you must hurry, for one never knows in this country. Individuals and gorillas are not indispensable . . ."

At the time, in 1971, no one was quite sure how many gorillas had survived the disorder of the last few years. Estimates ranged from a population of seventy in the Impenetrable Forest of Uganda, two hundred in Rwanda, and between two thousand and twenty thousand in Zaire. There was much more guesswork in Zaire than in any of the other countries for it is vast, unconnected by proper roads, covered by dense and often unexplored forests and swamps. Nobody to date had conducted a proper gorilla count. Nobody but Deschriever lived with them on intimate terms.

In Nairobi only a few people knew of Deschriever. One safari guide admitted that he had been gorilla-stalking with him, but, determined to keep the man and his animals a secret to only his clients, he volunteered little else. Others were curious once I started asking questions about Deschriever. A new quarry, another eccentric were always of interest to Kenyan wildlife voyeurs. Out of friendly crowds, strangers appeared eager to accompany me into the Congolese blue. Instead, I went to ABC in New York, told the producers about the gorillas, produced a Michelin map of Central Africa and pointed to the B in Bukavu. "Pockets of them everywhere," I muttered conspiratorially. "Man by the name of Deschriever knows them best. Sort of an oddity. Doesn't talk much. Said to be suspicious of strangers. Super shy. That sort of thing. No guarantee we'll see gorillas, mind you. High-risk film. Of course, if we do succeed, we'll be the first ever to get wild gorillas onto a television screen. See what I mean? It all depends on whether you're up to it."

The production survey was approved within the hour, and two weeks later four of us were driving from Entebbe, Uganda, southwest through Rwanda into Zaire. Burt Morgan, the producer, was an earnest, bald man who was never happy even with miracles. Also included was Liam Lynn, the comic balladeer of the hard-drinking white hunters of East Africa. Rob Glenn was a sculptor who had always dreamed of doing a study of mountain gorillas in the wild: for the network executives, the ideal human-interest story to punctuate footage of gorilla behavior. Rob was a good naturalist as well as an obsessive rally driver. He drove fast, told graveyard jokes and identified small weaver birds all at the same time.

The journey from Entebbe took us three days. The roads were red, and at the end of each day we were red too. In Uganda, driving through farm country, there is the sense that any crop can be planted and harvested in the space of twenty-four hours. Bananas are always ripe, the tea stands head-high and the coffee smells of fine Italian espresso. In those days, nobody, it seemed, could be truly poor in Uganda. Children sprinted through fields, arms waving, to shout "jambo" at us as we passed. The little ones were well rounded and never without a smile—the fertile human crop in a fertile land. Good rains, neat fields, proffered hands—Uganda was then a very comfortable country. Within a few years, all was to change, of course, but to have known Uganda then is to feel sure now that the violence under Amin was never a product of the Ugandan temperament. Amin was from the north. Some say he was not even a Ugandan.

We passed not far from Travellers' Rest, by now derelict, and then crossed the border into Rwanda. As soon as we passed the frontier we might have been on another continent. The roads were jammed with foot travelers, the fields were cluttered with tin-roofed huts. To find an open, unpopulated savannah took me twenty-four hours of looking, and even then it was marred by haze from fires. With a giant and ravenous population, the land suffers from erosion, overgrazing and overburning. It seemed abraded and festering from one horizon to the next. The tall Watusi, beautifully coiffed, their skin copper-colored, appeared fey and unrealistic next to the small and avaricious Hutu, who make up the bulk of the population and who have, since the expiration of the Belgian mandate over the territory, retained political control. I never felt a camaraderie with the Rwandese as I had with the people of Uganda; all I could do was to play tricks on them—cruel jokes involving a realistic gorilla mask I had bought on my last visit to Broadway. In Rwanda I convinced myself that the tricks constituted a study, of great sociological import, to determine people's awareness of gorillas on our approach to real gorilla country. In truth, we just had a good laugh. On one occasion when I actually started brachiating, beating on my chest and scuttling gorillalike across a village square, I successfully cleared more than a hundred people out of the village. I could see little from inside the mask and I did not realize until after I had done a lot of chest-thumping just how successful I had been. I looked around and I realized everybody had fled. Removing my mask, I uttered a few words of apology. A hundred faces remained glued behind huts and storefronts. "Just a joke," I repeated as I clambered back into the Land Cruiser. Then they came for the car, waving fists, hurling abuse and stones.

As we drove out of the village, I was debating whether or not to continue my research when Rob and I spotted a very elderly woman on the road. We slowed to a halt as I pulled on the mask, and when she was abreast of us I caught her attention by beating on the side of the car with hairy "gorilla" gloves. By the way her back was stooped the old woman, I thought, must be over eighty, and on her head, she carried a huge stalk of green bananas. Her eyes to the ground, she probably would never have looked my way had I not barked at her. When she turned and saw that a gorilla, dressed in a safari jacket, was seated as passenger in a wonderfully modern Toyota Land Cruiser, she decided in an instant that she wanted nothing more to do with the twentieth century. Without a pause, the bananas flew straight up, as though launched from her head, while she hurled off the road, over a ten-foot cliff, into a pyrethrum plantation where we followed her course for the next ten minutes by the sight of her head bobbing and weaving, heading toward the Indian Ocean, a thousand miles away.

We arrived in Bukavu that evening. The hotel where Adrien Deschriever promised to meet us had the unmistakable imprimatur of past elegance. In the meantime it seemed to have suffered a series of violent furniture moves. Portions of Regency beds were scattered about, but most chairs and tables were now of local manufacture. A vitrine that once had housed collections of French jewelry and Swiss watches now contained sixteen empty beer bottles. The manager explained that the hotel had been looted three times—first by rebels, once by the regular army and the last time by yet another group of rebels. The only article overlooked by the looters was in the manager's office. It was a Louis XVI Directoire desk, too large to fit through any doors. In any case, one could see immediately that it would not have suited a field commander's tent. Above my bed in my room there was an angry rainbow of machine-gun bullet holes whose presence spelled insomnia.

From the minute Adrien Deschriever walked into the dining room he looked tortured. He grimaced from the sound of the rock 'n' roll, he acted as if he even distrusted the chair he sat on and he treated us as if we were a conquering army. Adrien appeared about forty and there was nothing decorative about his looks. His hair was cut short for efficiency and left unwashed out of necessity. Like Verschuren, he had the pallor of a mushroom—not because he lived indoors but because he haunted the jungle. His clothes ranged in color from khaki to khaki. He mentioned his wife just once and he made it clear she preferred staying at home. Most of the time he stared at uneaten strawberries on his plate. Even talk of gorillas failed to animate him. During the two hours we sat together he voiced only one opinion that his fellow whites in Bukavu were interested only in money. The remark,

I believe, had been sparked by the sight of the white headwaiter accepting a tip from one of the guests. There was little to be added, so the dinner was conducted mostly in silence, and Bud Morgan grew more and more nervous that the star of his film was to be a man who was unable to talk.

The next morning when Adrien met us, there was a change. Although he still said very little, he was definitely in command. He looked at my Special Forces beret and obliquely asked me to remove it: "The rebels wear those berets. You'll be shot dead if soldiers see you." I delayed a fraction of a second before burying it at the bottom of my knapsack.

The Zaire government, for all its inefficiency and corruption under Joseph Desiré Sese Seko Mobutu, had at the time committed a greater percentage of real estate to national parks than had any other country of the world. A map of Zaire reveals a huge checkerboard of public lands held in trust for wildlife. That these parks were unmanageable and unmanaged was a matter of little concern. In Africa often the less management, the more the game prospers.

Kahuzi Biega National Park, protecting two small mountains and over six hundred square kilometers of forest, is probably managed better than any other park in Zaire, thanks to Adrien Deschriever. Nearly two hundred gorillas, possibly 10 percent of all those left in Zaire, are said to live here. Because there is a considerable human population inhabiting the contiguous country, there is probably more need here for human surveillance than in the other more desolate parks of Zaire.

Once our car has passed the gates of the park, the road becomes a dark hallway. Adrien's eyes, once so dull, now seem to shine with a sunlight of their own making, and I can see that each stately tree—thousands of them, their high branches our ceiling—is instantly recognizable to him. Twice he sticks his head out of the window of the car to orient himself by the smell of the forest, and the third time, he brakes to a halt. "Here," he says, inhaling deeply. The place is as distinctive to him as if it were marked by a signpost. We leave the car and follow him into the forest. Only hours later when I catch him looking distracted do I dare ask him why he has stopped at that particular spot. "Because," he replies, "there were gorillas on the wind. I smelled where they had crossed the road the day before."

Their trail is apparent only to Adrien and the pygmy game guard—broken branches, droppings smeared on leaves. Our footing is uncertain because of the fallen trunks of great trees concealing vines and barbs. For four hours we make damp and clumsy progress with never a chance to stand upright without brushing against a branch or a liana. Never once in all that time do I detect a view. Finally, exactly at noon, Adrien waves his hand. "They are ahead," he announces flatly. He has stopped exactly where he made the revelation—in a narrow flute of sunlight. "We wait," he adds, crossing his arms and folding himself into the shrubbery, still in the bull's-eye of sun. The pygmy tracker, bowing to historic convention, withdraws a short distance and sits alone in self-imposed exile.

If the tracking has been painful, the waiting will be worse. Adrien accepts our ennui with characteristic fatalism. He makes no effort to silence Liam's roaring stories of great sexual exploits nor Rob's smoking of an Upmann cigar. Adrien might just as well be carved from one of the giant newtonia trees as he stares from his private sunshine into the tangle of ferns directly ahead of him, where the troop of twenty-two are said to be sleeping. Just once he acknowledges Liam's not so droll remarks abut Mad Mike Hoare's resurgent popularity in Bukavu with a seditious clicking of his tongue, but otherwise he is indifferent. He accepts Liam's flippancy as most people do bad weather.

I am silent too, but for other reasons. I believe Adrien when he assures us we are within one hundred feet of gorillas. I believe him, yet I cannot accept that the moment that died aborning some ten years ago will be brought to its rightful conclusion today. Adrien has already identified the gorilla troop ahead of us as the one led by Kazimir, a large male silverback gorilla. I question whether a man can be so certain of something just from sounds. Occasionally I hear what I take to be a rumbling stomach, a fart, a belch. With each new noise Adrien nods in affirmation. Such and such sound was made by the silverback, or by a youngster or by the oldest member of Kazimir's harem. If today is to be the climax of my childhood quest, then I am somehow not prepared for it. I sense no drama, just bloody-minded self-assurance.

Previously Adrien has explained that the worst encounter with a gorilla is the surprise one (such as mine on the Virunga volcanoes). If a group is familiar with humans they should not run. To them, he believes, we are a mere subspecies—crude, unsophisticated and thoroughly clumsy—to be pitied, if nothing else. Gorillas are not in awe of humans and they treat us as we might animals in a zoo.

Adrien has spent the last five years "habituating" (familiarizing) two groups of gorillas in Kahuzi Biega. The smaller troop, numbering eighteen, is still shy and difficult to approach. The other—the one now before us—has been more successfully habituated. Adrien insists that the gun he carries is not intended for use against gorillas. Rather it is to deter poaching. "Poachers," he said, affecting a look of such extreme ambivalence that only afterward did I realize it was Adrien's way of expressing contempt. "Poachers," he added with a spit. Such was the beginning of a short tale describing how three years before, while driving through the park in a Land Rover, poachers had taken a shot at him. The bullet missed him, but killed his brother. When Adrien's story was done, the look of resigned neutrality once again fiddled across his face.

Now, after two hours of waiting, Adrien stands up. He beckons to the pygmy to cut a path toward the sound of belches in the underbrush and within a few seconds the two of them are lost to view, only the slicing sound of the *panga* marking their route.

Unexpectedly, a few minutes later, Adrien returns, almost a smile on his face. "I nearly tripped over a sleeping female," he signs. "Very bad country for viewing gorillas." He nods his head for us to follow, saying that the gorillas are now on the move, and that we should track them until they reach more open country.

Within fifteen minutes we stop again, for Adrien believes we have overtaken the troop. Although he keeps telling us to talk in normal tones, I continue whispering, conditioned as I am to the convention of quiet on the stalk. Adrien sits on the rough ground, his back as stiff as if he were attending a Papal audience. The pygmy hacks away at the vegetation on the edge of our minute clearing, allowing us a better view. "We will make contact," Adrien says with absolute conviction. His hands are folded in quiet expectation. Now, the gorillas must choose their moment.

"Talk," Adrien insists, like a pushy host. I look at him, pale and placid. I check the others: Bud unimpressed, Rob determined to finish his Upmann cigar, Liam still whispering about a girl called Maggie. Suddenly I am scared. Everybody must be able to hear the beating of my heart over the hush of the jungle. I wonder if they sense how much we are at the mercy of these gorillas. No matter that Kazimir may be three times our weight or that he might possess ten times our strength. What matters is that the gorillas have the option of choice, timing, command. We humans are merely awaiting their pleasure. They can do anything they wish to us. I begin to shake, like I never shook on the Virunga volcanoes.

Adrien raises a finger, as if he has just discovered the truth. "Do you hear?" he asks. "It is the silverback . . ." (he pauses to struggle with the English word) ". . . tapping, no beating at the ground." He listens some more. "They know . . . they know." He is looking at a high frond of fern, vigorously fanning, above all the rest. He cocks his head, pressing his ear against the wall of vegetation. "Cum, cum, cum, Kazimir," he says to the black tangle.

I pass the back of my hand across my mouth so the others will not hear my breathing. I am deafened by the gush and thud of blood in my neck. I imagine Kazimir everywhere: A shadow becomes a coiled arm, an oiled face forms from the wet bark of a tree. And then, I close my eyes. Suddenly I realize the waiting is over. A rank smell, half-skunk, half-underarm, settles over us. It is so powerful I open my eyes, only to see Rob grinning. Whatever we have been awaiting is happening.

At first there is one short bark. The bark becomes a shriek and the frond of fern above bounds from one tree to another. Branches snap and the cavernous roar becomes frantic. We are in the eye of a storm, unseen, but seeing, a force of insuperable but invisible power. Suddenly it stops. The jungle hushes. I search to see something—matted hair, eyes, a limb. Whatever created the chaos is now gone. We were, I fancy, being tested.

Slinging his rifle over his shoulder, Adrien nods to the pygmy to start cutting a path back to the car. "We have made contact," he announces without inflection. The gorillas have gone. Now, further contact with them must be cut short for yet another day.

Driving back to Bukavu, Adrien returns to the subject of poaching. "Read the official powers given to me by Mobutu," he says out of the blue. "When I catch a poacher I need not establish his legal guilt. Not necessary. If I suspect he is in the park for no good reason, then I call out to him to stop, once, twice, three times, and if he is still running when I call out the third time, then I have the right, not yet exercised, to shoot to kill." Here Adrien slaps his hands to dramatize the simplicity of execution. "There are few questions. No need even to know the man's name. 'Stop. Stop. Stop,' I yell. And then that is that. Simple." Again Adrien slaps his hands. "Just the other day my guards captured a poacher, and during the night the poacher tried to escape. My men stopped him with a knife between the ribs." Another slap of the hands. "My guard was thrown into prison for murder, but after a month we had him released, gave him a promotion and awarded him a medal. That's the way we work."

There is neither smugness nor cynicism when Adrien describes his absolute power. If anything, he wears a look of weary sadness. For him death is the inadmissible clincher of all bets, suspicions and beliefs. By carrying a gun he sees himself as the lawyer of wildlife, as the sole defender of animals in a court of bigots. Unarticulated but implicit is his belief that across the globe man has exceeded his authority. His story done, Adrien drives in silence, blinking only once between the park and Bukavu from the lights of an oncoming car.

Before I left Nairobi, someone who knew Adrien had spun a few legends about him for me. My informant was a man who sees only giants and dwarfs in life. For him, because all humans are on the brink of an apocalypse, the world must be divided between the heroes and the cads. Human motivation is tactile. "You must remember," he said, "that Adrien is married to an African woman, solidly built, barely literate and the mother of his many café-au-lait children. That she is the very antithesis of everything European is important. By taking her as his bride, you see, Adrien had, in effect, married Africa."

"But so do so many in French-speaking Africa. There, there is none of the stigma you have here in British Africa."

My friend was not listening. "That's only the beginning," he continued. "Adrien has been reduced to an essential form of life by the sheer necessity of having to deal with dog-eat-dog Africa. You see, he saw his own brother shot by poachers. Later he had to shoot his way out from his ruined farm when it was attacked by rebels. He's lived a life of war to such an extent he can no longer conceive of peace. Do you understand?" My friend did not wait for the answer.

"And then two years ago he fell in love. A sultry-eyed girl from California. His first white woman. She was working as an assistant to a German cameraman doing a film on gorillas. The cameraman left, the girl stayed on—just moved into Adrien's tent and that was that. From then on he dedicated himself to her. When she began their film about elephants he was there as her gofer. He learned about cameras, carried her tripod, set up her tent. Quite a twosome, those two. She was in her mid-twenties, he nearly forty.

"You're probably wondering about the venerable Madame Deschriever back at the hut with the kids. Quite simply this: The moment she got wind of her husband's infidelity, she went straight to the witch doctor. Told him she wanted the girl rubbed out. Maybe they stuck pins into a doll or something. Not quite sure. But the witch doctor agreed to her instructions and assured her that the girl had only a few days to live.

"Sure enough. Just at that moment, the girl was with her elephants in Rwanda. She was filming them first being airlifted from some *shambas* to a national park, and then released from a big *boma*, back into the wild. Smallest and last elephant of the day—couldn't have been more than four feet tall, just a little guy—he raced out of the *boma*, kind of crazed, and came straight for the girl. You see, her problem was that she was looking down a long lens. Didn't see how close the elephant was. And the moment she did—well, it was all over. That little bastard was pounding her. The girl had this damn battery belt attached to her camera and tripod and when she tried to escape there wasn't a thing she could do. Incredible, the power and weight of those elephants. Just killed her instantly.

"I guess Madame Deschriever was happy. Adrien was wrecked. He found a lonely spot in the park, with a magnificent view, and he buried the girl there. From then on he's been a little more sour, a little more contained. He's back with Madame now, but he's even more private than before . . ."

In the morning of the second day of our search, Adrien does not utter one word for the first two hours. He mutters occasionally to the pygmy, whose face is deformed by childhood leprosy. This game guard is wearing a pair of girl's boots, abandoned, no doubt, by a grateful gorilla-watcher who had done her safari outfitting on Rodeo Drive. The pygmy looked better yesterday when he was barefoot. Dressed either way, he is the nimblest of us all, flowing through the forest, over logs, under knotted foliage as if he were a panther.

Our path takes us along the edge of a tea plantation contiguous to the park. Late yesterday, Adrien explains at last, the gorillas skirted the clearings and made their way toward a narrow wedge of forest that still juts into farmland. They should be just ahead, for on most days they do not travel far. Depending on whether or not it is raining they generally leave their nests two hours after dawn, traveling and feeding continuously until about midday when, once again, they take time out for a nap. At about four in the afternoon they resume their feeding orgy, advancing slowly until they are overtaken by night. Almost invariably the children and females sleep in the trees, while the males build nests for themselves on the ground. Theirs is, by most standards, a life of leisure, only threatened by leopards and man. By disposition gorillas are gentle, preferring to bluff than to fight. Even when two males are antagonists, they resort to combat only as a final measure. The power to kill, which they have in abundance, is one they prefer not to exercise.

We arrive at last night's bedroom. It is marked by considerable devastation. Branches are ripped from hagenia trees, with berries scattered across the ground, half-eaten. Two small trees, on the edge of the clearing, lie uprooted. The gorillas will never come this way again, sensing somehow, as many animals do, that their habitat must be allowed time to heal. Only in cases when man meddles have gorillas ever been known to abandon these time-honored wisdoms.

The trail cut for us by the pygmy is pygmy-size. We who are over six feet tall must scuttle like crabs, our field glasses and cameras, hung from necks, scooping up mud and banging one against the other. "*Siafu*," Rob yells suddenly. "Safari ants." We bolt, high-stepping over the tunnel of skin-eating ants, and when the danger is past I pause to pluck leaves from my hair. Adrien is ahead, much more calm. A shaft of light now pokes me, first in one eye, then the other. If I squint I can see a cobweb, brushing against my nose; at the other extreme of focus I can follow a hypolimnious butterfly floating from branch to branch, five feet away. Out and in, back and forth, the jungle is an exercise in perspectives.

We follow Kazimir's family along the park boundary. Adrien is slightly unsettled, for he knows that when gorillas leave the protection of the jungle and the park, they risk a confrontation with farmers. Whenever they damage crops, Adrien must make reparations to the farmers, and already lines seem drawn between the two species of primates—the great apes and us. "Cousins," Adrien had once explained to me sadly.

When Adrien sees gorilla droppings, still steaming, he admits he is worried. Three months ago when the farms had not yet been cleared from the forest, the gorillas followed more or less this same route. Now the farmers have seriously encroached on the forest just outside the park. In all likelihood the gorillas do not know they are traveling into a promontory of thick cover which soon will leave them stranded with nowhere but open fields to cross. "They will be . . ." Adrien searches for the word.

"Frustrated."

"Yes. Frustrated. Sometimes they behave not well when they are out in the open. Last year a farmer threatened them and they attacked. He was not killed but he was injured." Adrien advances, shaking his head, as if this new plight of the gorillas might have been through his fault.

From the east come the singsong cries of farmers, calling from field to field. For the first time, perhaps as a result, we talk in whispers.

When we halt again, I watch a fly. It circles Adrien's head and then settles on his cheek beneath the right eye. It wanders his face, poking his eye, spelunking a nostril, buffeted by his breath on a lip. For five minutes he lets it explore. Soon it is joined by others and half his face becomes obscured by flies. Only then does he act. His is a halfhearted measure—not a slap, but an abracadabra wave of his hand which makes five flies circle his face and attracts ten more. For a man of war, I meditate, Adrien surely has found a peace. In comparison, I feel venal. Just my presence here jeopardizes the jungle. I am unable to walk, it seems, without snapping a branch. I cannot contemplate my surroundings without the desire to steal something—a leaf, a fungus, a gorilla dropping, a story, a photograph. I need to leave this jungle with proof. Adrien, however, is different. He does not know how to tell a story, much less to reduce a gorilla to a still photograph. He neglects all his tenses but his present, becoming part of the jungle itself.

Somebody else—not Adrien—told me about the gorilla baby. It had been brought to him by farmers who had discovered it next to its mother, killed by poachers. By the time it reached park headquarters, the child was almost wasted. Adrien and his wife nursed it back to health. At first, the milk formula was a problem, but when they finally achieved the right recipe, the gorilla began to grow. In six months, Adrien decided, it would be independent enough to be reintroduced to the wild, perhaps into Kazimir's troop of twenty-two gorillas.

Every day Adrien trained it to behave as a gorilla. One day he brought it to the jungle, introducing it to its natural environment, and while there, quite by accident, Adrien ran into Kazimir's troop. Clutching the youngster to his chest he tried to slip away but he was spotted. Without warning, the six-hundred-pound gorilla lunged at Adrien, wrenched the orphan from Adrien's hands and then sprang back into the forest. Kazimir looked back only once, defiantly holding the tiny infant in one large arm. For the next two weeks Adrien pursued the kidnappers, knowing that the little gorilla was not equipped to survive the forest, and hoping, one supposes, for magic. At the end of the second week, the infant was no longer with Kazimir's troop. The rains had been heavy and every day the forest was cold and covered in mist. Adrien was never again to see the orphaned gorilla.

Now, after two hours of waiting, the flies have assumed almost complete control of Adrien's face. We know we are a hundred feet from the gorillas, but they have been remarkably quiet. Suddenly, I hear thudding. The silverback kidnapper, Kazimir, is pounding the ground and soon, sure enough, his rank odor envelops us. The most massive of all gorillas is now no distance and, as always, he remains invisible. He screams to show us just how near: no more than fifty feet, I estimate. For the next half hour he and his family belch, fart, hammer the ground, rattle lips and bark. Never once do we see them. I am wondering if my story has no ending, after all.

Impatient, I crawl along the edge of our small clearing to where I can peer through a tunnel piercing the undergrowth. At its end, some thirty feet away, a shaft of light illuminates a square yard of jungle. I had sensed I might see something, but the tunnel is empty. One cannot fail to be impressed how these massive creatures can tantalize you with their sound effects, yet remain so completely concealed. I crawl back to the others. I know I am being watched, yet I cannot find the eyes.

Almost immediately I return to the maw of that tunnel. Perhaps I am merely trying to occupy myself; perhaps I have an intuition. I look into the blackness, past the beam of sunlight, into the very throat of the jungle. Just where it is blackest of all, two yellow eyes, sunken into their own syrup, return my stare. The eyes are inflexible, unblinking, glowing out of blackness like moons. Soon, amid those shadows, I see two arms, as massive as legs, reaching to the ground. Midges form a halo over the oiled coat, and although no one identifies him by name, there is no doubt I am looking at Kazimir.

One by one, while the silverback guards their retreat, the others pass through the tunnel. For a few seconds they each have a chance to steal a look in our direction, but they hurry, under orders, it would seem, to pay us no attention. I count eighteen. (The other watchers later assured me I was wrong and that there were twenty-two in all.) The last gorilla to pass is a young male. For a moment he stands fully upright to stare at us, his head bobbing in and out of the sunlight, as if he believes the darkness can conceal him. His game could be one I played many years ago, just before I learned to read.

When they have all gone and the jungle again resumes its hum, I look around at my companions. Like me, I suspect they are not sure what to say or whether to say anything at all. Even Adrien is smiling.

My story begun ten years ago on the Virunga volcanoes may still not have an ending, but it now surely has more meaning. I have seen a gorilla face to face. And neither one of us had to run.

Bud at last breaks the spell to pull out his pad. He begins calculating film costs, days needed for production and size of film crew. All his previous fears have now been laid to rest. His eyes on the pad, he keeps repeating to himself, "Dynamite." His budget grows from page to page. "How much is the hotel?" he asks me. He is shaking his head with rare conviction. "I'm betting that in ten days we'll have it in the can." He explains to Adrien the meaning of "marquee value," and then he gives him his legal opinion about the use of the film for nonpaying audiences. "All those myths that King Kong got going—this film will settle the score. Let me tell you, it will be a spellbinder."

I doubt whether Adrien is trying to understand the jargon. He is listening for the last sounds of the gorillas' retreat. Soon he beckons us to follow him. Within a short distance the forest ends and we find ourselves perched on a small knoll overlooking a gorge and a glade. Adrien indicates for us to sit, and for an hour we wait, assured by him that the gorillas are likely to pass through this clearing, en route to their forest. If we are fortunate we shall see the whole troop together. Occasionally, through the wait, Bud sings out the cost of a soundman, the price of an air ticket, the overtime needed by an assistant editor. Soon he is done, just in time to see the worry in Adrien's eyes. Without saying a word, Adrien looks to the smoke haze in the west and then turns to glance over his shoulder. At last he talks: "I think the gorillas have gone the other way." He points behind us to the rise, concealing a distant tea plantation. "They must have crossed that field. You see, at this hour of the day, they know that the farmers have gone home. They know they won't be bothered crossing the fields."

As if to acknowledge his words, there is a burst of barking from the direction of the tea field. At first the voice is deep and commanding, belonging perhaps to Kazimir, but then the others, less restrained than he, form a giant chorus. The symphony floats over hill, into ravine, through forest and the farther it travels, the longer it lasts, the louder it becomes. "They only scream like that," explains Adrien, "when they are back in the forest, when they feel safe. It is like victory."

We rise to our feet. The air has turned cool now, and if we do not hurry we will be caught by night. When we reach the bottom of the ravine, Adrien is the first to break the silence. He takes me aside and, pointing to where the gorillas had sounded their retreat, says, "They are the kings of these hills. And," he adds, "they know it."

For the first time, he laughed.

Bernhardsdorp

From Biophilia *(1984)*
By Edward O. Wilson

≈

E. O. Wilson, the soft-spoken Harvard University Professor of Science, is without question one of the great minds of our time. Dr. Wilson is also a gifted writer; he has received two Pulitzer Prizes, in 1979 for On Human Nature *and in 1991 for* The Ants.

Each of Dr. Wilson's works has profoundly shaped my own thoughts on conservation. In lecture halls across the country, I have reiterated his view that the loss of species is the greatest threat facing the world today. "The one process now going on that will take millions of years to correct is the loss of genetic and species diversity by the destruction of natural habitats. This is the one folly our descendants are least likely to forgive us."

In the following piece, we find Dr. Wilson reflecting on the richness of the tropics in Bernhardsdorp, a village in the South American country of Surinam (now spelled Suriname). One of his more personal pieces, this essay illustrates our "human bond with other species." It is a pity that all of the other explorers and naturalists who lived before him did not have a chance to sit awhile with E. O. Wilson. (DRK)

At Bernhardsdorp on an otherwise ordinary tropical morning, the sunlight bore down harshly, the air was still and humid, and life appeared withdrawn and waiting. A single thunderhead lay on the horizon, its immense anvil shape diminished by distance, an intimation of the rainy season still two or three weeks away. A footpath tunneled through the trees and lianas, pointing toward the Saramacca River and far beyond, to the Orinoco and Amazon basins. The woodland around the village struggled up from the crystalline sands of the Zanderij formation. It was a miniature archipelago of glades and creekside forest enclosed by savanna—grassland with scattered trees and high bushes. To the south it expanded to become a continuous lacework fragmenting the savanna and transforming it in turn into an archipelago. Then, as if conjured upward by some unseen force, the woodland rose by stages into the triple-canopied rainforest, the principal habitat of South America's awesome ecological heartland.

In the village a woman walked slowly around an iron cooking pot, stirring the fire beneath with a soot-blackened machete. Plump and barefoot, about thirty years old, she wore two long pigtails and a new cotton dress in a rose floral print. From politeness, or perhaps just shyness, she gave no outward sign of recognition. I was an apparition, out of place and irrelevant, about to pass on down the footpath and out of her circle of required attention. At her feet a small child traced meanders in the dirt with a stick. The village around them was a cluster of no more than ten one-room dwellings. The walls were made of palm leaves woven into a herringbone pattern in which dark bolts zigzagged upward and to the onlooker's right across flesh-colored squares. The design was the sole indigenous artifact on display. Bernhardsdorp was too close to Paramaribo, Surinam's capital, with its flood of cheap manufactured products to keep the look of a real Arawak village. In culture as in name, it had yielded to the colonial Dutch.

A tame peccary watched me with beady concentration from beneath the shadowed eaves of a house. With my own taxonomist's eye I registered the defining traits of the collared species, *Dicotyles tajacu*: head too large for the piglike body, fur coarse and brindled, neck circled by a pale thin stripe, snout tapered, ear erect, tail reduced to a nub. Poised on stiff little dancer's legs, the young male seemed perpetually fierce and ready to charge yet frozen in place, like the metal boat on an ancient Gallic standard.

A note: Pigs, and presumably their close relatives the peccaries, are among the most intelligent of animals. Some biologists believe them to be brighter than dogs, roughly the rivals of elephants and porpoises. They form herds of ten to twenty members, restlessly patrolling territories of about a square mile. In certain ways they behave more like wolves and dogs than social ungulates. They recognize one another as individuals, sleep with their fur touching, and bark back and forth when on the move. The adults are organized into dominance orders in which the females are ascendant over males, the reverse of the usual mammalian arrangement. They attack in groups if cornered, their scapular fur bristling outward like porcupine quills, and can slash to the bone with sharp canine teeth. Yet individuals are easily tamed if captured as infants and their repertory stunted by the impoverishing constraints of human care.

So I felt uneasy—perhaps the word is embarrassed—in the presence of a captive individual. This young adult was a perfect anatomical specimen with only the rudiments of social behavior. But he was much more: a powerful presence, programmed at birth to respond through learning steps in exactly the collared-peccary way and no other to the immemorial environment from which he had been stolen, now a mute speaker trapped inside the unnatural clearing, like a messenger to me from an unexplored world.

I stayed in the village only a few minutes. I had come to study ants and other social insects living in Surinam. No trivial task: over a hundred species of ants and termites are found within a square mile of average South American tropical forest. When all the animals in a randomly selected patch of woodland are collected together and weighed, from tapirs and parrots down to the smallest insects and roundworms, one third of the weight is found to consist of ants and termites. If you close your eyes and lay your hand on a tree trunk almost anywhere in the tropics until you feel something touch it, more times than not the crawler will be an ant. Kick open a rotting log and termites pour out. Drop a crumb of bread on the ground and within minutes ants of one kind or another drag it down a nest hole. Foraging ants are the chief predators of insects and other small animals in the tropical forest, and termites are the key animal decomposers of wood. Between them they form the conduit for a large part of the energy flowing through the forest. Sunlight to leaf to caterpillar to ant to anteater to jaguar to maggot to humus to termite to dissipated heat: such are the links that compose the great energy network around Surinam's villages.

I carried the standard equipment of a field biologist: camera; canvas satchel containing forceps, trowel, ax, mosquito repellent, jars, vials of alcohol, and notebook; a twenty-power hand lens swinging with a reassuring tug around the neck; partly fogged eyeglasses sliding down the nose and khaki shirt plastered to the back with sweat. My attention was on the forest; it has been there all my life. I can work up some appreciation for the travel stories of Paul Theroux and other urbano-phile authors who treat human settlements as virtually the whole world and the intervening natural habitats as troublesome barriers. But every-where I have gone—South America, Australia, New Guinea, Asia—I have thought exactly the opposite. Jungles and grasslands are the logical destinations, and towns and farmland the labyrinths that people have imposed between them sometime in the past. I cherish the green en-claves accidentally left behind.

Once on a tour of Old Jerusalem, standing near the elevated site of Solomon's Throne, I looked down across the Jericho Road to the dark olive trees of Gethsemane and wondered which native Palestinian plants and animals might still be found in the shade underneath. Thinking of "Go to the ant, thou sluggard; consider her ways," I knelt on the cobblestones to watch harvester ants carry seeds down holes to their subterranean granaries, the same food-gathering activity that had im-pressed the Old Testament writer, and possibly the same species at the very same place. As I walked with my host back past the Temple Mount toward the Muslim Quarter, I made inner calculations of the number of ant species found within the city walls. There was a perfect logic to such eccentricity: the million-year history of Jerusalem is at least as compelling as its past three thousand years.

At Bernhardsdorp I imagined richness and order as an intensity of light. The woman, child, and peccary turned into incandescent points. Around them the village became a black disk relatively devoid of life, its artifacts adding next to nothing. The woodland beyond was a luminous bank, sparked here and there by the moving lights of birds, mammals, and larger insects.

I walked into the forest, struck as always by the coolness of the shade beneath tropical vegetation, and continued until I came to a small glade that opened onto the sandy path. I narrowed the world down to the span of a few meters. Again I tried to compose the mental set—call it the naturalist's trance, the hunter's trance—by which biologists locate more elusive organisms. I imagined that this place and all its treasures were mine alone and might be so forever in memory—if the bulldozer came.

In a twist my mind came free and I was aware of the hard workings of the natural world beyond the periphery of ordinary attention, where passions lose their meaning and history is in another dimension, without people, and great events pass without record or judgment. I was a transient of no consequence in this familiar yet deeply alien world that I had come to love. The uncounted products of evolution were gathered there for purposes having nothing to do with me; their long Cenozoic history was enciphered into a genetic code I could not understand. The effect was strangely calming. Breathing and heartbeat diminished, concentration intensified. It seemed to me that something extraordinary in the forest was very close to where I stood, moving to the surface and discovery.

I focused on a few centimeters of ground and vegetation. I willed animals to materialize, and they came erratically into view. Metallic-blue mosquitoes floated down from the canopy in search of a bare patch of skin, cockroaches with variegated wings perched butterfly-like on sunlit leaves, black carpenter ants sheathed in recumbent golden hairs filed in haste through moss on a rotting log. I turned my head slightly and all of them vanished. Together they composed only an infinitesimal fraction of the life actually present. The woods were a biological maelstrom of which only the surface could be scanned by the naked eye. Within my circle of vision, millions of unseen organisms died each second. Their destruction was swift and silent; no bodies thrashed about, no blood leaked into the ground. The microscopic bodies were broken apart in clean biochemical chops by predators and scavengers, then assimilated to create millions of new organisms, each second.

Ecologists speak of "chaotic regimes" that rise from orderly processes and give rise to others in turn during the passage of life from lower to higher levels of organization. The forest was a tangled bank tumbling down to the grassland's border. Inside it was a living sea through which I moved like a diver groping across a littered floor. But I knew that all around me bits and pieces, the individual organisms and their populations, were working with extreme precision. A few of the species were locked together in forms of symbiosis so intricate that to pull out one would bring other spiraling to extinction. Such is the consequence of adaptation by coevolution, the reciprocal genetic change of species that interact with each other through many life cycles. Eliminate just one kind of tree out of hundreds in such a forest, and some of its pollinators, leafeaters, and woodborers will disappear with it; then various of their parasites and key predators, and perhaps a species of bat or bird that depends on its fruit—and when will the reverberations end? Perhaps not until a large part of the diversity of the forest collapses like an arch crumbling as the keystone is pulled away. More likely the effects will remain local, ending with a minor shift in the overall pattern of abundance among the numerous surviving species. In either case the effects are beyond the power of present-day ecologists to predict. It is enough to work on the assumption that all of the details matter in the end, in some unknown but vital way.

After the sun's energy is captured by the green plants, it flows through chains of organisms dendritically, like blood spreading from the arteries into networks of microscopic capillaries. It is in such capillaries, in the life cycles of thousands of individual species, that life's important work is done. Thus nothing in the whole system makes sense until the natural history of the constituent species becomes known. The study of every kind of organism matters, everywhere in the world. That conviction leads the field biologist to places like Surinam and the outer limits of evolution, of which this case is exemplary:

The three-toed sloth feeds on leaves high in the canopy of the lowland forests through large portions of South and Central America. Within its fur live tiny moths, the species *Cryptoses choloepi*, found nowhere else on Earth. When a sloth descends to the forest floor to defecate (once a week), female moths leave the fur briefly to deposit their eggs on the fresh dung. The emerging caterpillars build nests of silk and start to feed. Three weeks later they complete their development by turning into adult moths, and then fly up into the canopy in search of sloths. By living directly on the bodies of the sloths, the adult *Cryptoses* assure their offspring first crack at the nutrient-rich excrement and a competitive advantage over the myriad of other coprophages.

At Bernhardsdorp the sun passed behind a small cloud and the woodland darkened. For a moment all that marvelous environment was leveled and subdued. The sun came out again and shattered the vegetative surfaces into light-based niches. They included intensely lighted leaf tops and the tops of miniature canyons cutting vertically through tree bark to create shadowed depths two or three centimeters below. The light filtered down from above as it does in the sea, giving out permanently in the lowermost recesses of buttressed tree trunks and penetralia of the soil and rotting leaves. As the light's intensity rose and fell with the transit of the sun, silverfish, beetles, spiders, bark lice, and other creatures were summoned from the sanctuaries and retreated back in alternation. They responded according to receptor thresholds built into their eyes and brains, filtering devices that differ from one kind of animal to another. By such inborn controls the species imposed a kind of prudent self-discipline. They unconsciously halted their population growth before squeezing out competitors, and others did the same. No altruism was needed to achieve this balance, only specialization.

Coexistence was an incidental by-product of the Darwinian advantage that accrued from the avoidance of competition. During the long span of evolution the species divided the environment among themselves, so that now each tenuously preempted certain of the capillaries of energy flow. Through repeated genetic changes they sidestepped competitors and built elaborate defenses against the host of predator species that relentlessly tracked them through matching genetic countermoves. The result was a splendid array of specialists including moths that live in the fur of three-toed sloths.

Now to the very heart of wonder. Because species diversity was created prior to humanity, and because we evolved within it, we have never fathomed its limits. As a consequence, the living world is the natural domain of the most restless and paradoxical part of the human spirit. Our sense of wonder grows exponentially: the greater the knowledge, the deeper the mystery, and the more we seek knowledge to create new mystery. This catalytic reaction, seemingly an inborn human trait, draws us perpetually forward in a search for new places and new life. Nature is to be mastered, but (we hope) never completely. A quiet passion burns, not for total control but for the sensation of constant advance.

At Bernhardsdorp I tried to convert this notion into a form that would satisfy a private need. My mind maneuvered through an unending world suited to the naturalist. I looked in reverie down the path through the savanna woodland and imagined walking to the Saramacca River and beyond, over the horizon, into a timeless reconnaissance through virgin forests to the land of magical names, Yékwana, Jívaro, Sirionó, Tapirapé, Siona-Secoya, Yumana, back and forth, never to run out of fresh jungle paths and glades.

The same archetypal image has been shared in variations by others, and most vividly during the colonization of the New World. It comes through clearly as the receding valleys and frontier trails of nineteenth-century landscape art in the paintings of Albert Bierstadt, Frederick Edwin Church, Thomas Cole, and their contemporaries during the crossing of the American West and the innermost reaches of South America.

In Bierstadt's *Sunset in Yosemite Valley* (1868), you look down a slope that eases onto the level valley floor, where a river flows quietly away through waist-high grass, thickets, and scattered trees. The sun is near the horizon. Its dying light, washing the surface in reddish gold, has begun to yield to blackish green shadows along the near side of the valley. A cloud bank has lowered to just beneath the tops of the sheer rock walls. More protective than threatening, it has transformed the valley into a tunnel opening out through the far end into a sweep of land. The world beyond is obscured by the blaze of the setting sun into which we are forced to gaze in order to see that far. The valley, empty of people, is safe: no fences, no paths, no owners. In a few minutes we could walk to the river, make camp, and afterward explore away from the banks at leisure. The ground in sight is human-sized, measured literally by foot strides and strange new plants and animals large enough to be studied at twenty paces. The dreamlike quality of the painting rolls time forward: what might the morning bring? History is still young, and human imagination has not yet been chained by precise geographic knowledge. Whenever we wish, we can strike out through the valley to the unknown terrain beyond, to a borderland of still conceivable prodigies—bottomless vales and boundless floods, in Edgar Allan Poe's excited imagery, "and chasms, and caves and Titan woods with forms that no man can discover." The American frontier called up the old emotions that had pulled human populations like a living sheet over the world during the ice ages. The still unfallen western world, as Melville wrote of the symbolizing White Steed in *Moby Dick*, "revived the glories of those primeval times when Adam walked majestic as a god."

Then a tragedy: this image is almost gone. Although perhaps as old as man, it has faded during our own lifetime. The wildernesses of the world have shriveled into timber leases and threatened nature reserves. Their perilous state presents us with a dilemma, which the historian Leo Marx has called the machine in the garden. The natural world is the refuge of the spirit, remote, static, richer even than human imagination. But we cannot exist in this paradise without the machine that tears it apart. We are killing the thing we love, our Eden, progenitrix, and sibyl. Human beings are not captive peccaries; natural creatures torn from a sylvan niche and imprisoned within a world of artifacts. The noble savage, a biological impossibility, never existed. The human relation to nature is vastly more subtle and ambivalent, probably for this reason. Over thousands of generations the mind evolved within a ripening culture, creating itself out of symbols and tools, and genetic advantage accrued from planned modifications of the environment. The unique operations of the brain are the result of natural selection operating through the filter of culture. They have suspended us between the two antipodal ideals of nature and machine, forest and city, the natural and the artifactual, relentlessly seeking, in the words of the geographer Yi-Fu Tuan, an equilibrium not of this world.

So at Bernhardsdorp my own thoughts were inconstant. They skipped south to the Saramacca and on deep into the Amazon basin, the least spoiled garden on Earth, and then swiftly back north to Paramaribo and New York, greatest of machines. The machine had taken me there, and if I ever seriously thought of confronting nature without the conveniences of civilization, reality soon regained my whole attention. The living sea is full of miniature horrors designed to reduce visiting biologists to their constituent amino acids in quick time. Arboviruses visit the careless intruder with a dismaying variety of chills and diarrhea. Breakbone fever swells the joints to agonizing tightness. Skin ulcers spread remorselessly outward from thorn scratches on the ankle. Triatoma assassin bugs suck blood from the sleeper's face during the night and leave behind the fatal microorganisms of Chagas' disease—surely history's most unfair exchange. Leishmaniasis, schistosomiasis, malignant tertian malaria, filariasis, echinococcosis, onchocerciasis, yellow fever, amoebic dysentery, bleeding bot-fly cysts . . . evolution has devised a hundred ways to macerate livers and turn blood into a parasite's broth. So the romantic voyager swallows chloroquine, gratefully accepts gamma globulin shots, sleeps under mosquito netting, and remembers to pull on rubber boots before wading in freshwater streams. He hopes that enough fuel was put into the Land Rover that morning, and he hurries back to camp in time for a hot meal at dusk.

The impossible dilemma caused no problem for ancestral men. For millions of years human beings simply went at nature with everything they had, scrounging food and fighting off predators across a known world of a few square miles. Life was short, fate terrifying, and reproduction an urgent priority: children, if freely conceived, just about replaced the family members who seemed to be dying all the time. The population flickered around equilibrium, and sometimes whole bands became extinct. Nature was something out there—nameless and limitless, a force to beat against, cajole, and exploit.

If the machine gave no quarter, it was also too weak to break the wilderness. But no matter: the ambiguity of the opposing ideals was a superb strategy for survival, just so long as the people who used it stayed sufficiently ignorant. It enhanced the genetic evolution of the brain and generated more and better culture. The world began to yield, first to the agriculturists and then to technicians, merchants, and circumnavigators. Humanity accelerated toward the machine antipode, heedless of the natural desire of the mind to keep the opposite as well. Now we are near the end. The inner voice murmurs *You went too far*, and disturbed the world, and gave away too much for your control of Nature. Perhaps Hobbes's definition is correct, and this will be the hell we earned for realizing truth too late. But I demur in all this. I suggest otherwise: the same knowledge that brought the dilemma to its climax contains the solution. Think of scooping up a handful of soil and leaf litter and spreading it out on a white ground cloth, in the manner of the field biologist, for close examination. This unprepossessing lump contains more order and richness of structure, and particularity of history, than the entire surfaces of all the other (lifeless) planets. It is a miniature wilderness that can take almost forever to explore.

Tease apart the adhesive grains with the aid of forceps, and you will expose the tangled rootlets of a flowering plant, curling around the rotting veins of humus, and perhaps some larger object such as the boat-shaped husk of a seed. Almost certainly among them will be a scattering of creatures that measure the world in millimeters and treat this soil sample as traversable: ants, spiders, springtails, armored oribatid mites, enchytraeid worms, millipedes. With the aid of a dissecting microscope, proceed on down the size scale to the roundworms, a world of scavengers and fanged predators feeding on them. In the hand-held microcosm all these creatures are still giants in a relative sense. The organisms of greatest diversity and numbers are invisible or nearly so. When the soil-and-litter clump is progressively magnified, first with a compound light microscope and then with scanning electron micrographs, specks of dead leaf expand into mountain ranges and canyons, soil particles become heaps of boulders. A droplet of moisture trapped between root hairs grows into an underground lake, surrounded by a three-dimensional swamp of moistened humus. The niches are defined by both topography and nuances in chemistry, light, and temperature shifting across fractions of a millimeter. Organisms now come into view for which the soil sample is a complete world. In certain places are found the fungi: cellular slime molds, the one-celled chitin-producing chytrids, minute gonapodyaceous and oomycete soil specialists, Kickxellales, Eccrinales, Endomycetales, and Zoopagales. Contrary to their popular reputation, the fungi are not formless blobs, but exquisitely structured organisms with elaborate life cycles. The following is a recently discovered extreme specialization, the example of the sloth moth repeated on a microscopic scale:

> In water films and droplets, attack cells of an oomycete, *Haptoglossa mirabilis*, await the approach of small, fat wormlike animals the biologists call rotifers. Each cell is shaped like a gun; its anterior end is elongated to form a barrel, which is hollowed out to form a bore. At the base of the bore is a complicated explosive device. When a rotifer swims close, the attack cell detects its characteristic odor and fires a projectile of infective tissue through the barrel and into its body. The fungal cells proliferate through the victim's tissues and then metamorphose into a cylindrical fruiting body, from which exit tubes sprout. Next tiny spores separate themselves inside the fruiting body, swim out the exit tubes with the aid of whip-shaped hairs, and settle down to form new attack cells. They await more rotifers, prepared to trigger the soundless explosion that will commence a new life cycle.

Still smaller than the parasitic fungi are the bacteria, including colony-forming polyangiaceous species, specialized predators that consume other bacteria. All around them live rich mixtures of rods, cocci, coryneforms, and slime azotobacteria. Together these microorganisms metabolize the entire spectrum of live and dead tissue. At the moment of discovery some are actively growing and fissioning, while others lie dormant in wait for the right combination of nutrient chemicals. Each species is kept at equilibrium by the harshness of the environment. Any one, if allowed to expand without restriction for a few weeks, would multiply exponentially, faster and faster, until it weighed more than the entire Earth. But in reality the individual organism simply dissolves and assimilates whatever appropriate fragments of plants and animals come to rest near it. If the newfound meal is large enough, it may succeed in growing and reproducing briefly before receding back into the more normal state of physiological quiescence.

Biologists, to put the matter as directly as possible, have begun a second reconnaissance into the land of magical names. In exploring life they have commenced a pioneering adventure with no imaginable end. The abundance of organisms increases downward by level, like layers in a pyramid. The handful of soil and litter is home for hundreds of insects, nematode worms, and other larger creatures, about a million fungi, and ten billion bacteria. Each of the species of these organisms has a distinct life cycle fitted, as in the case of the predatory fungus, to the portion of the microenvironment in which it thrives and reproduces. The particularity is due to the fact that it is programmed by an exact sequence of nucleotides, the ultimate molecular units of the genes.

The amount of information in the sequence can be measured in bits. One bit is the information required to determine which of two equally likely alternatives is chosen, such as heads or tails in a coin toss. English words average two bits per letter. A single bacterium possesses about ten million bits of genetic information, a fungus one billion, and an insect from one to ten billion bits according to species. If the information in just one insect—say an ant or beetle—were to be translated into a code of English words and printed in letters of standard size, the string would stretch over a thousand miles. Our lump of earth contains information that would just about fill all editions of the *Encyclopædia Britannica*.

To see what such molecular information can do, consider a column of ants running across the floor of a South American forest. Riding on the backs of some of the foragers are minute workers of the kind usually confined to duties within the underground nursery chambers. The full significance of hitchhiking is problematic, but at the very least the act helps to protect the colony against parasites. Tiny flies, members of the family Phoridae, hover above the running foragers. From time to time a fly dives down to thrust an egg into the neck of one of them. Later the egg hatches into a maggot that burrows deeper into the ant's body. The maggot grows rapidly, transforms into a pupa, and eventually erupts through the cuticle as an adult fly to restart the life cycle. The dive-bombers find the runners easy targets when they are burdened with a fragment of food. But when one also carries a hitchhiker, the smaller ant is able to chase the intruder away with its jaws and legs. It serves as a living fly whisk.

The brain of the fly or of the fly-whisk ant, when dissected out and placed in a drop of saline solution on a glass slide, resembles a grain of sugar. Although barely visible to the naked eye, it is a complete command center that choreographs the insect's movements through its entire adult cycle. It signals the precise hour for the adult to emerge from the pupal case; it processes the flood of signals transduced to it by the outer sensors; and it directs the performance of about twenty behavioral acts through nerves in the legs, antennae, and mandibles. The fly and the ant are hardwired in a manner unique to their respective species and hence radically different from each other, so that predator is implacably directed against prey, flier against runner, solitaire against colony member.

With advanced techniques it has been possible to begin mapping insect nervous systems in sufficient detail to draw the equivalent of wiring diagrams. Each brain consists of somewhere between a hundred thousand and a million nerve cells, most of which send branches to a thousand or more of their neighbors. Depending on their location, individual cells appear to be programmed to assume a particular shape and to transmit messages only when stimulated by coded discharges from neighbor units that feed into them. In the course of evolution, the entire system has been miniaturized to an extreme. The fatty sheaths surrounding the axon shafts of the kind found in larger animals have been largely stripped away, while the cell bodies are squeezed off to one side of the multitudinous nerve connections. Biologists understand in very general terms how the insect brain might work as a complete on-board computer, but they are a long way from explaining or duplicating such a device in any detail.

The great German zoologist Karl von Frisch once said of his favorite organism that the honeybee is like a magic well: the more you draw from it, the more there is to draw. But science is in no other way mystical. Its social structure is such that anyone can follow most enterprises composing it, as observer if not as participant, and soon you find yourself on the boundaries of knowledge.

You start with the known: in the case of the honeybee, where it nests, its foraging expeditions, and its life cycle. Most remarkable at this level is the waggle dance discovered by von Frisch, the tail-wagging movement performed inside the hive to inform nestmates of the location of newly discovered flower patches and nest sites. The dance is the closest approach known in the animal kingdom to a true symbolic language. Over and over again the bee traces a short line on the vertical surface of the comb, while sister workers crowd in close behind. To return to the start of the line, the bee loops back first to the left and then to the right and so produces a figure-eight. The center line contains the message. Its length symbolically represents the distance from the hive to the goal, and its angle away from a line drawn straight up on the comb, in other words away from twelve o'clock, represents the angle to follow right or left of the sun when leaving the hive. If the bee dances straight up the surface of the comb, she is telling the others to fly toward the sun. If she dances ten degrees to the right, she causes them to go ten degrees right of the sun. Using such directions alone, the members of the hive are able to harvest nectar and pollen from flowers three miles or more from the hive.

The revelation of the waggle-dance code has pointed the way to deeper levels of biological investigation, and a hundred new questions. How does the bee judge gravity while on the darkened comb? What does it use for a guide when the sun goes behind a cloud? Is the waggle dance inherited or must it be learned? The answers create new concepts that generate still more mysteries. To pursue them (and we are now certainly at the frontier) investigators must literally enter the bee itself, exploring its nervous system, the interplay of its hormones and behavior, the processing of chemical cues by its nervous system. At the level of cell and tissue, the interior of the body will prove more technically challenging than the external workings of the colony first glimpsed. We are in the presence of a biological machine so complicated that to understand just one part of it—wings, heart, ovary, brain—can consume many lifetimes of original investigation.

And if that venture were somehow to be finished, it will merely lead on down into the essence of the machine, to the interior of cells and the giant molecules that compose their distinctive parts. Questions about process and meaning then take center stage. What commits an embryonic cell to become part of the brain instead of a respiratory unit? Why does the mother's blood invest yolk in the growing egg? Where are the genes that control behavior? Even in the unlikely event that all this microscopic domain is successfully mapped, the quest still lies mostly ahead. The honeybee, *Apis mellifera*, is the product of a particular history. Through fossil remains in rock and amber, we know that its lineage goes back at least 50 million years. Its contemporary genes were assembled by an astronomical number of events that sorted and recombined the constituent nucleotides. The species evolved as the outcome of hourly contacts with thousands of other kinds of plants and animals along the way. Its range expanded and contracted across Africa and Eurasia in a manner reminiscent of the fortunes of a human tribe. Virtually all this history remains unknown. It can be pursued to any length by those who take special interest in *Apis mellifera* and seek what Charles Butler called its "most sweet and sov'raigne fruits" when he launched the modern scientific study of the honeybee in 1609.

Every species is a magic well. Biologists have until recently been satisfied with the estimate that there are between three and ten million of them on Earth. Now many believe that ten million is too low. The upward revision has been encouraged by the increasingly successful penetration of the last great unexplored environment of the planet, the canopy of the tropical rainforest, and the discovery of an unexpected number of new species living there. This layer is a sea of branches, leaves, and flowers crisscrossed by lianas and suspended about one hundred feet above the ground. It is one of the easiest habitats to locate—from a distance at least—but next to the deep sea the most difficult to reach. The tree trunks are thick, arrow-straight, and either slippery smooth or covered with sharp tubercles. Anyone negotiating them safely to the top must then contend with swarms of stinging ants and wasps. A few athletic and adventurous younger biologists have begun to overcome the difficulties by constructing special pulleys, rope catwalks, and observation platforms from which they can watch high arboreal animals in an undisturbed state. Others have found a way to sample the insects, spiders, and other anthropods with insecticides and quick-acting knockdown agents. They first shoot lines up into the canopy, then hoist the chemicals up in canisters and spray them out into the surrounding vegetation by remote control devices. The falling insects and other organisms are caught in sheets spread over the ground. The creatures discovered by these two methods have proved to be highly specialized in their food habits, the part of the tree in which they live, and the time of the year when they are active. So an unexpectedly large number of different kinds are able to coexist. Hundreds can fit comfortably together in a single tree top. On the basis of a preliminary statistical projection from these data, Terry L. Erwin, an entomologist at the National Museum of Natural History, has estimated that there may be thirty million species of insects in the world, most limited to the upper vegetation of the tropical forests.

Although such rough approximations of the diversity of life are not too difficult to make, the exact number of species is beyond reach because—incredibly—the majority have yet to be discovered and specimens placed in museums. Furthermore, among those already classified no more than a dozen have been studied as well as the honeybee. Even

Homo sapiens, the focus of billions of dollars of research annually, remains a seemingly intractable mystery. All of man's troubles may well arise, as Vercors suggested in *You Shall Know Them*, from the fact that we do not know what we are and do not agree on what we want to become. This crucial inadequacy is not likely to be remedied until we have a better grasp of the diversity of the life that created and sustains us. So why hold back? It is a frontier literally at our fingertips, and the one for which our spirit appears to have been explicitly designed.

I walked on through the woodland at Bernhardsdorp to see what the day had to offer. In a decaying log I found a species of ant previously known only from the midnight zone of a cave in Trinidad. With the aid of my hand lens I identified it from its unique combination of teeth, spines, and body sculpture. A month before I had hiked across five miles of foothills in central Trinidad to find it in the original underground habitat. Now suddenly here it was again, nesting and foraging in the open. Scratch from the list what had been considered the only "true" cave ant in the world—possessed of workers pale yellow, nearly eyeless, and sluggish in movement. Scratch the scientific name *Spelaeomyrmex*, meaning literally cave ant, as a separate taxonomic entity. I knew that it would have to be classified elsewhere, into a larger and more conventional genus called *Erebomyrma*, ant of Hades. A small quick victory, to be reported later in a technical journal that specializes on such topics and is read by perhaps a dozen fellow myrmecologists. I turned to watch some huge-eyed ants with the formidable name *Gigantiops destructor*. When I gave one of the foraging workers a freshly killed termite, it ran off in a straight line across the forest floor. Thirty feet away it vanished into a small hollow tree branch that was partly covered by decaying leaves. Inside the central cavity I found a dozen workers and their mother queen—one of the first colonies of this unusual insect ever recorded. All in all, the excursion had been more productive than average. Like a prospector obsessed with ore samples, hoping for gold, I gathered a few more promising specimens in vials of ethyl alcohol and headed home, through the village and out onto the paved road leading north to Paramaribo.

Later I set the day in my memory with its parts preserved for retrieval and closer inspection. Mundane events acquired the raiment of symbolism, and this is what I concluded from them: that the naturalist's journey has only begun and for all intents and purposes will go on forever. That it is possible to spend a lifetime in a Magellanic voyage around the trunk of a single tree. That as the exploration is pressed, it will engage more of the things close to the human heart and spirit. And if this much is true, it seems possible that the naturalist's vision is only a specialized product or a biophilic instinct shared by all, that it can be elaborated to benefit more and more people. Humanity is exalted not because we are so far above other living creatures, but because knowing them well elevates the very concept of life.

Interview with Ailton Krenak

From The Fate of the Forests *(1989)*
By Susanna Hecht and Alexander Cockburn

In 1989, Susanna Hecht, a noted Amazon expert and geographer from UCLA, and Alexander Cockburn, writer for The Nation, *teamed up to write a political history of the Amazon. Within their excellent book is an interview with Ailton Krenak, a well-known spokesperson for traditional peoples of the Amazon.*

In this interview, Krenak speaks on behalf of extractive reserves in Brazil. These reserves are public lands used by local communities to harvest forest products such as Brazil nuts and rubber. Extractive reserves give legal rights to use the lands in a well-managed way for long periods of time.

The words of Ailton Krenak are important to remember. One can only imagine what the world would be like if the words and wisdom of traditional peoples were heeded.

It is also worth noting again that most of the passages in this collection are Western views on jungle lore. A collection of tales by the peoples indigenous to the forest—those who know the forest best and who have lived there the lon-

gest—would certainly yield rich reading. More importantly, these stories would surely provide many important lessons to be learned about the past, the present, and the future. The following is but one example. (DRK)

Ailton Krenak, 34, belongs to a small tribe of the Krenak Indians who lived in the Vale do Rio Doce at the frontier of Minas Gerais and Espírito Santo. This group is also known generically as the Botocudos. In 1920 the Krenak people were estimated to have a population of about 5,000, and lived in an area of 200 square miles. Today they are reduced to 150 Indians who live on an area of some 15 square miles which has been almost entirely invaded by ranchers.

Ailton Krenak has lived in the city since he was about eighteen, which was when he learned to read. He has worked as a journalist and in public relations. Since 1980 he has placed his skill and knowledge of the press at the disposition of Indian peoples. In recent years he has coordinated the Indian Program of the radio of São Paulo distributed by about five networks in Brazil.

When talking of native science it's impossible to separate it out of its context. If I pull one of the shells off a bracelet, the entirety is less beautiful, and the shell itself, however beautiful, has less meaning. We can miss so much of what a shell actually is if we cut it away from myths, practices, the people who discovered and named the shell and other similar shells, and the rituals and stories and secrets of that shell. That's only one part of the bracelet, and that shell—let's say it's agriculture—is only one part of the special knowledge we have about nature. There are strands of life and history and nature and what it means to be an Indian that tie that shell to the others.

In the indigenous cycle of things, when we stayed too long in an area we would see that the game fled and that people's dreams were no longer good, and so we would leave, and let the *maloca* collapse. But that place was not lost to us or abandoned because sometimes we had our dead there, and we knew that we would always return, and so for this reason we would plant fruits, medicines and magic plants for this life and for the other forest lives that would follow us. We saw that forest not as a wild bunch of trees, but as a place in which our history and our future was written; the trees planted to remember the dead or to provide someday for our sons and daughters. The forest is not a wild thing to us. It is our world.

At the Altamira meeting, a Kayapó woman in full regalia raced up to the head of Eletronorte, brandishing her machete, and with a scream raised it and brought it down just short of each of his shoulders. She swore at him, full of bitter contempt: "Do you think that we're so stupid, do you think that we don't know what your plans are for us, what your plans are for this forest? Here we have been for millennia and you think that your silly plans are beyond our understanding. If you are a person of so much courage, knowledge and understanding, why don't you come and say what you have to say there and we'll kill you once and for all. Come with all your ministers and we'll take care of you once and for all. But for godsake don't think for a moment that we are somehow going to disappear between now and 1995 when you plan to flood these lands."

Well, yes, they are theatrical gestures. There are moments when theatrical gestures are very necessary. But because we occasionally engage in such gestures, people think that when we don't do them all the time we are adapting ourselves to the plans the Brazilian government has in mind for us. That's not really the case. One must choose the moments in which theatrical gestures will be most effective, and everything is achieved by dramatic presentation. But just because things are calm and quiet doesn't mean that we're quiescent. All of these things show that we are vibrant and living cultures and we won't be undone by what the Brazilian government has in mind for us.

For a long time the press was taken with a certain exotic and romanticist view of what Indians were. So when someone managed to contact a tribe that had never been heard of before, this was heralded with much applause for the great "indigenists"—the Villas-Boas brothers or whoever—and those Indians were viewed as residue of some stone-age past, whether this bore any relation to the cultural reality or not. On the other hand, magazines like *Machete* would photograph bucolic scenes of Indian kids diving into beautiful forest ponds, with headings like "Brazil preserves its native heritage," noble warriors, or beautiful women. So what one saw was the savage and the exotic.

For a long time the spokesmen about Indian affairs were people from FUNAI [Fondação Nacional do Indio, the National Indigenous Agency of Brazil], that is to say the government itself, who would speak of the lost innocence of the world, the Rousseauian idea. Then we had anthropologists who studied us and spoke for us for a while. For a long time only the anthropologists were able to get into the Indian areas and describe what was going on. Since the 1970s this has all changed. This is due to changes in the government policy itself. As they penetrated more deeply into Amazônia, any time they cut a road Indians would leap out of the way. Thousands of Indians would be running out of the way of bulldozers. People didn't realize that the area was full of Indians. Another factor is technological. The level of communication improved and people could hear what was going on and began to realize that all over the region Indian groups were experiencing the same problems. What began to happen was the emergence of a true indigenous voice. We had our own analysis and point of view that we ourselves could articulate. We didn't want to be presented only by anthropologists. Before the 1970s, few Indians were off the reservations, and an Indian off the reservation was a dead Indian. With the 1970s, Indians began to move into other parts of Brazil as Indians rather than half-breeds, and to participate as an autonomous political force, to send people down to Brasília.

The big thing is to turn Brazilian history on its head, the history of colonization. You are a forest person, from some tribe, and then some "civilizing agent" enters the region, whether it's the Church, a political party, or an association of whites. Then they go "discover" this tribe of Indians in the same way they have done with other tribes. Once the contact is made, then begins the progressive, actually repressive infection, "civilizing" the tribe. Each day the tribe becomes less of the forest, of the rural zones, and more of the city. This is a progressive story— one day the tribe will be absolutely integrated. They will have learned how to talk Portuguese, to buy clothes, gasoline and a series of products that they don't produce. This obliges them to migrate from the land, or to apply a type of economy which will turn them into a village, town, and so forth. This is the history of the world.

Extractive reserves bring into play part of the population which came to the Amazon to "civilize" it along with the Indians, but who instead learn from them a new way of living with nature. Rubber tappers learn how to humanize nature and themselves. Thus the reserve brings a new form of social culture, and economic character. Migrants to this region came in search of land, but the property of the people cannot be commercialized. An extractive reserve is not an exchange item, and it isn't property. It is a good that belongs to the Brazilian nation, and people will live in these reserves with the expectation of preserving them for future generations. This is tremendously innovative.

Imagine if all the people in Amazônia decided in the next decade that they didn't want to treat the places they lived in as a commodity but rather as a sacred place! How does one guarantee a reserve's effective occupation? A fruit as it ripens goes through several different processes. I think that the first step is to get the reserves established. We are determined now to do a survey of the practices of rubber tappers and Indians in reference to real economic dynamics. From this inventory we are going to observe which activities are being done in a form in which resources are underutilized, and what their potential is. If there is a process in extractivism that can be mechanized, then let's see if we can develop a structure to use it.

Of course there are a lot of people waiting for the hour in which they can proclaim the whole thing a failure. We have to view this as normal. There are days when things are cloudy but the sun is shining above it all. The wind comes and blows these clouds away. It's entirely normal that there are other intentions about how to occupy the Amazon. One cannot in any way treat with disrespect and violence the thoughts of others. I think that this is the most generous aspect of the Forest Peoples' Alliance— to unite people who've been killing each other for a century. Do you think that back then rubber tappers wanted to throw in their lot with Indians? Let's just suppose that the people who are today against this most reasonable form of land occupation perceive that they can make money; that municipalities, potential producers supplying large markets, bring large taxes. We have to convince them of this. The alliance has to show its fruits, we cannot only keep talking.

Sympathy for the Devil

From Natural Acts *(1985)*
By David Quammen

When people name the creatures they'd least like to meet face-to-face in a lonely part of the jungle, the names of snakes, big cats, and toothed fish are far more likely to spring forth than that of a creature that cannot even stand up to the slap of the human hand. But what animal is really more ferocious than the tiny, intrepid, and utterly infuriating mosquito?

In this essay, David Quammen tells us everything we ever wanted to know about this nasty insect . . . and then some. The author who shed some light on snakes in Rumors of a Snake *tells us why the mosquito deserves a better reputation than it has, arguing convincingly that conservationists should recognize the much-maligned pest as a true "Rainforest Hero." (DRK)*

Undeniably they have a lot to answer for: malaria, yellow fever, dengue, encephalitis, filariasis, and the ominous tiny whine that begins homing around your ear just after you've gotten comfortable in the sleeping bag. All these griefs and others are the handiwork of that perfidious family of biting flies known as Culicidae, the mosquitos. They assist in the murder of millions of humans each year, carry ghastly illness to millions more, and drive not a few of the rest of us temporarily insane. They are out for blood.

Mosquitos have been around for 50 million years, which has given them time to figure out all the angles. Judged either by sheer numbers, or by the scope of their worldwide distribution, or by their resistance to enemies and natural catastrophe, they are one of the great success stories on the planet. They come in 2,700 different species. They inhabit almost every land surface, from Arctic tundra to downtown London to equatorial Brazil, from the Sahara to the Himalaya, though best of all they like the tropical rainforests, where three-quarters of their species lurk. Mosquitos and rainforests, in fact, go together like gigolos and bridge tournaments, insurance salesmen and Elks lunches, panhandlers and . . . But more on all that in a moment.

They hatch and grow to maturity in water, any entrapment of quiet water, however transient or funky. A soggy latrine, for instance, suits them fine. The still edge of a crystalline stream is fine. In the flooded footprint of an elephant, you might find a hundred mosquitos. As innocent youngsters they use facial bristles resembling cranberry rakes to comb these waters for smorgasbord, but on attaining adulthood, they are out for blood.

It isn't a necessity for individual survival, quenching that blood thirst, just a prerequisite for motherhood. Male mosquitos do not even bite. A male mosquito lives his short, gentle adult life content, like a swallowtail butterfly, to sip nectar from flowers. As with black widow spiders and mantids, it is only the female that is fearsome. Make of that what larger lessons you dare.

She relies on the blood of vertebrates—mainly warm-blooded ones but also sometimes reptiles and frogs—to finance, metabolically, the development of her eggs.

A female mosquito in a full lifetime will lay about ten separate batches of eggs, roughly 200 in a batch. That's a large order of embryonic tissue to be manufactured in one wispy body, and to manage it the female needs a rich source of protein; the sugary juice of flowers will deliver quick energy to wing muscles, but it won't help her build 2,000 new bodies. So she has evolved a hypodermic proboscis and learned how to *steal* protein in one of its richest forms, hemoglobin. In some species her first brood will develop before she has tasted blood, but after that she must have a bellyful for each set of eggs coming to term.

When she drinks, she drinks deeply: The average blood meal amounts to 2½ times the original weight of the insect. Picture Audrey Hepburn sitting down to a steak dinner, getting up from the table weighing 380 pounds; then, for that matter, flying away. In the Canadian Arctic, where species of the genus *Aedes* emerge in savage, sky-darkening swarms like nothing seen even in the Amazon, and work under pressure of time because of the short summer season, an unprotected human could be bitten 9,000 times per minute. At that rate a large man would lose half his total blood in two hours. Arctic hares and reindeer move to higher ground, or die. And sometimes solid mats of *Aedes* will continue sucking blood from a carcass.

Evidently the female tracks her way to a blood donor by flying upwind toward a source of warmer air, or air that is both warm and moist, or that contains an excess of carbon dioxide, or a combination of all three. The experts aren't sure. Perspiration, involving both higher skin temperature and released moisture, is one good way to attract her attention. In Italy it is established folk wisdom that to sleep with a pig in the bedroom is to protect oneself from malaria, presumably because the pig, operating at a higher body temperature, will be preferred by mosquitos. And at the turn of the century, Professor Giovanni Grassi, then Italy's foremost zoologist, pointed out that garrulous people seemed to be bitten more often than those who kept their mouths shut. The experts aren't sure, but the Italians are full of ideas.

Guided by CO_2 or idle chatter or distaste for pork or whatever, a female mosquito lands on the earlobe of a human, drives her proboscis (actually a thin bundle of tools that includes two tubular stylets for carrying fluid and four serrated ones for cutting) through the skin, gropes with it until she taps a capillary, and then an elaborate interaction begins. Her saliva flows down one tube into the wound, retarding coagulation of the spilled blood and provoking an allergic reaction that will later be symptomized by itching. A suction pump in her head draws blood up the other tube, a valve closes, another pump pulls the blood back into her gut. And that alternate pumping and valving continues quickly for three orgiastic minutes, until her abdomen is stretched full like a great bloody balloon, or until a fast human hand ends her maternal career, whichever comes first.

But in the meantime, if she is an *Anopheles gambiae* in Nigeria, the protozoans that cause malaria may be streaming into the wound with her saliva, heading immediately off to set up bivouac in the human's liver. Or if she is *Aedes aegypti* in Costa Rica, she may be drooling out an advance phalanx of the yellow fever virus. If she is *Culex pipiens* in Malaysia, long tiny larvae of the filaria worm may be squirting from her snout like a stage magician's spring-work snakes, dispersing to breed in the unfortunate person's lymph nodes and eventually clog them, causing elephantiasis. Definitely, this is misanthropic behavior.

No wonder, then, that in the rogues' pantheon of those select creatures not only noxious in their essential character but furthermore lacking any imaginable forgiving graces, the mosquito is generally ranked beyond even the wood tick, the wolverine, or the black toy poodle. The mosquito, says common bias and on this the experts agree, is an unmitigated pain in the ass.

But I don't see it that way. To begin with, the family is not monolithic, and it does have—from the human perspective—its beneficent representatives. In northern Canada, for instance, *Aedes nigripes* is an important pollinator of arctic orchids. In Ethiopia, *Toxorhynchites brevipalpis* as a larva preys voraciously on the larvae of other mosquitos, malaria carriers, and then *Toxo* itself transforms to a lovely huge iridescent adult that, male or female, drinks only plant juices and would not dream of biting a human.

But even discounting these aberrations, and judging it by only its most notorious infamies, the mosquito is taking a bad rap. It has been victimized, I submit to you, by a strong case of anthropocentric press-agentry. In fact the little sucker can be viewed, with only a small bit of squinting, as one of the great ecological heroes of planet Earth. If you consider rainforest preservation.

The chief point of blame, with mosquitos, happens also to be the chief point of merit: They make tropical rainforests, for humans, virtually uninhabitable.

Tropical rainforest constitutes by far the world's richest and most complex ecosystem, a boggling entanglement of life forms and habits and equilibriums and relationships. Those equatorial forests—mainly confined to the Amazon, the Congo basin and Southeast Asia—account for only a small fraction of the Earth's surface, but serve as home for roughly *half* of the Earth's total plant and animal species, including 2,000 kinds of mosquito. But rainforests lately, in case you haven't heard, are under siege.

They are being clear-cut for cattle ranching, mowed down with bulldozers and pulped for paper, corded into firewood, gobbled up hourly by human development on the march. The current rate of loss amounts to eight acres of rainforest gone poof since you began reading this sentence; within a generation, at that pace, the Amazon will look like New Jersey. Conservation groups are raising a clamor, a few of the equatorial governments are adopting plans for marginal preservation. But no one and no thing has done more to delay this catastrophe, over the past 10,000 years, than the mosquito.

The great episode of ecological disequilibrium we call "human history" began, so the Leakey family tell us, in equatorial Africa. Then immediately the focus of intensity shifted elsewhere. What deterred mankind, at least until this half of this century, from hacking space for his farms and his cities out of the tropical forests? Yellow fever did, and malaria, dengue, filariasis, o'nyong-nyong fever.

Clear the vegetation from the brink of a jungle waterhole, move in with tents and cattle and Jeeps, and *Anopheles gambiae*, not normally native there, will arrive within a month, bringing malaria. Cut the tall timber from five acres of rainforest, and species of infectious *Aedes*—which would otherwise live out their lives in the forest canopy, passing yellow fever between monkeys—will literally fall on you, and begin biting before your chainsaw has cooled. Nurturing not only more species of snake and bird than anywhere else on Earth, but also more forms of disease-causing microbes, and more mosquitos to carry them, tropical rainforests are elaborately booby-trapped against disruption.

The native forest peoples gradually acquired some immunity to these diseases, and their nondisruptive hunting-and-gathering economies minimized their exposure to mosquitos that favored the canopy or disturbed ground. Meanwhile the occasional white interlopers, the agents of empire, remained vulnerable. West Africa, in high colonial days, became known as "the white man's grave."

So as Europe was being stripped of its virgin woods, and India and China, and the North American heartland, the rainforests escaped, lasting into the late twentieth century—with some chance at least that they may endure a bit longer. Thanks to what? Thanks to ten million generations of jungle-loving, disease-bearing, blood-sucking insects: the Culicidae, nature's Viet Cong.

And a time, says Ecclesiastes, to every purpose.

Why Save Tropical Forests?

From The Primary Source *(1984)*
By Norman Myers

~~~

The Primary Source, *by Dr. Norman Myers, is the bible of modern-day rainforest conservation and has been a conservation classic since it first hit the stores in 1984.*

I read a review of it while living in Wuhan, China, and could not wait to get my hands on a copy. Ordering the book was one of the first things I did upon returning home to Cincinnati, Ohio—I could barely wait the week or so it took for the book to arrive. On the drive home from picking it up at the store, I couldn't resist peeking; I was so captivated by the contents that I pulled over to the side of the road and read, oblivious to the passing cars and passing time. I started the car again only when the sun went down and I could not see the printed words. The Primary Source *is that good.*

The book's introduction, excerpted here, is, of course, just the beginning. For Miles and me, however, it is the perfect way to close our collection. Dr. Myers says it all and says everything we hope to leave you with. (DRK)

Tropical forests rank foremost among my professional preoccupations. They fascinate me, they awe me. I probe their workings, investigate their makeup, undertake research of a dozen sorts, and am enthralled at the insights that must lie ahead. I likewise feel I have no more important professional endeavor than my inquiries into the status of tropical forests—how many we have left, how fast they are disappearing, what their outlook is for the year 2000, for the year 2100. I further feel that there is no more challenging task for me than to contribute to such conservation activities as assist the cause of tropical forests. In short, tropical forests excite me like no other subject in my work as a scientist and a conservationist.

Even more to the point, I feel, as an individual—not as a scientist or a conservationist, but as a human being—that this is a splendid time to be alive, when, at long, glorious last, we can penetrate the furthest reaches of tropical forests, not only their remote heartlands but also the zone that, paradoxically, has remained more concealed from us than have the depths of the Amazonia or Borneo and that forms the forest canopy scores of meters above the ground: the last, great unexplored frontier of life on Earth. The thought that we shall learn so many new secrets of life within the next few years appeals to me more than most things I can think of. There is one notable exception: I feel lucky to be alive at a time when I can take part in a great enterprise by people in many lands to safeguard this, the finest celebration of nature ever known on the planet.

Thus for me tropical forests serve as a primary source of inspiration, whether as a professional scientist and conservationist or a private citizen. I know the same applies to many of my friends and colleagues. Probably rather few people feel so excited by tropical forests, even though they might agree that tropical forests represent the outstanding sector of our planetary patrimony and deserve an exceptional effort to be saved. But tropical forests are a primary source of welfare for people everywhere, in ways they never suspect—especially through their material contributions to our everyday lives. Forming a green band around the equator, tropical forests cover only little more than nine million square kilometers—an expanse less than that of the United States, a mere one-sixteenth of the Earth's land surface. Their limited expanse notwithstanding, they supply far more to our well-being than does any other ecological zone of similar size. We benefit from them dozens of times each day and have done so for many years, many millennia: in fact since man first climbed down from his tropical forest trees.

Moreover, the best times lie ahead of us. If we manage to make full, sustainable use of the tropical forests' myriad products, we shall enjoy the fact of their existence in more ways than most people now dream. However little we may realize it, our future is likely to become ever-more closely linked to that of tropical forests. As a wellspring of products to sustain our sojourn on Earth, they are a primary source.

Decline of Tropical Forests

Only in recent times has the sense of concord been widely compromised. After the end of World War II, man started to exploit tropical forests in a manner that they cannot sustain. In many places, excessive harvesting of commercial timber is taking its toll. Undue demands for fuelwood are degrading one tract after another. Small-scale cultivators engage in slash-and-burn farming with an intensity that allows the forest little chance to renew itself. Large-scale ranchers cut down entire sections of forest, put a match to the felled timber, and then plant pastures on which to raise beef for the fast-food trade in the United States and elsewhere.

At present rates of depletion—and the rates are accelerating—our grandchildren may well witness the end of tropical forests, except for a few isolated patches of degraded remnants. Instead of having a band of greenery around the equator, the Earth may eventually feature a bald ring. The integrative relationships between humankind and tropical forests are being ruptured in a far more profound manner than has ever occurred in the past—and the effects may persist for thousands, if not millions, of years. These unique forests, which have served humankind as a fountainhead of welfare for many millennia, look likely to be all but destroyed in a single century. The primary source will be gone for good—a loss in more ways than many of us apparently care to think about right now.

Citizens of tropical forest countries will not be the only ones to suffer from the demise of the forests. We shall all be losers. Just as we are about to embark on a Gene Revolution to surpass the finest achievements of the Green Revolution, in Iowa as well as India, and many other parts of the world besides, the richest reservoirs of gene resources on the face of the planet are being eliminated. Similarly, a uniquely diversified stock of raw materials for innovative medicine and industry is being rapidly extinguished. Our lives and the lives of our descendants for untold generations will thereby be impoverished. Climates in all parts of the global ecosystem will undergo changes for thousands, perhaps millions, of years. The economic and political upheavals ensuing may well exceed those of any military conflicts we have known. If, as is not unlikely, a greenhouse effect caused by carbon dioxide leads to the ultimate melting of the polar ice caps, sea levels will rise and shorelines will retreat at a far faster rate than any we can discern in the prehistoric past, with adverse repercussions for one-fifth of humankind that will probably be living in coastal zones. Species will disappear in a mass extinction greater in its concentrated spasm than any since the emergence of cellular life, and the course of evolution will be fundamentally modified if not debilitated. So far as we can tell from the paleontological past, the planetary ecosystem will need between ten and twenty million years to restore the damage done to the fabric of life.

Thus the losers will include all inhabitants of Earth—no more than appropriate, some observers may reflect, since all are involved in the depletion of tropical forests. Misuse and overuse of the forests through timber harvesting reflects international marketplace demand for tropical hardwoods. The consumerist appetite of developed-world citizens for specialized timbers of tropical forests, with their many luxury applications in virtually every home of an affluent-world citizen, has expanded almost twenty times during the past three decades, until developed-world consumption has recently surpassed that of the developing world. Hence a key question: Whose hand is on the chainsaw at work in tropical forests? Furthermore, much of the excessive logging is conducted by giant timber corporations based in North America, Western Europe, and Japan. All the more we may ask, Whose hand is on the chainsaw?

The recent surge of cattle raising in forestlands of Latin America has been stimulated by the Americans' search for "cheap," that is, noninflationary, beef for hamburgers, frankfurters, television dinners, and other convenience foods. This trend is being replicated in both Western and Eastern Europe, Japan, and some of the newly rich nations of the Middle East. At the same time, certain of the ranching interests are based in those same nations that foster excessive demand for cheap beef. People around the world are involved in the decline of tropical forests.

Collective Campaign in Support of Tropical Forests

Since everybody will lose by the decline of tropical forests, and since everybody contributes to the process, it makes sense that everybody should become involved in safeguarding the forests. Of course we should not seek to keep them locked away, declaring them off limits to development. Sustainable use is feasible in many ways. We can derive far greater benefits from tropical forests than we have in the past, and derive them in perpetuity. We can even turn to tropical forests as a more significant primary source, of multiple sorts, than was thought possible by our forebears. Yet the task of safeguarding tropical forests represents a challenge as great as that of any other resource issue confronting humankind. The very prospect of trying to save tropical forests raises hosts of problems in one's mind. But problems also imply opportunities. A time of crisis, as the Chinese say, is a time for breakthrough, a time when we can move beyond the patterns and practices of the past and attempt bold, new strategies for the future. We shall need a whole series of initiatives by the tropical forest countries themselves, matched by a similar set of initiatives by the developed nations. Even more, we shall require a set of measures taken by the community of nations acting as a whole: a concerted endeavor of a nature and scale such as is rarely envisaged, let alone implemented, by the collectivity of citizens around the world.

Taxing as such measures will be, they do not compare with the steps we would have to take to compensate for the harm done to society if tropical forests continue to decline. In this prospect should lie our motivation. What better impulse for collective endeavor by the global citizenry than an effort to safeguard the extraordinary natural phenomena and the exceptional stock of natural resources inherent in tropical forests? When we consider what is at stake, how can we question whether we are up to the task?

If we seek further incentive, we need only contemplate these same forests. Surely they offer a primary source of inspiration for us to act together in defense of a salient segment of our One-Earth home.

Such thoughts often occupy my mind as I stand amid the grandeur of a tropical forest. Something of the scene outside me serves to stretch something inside me. It makes my faculties operate with a sharpness I do not generally sense; a host of additional nerve endings comes alive. I seem to sprout antennae to probe this new and fascinating world. At my finest moments in wild nature, such as I experience hour by hour in a tropical forest, I feel as if my whole being is standing on tiptoe. I shall not be the same again—thank goodness. I shall look at things differently, and not just the natural world, but cities, newspapers, friends, and unknown faces. I have grown a little—and what better place to do it than in that luxuriant community where growing, ever-more growing, is the essence of it all.

Perhaps what most stimulates me about a tropical forest is the notion that its diversity, its interactions, its sense of wholeness, all are so advanced that it is far beyond the scope of my imagination—let alone my intellect—to grasp how advanced they are. I feel cut down to size, even as I feel I stand taller than before.

Afterword

The Rainforest Alliance is an international nonprofit organization dedicated to the conservation of the world's tropical forests. Since 1987, the Alliance has been working to create long-term, economically viable alternatives to deforestation.

Based in New York City, the Alliance also has offices in California and Costa Rica. As of the publication of this volume, the Alliance's programs include the *Smart Wood Program*, which develops methods to decrease the adverse environmental effects of logging; the *ECO-OK Certification Program*, which does the same for the cultivation of tropical crops; the *Amazon Rivers Program*, which seeks to conserve the Amazon Basin and its vast fish resource; the *Conservation Media Center*, Latin America's primary clearinghouse for conservation information; and the *Natural Resources and Rights Program*, which works to ensure that the benefits of biodiversity support conservation while serving the needs of human communities.

By purchasing this book, you are making a direct contribution to the Rainforest Alliance—and to the conservation of rainforests worldwide.

For more information on the Alliance, please call 1 (800) 930–RAIN, or write: Rainforest Alliance, 65 Bleecker Street, New York, New York 10012.

We hope you have enjoyed this volume of *Tales from the Jungle*. For future projects, we welcome your own personal tales from the jungle, fact or fiction. Please write to us with your own stories, or your favorites from elsewhere (stories cannot be returned). Send them to: Daniel R. Katz and Miles Chapin, Rainforest Alliance, 65 Bleecker Street, New York, New York 10012.

Here is a chance to do more now!!

As a special thank-you for purchasing and reading this book, the Rainforest Alliance is offering you a one-year membership at a greatly reduced rate. As a member, you will receive the *Canopy*, the Alliance's quarterly newsletter—just what you need to keep abreast of the latest in rainforest conservation activities—and special updates and notices throughout the year. As a bonus, you will receive a free colorful T-shirt.

To join today, simply fill out and mail the enclosed form with a check for $15.00 (a $10 savings over the regular annual membership rate of $25—which doesn't include the T-shirt). This offer is valid only for owners of *Tales from the Jungle*.

Please specify your T-shirt size.

_____

_____Yes! Please count me in as a member of the Rainforest Alliance. My $15 special membership fee is enclosed.

_____Also enclosed is a special tax-deductible contribution to support rainforest conservation activities.

Name: _____

Address: _____

City, State, Zip Code: _____

Phone Number: _____

T-shirt Size: _____

Please make checks payable to the Rainforest Alliance and mail to 65 Bleecker Street, New York, New York 10012. Thank you.

_____

Permissions

The editors have made every effort to secure permission for the publication of the works contained in this volume. If we have inadvertently overlooked securing the proper permission for a selection that appears here, we apologize, and ask that you contact us at the Rainforest Alliance for correction in subsequent printings.

Thanks are due to the following authors, publishers, and publications, for permission to use the material indicated.

"The Snake Doctor," from *Last Chance to See,* by Douglas Adams and Mark Carwardine. Copyright © 1990 by Serious Productions Ltd. and Mark Carwardine. Reprinted by permission of Harmony Books, a division of Crown Publishers, Inc.

"Hammock Nights," from *The Edge of the Jungle,* by William Beebe. Copyright © 1921, 1949, by William Beebe.

"Cahill Among the Ruins in Peru," from *Jaguars Ripped My Flesh,* by Tim Cahill. Copyright © 1987 by Tim Cahill. Used by permission of Bantam Books, a division of Bantam Doubleday Dell Publishing Group, Inc. .

"The Black Beach," from *The Windward Road,* by Archie Carr. Copyright © 1979 by Archie Carr. Reprinted by permission.

"A Black Stream of Death," by Arkady Fiedler. Copyright © 1951 by Arkady Fiedler.

"Jerry's Maggot," reprinted with permission of Charles Scribner's Sons, an imprint of Macmillan Publishing Company, from *Tropical Nature,* by Adrian Forsyth and Ken Miyata. Text copyright © 1984 Adrian Forsyth and Ken Miyata.

"A Chance for Mr. Lever," copyright 1936, renewed © 1968 by Graham Greene, from *Collected Stories of Graham Greene* by Graham Greene. Used by permission of Viking Penguin, a division of Penguin Books USA Inc.

"Pa Lampung Padan's Sewing Machine," from *Stranger in the Forest,* by Eric Hansen,